INSIGHT GUIDES
ESTONIA
LATVIA & LITHUANIA

APA PUBLICATIONS L

Part of the Langenscheidt Publishing Group

※ INSIGHT GUIDE

ESTONIA, LATVIA & LITHUANIA

Editorial

Project Editor
Tom Le Bas
Art Director
Steven Lawrence
Picture Manager
Tom Smyth
Series Manager
Rachel Lawrence

Distribution

UK & Ireland
GeoCenter International Ltd
Meridian House, Churchill Way West
Basingstoke, Hampshire RG21 6YR
sales@geocenter.co.uk

United States
Ingram Publisher Services
1 Ingram Blvd, PO Box 3006
La Vergne, TN 37086-1986
customer.service@ingrampublisher
services.com

Australia
Universal Publishers
PO Box 307
St. Leonards NSW 1590
Ph: (02) 9857 3700
Email: sales@universalpublishers.com.au

New Zealand
Hema Maps New Zealand Ltd (HNZ)
Unit 2, 10 Cryers Road
East Tamaki, Auckland 2013
sales.hema@clear.net.nz

Worldwide
Apa Publications GmbH & Co.
Verlag KG (Singapore branch)
7030 Ang Mo Kio Avenue 5
08-65 Northstar @ AMK
Singapore 569880
apasin@signet.com.sg

Printing

CTPS - China

©2011 Apa Publications GmbH & Co.
Verlag KG (Singapore branch)
All Rights Reserved

First Edition 1992
Fourth Edition 2011

CONTACTING THE EDITORS
We would appreciate it if readers
would alert us to errors or outdated information by writing to:
**Insight Guides, PO Box 7910,
London SE1 1WE, England.**
insight@apaguide.co.uk

www.insightguides.com

ABOUT THIS BOOK

The first Insight Guide pioneered the use of creative full-colour photography in travel guides in 1970. Since then, we have expanded our range to cater for our readers' need not only for reli-able information about their cho-sen destination but also for a real understanding of the culture and workings of that destination. Now, when the internet can supply inex-haustible (but not always reliable) facts, our books marry text and pictures to provide those much more elusive qualities: knowledge and discernment. To achieve this, they rely heavily on the authority of locally based writers and pho-tographers.

How to use this book

The book is carefully structured both to convey a proper understanding of Estonia, Latvia and Lithuania and to guide readers through their sights and activities:

◆ To understand the three countries today, it is important to know about their past. The first section of Fea-tures, with a pink band at the top of each page, covers the countries' history of occupation and its people, with essays on culture, nature and food. These lively, authoritative essays are all written by specialists.
◆ The main Places section, with a blue band at the top of the page, covers each country and their his-tory since independence. There is then a full run-down of all the attrac-tions worth seeing. Principal places of interest are co-ordinated by number with full-colour maps.
◆ The Travel Tips listings section, colour-coded in yellow, provides a convenient point of reference for information on travel, accommoda-tion, restaurants, activities and fes-

LEFT: a traditional rural dwelling in Lithuania.

to contribute to travel publications. He is currently posted with Estonian Public Broadcasting.

Richard Schofield has been based in Lithuania since 2001. At the time of writing he is the editor of the locally-produced *Vilnius In Your Pocket* city guide, as well as a contributing editor to countless other In Your Pocket guides throughout Eastern Europe. Something of an expert on life behind the former Iron Curtain, Richard is also a professional photographer and is currently at work photographing Russia for Insight Guides.

Martins Zaprauskis is the editor of the highly acclaimed city guide *Riga In Your Pocket* and has lived in Riga, Latvia since 1998. He has also edited or authored guides for In Your Pocket in the Netherlands, Czech Republic, Germany, Croatia, Hungary and Romania.

The Features chapter were updated by **Roger Williams**, who compiled the original edition – was the first colour guide book to the then newly independent countries. Roger also provided the new photo essays on The Baltic Sea and Saunas.

Much of the photography for the book was supplied by **Micah Sarut**, winner of the Insight Guides/Independent on Sunday photography competition. An architect, writer and photographer who writes a monthly travel column for Iamstaggered.com USA, and has exhibited his photography at numerous galleries. Many of the other images are the work of Insight regulars **Anna Mockford** and **Nick Bonetti**. Picture research was undertaken by **Tom Smyth**.

The book was proofread by **Neil Titman** and indexed by **Helen Peters**.

Map Legend

___ ..	International Boundary
_ _ _ _	Province Boundary
⊖	Border Crossing
_ ._ ._	National Park/Reserve
_ _ _ _	Ferry Route
✈ ✈	Airport: International Regional
🚌	Bus Station
❶	Tourist Information
✉	Post Office
🏛 † ⛪	Church/Ruins
†	Monastery
☾	Mosque
✡	Synagogue
🏰 🏯	Castle/Ruins
🏠	Mansion/Stately home
∴	Archaeological Site
∩	Cave
𝐈	Statue/Monument
★	Place of Interest

The main places of interest in the Places section are coordinated by number with a full-colour map (eg ❶), and a symbol at the top of every right-hand page tells you where to find the map.

tivals. Travel Tips information may be located quickly by using the index printed on the back cover flap – and the flaps also serve as bookmarks.
◆ Photographs are chosen not only to illustrate landscape and attractions but also to convey the moods of the countries and the activities of their people.

The contributors

This fourth edition of the book was managed by **Tom Le Bas** at Insight's London office and comprehensively updated by **Steve Roman** in Tallinn, **Martins Zaprauskis** in Rīga, and **Richard Schofield** in Vilnius.

Steve Roman, a journalist from San Francisco, has been living in Estonia for more than a decade. After spending several years as Editor in Chief of the *Tallinn In Your Pocket* city guides, he now works as a freelance journalist and continues

Contents

LEFT: 18th-century splendour at Latvia's Rundāle Palace.

Maps

THE BEST OF ESTONIA, LATVIA AND LITHUANIA: TOP ATTRACTIONS

From saunas, sandy beaches and untouched islands to state-of-the-art galleries and old-world architecture, the three countries have plenty to offer, both in the towns and in the countryside

△ **Tallinn Old Town** This is as pretty as Old Towns get, with cobbled streets, a harmonious square and attractive buildings such as The Three Sisters. Like the other two capitals, Tallinn is a Unesco World Heritage Site. *See page 113*

▷ **Palmse Manor** One of the finest restored manors, the house and grounds show the luxurious lifestyle of the Baltic German nobles who bought it in 1873. There is a coach and car museum here, too. *See page 165*

◁ **Museum of the History of Rīga and Navigation** The best historical museum in the Baltics, it explains the Latvian capital's rich past acquired by the Hansa merchants, with paintings, furniture and decorative arts. *See page 206*

▽ **The Curonian Spit** This magnificent 98km (60-mile) spit is a dazzling white sandy hill alongside the Lithuanian coast. "One must see it to give pleasure to one's soul," wrote Alexander von Humboldt. *See page 320*

△ **Gauja National Park** This is the place to go for outdoor activities, from bobsleighing to canoeing, horse riding to bungee-jumping. It's a favourite of Latvians, who, like all Baltic people, love the outdoor life. *See page 241*

◁ **Amber Museum, Palanga** This extraordinary fossil of pine resin is a feature of the Baltic coast, where it made many fortunes. The museum in Palanga, Lithuania, is the place to find out all about it. *See page 319*

△ **Saunas** Don't visit without trying a sauna. Traditionally, these lie at the heart of country homes, but today can be found in hotels and locations throughout the three countries. *See page 62*

△ **Saaremaa** The largest of Estonia's many islands is a real rural retreat, with a new marina, meteorite craters and the castle at Kuressaare (interior detail pictured), the only complete medieval fortress in the Baltics. *See page 154*

△ **Art Nouveau, Rīga** Latvia's capital is known for its Art Nouveau, which flourished here at the turn of the 20th century. Among its architects was Mikhail Eisenstein, father of the great filmmaker. *See page 208*

▷ **Trakai** Built just outside Vilnius in the 14th century by Grand Duke Vytautus, this imposing brick Gothic castle, beautifully set on a lake, embodies Lithuania's glorious past. *See page 284*

THE BEST OF ESTONIA, LATVIA AND LITHUANIA: EDITOR'S CHOICE

First-rate cultural attractions, emotive pilgrimage sites, colourful markets, peaceful forests and long, sandy beaches... here at a glance are our recommendations of what to prioritise to make the most of your trip

BEST BEACHES

● **Pärnu**
Estonia's "summer capital" buzzes with beach parties and barbecues to make the most of the white nights. *See page 143*

● **Jūrmala**
This string of small towns lies just outside Rīga, attracting a holiday crowd. The name in Latvian simply means "seaside". *See page 215*

● **Ventspils**
This prosperous small town on Latvia's coast has a fine beach, an outdoor museum of old fishing boats and a narrow-gauge railway. *See page 225*

● **Palanga**
This Lithuanian settlement of fishermen and amber-gatherers is now a popular resort. *See page 319*

● **Nida**
The main resort of Lithuania's Curonian Spit has sandy beaches and several museums, including the summer home of Thomas Mann. *See page 321*

FAMILY ATTRACTIONS

● **Open-Air Museums**
All three countries have open-air museums where traditional buildings have been brought together. Here, costumed blacksmiths, potters and other craftspeople show their skills. *See Tallinn page 128, Rīga page 213, Rumšiškės page 294*

● **Estonian Puppet Theatre**
A popular local attraction, and although shows are in Estonian, they are not hard to follow. There is also a high-tech museum of puppet history, and theatres in Rīga and Kaunas, too. *See Travel Tips, Activities, page 358*

● **Zoos**
Zoos in Tallinn, Rīga and Kaunas have large animal collections, and with children's playgrounds they are orientated towards families. *See Travel Tips, Activities, pages 358–9*

● **Horse Riding**
The quiet lanes and forest tracks are ideal for hacking, and there are stables throughout the three countries. *See page 75 and Travel Tips, Activities, page 364*

TOP: in costume at Tallinn's open-air museum. **ABOVE:** puppet theatre, Tallinn. **LEFT:** on the beach at Palanga.

BIRD-WATCHING

• **Matsalu National Park**
The flatlands of Matsalu Bay in Estonia attract waders, terns and white-tailed eagles. *See page 148*

• **Vilsandi National Park**
Covering 150 islets off the coast of Estonia, this is a hatching ground for many European species. *See page 157*

• **Pape Nature Park**
This is the best place to see migrating birds in Latvia. *See page 226*

• **Engure Lake and Nature Reserve**
Around 50,000 birds a year visit Latvia's 18km (12-mile) long lake, which has a floating ornithological station. *See page 236*

• **Nemunas Delta Regional Park** (Lithuania)
Base of the Vente Horn ornithological ringing station, Nemunas is notable for its migratory birds. *See page 322*

ABOVE: Stalin's car at the Occupation Museum in Rīga.
LEFT: a black stork, summer visitor to the region.

PILGRIM SIGHTS

• **Pühajärv Oak**
The biggest and oldest oak in Estonia is said to possess magical powers. *See page 137*

• **Occupation Museum, Rīga**
The museum depicts life under the Soviets, with a railway wagon to show how, from 1941 to 1949, 15,000 were deported from Rīga to Siberia and elsewhere. *See page 202*

• **The Virgin of Aglona**
This venerated Byzantine figure is the object of Latvia's largest annual pilgrimage. *See page 232*

• **Madonna of the Gates of Dawn**
Lithuanians and Poles come every year to pray before Vilnius' most venerated icon. *See page 276*

ART GALLERIES

• **Kumu, Tallinn**
This multi-functional maze of copper, limestone and glass is the highlight of the Art Museum of Estonia. *See page 126*

• **Viinistu Art Museum**
The largest private collection of Estonian paintings was acquired by the former financial manager of Abba and is now housed in the village's canning factory. *See page 167*

• **Užupis Gallery, Vilnius**
Contemporary exhibitions are held here at the heart of the arty, breakaway republic of Užupis. *See page 275*

• **National Art Gallery, Vilnius**
Newly refurbished, the gallery includes a collection of folk art. Its changing exhibitions are worth a look. *See page 281*

• **The MK Čiurlionis Art Museum, Kaunas**
Some 360 works by Lithuania's best-known artist-composer, with the chance to hear some of his work in the "listening hall". *See page 293*

• **Museum of the Holocaust, Vilnius**
This tells the story of the thousands of Jews in "the Jerusalem of Lithuania" who were forced into ghettos, then sent to their deaths. *See page 279*

• **The Ninth Fort, Kaunas**
A haunting memorial to the 30,000 Jews who were shot in the 19th-century fort that became the burial ground for the victims of Kaunus' ghetto. *See page 294*

• **Hill of Crosses, Šiauliai**
A remarkable symbol of the resilience and faith of the Lithuanians, this hill has collected thousands of crosses, brought here by ordinary people. *See page 326*

ABOVE: statue at Kumu, Tallinn. **RIGHT:** the Hill of Crosses, Šiauliai, Lithuania.

THE BALTIC STATES

Estonia, Latvia and Lithuania, each with its own strong individual identity and rich in culture, are lands of vibrant capitals, exquisite architecture, pristine beaches and unspoilt rural landscapes

The term "Baltic States" groups together three small neighbouring northern European countries that have shared histories, similar geographies, different languages and quite separate identities. Lying between Scandinavia in the north and Poland in the south, with Russia looking on from the east, they are in helpful alphabetical order north to south – Estonia, Latvia and Lithuania, the order they appear in this guide. Their combined total area of 175,000 sq km (67,500 sq miles) makes them smaller than Austria and about the size of Oklahoma.

Travelling between the three is relatively simple by road, on the Via Baltica, but north–south transport has never been developed: there is no rail link between the capital cities of Estonia and Latvia, 300km (186 miles) apart, and it takes 40 hours and six train changes to travel from Warsaw to Tallin, though a new "Rail Baltica" is promised.

Fairytale Old Towns

Many visitors will head for the capitals to see the extraordinarily attractive and well-preserved Old Towns that have won each of them a place on the Unesco World Heritage list.

They have distinct flavours: Estonia's fairytale Tallinn with cobblestones, Lutheran church spires and any excuse for a song; Latvia's busy Rīga on the Daugava, largest of the capitals (pop. 710,000), with guild halls, an impressive Gothic cathedral and a great market in former Zeppelin hangars; and Lithuania's Baroque Vilnius, where there is an emphasis on art and a background of Catholic shrines. Beautiful to look at and easily assimilated, with cultural attractions and some good bars and restaurants, it is not surprising that they

PRECEDING PAGES: views across the rooftops of old Tallinn; on the beach at Jūrmala, Latvia; Aukštaitija, Lithuania. **LEFT:** rural Estonia. **TOP:** birch forest in eastern Latvia. **ABOVE RIGHT:** Tartu Cathedral. **ABOVE LEFT:** festivals are a feature of Baltic life.

have become popular short-break destinations. Tallinn is European Capital of Culture in 2011, Rīga in 2014.

The summer holiday resorts of Pärnu (Estonia), Jūrmala (Latvia) and Palanga (Lithuania) have been popular since the 19th century, and you will still hear Russian spoken on their promenades, as sea-starved neighbours return for a traditional break. Backed by dunes and pine woods, the blond sands of the islands and coasts are washed by the safe, shallow Baltic Sea. Having spent half a century out of bounds, the shore has been kept free of development until only recently, when smart hotels and spa facilities have been installed to cater for the modern tourist's demands. There is plenty of waterborne activity, with the myriad islands of Estonia to explore, though a proper sailing culture has yet to take off.

Manors and myths

A longer break might take in more than one capital, or a second city: Tartu, the university town of Estonia, ancient Cēsis in Latvia, or Kaunas, the former capital of Lithuania, all rich in culture and traditions. Castles and manor houses will also tempt people out of town: the handsomely restored Palmse Manor in Estonia; Rundāle Palace in Latvia, built by Bartolomeo Rastrelli, architect of St Petersburg's Winter Palace; or the beautifully situated island castle of Trakai in Lithuania. Most

towns have a civic gallery or museum that will tell you about the life of the area. All three countries maintain the kind of pride in their past that newly re-established nations so often feel the need for. Myths and legends, stories of local heroes and bold defenders of freedom lurk in every ruin and monument. Sometimes the ghastly events of the 20th century, which wrenched the countries in all directions, don't seem far away.

From e-capital to rural retreat

Life in the capitals is much like life in any modern city, and highly wired Tallinn, where Skype was invented and where the world's first paperless parliament was introduced, is in advance of most. But the urban dwellers feel a need to escape to the countryside, and most weekends see an exodus to friends or relations who have a patch of land and some space. Here is peace and quiet, in some quite untouched places, in woodland and forest inhabited by elk and boar, in meadows and marshes where many birds gather, and by countless lakes and rivers.

TOP: painted doorway, Tallinn. **ABOVE RIGHT:** Žemaitija sculpture. **ABOVE LEFT:** rural scene in southern Lithuania.

In Lithuania shrines sprout from roadsides, and each country has its open-air rural museums where you can see how life was lived before the Industrial Revolution, when houses and churches were hewn with axes and the Baltic serfs had to live under their foreign masters. Attendants are dressed in traditional costumes, which are worn on any of the many festive occasions that have kept the nations singing and dancing through hard times.

People remain deeply attached to their rural roots, and visiting the countryside or staying on a farm is most certainly the best way to enter the local soul. Here are plots of land, carefully tended for local use, with flowers planted alongside vegetables and fruit, and perhaps some chicken and fowl for the pot.

Long summer days

The seasons are pronounced, and life follows them closely. Winters are deep and dark, so when days lengthen and the sun shines, people are more than ready to get outdoors. Children have a full three months' holiday in summer, and there are myriad attractions and activities

on offer in the widespread national parks, from canoeing and horse riding to archery, and even kiiking, a hair-raising swing invented by an Estonian. Beach parties make the most of light evenings, with barbecues, DJs and occasional skinny dipping. There are many macho events to choose from too, from paintballing and karting to army-style activities, laid on for the stag-party and team-building crowds.

Whether in the city or down on the farm, don't leave without experiencing a sauna, one of the Baltic States' great institutions. ❏

Top: summer pleasures on the Žemaitija lakes, Lithuania. **Above Left:** the Hilmuaa Islands, Estonia.

THE BALTIC PEOPLES

In terms of history and geography, these countries have much in common – and yet each retains a strong national characteristic in its approach to life

The people of the three Baltic nations are as different from each other as the Poles are from the Norwegians, or the Irish from the Dutch, but one characteristic that showed itself immediately after independence, in common with all newly emergent or re-emergent states, was a tendency for self-absorption, accompanied by a constant need to discuss their plight. In part, this is a general complaint of small countries, but, more importantly, it was the result of the systematic, and partially successful, attempt by Russia to exterminate them, leaving many with a strong sense of doubt as to their own worth, and to the worth of their countries on the world stage.

If repression had been any harsher, Estonians, Latvians and Lithuanians might have met the same fate as the Ingrians, Kalmuks, Tatars and other small nations who got in Stalin's way. As it was, the debasement of the language and national culture through Russification and Sovietisation left a deep-rooted scar on the collective psyche.

New-found confidence

But as they began to make a name for themselves, from winning and staging the Eurovision Song Contest (a dubious honour, but certainly a way of becoming noticed), gaining medals at the Olympics and sending forces to Afghanistan, the endless soul-searching diminished.

Having a shared recent past has done little to diminish national differences. For instance, Lithuanians remain stereotypically the most outgoing people from the three countries, and

In the first decade after independence all three countries suffered a decline in population, taking their numbers back to where they were before the intense Russification of the 1970s.

are perhaps the most nationalistic. A memory of the Grand Duchy that ran from the Baltic to the Black Sea still exerts a profound influence over people. Sometimes the result is attractive: national self-confidence gives Lithuanians a zeal to succeed and regain their rightful place among what they consider to be Europe's "real" countries. The desire not to be outstripped

LEFT: singers at a cultural festival in Estonia.
RIGHT: Latvian football fan on midsummer's eve.

economically by Poland, their historical partner and sometime coloniser, is deep.

"The world may not know much about us, but it should," is a deeply ingrained attitude – though anyone who follows basketball will know its stars well. This "think big" *Weltanschauung* meshes neatly with a continuing fixation with the USA, the Promised Land to which many tens of thousands of Lithuanians have emigrated over the past 100 years. Despite its distance, the USA remains a dominant cultural influence: televised NBA basketball games attract an avid following, while the American ambassador's comings and goings are front-

ignorance. Contacts between Estonians and Lithuanians, when they happen, seem to be the warmest, with the austere Nordic character of the former complementing the exuberance of the latter. But all three Baltic republics share a certain shrewd scepticism in their humour.

One renowned Lithuanian political commentator remarked during the scandal surrounding the populist President Rolandas Paksas, who was impeached for awarding Lithuanian citizenship to a rich Russian financial backer, "We used to joke about how Lithuanians couldn't defend themselves against a few million Russians. Now we joke about how we

page news. Conversely, Lithuanians tend to be remarkably uninterested in their neighbours. Few could name the prime ministers of major neighbours such as Poland, Sweden or Belarus. The idea, therefore, that economic or political self-interest should lead to a close engagement with such countries is regarded with amused indifference, or, in the case of Poland, with suspicion and defensiveness.

Lithuanians like talking about Baltic co-operation, but they are generally much less enthusiastic about following it up in practice. Despite close linguistic ties with their Baltic cousins, the Latvians, Lithuanians treat their northern neighbours rather as Americans treat Canadians: benignly and with sweeping

can't defend ourselves against a few Russians and their millions."

Solid stock

The stereotype goes that the Latvian national character lies somewhere in between the reserved Estonians and the outgoing Lithuanians, but this really doesn't begin to do them justice. The German, Protestant influence, as in Estonia, results in a solid, reliable work ethic that has largely survived the effects of Soviet Communism. Slow starters, Latvians initially lagged behind their Baltic neighbours in economic

ABOVE: a military parade, Rīga. **RIGHT:** dining out on a summer's evening in Vilnius.

reform, but soon easily overtook Lithuania in attracting investment from abroad, and on several scores were doing even better than Estonia, the unquestioned star performer. But when the downturn struck, they were hardest hit.

Latvians' roots are traditionally in the countryside – something apparent in everything from folk art to the national cuisine. But while the Latvians treasure their rustic roots, they have also taken to their new way of life with aplomb. Most work hard in their determination to make a better life for themselves, and it is perfectly common for young people to hold down a demanding full-time job, study for a

> Today there are around 5,000 Jews in Vilnius. Until World War II there were some 100,000, nearly half the population of the city described as the Centre of Jewry in Europe; and 250,000 Lithuanian Jews died in the Holocaust.

higher degree, attend language lessons and go to the gym, while still maintaining a full social life. Latvians' good nature is sometimes said to be their undoing. Whereas the Estonians maintained a stony inner resistance to Russification, this process advanced far further in Latvia: mixed marriages were more frequent, and national consciousness seemed the weakest in the Baltics when the independence struggle began in the late 1980s. Whereas Lithuanians make up 80 percent of the population of their country, Latvians are in a bare majority (just under 60 percent at the last count) in theirs – which adds a bitter edge to the question of naturalising the hundreds of thousands of postwar settlers, many of whom have taken up their entitlement for Latvian citizenship.

Not to be forgotten among the Latvians are the Livs, a handful of descendants of the original coastal tribe, who like the Estonians speak a Finno-Ugric language. Latvians have a special respect for this almost extinct race and its mystical link with the past.

Linguistic differences

The difference between Estonians and their Baltic neighbours – and indeed most of Europe – is well illustrated by the language. Whereas Latvian and Lithuanian have some elements in common, Estonian, with its unfamiliar vocabulary, chirruping intonation, ultra-complex grammar and distinctive word order, is as impenetrable to most European ears as Hungarian or Finnish. This is not surprising: Estonians, like these two nations, are members of the Finno-Ugric ethnic family, whose origins lie deep in the marshes of Siberia. Despite substantial influences from their Swedish, Danish, German and Russian rulers over the past six centuries, Estonians prize their bloodline – sometimes comically: "War is an Indo-European phenomenon," one visitor was startled to hear. "It's because of your settlement pattern: you live in villages, while we prefer solitary forest clearings."

Equally incongruously, the Estonians' Finno-Ugric near neighbours, the Finns, are regarded rather disparagingly, frequently referred to as "elk". Of course, there have long been close ties between the two countries. During Soviet times Estonians could not be prevented from tuning in to Finnish television, and Finland's helping hand in the early days of independence was invaluable. But the long-standing tradition of boatloads of Finns turning up in Tallinn for a weekend of heavy drinking is as strong as ever, and for many Estonians, this is the image they have of their neighbours. Estonians have had many years to brood on the misfortune that has soured their history. Just as Lithuanians like to tell you that their country is at the geographical centre of Europe, that their language is archaic and their folk art extraordinary, and just as Latvians will point out that in the pre-war years of their first independence they were one of Europe's great dairy exporters, so Estonians relish any chance to explain that their country was, before the war, more prosperous than Finland.

Looking to Scandinavia

Estonia has its face set squarely towards Helsinki and Stockholm. The majority of young, economically active Estonians have visited one or both of these cities. Unlike Lithuanians or Latvians, whose emigrations are far more dis-

persed – Ireland is an especially popular destination in recent years – in other hemispheres, one of the most active Estonian diasporas lies

> Though the idea that real friendship is like a precious cordial which should only be offered to one's nearest and dearest can be off-putting to foreigners, Estonians are not unfriendly: once the friendship is actually made, it is solid and lasting.

just across the Baltic Sea, in Sweden. Estonians are only too aware of the importance of their Scandinavian neighbours: indeed, many Estonians would be glad to shed their "Baltic" tag altogether and are more likely to describe themselves as being Scandinavian.

However, even if Estonia does consider itself the "least" Baltic of the three states, no Estonian would deny that their country is historically inextricable from both Latvia and Lithuania. Estonia sometimes chooses to see itself as more Scandinavian simply to differentiate itself from its southern neighbours. It is not a rational attitude to geopolitics that distinguishes the Estonian national character, but rather its degree of reserve, which is in stark contrast to the other Baltic states. Staying for more than a few days in Vilnius, for example, a foreigner is likely to be invited into a Lithuanian household, stuffed with food, offered presents, taken on guided tours, introduced to family, friends and pets, and generally made to feel at home. In Latvia the visitor will find hospitality, too, though the atmosphere will be more relaxed and not quite so intense. Invited to a house, you will not escape without sampling home produce, some of which may be pressed on you to take away.

More hugs and kisses

Estonians, however, have mastered the art of being impeccably polite without being friendly, and an invitation to an Estonian home is rare. Friendship, an Estonian may tell you, is for life, and it would not be right for a new acquaintance to be invited into their home when they know that sooner or later he or she will go away.

But, as with so much else in the Baltics, old habits are changing, especially with the young and more widely travelled generation. Public displays of affection were once disdainfully regarded as a "Russian thing", but young Estonians increasingly kiss each other on the cheeks or hug by way of greeting each other and generally behave like most other Europeans in public settings.

Despite their differences, Estonians, Latvians and Lithuanians are united by a love of nature and the outdoors. Admittedly, they enjoy it in different ways. Lithuanians will drive their car to a beauty spot and blast their surroundings with pop music, whereas Latvians will organise barbecues or swimming parties. Estonians tend to regard such habits with horror, going to great lengths to find a truly solitary spot where they can sit in silence. ❑

LEFT: most urban residents in all three countries have their roots in the countryside.

The Russians

Relationships with the largest minority are not always easy on a political level, and equality laws are on the agenda

Russian-speakers make up substantial communities in Estonia and Latvia. Citizenship laws introduced since independence have reduced their official number in Estonia from 32 percent to just under 8 percent today. In Latvia, which brought in similar laws, ethnic Russians make up around 27 percent of the population – about 40 percent of Rīga, and just over half of Daugavpils – and more than half have Latvian citizenship.

Relations between Balts and Russians can be seen on two levels. On a personal level, as friends and neighbours, they tend to get along fine. Russians are, on the whole, easygoing and cause few problems in the countries that are their homes. Politically, matters are easily stirred. History is a cause of great contention. Russia continues to portray Stalin as the countries' saviour. The Baltic States see him as their destroyer. Both sides are capable of seeing themselves as the oppressed.

Waves of immigration

Small communities of Russians had lived in the area since the early Middle Ages, when some Baltic tribes paid tribute to Russian princes. After the conquest by Peter the Great, these were joined by Russian soldiers, merchants and officials. At the end of the 19th century a major influx of Russian workers began. This was interrupted by World War I and the Russian Revolution, which drove considerable numbers of White Russian refugees to the Baltics. Before 1940, Rīga was the greatest Russian émigré centre after Paris.

When Stalin occupied the Baltic States in June 1940, these émigrés were among the first to suffer from the secret police. Newspapers and cultural centres were closed and churches converted for secular purposes. In 1944–5 the reconquest of the Baltics by the Soviet Union (or the liberation, as Russia today would have it) began a process of Russian immigration that drastically altered the region's demography. The great majority of Russians now living in the Baltic area are immigrants

RIGHT: Tallinn's Nevsky Cathedral, a focal point for the city's Russian Orthodox community.

from the Soviet period – many sent here against their will – or their descendants.

A question of citizenship

Lithuania, with far fewer Russians (14 percent of Vilnius, 21 percent of Klaipėda) granted citizenship to all of its residents during the early 1990s, but the Latvian and Estonian governments decided that its "non-citizens" would not be allowed such automatic rights. Once the European Union spotlight fell on the Baltic States, however, all three governments had to deal with the minority issue.

Tensions today remain. None of the countries have ministers with responsibilities for minorities,

and it was only in 2009 that the first law dealing with discrimination – The Equal Treatment Act – came into force in Estonia, where a progressive programme of naturalisation has been backed up by the creation of a large, state-funded Russian cultural centre in Tallinn. Meanwhile, public administration employees, such as nurses, police and prison officials, are required to have a minimum level of Estonian-language ability and, with the exception of Narva, which has a high Russian population, all public administration is in Estonian. Ethnic Russians must pass a citizenship test, which includes a language test, and there are complaints that they are discriminated against over jobs and housing. In Latvia and Estonia 60 percent of all classes must be held in Latvian and Estonian. ❏

DECISIVE DATES

6000 BC
Finno-Ugric peoples from southeast Europe reach Estonia.

2500 BC
Indo-European culture merges with indigenous population in Latvia and Lithuania. Kurs, Semigallians, Letgallians, Sels and Finno-Ugric Livs settle.

9th–10th centuries
Vikings establish trade routes to Byzantium via the River Daugava.

1201
German crusaders establish a bishopric in Liv settlement at Rīga, which becomes capital of Livonia (Terra Mariana), part of the Holy Roman Empire.

1219
Danes take Tallinn.

CHRISTIAN CRUSADERS
1230
Mindaugas unites the Grand Duchy of Lithuania. He adopts Christianity and is crowned king (1253).

1236
Latvian and Lithuanian forces defeat crusaders at Saulė.

1282
Rīga joins Hanseatic League; Tallinn joins three years later.

1316
Lithuanian expansion begins.

1346
Danes sell Duchy of Estonia to the Teutonic Order.

1386
Duke Jogaila and Queen Jadwiga marry, uniting Poland and Lithuania until 1795.

1410
Joint Polish-Lithuanian forces defeat the Teutonic Knights in the Battle of Grunwald/Tannenberg/Žalgiris.

1520s
The Reformation establishes Lutheranism in Latvia and Estonia.

SHIFTING POWERS
1558–83
Livonian Wars. Northern Estonia comes under Swedish

rule, southern Estonia under Polish. Polish duchies established in Kurzeme (Courland) and Pārdaugava in Latvia. German bishop of Piltene (Latvia) and Oesel (Saaremaa Island) sells land to Denmark.

1579
Vilnius University founded.

1600–29
Polish-Swedish War leaves Estonia and northern Latvia in Swedish hands; southern Latvia and Lithuania in Poland's.

1694
St Peter's steeple, Rīga, the "tallest in the world", is completed.

1700–21
Great Northern War between Charles XII of Sweden and Peter the Great results in Russian victory. Russia occupies Estonia and Latvia.

1712
Martha Skavronska, a peasant from Latvia, marries Peter the Great and is later crowned Empress of Russia.

1795
Lithuania becomes part of the Russian Empire. Lithuania Minor (modern-day Klaipėda and Kaliningrad) falls to Prussia.

NATIONAL AWAKENING
1812
Napoleon marches through Lithuania en route to Moscow, raising hopes of freedom from Russia.

1860–85
The era of National Awakening. Abolition of serfdom and new educational opportunities lead to literary and artistic flowering.

1885
An era of intense Russification begins following unsuccessful uprisings against Russia; local languages displaced.

1905
The first socialist revolution demands independence. Manors are burnt and hundreds of citizens executed.

1914–18
World War I. War is waged on three fronts, between Germans and White and Red Russians. Bolsheviks seize power in bloodless coup in Estonia, but are unable to maintain control. Germany occupies Latvia and Lithuania.

FIRST INDEPENDENCE
1918
Republics declared in Estonia and Latvia. German Army moves in, and power briefly

returns to German aristocracy. Soviets move in, but with some Allied help are fought back.

1920
Independence in Estonia, Latvia, and Lithuania. Poland, also newly independent, seizes Vilnius.

1923
Lithuania reclaims Klaipėda.

1939
Hitler–Stalin Pact puts the Baltic States under the Soviet sphere of influence; Soviet soldiers arrive. Baltic Germans are ordered back to Germany.

1940–41
Red Army terror rages. Thousands are deported or shot.

1941–4
German occupation of Baltics. Concentration camps are set up. Almost the entire Jewish population is exterminated.

1944
The Soviets reoccupy the Baltics and turn them into Soviet republics. Mass reprisals, and deportations to Siberia.

1953
Death of Stalin.

THE END OF OCCUPATION
1988
Opposition parties established.

1989
A 690km (430-mile) human chain, from Tallinn to Vilnius, links up in protest in the "Singing Revolution".

1991
Soviet intervention. Independence restored.

1993
Pope John Paul II pays a visit to Lithuania's Hill of Crosses.

1994
Last Russian troops depart. Tallinn–Helsinki ferry, *Estonia*, sinks with loss of 852 lives.

2003
Rolandas Paksas, president of Lithuania, is impeached.

2004
All three countries become members of NATO and the European Union.

2008
"Baltic tiger" boom ends.

2011
Estonia joins the Eurozone. Tallinn is the European Capital of Culture.

TOP LEFT: tomb of a crusader bishop in Dundaga Castle, Latvia. LEFT: Peter the Great. ABOVE: German troops in Latvia, 1917. RIGHT: Estonia is leading the way into the Eurozone.

A SHARED HISTORY

Before independence, Estonia and Latvia had lived under occupation for the best part of eight centuries, while Lithuania flourished in a union with Poland

One of the most perplexing problems facing the Paris peace conference in 1919 was what to do about the Baltic provinces of tsarist Russia which the Bolsheviks, not without a fight, had consented to let go. Lithuania had once ruled the largest empire in Europe. It was somewhat overwhelmed by Poland before both were swallowed, almost but not quite whole, by Russia in the 18th century. Estonia and what was put forward to the peace conference as an independent state which called itself Latvia were, by any historical or political criteria, equally elusive.

Nevertheless, three independent states were internationally recognised under these names, although first the Bolsheviks and then Stalin made it plain that it was not a situation that could be tolerated for ever.

Their independence was sentenced to death by the Nazi–Soviet Pact just before World War II. The pact implied that the Baltic States would be parcelled out between the two, but it was overtaken by events with Hitler's invasion of the Soviet Union.

The three states were incorporated into the Soviet Union in 1940 and at the end of the war they were reconquered, and though there were some minor concessions to autonomy, they became virtual Russian provinces once again.

Russia's grand designs

Among few other peoples did the Soviet mill grind finer than in Estonia, Latvia and Lithuania. They occupied a special place in Soviet

strategy, an updated version of Peter the Great's "window to the West", which began with the founding of St Petersburg but envisaged expansion southwards to maximise Russia's access to the Baltic, often referred to as the "Northern Mediterranean". Russia had initially been held to ransom by German Balts who controlled the Estonian and Latvian ports, and Peter the Great was determined that it would never happen again, a view with which the Soviet regime totally concurred.

Lithuania was regarded in exactly the same light, and it was agents of the tsar, long before any thought of Soviet Man, who vowed to obliterate all signs of national Baltic identities.

LEFT: the end of occupation – a painting in Lithuania's parliament building of a 1991 rally in Vilnius.
RIGHT: starting the occupation, Teutonic Knights.

The Russification of the Baltic provinces in the 19th century was so successful that when the matter of their independence came up at the Paris peace conference one question asked was sublimely naive: "Who are these people and whence did they come?" For three nations buried so deep in the history of others that their identities were long presumed to have been lost, they have surprisingly robust tales to tell.

Three languages

The countries also have common bonds. With their backs to the Baltic Sea, they have been hemmed in by the great powers of Sweden,

was a long time before the languages, with their extended alphabets and complex word endings, were written down.

Religion follows trade

Baltic peoples also took longer than the rest of Europe to embrace Christianity, preferring their sacred oaks and thunderous gods. Some of the earliest Christian teaching came from Orthodox traders from the east. The trade routes were well established, up the River Daugava and down the Dnieper to the Black Sea. Amber was the singular commodity the Balts possessed, and others wanted it. This gem,

Denmark, Germany and Russia, who have all interfered in their affairs for 800 years. In fact, the peoples of the three countries come from two distinct groups, neither Slavic like the Russians nor Teutonic like the Germans. In the north there were the Finno-Ugric tribes of Estonia and the Livs of Latvia, of whom only a handful remain.

Latvia was otherwise peopled by Letts, who, like Lithuanians, were Indo-European Balts whose language has some similarities with Sanskrit. For instance, the words for "god", "day" and "son" in Lithuanian are *dievas*, *diena* and *sunus* and *devas*, *dina* and *sunu* in Sanskrit. In Estonian, which has similarities with Hungarian, those words are *jumal*, *poeg* and *päev*. But it

made of fossilised pine resin, made its way to ancient Egypt and Greece.

Among those taking this trade route were the Vikings, and it was their leader, Vladimir I, who first united the Slavic Russians and made a capital on the Dnieper at Kiev. When the Scandinavians settled down on the Baltic coast, they did so in Estonia: *Taani Linn* (Tallinn) is Estonian for Danish town. By then the real conquering force of the Baltics was beginning to dig in. The German crusaders appeared in 1201 in Rīga, where they installed a bishopric for Albrecht of Bremen. From there, they set down roots of

ABOVE: the Danes' capture of Tallinn.
RIGHT: Peter the Great prized the coast highly.

The Latin Mare Balticum is known as the West Sea by Estonians and the East Sea by Scandinavians and Germans. English-, Lithuanian-, Latvian- and Romance-language-speakers call it the Baltic Sea.

a ruling class in all three countries that lasted into the 20th century.

This elite arrived in religious orders, which fought among themselves as much as they fought against those who opposed them. There were the ministers of the archbishop, the burghers of the city and the Knights of the Sword, who became Knights of the Livonian Order. The country of Livonia that they created put the different peoples of Latvia and Estonia under the same authority and established a healthy and lucrative environment for the Hanseatic League's merchants, the powerful German trading confederation that followed in their wake.

Lithuania, however, was not so easily brought to heel, and it frequently joined forces with the Kuronian and Semigallian Letts in clashes with the German knights. By the middle of the 13th century the Lithuanian tribes had been unified under Mindaugas, who briefly adopted Christianity so that the Pope, in 1252, could crown him king. When the German knights opposed him, he reverted to his pagan beliefs, and stood his ground against the knights. In 1325 the Lithuanian ruler Gediminas allied himself to the Poles, who had similar problems with the Teutonic Knights.

This union also gave Poland invaluable access to the sea. At its height the duchy was one of Europe's largest countries, stretching from the Baltic to the Black Sea. Gediminas' grandson married the Polish queen and the two houses were united for the next 400 years.

Jesuit builders

Poland brought a strong Catholic influence to Lithuania, and the Jesuits arrived to build their schools and fancy Baroque churches, while the Reformation whipped through the Germanic northern Baltic lands in a trice, converting everyone overnight. In the brief period when half of Latvia became a Polish principality, everyone converted back to Catholicism. The Balts had little say in this matter as in everything else.

Compulsory church attendance made them indifferent as to how the service was conducted. The local inhabitants were denied virtually every privilege and for centuries were not permitted to build houses of stone nor live within the city walls. Membership of the greater guilds was forbidden; even semi-skilled workers, such as millers and weavers, were brought in from abroad. The ruling society was impenetrable. In Estonia and Latvia the German descendants of the knights ruled; in Lithuania there was a rigid aristocracy of Poles. This survived even the break-up of Livonia by the Swedes during the mid-16th century.

The Swedish period is sometimes looked on as an enlightened one, in spite of wars against Poland, then Russia. But there was more talk than action. In Tallinn in 1601 Charles IX demanded peasant children be sent to school and learn a trade. "We further want them to be allowed, without hindrance, to have themselves put to use as they like, because to keep children as slaves is not done in Christendom and has been discontinued there for many years." Despite noble intentions, however, his words fell on deaf ears.

Serfs exchanged for dogs

Further upheaval followed in the 18th century. When Charles XI threatened to take away more than 80 percent of the domains occupied by the descendants of the Teutonic Knights, these German Balts called him a "peasant king" and turned to their other enemy for help. Russia was soon in charge and thereafter took control of Lithuania as well.

In 1764 Catherine the Great visited Estonia and Latvia and found serfs still being sold or exchanged for horses or dogs, and fugitives branded and even mutilated. Little became of her demands for change. In 1771 public auctions of serfs became illegal, but there are records of auctions for years afterwards, while in Lithuania a noble who killed a serf faced only

time. Tartu University, near the Latvian border, was the intellectual force behind the National Awakening in both Estonia and Latvia. However, Lithuania suffered a setback with the closing of its university in 1832, followed by a ban on printing Lithuanian books, which was a punishment for uprisings against the tsar. Paradoxically, throughout the Baltics there was as much Russification towards the end of the century as there was national fervour.

The peasants revolt

Discontent with the unenlightened tsars broke out into the Russian Revolution of 1905. This

a fine. The barons remained powerful, making laws and practising their *droit de seigneur*. Serfdom was not finally abolished until the middle of the 19th century.

Nationalist ideals

In the 18th century the idea of nationhood was fomented by teachers such as J.G. Herder, but it wasn't until the 19th century and the Romantic movements, with towering poets and intellects such as Lithuania's Adam Mickiewicz, that the idea really started gaining ground. There was much lost time to catch up on. The more enlightened German landlords did their best to make amends, starting schools and themselves learning the local languages perhaps for the first

IMPOSSIBLE DECISIONS

One recent event confirms the impossible choices people had to make at the start of World War II. In Lihula in Estonia a former dissident who had become mayor allowed a statue of a soldier in German (Nazi) uniform to be erected. Though disagreeing with Nazi ideology, many veterans see the Germans as delaying Stalin's return and providing a breather in which to try to re-establish independence as well as allowing people to escape abroad. Many of this dwindling band of "freedom fighters" spent years in Soviet labour camps and argue that if Soviet army monuments can remain, the Germans should have one, too. The mayor was told to take it down.

peasants' revolt was a horrifically violent time that affected all the Baltic States, where many were delighted to torch the grand palaces, manors and other buildings of the ruling class. The destruction sparked was the start of a savage century. The two world wars were particularly fiercely fought.

The Red Army, retreating before the German advance, scorched its way homewards at the end of World War I, leaving the land in ruins. Again ravaged by the two sides in World War II, only a few dozen people crawled from the rubble of major ports such as Klaipėda, Ventspils and Narva. Vilnius, the Jerusalem of Lithuania,

state. From 1918 to 1939 the land belonged to the people of the Baltics for the first time for more than seven centuries. The German Balts were sent home, first through land reforms, and in the end by Hitler who, under his pact with Stalin, ordered them out. There was great

There are strong feelings about the Red Latvian Riflemen statue in Rīga. Some see the riflemen as part of the Soviet oppression, others as patriotic fighters against Germany, while some Russians view them as foreign mercenaries.

witnessed the wholesale extermination of the 50,000 Jewish population.

The final injustice was the permanent imposition of Soviet rule and Stalinist terror. Anyone a visitor meets today in the Baltics is likely to have a relation who was sent to Siberia or shot.

Flowering between the wars

The period between the two world wars saw the extraordinary flowering of three quite separate cultures, each coming into its own as a nation

hardship to overcome, but the economies, based on agriculture, grew to match those in the West. Political life was not all roses, but at least it was their own.

This golden age of political autonomy was an era that the Balts looked back to for 50 years thereafter. Only in the late 1980s did they turn away from the past and start to build a new future for themselves.

The struggle for independence during this period cost many lives, but secured for Estonia, Latvia and Lithuania the freedom of self-determination and a future over which they were to have control.   ❑

• *For the three nations' individual histories, see the relevant country chapters in the Places section.*

LEFT: conscription of Estonians into the Russian Army in the 19th century. **ABOVE:** Hitler leads German troops in the occupation of Klaipėda (Memel), Lithuania, on 23 March 1939.

LIFE TODAY

Struggling to overcome the recession whilst embarking on membership of the Eurozone, the countries are finding a new reality with independence

On 13 January 2009 around 10,000 angry Latvians gathered before parliament in Rīga. For the first time since ejecting the Russians nearly 20 years earlier, there were riots and windows were shattered, a shocking thing in a country whose people are not known for their aggression. But the government of Ivars Godmanis was under pressure, and there were tales of corruption. Three days later, Lithuanians were out on the streets of Vilnius, though their government, not long in power, had an easier ride, while Estonians took their cuts stoically and, having had a budget surplus for 18 years, it passed all economic tests to join the Eurozone in 2011.

It was never going to be too easy for the people of the three small Baltic countries to find wealth as well as health and happiness in the modern world, and the recession of 2008 came as a bitter blow after the "Baltic tiger" had come roaring out into the full light of Europe. While preparing to join the Eurozone on 1 January 2011, GDPs fell like stones and unemployment soared. The worst hit by the crisis was Latvia. A year after it had the fastest-growing economy in Europe, it was forced to take on a $7.5 billion-dollar loan from the International Monetary Fund.

The fact is that the three countries had invested their hopes in the European Union. The vote to become members of the EU in 2004 had an enormous effect on national pride. It was final proof that they had surfaced from the great crushing boulder of the Soviet Union into the light of the democratic West. Personal self-confidence and self-esteem were restored.

PRECEDING PAGES: goodbye Lenin, Rīga, 1991.
LEFT: selling flowers for the Midsummer Festival, Rīga. **RIGHT:** keeping an eye on share prices.

Free press and civic pride

In order to accede to the EU, the countries had been made to demonstrate that they were both socially and economically fit. The intervening decade had been far from easy. They were years characterised by divisive political infighting, institutionalised corruption, rampant crime, high prices and appalling wages, all of which contributed to a sense of malaise. Now, a generation after independence, the most pressing remaining social problems have largely been addressed. The mafia and other crooks, always in the vanguard of capitalism's advance, are generally under control, and those who have spent their lives involved in crime and corruption are simply starting to die out. The press is free. There are fewer political parties, and those that remain are more clearly defined.

In many different areas hard work has paid off. A civic pride has revitalised old buildings and kept the streets clean and litter-free, making a necessarily dignified backdrop to progress. Many people have more than one job – not always paid legally – and will often tell you how busy they are. Despite this new-found dynamism, there is a pleasantly relaxed rhythm about day-to-day life.

Estonia prides itself at being at the cutting edge of technology, and it is certainly one of

> To take Latvians' minds off their economic woes, Swedish mobile operator Tele2 organised a hoax meteor crash in the country. The emergency services were not amused.

system, where salary cuts have been deep, particularly in Latvia, where public-sector wages were slashed by 28 percent at the time of the IMF loan. Although often underfunded, the education system is good and the literacy rate is high. Many teachers from school right through to university tenaciously cling on to traditional

the most wired countries in the world, while Lithuania's prime minister Andrius Kubilious has told the IMF of his "ambitious vision" of the Baltic States becoming a world high-tech service hub by 2020.

Health and education

There is still need for improvement, particularly in the basic services of education, healthcare and transport. The public healthcare systems in the main work well. Hygiene is strict, and there are no problems with medical supplies. Scandinavians book into Estonia for cosmetic surgery, and all three countries offer inexpensive medical tourism. But austerity measures are biting here, as they are in the the education

CYBER ATTACK

Relations with Russia, often tense, were brought to a head after the removal of a statue of a Soviet soldier on a war memorial in the centre of Tallinn in 2007. Around 1,300 ethnic Russians living in Estonia were arrested when they protested, and Estonia came under a concerted three-week cyber attack, aimed at government, banking and the media, as well as the Estonian embassy in Russia. It was the first such onslaught in history, and it was particulary important for Estonia, which is probably the most wired country in the world (see E-stonia, page 141). At its height it paralysed the internet system, and froze bank and credit cards and mobile phones.

pedagogy, which gives children a sound schooling in maths, literacy and science. In many ways Balts are better educated than some of their Western counterparts.

The majority of people are fluent in two languages, and a great many are proficient in three. Most Estonians and Latvians are fluent in Russian, a language spoken by some 250 million people. After years of going out of fashion, it is being taken up again by the young. English is taught in almost every school, beginning at an early age, and there are few young people who are not reasonably fluent. Many older people increasingly choose to study German, French,

was lowered to encourage business. Of the three countries, Estonia has the lowest unemployment, its debt levels are among the lowest in Europe and its GDP is around twice that of Latvia.

Following the seasons

Capitalism has not, on the whole, made people particularly greedy. Few people are overly materialistic. While people cherish comfort and certainly enjoy material wealth, most retain a strong sense of what's really important in life, such as family, friends and the need to spend time communing with nature. The changing seasons are very much a part of

Spanish and other European languages, either for work or pleasure.

If public-sector wages are still critically low, private-sector wages for professionals are relatively good. All three countries have a minimum wage, and a statutory 28 days holiday a year. Many foreign companies have set up in the Baltics, taking advantage of the highly educated workforce and helping to create a modernised and efficient working culture. Estonia had pioneered the introduction of a flat tax to get the economy off the ground, and the other countries followed suit. After accession to the EU, the rate

LEFT: clubbing in a disused chemical plant near Tallinn. **ABOVE:** symbolic old and new.

the rhythm of their lives, from the arrival of storks in the spring, when ice melts can lead to floods, to the celebration of midsummer, the most important event in the calendar. The berry- and mushroom-picking of early autumn are followed by the hunkering down of winter, when skis, skates and sledges provide mobility and fun for several months.

Many town dwellers head for the country at weekends, arriving back with baskets full of provisions. Some have bought the allotment plots provided by factories and companies during Soviet times, and many city blocks have cellars in which to store produce. These rural connections are important, as country fare can help city dwellers through hard times.

Population

The average life expectancy for both sexes has risen to around 70 in Estonia and 69 in Latvia and Lithuania, and this is forecast to rise further. Obesity is notable by its absence in all three Baltic countries, perhaps due to the fact that eating habits remain by and large healthy. Many Balts lead an active life. Saunas are regularly taken, and if you are invited to have one, especially in the country, it's an offer worth accepting. However, alcoholism is still serious, despite government legislation to try to tackle the problem, such as banning the sale of alcohol in shops after 10pm in Latvia and

some parts of Estonia. Among society's poorest members, there is still a widespread culture of consuming cheap, potent and sometimes lethal home-made alcohol.

There is also concern about the decrease in populations. Public figures have urged procreation as a matter of patriotic duty, as figures in all three countries since 1991 have shown a gradual decline, with a drift away from rural populations. However, as the three economies improved and people became more reluctant to go abroad to find work, this is becoming less of a problem.

Unemployment has risen as a result of the recession. It has been a driving force behind sex trafficking, particularly in Latvia and Lithuania, from where women are sent to work in the UK, Scandinavia and elsewhere. The countries also provide other EU countries with cheap labour.

Home life

A burgeoning middle class has built homes, taking out mortgages and loans. A mass programme of re-privatising state-owned homes in the years following independence gave them a good start. Property prices were incredibly cheap throughout the 1990s and there were strict state regulations in relation to the purchase of property by foreigners. If you could prove familial ownership of a property prior to the Soviet occupation, you could reclaim the property. Many people who didn't have any claim took advantage of the relatively cheap prices to take on a mortgage.

Property prices in the capital cities have, however, rocketed, thanks in no small part to EU membership and the willingness of some foreigners to pay anything asked. However, prices are still very low in the provinces and in smaller towns. The mortgage market is steadily growing year on year, especially among young people who want to live independently of their families. The average cost of renting and a mortgage are roughly the same. Many families are increasingly choosing to build larger, more spacious houses in the countryside, from where they then commute to the cities.

You can clearly tell when a new home is nearly complete – oak wreaths are displayed when a building is "topped out". There is little or no inheritance tax, a huge incentive for parents to pass their wealth on.

DEMOCRATIC REPUBLICS

The Baltic republics are all parliamentary democracies with a president as the head of state, and the elected governments are led by prime ministers.

The president of Estonia is called the Riigivanem (state elder). The parliament, the Riigikogu, is responsible for all national legislative matters. In Latvia, a 100-member parliament, the Saeima, elects government personnel, including the prime minister. In Lithuania, the Seimas has 141 seats, of which 71 members are elected by popular vote and 70 by proportional representation. The prime minister is appointed by the president on the approval of parliament. Elections are held every four years.

Yet poverty remains in rural areas. In Lithuania half the population does not have an indoor toilet and only a quarter of rural households have running water; out of a population of 3,350,000, some 400,000 have deserted the countryside since independence.

Television and sex

At home, television is a staple entertainment, and there are a number of public and private channels on a regional as well as a local basis; Estonia has seven free digital TV channels. Schedules are a mixture of home-grown programmes and US and Russian imports. Popular programmes

that he did it "for Lithuania", while the woman was so vilified in the media for her actions that she moved abroad.

Equality of the sexes still has a way to go in this predominantly male culture. Homosexuality is something that is often declared only behind firmly closed doors. The attitude towards gays remains unequivocal and attempted Gay Pride marches in all three countries have either met with violence or been banned.

Lithuania, the most morally conservative of the three countries, is loosening its Catholic ties. While Tallinn and Rīga have a widespread reputation for their wild nightlife, Vilnius isn't

have included budget-friendly reality TV shows, such as *Robinson*, in which young people had to eke out an existence on an Estonian island.

> Since independence, Lithuania has become the country with the highest suicide rate in the world. This is largely a rural phenomenon.

And there was a national scandal when a young couple had sex on a Lithuanian reality TV show. The young man involved proudly proclaimed

LEFT: Soviet-era housing block, Rīga. **ABOVE:** standards of education are high in all three countries.

far behind. Estonia and Latvia are generally liberal in relation to sex.

Looking back

As time moves on, and where economic conditions make life for some a struggle, a nostalgia for the Soviet era gnaws at a few folk. Grūtas Park, the Soviet "theme park" in Lithuania, has attracted world attention, and Lenin memorabilia has become collectable. Some say that people have short memories, others that it is a sign of no longer being ashamed of having been "Soviet". Some miss the fact that people had more time, that friendships were more treasured in that atmosphere of mistrust. Others like to talk about that "crazy" time with those who understand. ❏

niv mein de doer wil n nv dit vet so wat   Cuteunor hoch nu weten uy dunchet dn bat nymir un adeven
ebe ſi incht al bi ſine hun th Doer ſuit vn ob n keiſchr   Tid hir au ir is nit ve tye na mendet ik ſolde vi ſcheldeu
e ik heide vele macht up em hebbe ik uv gedacht   Den al welſcti noch ſo vele dn molt uyrto deſem ſude
mor dode wan na ott lat nu noch loir des bodde ik u   Bude m ardeien dtn male hoit an volge nv hre heidenale

THE CHURCH AND RELIGION

The variety of Christian and Jewish beliefs practised has helped define the architecture of the three countries, and major restoration programmes have uncovered superb examples of decorative Baroque and simple Gothic

Throughout the Baltics, religion is often the defining architectural style of a place, from simple wooden Lutheran churches in the north to lavish Baroque masterpieces in the south. Their restoration has been a major part of independence and has helped the Old Towns of the three capitals become World Heritage Sites.

Ever at the mercy of changing spheres of influence, the Baltics have amassed a collection of churches with an extraordinary variety of styles. Their history has also left the countries with some two dozen differing belief codes and has created such a tolerance towards other people and their religions that there are Lutherans who regularly attend Catholic Mass and Catholics who sing in Orthodox choirs. In Tallinn, for example, Methodists and Seventh Day Adventists both share the same church.

Orthodox beginning

With the help of Greek Orthodox Russian merchants, the first teachings of Christ were voiced here in the 11th and 12th centuries, but Christianity did not arrive in full force until the early 13th century when the German crusaders subjugated Estonia and Latvia. This belated start meant that the early European ecclesiastic style, Romanesque, was on the decline. Only St George's in Rīga and the remains of Ikšķile church on an island on the River Daugava give a glimmer of that expiring style. Church architecture in the Baltics begins with Gothic.

In Estonia the earliest stone churches, built of limestone and dating from the end of the

13th century, are on the islands. These were simple Gothic buildings without towers, and were used for protection. On Saaremaa the churches at Kaarma and Valjala have interesting murals and the one at Karja has beautiful sculptures.

Lithuania converted to Christianity nearly two centuries after its Baltic neighbours, in 1387. Although nothing remains of Vilnius' first church, it must have echoed the red-brick building of the castle. When St Anne's and the Bernardine monastery were built in the 15th century, its bricks would not have looked as out of place as they do today.

The Reformation took hold almost immediately after Martin Luther published his thesis in

LEFT: Bernt Notke's *Dance of Death* (detail; 1463) in Tallinn's Niguliste Church Museum.
RIGHT: carving on the organ in Ugāle church, Latvia.

1520 and its first centres were Tallinn and Rīga, where sacred paintings began to be destroyed. There is a strong painterly tradition in Baltic churches, and many churches had decorated walls and ceilings. These were mostly done by Balts, and only the "easel" paintings were produced by foreigners.

In Tallinn, the late 15th-century Baltic painter Bernt Notke, who produced the high altar of Aarhus Cathedral, Denmark, and Lübeck cathedral's great cross, was responsible for the folding altar at the Holy Spirit Church (1483), which has more paintings than any other in the Baltics. He also produced the macabre *Dance of Death* painting now in the Niguliste Church Museum. In the middle of the 16th century the newly formed Duchy of Courland sought to secure its power base by ordering the building of 70 new Lutheran churches.

Catholic Baroque

Catholics sought refuge in the Polish territories of southern and eastern Latvia and Lithuania where the Jesuits began to build their sumptuous churches. Many of Vilnius' 40 Catholic churches are in the highly decorative Baroque style. The first, begun in 1604, was dedicated to Lithuania's patron saint, Casimir. Among the finest is Sts Peter and Paul Church, supposedly built on the pagan temple to the goddess Milda. Its Italian sculptors adorned it with more than 2,000 white stucco figures. The churches, which typically feature a twin-towered facade, show Hispanic influence. In the Latgale region both St Peter's in Daugavpils and the huge, isolated church at Aglona, which attracts pilgrims from all over eastern Europe on the Feast of the Assumption, are in this style.

Catholics were not the only refugees. A split in the Russian Church in the 17th century brought an influx of Old Believers to the Baltics and elsewhere (*see box, below*). They belong to the *bezpopovci* (without ministers) faction: during Russia's great repressions against the Church all trustworthy bishops were eliminated and it was impossible to ordain new priests. Today the world's largest Old Believers congregation, numbering some 5,000, is in the gold-domed Grebenschikova temple in the Moscow district of Rīga, which is the largest landowner in the city. The church's walls are lined with stunning icons depicting only the saints' faces, and services are led by someone from the congregation, elected teachers (*nastavniki*) of the church.

Wooden churches

Though they tend not to last as long, there are still a number of wooden churches throughout the three countries, mostly in Lithuania. The oldest examples date from the middle of the 18th century. The Ethnographic Museum near Rīga has a typical example. Its figurative carvings and round log walls were all hewn with nothing more refined than an axe. It has a special fancy seat for the local German landlord and the front pews were more elaborately made

OLD BELIEVERS OF LAKE PEIPSI

Some of the Old Believers who fled persecution under successive Russian rulers settled beside Lake Peipsi in Estonia in the late 17th century. Here, just south of Mustvee, a shore-side road connects the villages of Raja, Kükita, Tiheda and Kasepâa, where four functioning Old Believers churches can be seen. Houses are two-storeyed, with towers and wooden balconies, and contain icons. Gavrila Frolov (1854–1930) was a well-known icon painter from Raja, and there is an Old Believers Museum, with icons, at Kolkja. In Estonia there are around 15,000 Old Believers in 11 congregations, and they receive state support for preserving their culture.

for German workers; the native peasants were obliged to sit at the back – and were put in the stocks if they failed to attend services.

Because the Lutheran churches in Estonia and Latvia served the interests of the overlords, the Herrnhuters, or United Brethren Church, gained many followers during the 18th and 19th centuries. Services were conducted in farmers' houses or specially built prayer halls, and it became known as "the people's church", with an emphasis on education and religious enlightenment. The United Brethren's activities diminished during the middle of the 19th century as pressure was put on them by both

in Tallinn (1900). Many can be seen, abandoned, throughout the countryside today. There are still a few practising Orthodox Latvian and Estonian churches, though commercial links with Moscow have been severed.

Towards the end of the 19th century the first Baptist churches appeared in Estonia and Latvia, and around the beginning of the 20th century

The Pilgrim Route of John Paul II links 16 religious sites across Lithuania, including those visited by the Pope in 1993.

the Lutheran Church and the tsar, who won some conversions to Orthodoxy after promising support to farmers against the demands of German land barons. After Poland failed to gain independence in the 1863 uprising, the tsarist government also came down heavily on Old Believers, whom it looked on as renegades, and Catholics, whom it thought were a threat to the empire.

A huge building programme brought a crop of onion-domed churches, including the Orthodox cathedrals of the Holy Theophany of Our Lord in Rīga (1844) and the Alexander Nevski

Seventh Day Adventists and other Protestant sects arrived. After World War I and the break with Russia the countries formed independent Evangelical Lutheran Churches, while all the Catholic Churches came under the direct subordination of the Pope.

Demise of the synagogues

Jewish populations were well established in the Baltic region, which was one of the world's largest Yiddish language centres. Vilnius, the "Jerusalem of Lithuania", had 98 synagogues, some of them elaborate wooden buildings, and there were synagogues in nearly every town in the countryside, where small businesses were often Jewish-run. Almost the entire population was

LEFT: the Jewish synagogue, Vilnius.
ABOVE: Lithuania's Hill of Crosses.

> *After independence smart-suited evangelists arrived in the Baltics with a zeal to match the early Crusaders.*

deported or killed during the Nazi occupation: more than 200,000 died in Vilnius. Though some of the synagogue buildings around the countries remain, it is hard to identify them. One or two have reopened in the capitals and the one in Rīga has been beautifully restored. Optimistic plans to rebuild the Great Synagogue in Vilnius have been mooted.

The Church underground

During the Soviet years, all Church properties and holdings were nationalised and many churches became concert halls or museums. St Casimir's in Vilnius was turned into a Museum of Atheism, and Rīga's Orthodox cathedral became a planetarium. Those who attended church found their careers threatened, and their children were banned from higher education.

Local authorities in the Baltic countries were more lenient and liberal compared with the Soviet heartland. There were many more working churches in Rīga than in Leningrad (St Petersburg). Because it was easier to register a church and educate children in the Baltics, many Baptists, Adventists, Pentecostals and other believers emigrated here from Russia, the Ukraine and elsewhere.

The Roman Catholic Seminary in Rīga educated all new priests from the Soviet Union, except for Lithuania. Other institutions survived, such as the only Orthodox nunnery in the Soviet Union, at Kuremäe in Estonia. Many priests, evangelists and activists were imprisoned for their work. Estonia lost more than two-thirds of its clergy in the early Soviet years.

Some churches were most successful in organising their opposition. A group of Catholic priests regularly published the underground *Chronicles of the Lithuanian Catholic Church*, which informed the world about repression and human-rights violations. The people, too, remained resilient. The Hill of Crosses, just north of Šiauliai on the Kaunas–Rīga highway, was bulldozed by the Soviets three times, but each time the crosses were rebuilt. Encouraged by the late Pope John Paul II's visit in 1993, a Franciscan monastery has been built beside it.

Changing congregations

Today the Baltics are still centres of religion, with a bishop's chair for the German Evangelical Lutheran church in Rīga, and Vilnius re-established as one of Catholicism's citadels in Europe. People have returned to the church but things have changed. The Lutheran and other Protestant congregations have fallen in the intervening years. By contrast, the Catholic Church has held its flock.

Everywhere there are still signs of the religious mix. In Trakai and Vilnius are two *kenessas*, prayer houses of the Karaites, a surviving Jewish sect of Tatars who arrived in the 14th century at the behest of Grand Duke Vytautas. There are Muslims and Mormons, Uniats and *dievturi*, pagan Latvians whose churches are holy places built around sacred oaks.

Not all the ecclesiastic splendours are on the beaten track. The wonderful Pazaislis monastery should be sought out near Kaunas. One of Rīga's architectural secrets is hidden behind the Academy of Sciences: the 1822 Church of Jesus, the Lutheran bishop's seat, is a wooden octagonal building in the Empire style. The largest wooden church in the country, it measures 27 metres (90ft) wide and has eight Ionic columns supporting elliptical domes. ❑

LEFT: prayer house of Lithuania's Tatar community.

Timber Buildings

Combining craftsmanship with folk art, the wooden buildings of the Baltics are all highly individual, exuding character and style

Wood is the natural building material of the Baltics. Spruce, pine and oak are the main materials used in buildings that have survived from as far back as the 16th century. Some were constructed on foundations of alder logs, with oak shingle roofs and pine floorboards 30cm (12in) wide. The oldest existing wooden buildings tend to be churches. None of the elaborate synagogues of Lithuania survive, but the country has 265 wooden churches and its roadside shrines are an art in themselves. It is intriguing to think that the very trees that have always brought out the pagan in Balts should be doing duty supporting so many faiths.

Farmsteads and villas

The best places to see wooden folk architecture is in the larger of the open-air ethnographic museums, just outside Tallinn, Rīga and Kaunas. Here, farmhouses, barns, saunas, windmills and workshops can all be seen in one place.

Traditional farmsteads were built to share with livestock and dry storage, and the comfort of their hearths was enhanced with smoking meat or fish. Few large farmsteads have survived. In the 19th century, with the drift towards the cities, timber suburbs grew up and though many of these are now dilapidated, they are full of character. Rīga's Moscow district, for example, is attracting a young, arty crowd. Across the river is Pārdaugava, a suburb of delightful wooden buildings that are increasingly sought after. In its citation of Rīga as a World Heritage Site, Unesco made particular mention of the city's "19th-century architecture in wood".

Timber houses in other suburbs, such as Kalamaja in Tallinn *(see page 128)*, are also beginning to be fully appreciated and the restorer's crafts have been revived, often with help and expertise from Scandinavia.

With the 19th-century railways came the burgeoning of resorts. Grand villas grew beside the sea in places such as Pärnu and Narva-Jõesu in Esto-

nia, Jūrmala and Liepāja in Latvia and Palanga and Drusininkai in Lithuania. Chisel and saw added finesse that axes could not match, with fancy finials, balustrades, duckboards, verandas, balconies, towers and turrets, all prettily painted. Among the best-known architects-in-wood was the multi-talented artist Stanislaw Witkiewiecz (1851–1915), inventor of the Zakopane style, whose flights of fancy decorated the villas of Palanga. Railway stations, such as the one in Haapsalu that now houses a railway museum, were architectural gems.

When the 20th century arrived, prospering cities continued to use wood as a building material. The eclectic European revival styles – classicism, Gothic,

Baroque – could all be replicated in timber. Among the masters of the craft was Alexander Vladovski, whose handiwork can be seen in Tallinn's Art Nouveau, a movement that had a strong folkloric, back-to-nature element that suited wooden buildings.

Thatched roofs

Many buildings suffered from neglect in Soviet times. Thatched roofs were replaced with corrugated iron, and the rot set in. But renovation in recent years has shown just how attractive these buildings can be, and there is a great enthusiasm to see them restored. Thatch is coming back – and few villages are more picturesque than Altja, on the coast east of Tallinn, where trees and reeds combine in the most harmonious country style. ❏

CULTURE

The contemporary arts scene may sometimes poke fun at the past, but it's the rich cultural inheritance of the Baltic States that makes music and literature so forceful today

ertolt Brecht wrote: "Unhappy the land that needs heroes." Yet the Baltic states could hardly have political and cultural subjugation without consolation from folklore and literature. Heroes from old legends embodying the national fate, and those from painting, poetry and music, offered freedom and a refuge. Theatre, opera and ballet performances were packed, and writers exploited subsidies to keep national pride and independent thought alive. They fostered a climate for independence that was brought to the surface in the 1980s by rock music, which united classical composers, politicians and people in a mass gesture of defiance, which is why prime ministers can join the stage with bands today.

A wave of new experience

Artists no longer need national myths to sustain them. The freedom to travel west as well as east led to a tidal wave of influences, and those best able to handle this have often been those old enough to have experienced two very different cultural worlds. Artists struggle to balance aesthetic aspirations with the need to stay financially afloat, to secure grants, find agents to promote their work and, in theatre and film, forge co-productions with foreign participation.

Culture, happily, is not for the few. Theatres, festivals, exhibitions and concerts are well attended, and governments have realised that small countries need strong cultural initiatives to earn respect in the wider world. Baltic writers, painters, musicians, sculptors, composers and philosophers have, historically, been prime movers in public life. Being a musicologist was no bar to Vytautas Landsbergis becoming president of the newly independent Lithuania, nor

was a background as a novelist anything but an asset when Lennart Meri became Estonia's first post-war president. The former Latvian president Vaira Vīķe-Freiberga is well known as a folklorist and literature specialist, a psychologist and linguist.

Roots of literature

Intellectuals and artists have nurtured the idea of independent nationhood since it emerged in the early 19th century, when the three languages began to be recorded in written form. The freedom to write and to express a national sentiment in this manner arrived in a burst of romantic novels and epic verses from which the modern culture took off. Latvian Andrējs

Pumpurs told in *Lāčplēsis* the tale of the bear-slayer drowned in the River Daugava, who, on returning to life, will ensure the eternal freedom of his people. Friedrich Kreutzwald fathered the national Estonian epic, *Kalevipoeg*, which ends with the hero trapped in hell but vowing to rise again and build a new Estonia.

Despite a tsarist ban on printed Baltic languages, the lyrics to *Pavasario balsai* (*Voices of Spring*, 1885), by a Lithuanian priest, perfectly encapsulated national striving and romantic sentiment. Indeed, priests, doctors and professors played a large part in establishing the region's written cultures, first in German, then later in Estonian, Latvian and Lithuanian. The

delightful Art Nouveau residence where the philosopher Isaiah Berlin (1909–97) was born.

When the Russians closed Vilnius University, between 1832 and 1905, many culturally active Lithuanians moved to Rīga, while Tartu educated Balts of all origins. Students of the 1850s included Latvian Krišjānis Barons, who collated the Latvian folk songs called *dainas*, and Krišjānis Valdemārs and Juris Alunāns, who founded Latvian theatre. Much Latvian effort went into overcoming perceived German colonial condescension. Budding Estonian culture was less confrontational, and many Germans teaching and studying in Tartu were fascinated with the native language

Baltic peoples could boast early of high-quality European centres of learning and a fertile intellectual ambience. In Lithuania, the Jesuits created Vilnius University in 1579, and in 1632 the Swedes established a university in Tartu, southern Estonia.

Rīga, meanwhile, acquired a cosmopolitan cultural importance. The East Prussian-born Johann Gottfried Herder (1744–1803), author of the idea of folklore, was a popular young preacher at its Dom cathedral, while from 1837–8, Wagner managed the German Opera and Drama Theatre. Today, you can see the

LEFT: Estonian composer Arvo Pärt. **ABOVE:** monument to the Estonian poet Kristjan Jaak Peterson.

MUSIC AT THE TOP

Musical accomplishments are generally accepted in the Baltic States – even among the highest offices in the land.

At the 2008 Punk Song Festival in Rakvere, Estonia's President Toomas Hendrik Ilves got on stage to sing the Sex Pistols' *Anarchy in the UK* – he knew all the words. Later that year Latvian Prime Minister Ivars Giodmanis took over Roger Taylor's famous Queen drum kit to play *All Right Now* at the Queen + Paul Rodgers concert in Rīga.

In Lithuania Prime Minister Andrius Kubilius is a classical music fan, and his wife, Rasa, is a violinist with the Lithuanian National Symphony Orchestra.

and themes. But for young Estonians the birth of their nation was above all romantic. As Kristjan Jaak Peterson (1801–22), a poet and Tartu graduate living in Rīga, declared:

Why should not my country's tongue
Soaring through the gale of song,
Rising to the heights of heaven,
Find its own eternity?

Peterson's question has remained relevant to the present day. The Baltic languages are no longer oppressed, but the populations are declining, while the post-war émigré communities abroad that have striven to keep those languages alive are dwindling.

Literature led the emerging 19th-century arts, with the novel of social realism, to the fore. In Lithuania, Jonas Biliūnas described peasant life under his own name; more familiar are three assumed names, Julija Žemaite, Juozas Vaižgantas and Antanas Vienuolis. In Estonia, novelist Eduard Vilde and playwright August Kitzberg ploughed a similar furrow, while the Brothers Kaudzīte wrote the first Latvian novel, *The Times of the Land Surveyors* (1879).

Exiled genius

Then suddenly, from Latvia, emerged a world-class talent, Jānis Pliekšāns (1865–1929), who assumed the pseudonym of Rainis. A complex, multifaceted figure, he was a lyrical poet, dramatist, translator (of *Faust*) and political activist. He wrote his best plays in Switzerland, where he fled after his involvement in the 1905 Revolution. *Fire and Night* (1905) is a dramatic statement of the Latvian spirit; *The Sons of Jacob* (1919), based on his own experience, deals with the conflict between art and politics. Jānis Tilbergs' portrait of Rainis in the State Musuem of Art conveys his authority as a national elder and the personal loneliness voiced in his poetry. Modern Latvian literature still rotates around this giant figure, while his wife, Aspazija (1868–1943), a romantic poet and feminist, is also revered. Both are remembered in a museum in their Jūrmala home.

Latvian literature, always influenced by folk traditions and rustic life, was given a lyrical quality by the terse, philosophical *daina*. The plays of Rūdolfs Blaumanis (1863–1908) also set a high artistic standard. His folk comedy *The Days of the Tailor* in *Silmači* (1902) is still staged in the open air every midsummer.

Affected by his German education and familiarity with the German poets, Jānis Poruks (1871–1911) introduced introspection, melancholy and dreams to Latvian poetry and prose. Kārlis Skalbe (1879–1945) was dubbed the Latvian Hans Christian Andersen for his allegorical tales; he was also an exquisite poet and short-story teller.

Other notable poets include the symbolist Fricis Bārda (1880–1919), Anna Brigadere (1861–1933) and Aleksandrs Čaks (1901–50), whose Imagist style burst forth with Latvia's 1918 independence and brushed the realities of urban life in Rīga with lyrical excitement.

Lithuanian literature did not develop such early power and variety, which may explain its greater openness to European influences. The literary group Four Winds, formed by Kazys Binkis (1893–1932), was devoted to Futurism; others imitated German Expressionism. Vincas Krėvė-Mickevičius (1882–1954) was a great prose writer and dramatist whose work continued in exile. Having briefly been foreign minister, he fled in 1940, and his epic *The Sons of Heaven and Earth* was never finished.

The Young Estonia Movement, devoted to raising Estonian literary standards to a European level, flourished in the decade after 1905. The traveller Friedebert Tuglas (1886–1971) brought the world to Estonian readers through his romantic, exotic stories. A.H. Tammsaare

(1878–1940), author of the epic *Truth and Justice*, was influenced by Dostoevsky, Knut Hamsun and Bernard Shaw. He has been called the greatest Estonian prose writer of the 20th century. Find out more about the modest lifestyle of this retiring, reflective man at the tumbledown villa in Kadriorg, Tallinn, where he once lived. A more radical experimental literary group, Siuru, nurtured the poets Jaan Oks (1884–1918) and Marie Under (1883–1977). Under, who spent the Soviet period in exile, is one of Estonia's most highly regarded poets, along with Betty Alver, whose poetry is generally darker, and whose husband was deported to Siberia.

Vytautas Landbergis, Lithuania's independence prime minister and a musicologist, was involved with the Fluxus group in the 1960s – an art movement that was joined by Yoko Ono – though he opposed the smashing of pianos.

Visual arts

Foreign influences and rural life stimulated the visual arts and music in the Baltic region. National Romanticism, imported from St Petersburg in the 1900s, ousted academic painting and influenced architecture, taking over from Art Nouveau. When that dreamy style became exhausted, new schools of national painting took over. The Baltic National Romantic style incorporates folk heroes and legends, with echoes of Munch, Beardsley, Klimt, Boecklin and Bakst.

In this vein, over Latvia's Vilhelms Purvïtis (1872–1945) and Estonia's Konrad Mägi towers the Lithuanian mystical painter and musician Mikalojus Konstantinas Čiurlionis (1875–1911), a Baltic William Blake. In thin, richly coloured pastels and tempera, he created symbolic landscapes suggesting a mystical universe, with motifs from Lithuanian folklore. He conceived many of his paintings as linked musical movements or as cycles of life and death, day and night. They are extraordinary, pantheistic, poetic distillations of human life. Čiurlionis' own nature was rich and varied. He travelled widely, wrote for newspapers and almost single-handedly founded the nation's cultural

life before dying at the age of 36. His pictures can be seen, and his music heard, at his own museum in Kaunas.

After Čiurlionis, Lithuanian painting, in the hands of the Kaunas-based Ars Group, grew into a satisfyingly complex art of landscape and portraiture, well informed on European developments and characterised by a rich, dark palette. Emerald green, dark pink, mauve and a touch of yellow evolved into national colours, and a persistent motif was the inclusion of folkloric wooden figures and toys.

The first Estonian school was realist, shaped by Russian and German artistic influence.

Impressionism came late, and is best seen in the works of Ants Laikmaa, Alexsander Vardi and Kondrad Mägi. Mägi co-founded the Pallas Art School in Tartu, which produced the highly individual painter Eduard Wiiralt (1898–1954), best known for his graphics, and Jaan Koort, whose deer sculpure stands at the foot of Toompea on Tallinn's Nunne Street. By the end of the 19th century, there was a strong interest in national romanticism and quasi-mythological themes, as in the symbolist-influenced works of Kristjan Raud, who illustrated *Kalevipoeg*. Ado Vabbe is the greatest Estonian Modernist of the early 20th century, while noteworthy Cubists include Karin Luts and Karl Pärsimägi. Any Baltic visitor interested in painting should head for

LEFT: Estonian writer Jaan Kross.
RIGHT: *Vyties preliudas* (detail) by M.K. Čiurlionis.

Latvia, where Vilhelms Purvītis, Jānis Rozentāls (1866–1917) and Jānis Valters (1869–1932) combined European Impressionist, Fauvist and German Expressionist tendencies with their own distinctive approach to landscape and portraiture. Their influence extended to Lithuania and to future generations of Baltic artists.

Purvītis, founder of the Rīga Art Academy, depicted the Latvian landscape, but most of his work was burnt in Jelgava during the war; Valters, who studied in Germany, painted landscapes tinged by subjective mood and represented in stark Fauvist colours; Rozentāls' work peaks with his portraiture. Generally,

the Latvian portrait tradition is outstanding. Rozentāls' depiction of his mother and a painting of opera singer Pāvils Gruzdna by Voldemārs Zeltiņš (1879–1905), using Purvītis' pale Latvian colours, lead into the highly coloured avant-garde movement. Artists such as Oto Skulme, Leo Svemps and Jānis Tīdemanis bring this rich period to life.

Notable composers

Čiurlionis contributed to modern Lithuanian culture not only through painting, but through music. An intensely active year at the Leipzig Conservatoire produced works still

recorded today, including the String Quartet in C minor and the first Lithuanian symphonic composition, *In the Forest*. To a modern ear, the symphonic work often recalls the music of Bruckner, Mahler and Sibelius, but Čiurlionis was a distinct talent in his own right. He later reworked folk songs, wrote choral pieces and organised the nation's musical life in Vilnius.

From the First National Awakening, all the Baltic cultures developed strong traditions in choral singing. The first operas were written on national themes in the early 20th century,

ABOVE LEFT: *Going to Church* (detail) by Janis Rozentāls. **ABOVE:** Alfrēds Kalniņš statue, Rīga. **RIGHT:** Latvian violinist Gidon Kremer.

establishing opera as a popular but conservative genre. Baltic symphonic music evolved from the St Petersburg Conservatoire, echoing the memory of Tchaikovsky and Rimsky-Korsakov. Outstanding composers of the era included Latvia's Emīls Dārziņš, best known for his *Melancholy Waltz*, and Estonia's Artur Kapp.

Latvians consider Alfrēds Kalniņš a musical father-figure for his varied work, both romantic and choral. His son Jānis also became a composer, later well known in Canada as John Kalniņš.

In all the arts, there was strong Scandinavian influence between the wars. An equally strong sense of alienation was felt from the Russian soul, the so-called "Asiatic principle". In the applied arts, the Balts excelled in graphic work, textiles, book publishing and illustration.

Post-war writing

All the Baltic cultures reach out to the larger world through theatre, frequently devoting half their repertoire to world classics, with many adaptations also from prose. A strong tradition of open-air performances, with real animals on stage, persists in Latvia, alongside rather verbose poetic theatre. After the war, alien ideology and the expulsion of several key figures cramped the development of the arts. Latvians Anšlavs Eglītis, Zenta Mauriņa and Mārtiņš Zīverts, Lithuanians Antanas Vaiculaitis and Kreve, and Estonian Marie Under continued the best pre-war traditions of theatre, prose and poetry abroad. But many writers died during the war or shortly after.

A literature of suffering and displacement, recounting the mass deportations to Siberia, emerged only in the 1980s, though in 1946, *The Forest of Gods*, by Balys Sruoga, recounted the experience of Lithuanian intellectuals in a German camp with irony and humour. The Estonian Jaan Kross (born 1920), who was imprisoned by the Nazis, spent nine years in Russian labour camps, and his novels and short stories provide poignant accounts of his country's history and of the awful compromises faced by a repeatedly occupied population.

Soviet avant-garde

A new creative generation emerged during the Khrushchev thaw, ready to exploit the advantages of being at the fringe of a centralised empire. The Baltics became the home of the Soviet avant-garde, with productions of Beckett

and Ionesco, and in Tallinn in 1969 the daring publication of Russian writer Mikhail Bulgakov's satirical masterpiece *The Master and Margherita*. An uncensored edition of George Orwell's *Nineteen Eighty-Four* appeared in the mid-1980s. The thaw also produced notable opera singers and ballet dancers, including Mikhail Baryshnikov, from Rīga, and anti-Establishment poetry. Musicians managed to experiment with atonality and minimalism. The coincidence of modern ideas with folksong was cleverly exploited, as in the haunting compositions of Estonia's Veljo Tormis and the ritualistic rhythms of Lithuania's Bronius Kutavičius. The late Soviet

period brought more abstractionism into painting, from Jonas Svazas and Dalia Kosciunaite in Lithuania to Latvia's Maija Tabaka and Ado Lill and Raul Meel in Estonia.

Contemporary music

Estonian music is flourishing at home and abroad. Best known is contemporary composer Arvo Pärt, exiled in the Soviet years but now back living in Tallinn. His minimimalist, sacred works includes the widely acclaimed *Tabula Rasa*, written for the great Latvian violinist Gidon Kremer. Other Estonians with a reputation beyond their borders are the former rock musician-turned-avant-garde composer Erki Sven Tüür and a stream of world-class conductors, among them Neeme Järvi and his son, Paavo. The Latvian conductors Mariss Jansons and Andris Nelsons have made their names with, respectively, the Royal Cincertgebouw Orchestra in Amsterdam and the City of Birmingham Orchestra. Lithuanian modernist Osvaldas Balakauskas also enjoys world renown, having earned the title of "Lithuanian Messiaen".

Performing arts

Lithuanian theatre, currently favouring radical takes on the classics, has generated several world-class producers, among them Jonas Vaitkus,

known film director is Laila Pakalniņa, whose work has been screened at Venice and Cannes. Latvia is also renowned for documentaries, a form championed by award-winning directors Ivars Seleckis and Herz Frank. Lithuania's best-

> 66 When the musicians saw the score of Tabula Rasa, they cried out: 'Where's the music?' But then they went on to play it very well. It was beautiful. It was quiet and beautiful. Arvo Pärt 99

Juozas Nekročius and Oskaras Korčunovas. Lithuanian dramatist Marius Ivaskevicius and Estonia's Andrus Kivirähk both delight in poking fun at national identity, while Adolfs Žapiro and Pēteris Petersons are two very active, cosmopolitan figures in Latvian theatre. The National Opera in Rīga is the most dynamic in the Baltic States, and contemporary dance now has a dedicated following in all three countries.

Film and video

Estonia has a particularly strong tradition in animated film, with directors such as Priit Pärn scooping prizes at international festivals. Rooftop cinema is a feature of Tallinn's 2011 European Capital of Culture. Latvia's best-

known film director is Sarunas Bartas, whose philosophical and minimalist films have won international acclaim. Bigger-budget historical films about the post-1917 fight for independence, the collapse of the first republics and post-war resistance are popular in all three nations.

Vilnius is home to the excellent Centre for Contemporary Arts, which has a reputation for being one of the most dynamic and innovative of its kind in the Nordic area, hosting the Baltic Triennials, the last one being in 2009, when Vilnius was the European Capital of Culture.

In all three countries, video art has taken over from painting. Estonia's Raoul Kurvitz and Jaan Toomik and Lithuania's Deimantas Narkevičius have all contributed to the Venice Biennale. In

Lithuania there has been particular focus on social issues and questions of female identity, as in a video by Egle Rakauskaite which investigates the recent experience of eastern Europeans working in the United States.

Filmmakers are making their mark, too, not least because the three countries provide exceptional backdrops. The unspoilt towns and countryside are ideal for period dramas. The Rīga Film Fund was established in 2010, and shortly afterwards shooting in the city began in a joint venture between Latvia's Film Angels Studio and Indian Bollywood filmmakers Illuminati Films.

very different, show the continuing attraction of folk themes. Critics in Latvia have spoken of the "rebirth of the short story", a form championed by writers Andra Neiburga and Nora Ikstena. Estonia's Jaan Kross and the poet Jaan Kaplinski have an international following and have both been nominated for the Nobel Prize for literature.

Moving on from explorations of the Soviet era, writers such as Estonia's Tõnu Õnnepalu's, whose *Border State* explores the experience of a young homosexual in Paris, examine contemporary life and adopt more experimental styles thanks to exposure to Western trends.

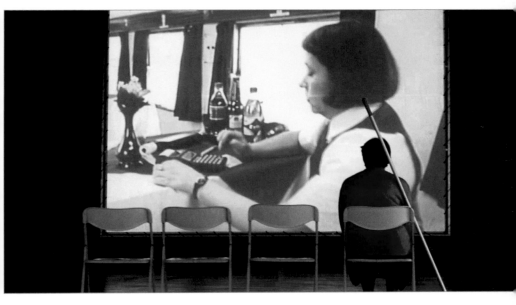

Modern literature

Popular present-day writers include Latvian poet and writer Imants Ziedonis and prose-writer Zigmunds Skujiņš. Writers who were censored and repressed during the Soviet era and who have since won wide acclaim include Latvian poet and writer Vizma Belševica, poet Knuts Skujenieks and Lithuania's Juozas Aputis. Traditionally dubbed "land of poetry", prose and innovative essay-writing is now flourishing in Lithuania. The novels of Lithuanians Vytautas Bubnys and Vytautas Martinkus, though

Lithuania's Jurga Ivanauskaite has tackled in ironic and provocative fashion contemporary issues such as consumerism, advertising and the dumbing down of culture, while also exploring Buddhism following travels in Tibet. A mystic tendency in Lithuanian literature contrasts with a strong, continuing cult of the grotesque, the absurd and magic realism in Estonia.

Spreading the word

Inevitably, Baltic literature suffers from a dearth of translation into foreign languages, although extracts are regularly published by the countries' literature centres and cultural institutes, which will happily inform the curious about the latest trends in the arts. ❑

LEFT: Priit Võigemast and Hele Kõre in *Names in Marble,* a film about Estonia's first independence.
ABOVE: watching a video installation, Lithuania.

FOLKLORE

From traditional tales, strange musical instruments and midsummer festivals to national costumes and sacred trees, the Baltic countries are steeped in folklore

Folklore is at the very heart of Baltic culture. Indeed, until the 19th century, folklore in effect *was* Baltic culture, because German and Polish rule from the Middle Ages onwards had meant that no real indigenous literary culture had been able to evolve. In the 19th and 20th centuries, the Baltic scholars and writers who developed the new Baltic cultural identity primarily used peasant folklore as their starting point.

Fortunately this folklore was of immense richness, especially in the field of music. Songs appear to have played an important part in the worship of the ancient Baltic gods, and ever since have been at the heart of the Balts' sense of themselves. Almost every village has its own choir, many of a professional standard. State and public occasions often begin with folk songs. As a Latvian *daina*, or folk song, has it:

I was born singing, I grew up singing,
I lived my life singing.
My soul went singing
Into the garden of God's sons.

> Has a people anything dearer than the speech of its fathers? In its speech lies its whole domain, its tradition, history, religion and basis of life, all its heart and soul.
> Johann Gottfried Herder

The Singing Revolution

A visit to a folk performance is recommended for any visitor. From the beginning, folklore

and the Baltic national movements were entwined. The first Estonian and Latvian song festivals, in 1869 and 1873 respectively, were also political events, celebrating the end of serfdom and symbolising the reawakening and unity of the new nations. The republics between 1920 and 1940 turned them into great symbolic events. Folklore festivals became key symbols of the national independence movements in a process which has been dubbed, especially in Estonia, the "Singing Revolution". It was at the Baltica Festival in 1987 that the old national flags of the former republics were publicly displayed together for the first time under Soviet rule and without those

LEFT: folk art painting, Lithuania.
RIGHT: Estonian wedding socks from Saaremaa.

responsible being promptly arrested. The national song festivals are astonishing affairs, with the choirs numbered in thousands and the audiences in tens or even hundreds of thousands. Folklore was also the key to rediscovering, or reinventing, the beliefs and society of the pagan Balts that existed before the Christian conquest. These seem to have been based on the idea that the world was itself created partly through song and story-telling: *Once upon a time, the Lord God walked through the world, telling stories and curses, asking riddles . . .* The 14th-century priest Peter of Duisburg wrote

over with gifts. Later, however, they came to be identified with the Christian devil. The Devils Museum in Kaunas, unique in the world, contains a magnificent collection of portrayals of the devil by Lithuanian folk artists. Unfortunately, this is also to some extent a museum of historical anti-Semitism, since most of the devils are meant to be Jewish.

By the 18th century, awareness of the old Baltic religions as such had disappeared or become completely mixed up with Christian beliefs. Thus the great pagan festival of Midsummer Night was renamed St John's Eve, but it has retained many of the old pagan legends and

that the Balts of his time "worship all of creation . . . sun, moon, stars, thunder, birds, even four-legged creatures down to the toad. They have their sacred forests, fields and waters, in which they do not dare to cut wood, or work, or fish."

Spirits of the forests

Until the 18th century, Catholic priests in Lithuania were still cutting down sacred oaks in an effort to stop their worship, and until the 20th century some of the ancient spirits lived on in folk tales about forest spirits such as the leprechaun-like *kaukai*, the *aitvarai* (who can lead people to hidden treasure) and the *barzdukai*, a form of bearded gnome. The *kaukai* were originally neutral spirits who could be won

JOHANN GOTTFRIED HERDER

Johann Gottfried Herder (1744–1803) was born in the Prussian town of Mohrungen (Morag), in the former Lithuanian-Polish Empire. He recognised that language played a key role in both a person's identity and thought. While working as a teacher in Rīga, he produced *Tract on the Origins of Language* (1772), and his appreciation of the folk songs he collected was based on a belief that they represented a purity of spirit in peoples before civilisation. However, he warned against blind nationalism: "National glory is a deceiving seducer. When it reaches a certain height, it clasps the head with an iron band. The enclosed sees nothing on the mist but his own picture."

customs, especially those connected with fertility. One of these is that on that particular night and only then, a flowering fern appears, and if a boy and a girl find it together, it will fulfil their heart's desire. Of course, ferns don't flower, but the tradition is a good excuse for young couples to go off into the forest at night.

For many centuries, Christian priests and ministers did their best to stamp out much of Baltic folklore, because it embodies so much paganism. The earliest records of Latvian folk songs are provided in evidence for 17th-century witch-trials, and it has been suggested that the "witches" of this period were the linear descendants of the old pagan priests and sorcerers.

"God is a Latvian"

In the 1920s and 30s, efforts were made by some people to resurrect the old pagan religions. In Latvia, this took the form of the Dievturība movement, which continues to this day. Because in the 1930s the movement was closely associated with Latvian fascism, it was savagely persecuted under Soviet rule. Its ideology today remains intensely nationalist. "We have always believed that Latvia should be only for the Latvians," one of its leaders has said. "God is a Latvian – or at least, our god is."

Its theology maintains the existence of a single godhead who takes different forms. This, however, is a modern construct derived from the real, but now almost forgotten, ancient pagan religion. The Dievturi number only a few hundred, but their past sufferings and the purity of their folk singing gives them a prestige.

A certain holistic, pagan-influenced mysticism, a willingness to see divinity in all the works of nature, has characterised all three cultures up to the present day. This is true both of those authors who hark back to the ancient traditions, and those, like the Estonian poet Jaan Kaplinski, who render them into wider, universal terms – in his case, neo-Buddhist.

The new attitude to folk traditions in Europe dates to the later 18th century and the rise of Romanticism. Baltic folklore played a part in this cultural shift, because a key figure in the movement was the German philosopher Johann Gottfried Herder, who was moved by Latvian folk songs and stories when he was a Protestant minister and teacher in Rīga in the 1760s (see box, opposite).

Oral folklore and folk art

Herder's influence led to generations of research by Baltic German scholars and, in the mid-19th century, the work was taken over by the first generations of native Baltic intelligentsia. Their task was the recording of this oral history. In Latvia, this process is linked above all with the name of Krišjānis Barons, who assembled the *dainas*, or Latvian folk songs. The 217,996 items form one of the largest collections of oral folklore in the world. After 1918, the governments and universi-

ties also set out to collect folk art. The Estonian National Museum in Tartu houses hundreds of thousands of examples, giving clues to an ancient tradition: for example, beer mugs were decorated with "male" symbols, such as suns and horses.

Lithuania has a particularly rich tradition of folk carving, which is illustrated by the intricate wooden crosses outside many villages. Covered with ancient symbols, they resemble pagan totem poles. The carved crosses on the famous Hill of Crosses at Šiauliai is an apotheosis of Catholic piety and of Lithuanian nationalism, but also of ancient pagan symbolism.

However, the task of recovering the meaning of such figures, and the ancient Baltic tradition in general, is an intensely difficult one, both

---

LEFT: Estonia's Voru Festival.
ABOVE RIGHT: Midsummer Festival in rural Latvia.

The Thinker (Rūpintojelis), *a mournful carved wooden figure often seen by the roadside in Lithuania, is presented as Christ, but is in fact much older than Christianity.*

because of the suppressive effect of Christianity, and the effects of modernisation, especially Soviet rule. One reason why many Estonians wish to recover the area of Petseri, captured by Estonia from Russia in 1920 and transferred back by Stalin in 1944, is that the small Setu minority who live there have preserved folk tra-

PAGAN GODS

Modern-day scholars, such as the great French-Lithuanian semiologist Algirdas Julien Greimas, have used surviving folk tales to try to establish the nature of the ancient gods and their worship. They have identified: **Dievs**, the principal deity; **Perkūnas** or **Pērkons**, god of thunder, akin to the Slavic Perun and the Scandinavian Thor; **Saule**, goddess of the sun; **Laima**, goddess of luck (good and bad, because Laima, like some Indian goddesses, also brings the plague); **Māra**, goddess of birth and death; **Usins**, the celestial charioteer, keeper of light; **Martins**, keeper of horses; **Janis**, who is responsible for the fertility of fields; and **Ausra**, goddess of the dawn.

ditions which have been lost in Estonia itself.

The first major guide to Estonian folk stories was *Old Estonian Fairy Tales*, published in 1866. It is still popular in Estonia, and is held to have contributed to the creation of an Estonian prose style that is independent of the German models it previously imitated.

In 1861, Kreutzwald published the "national epic" *Kalevipoeg* ("Son of Kalev"), a reworking in verse of stories about a giant hero; the work was intended to help build up a national spirit, and prove to a sceptical world that the Estonian folk tradition was capable of producing an epic – considered at that time to be the highest form of literature. As with the Finnish *Kalevala*, debate has raged over the merits of the work ever since.

Invented gods

The *Kalevipoeg* is still taught in every Estonian school, but otherwise its influence has progressively diminished. This has been far less the case with the Latvian national epic, *Lāčplēsis (The Bear-Slayer)*, by Andrējs Pumpurs, in which another mythical hero is made a leader of the medieval Latvian resistance against the German invaders. *Lāčplēsis* has since become the theme of a verse play by Jānis Rainis, a rock-opera and several other works. Under the first Latvian republic, the Order of Lāčplēsis was the highest state award. Kangars, the traitor in the epic, has become a generic name for traitors, while Laimdota, Lāčplēsis' beloved, has given her name to boutiques and hairdressers, and ships and yachts are named after Spīdola, the witch.

Pumpurs also gave the ancient Latvians a pantheon of pagan gods, like the classical Olympus – quite unhistorical, but another passport to European respectability in his time. The contemporary habit of giving children "traditional" pagan names, such as Laima or Vytautas (after the Lithuanian medieval Grand Duke), dates from this period.

Today, this rich folkloric tradition is threatened by modern mass culture and by a danger that the over-use of folklore on official occasions, in schools and so on, may drain it of the joyous spontaneity which kept Baltic folklore alive and part of the region's life. Folklore traditions have therefore become diluted, but this is the price that has to be paid for joining the global capitalist community. ❑

ABOVE: the Kreutzwald Monument, Tallinn.

The Singing Tree

A number of different instruments bring a distinctive sound to these lands of music and song; some have to be made with special rituals

Most traditional musical instruments are common throughout the Baltics and Eastern Europe: the goat-horn, whistle, flute, reed, violin, squeeze-box and zither. Other instruments belong to particular regions: the bagpipe in Estonia and Latvia's Protestant area, the hammer dulcimer in Lithuania and Latvia's Catholic part, and the *hiukannel* or bowed harp in the Estonian islands. But one instrument unique to the Baltic lands is a kind of board zither with between 5 and 12 iron or natural-fibre strings. Its history can be traced with some certainty back at least 3,000 years, and its Baltic names have supposedly originated from the proto-Baltic word *kantlés*, meaning "the singing tree": *kantele* in the Finnish language, *kannel* in Estonian, *kåndla* in Livonian, *kokles* in Latvian and *kankles* in Lithuanian.

This is a deified instrument and, according to folk beliefs, the tree for its wood must be cut when someone has died but isn't yet buried. In a fairy tale, a youth helps an old man who turns out to be God and rewards the good-hearted lad with this particular instrument.

The Apollonic, heavenly aura and the fine, deeply touching tone quality have made *kokles* a symbol of national music for Estonians, Latvians and Lithuanians. Unfortunately, the playing of the original instrument has almost died out. At the beginning of the 20th century, *kokles* developed into a zither of 25 to 33 strings, like a harp. "Modernisation" during the Soviet time resulted in a soprano, alto, tenor and bass *kokles* family. Compositions of questionable musical quality were played and presented as the national music.

Music festivals

A folklore revival in the 1970s and 80s restored an interest in traditional instruments. Many of them, such as the bagpipe, jew's-harp, whistle, flute, reed, horn, clappers and rattles, are made by enthusiasts and played informally. It is now hard to

---

RIGHT: the deified "singing tree", a traditional local instrument similar to a zither

imagine a celebration of calendar customs, folk-dance parties or folklore festivals without them.

The most important festivals are the summer and winter solstice celebrations, and there are large gatherings at such festivals as the Baltica, which involves all three Baltic republics. More local but no less exciting are Skamba (*skamba kankliai* in Lithuania) and the children's and young people's folklore festival, Pulkā eimu (*pulkā teku* in Latvia).

Sonoric meditation

In Lithuania visitors should try to listen to *sutartines*, which is endless sonoric meditation, both vocal and instrumental. The instrumental version

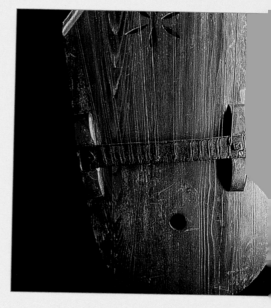

of *sutartines* is played on *kanklès*, pan-pipes, trumpets or horns.

Primitive musical instruments are usually made by the players themselves. The more sophisticated ones such as the *kokles*, bagpipes, flutes, violins, accordions and zithers are made by a few skilled masters. These are not easy to obtain, though they can be found at fairs and folk-crafts festivals where there is also a good variety of bird-, devil- and animal-shaped clay whistles. The most popular instruments are the accordion and guitar, played at family celebrations and informal parties.

Catholic and Lutheran churches mostly have organs with distinctive characteristics. Rīga Dom's organ is recognised worldwide, while those in rural areas can have their own unique charm. ❑

SAUNAS AND SPAS

If you are ever invited to a sauna, don't pass up this very Baltic experience, and if you are not invited, you should seek one out

Saunas have always been a way of life in the Baltic countries, and today they are undergoing a revival. Every farmstead once had one, usually by a river or pond for filling the pail for the fire and to cool off afterwards. Bathhouse walls were always made from logs, but the roof was often made from clay or earth with grass growing on top of it. There were two rooms, a dressing room at the front and a bathing room containing the oven and wooden benches.

The sauna was central to life: the goddess of fertility was thought to reside here, babies were born here and women would spend the eve of their wedding here. It was a spiritual as well as a healthy place: the word *gars* in Latvian means both spirit and the steam of a bathhouse.

Novices are advised to start off gradually, steaming for about 7–10 minutes, then cooling off and repeating the exercise three to five times. Only then should they start switching – a light flailing by birch branches – which helps blood circulation, increases perspiration, opens pores to help the skin to breathe and cleans out toxins. It is an excellent remedy for muscular pains and a good way to help get rid of extra weight. Either do this switching yourself or ask a friend – it's best to lie on the bench while someone else switches your back, starting from your feet and moving towards your head. Twigs should be soaked in cold water for up to 15 minutes before being used.

Cooling off can be done by taking a shower, relaxing for five minutes in a separate room or swimming in a lake. In winter, the hardy roll in the snow. But do take it easy after coming out of a sauna, as you might feel a little giddy. Herbal teas or beer are generally a part of the cooling-off process.

ABOVE: ideally, a sauna will be built by a lake, which provides to create the steam and a bath to cool off in. Traditionally, it wa place of life and death, where pagan spirits dwelt.

BELOW: felt hats come in various shapes and sizes and are wo insulate the head from the intensity of the heat, allowing a long period of steaming. A friendly switcher, using well-soaked bran of birch or oak, should start at the feet and work upwards.

LEFT: water ladelled from a bucket is thrown onto heated coals, bringing the room temperature to around 70°C (158°F).

SPAS

For two centuries water cures and mud treatments in the Baltic countries have been offered in traditional spas, based on the healing power of the sea, mud and mineral water. The first one was at Druskininkai, an inland spa of curative waters opened by King Stanislav Augustus in 1794. The seaside resorts such as Jūrmala in Latvia and Pärnu in Estonia, began in the 1820s, developing from the sanatoria built for veteran officers of the Napoleonic wars of 1812, and subsequently popularised by the Russian royal family. The tsars and Tchaikovsky stayed at Haapsalu, famous for its mud treatments – the wooden Kuursaal (Resort Hall) here is the original from 1825. These spas were of the traditional European variety, not the kind one associates with pampering and mystic stones, but based on scientific balneotherapy. Under the Soviets they became institutions where Politburo members and chosen factory workers would be rewarded with a week or two of rest and relaxation.

Today, these centres have burgeoned into large spa holiday complexes, offering excellent modern facilities, and the idea of the spa has spread to the major hotels throughout the three countries. Now you are just as likely to be offered a bath in chocolate rather than in extremely smelly mud.

LEFT: if there is no river or lake, jump into a cold tub. This one has scenic forest views. Novices are advised to start taking a sauna gradually, steaming for around 7–10 minutes, then cooling off, repeating the exercise three to five times.

: a floating summer sauna provides a focus for family life. e is in Soomaa National Park, Estonia, where floating saunas rented by the hour, and hold up to 15 people.

ABOVE: a mud bath is efficacious, if somewhat malodorous.

BELOW: felt hats, oak twigs, ferns and herbs: saunas are found in forests as well as in many modern hotels.

NATURE AND WILDLIFE

Though lacking in dramatic scenery, the region has some of the most unspoilt spaces in Europe, which are wonderful habitats for all manner of flora and fauna

In common with their neighbours in Scandinavia, people in the Baltics have an especially close relationship with nature. Many have a summer house and get away to the countryside during the warm weather as often as they can. A surprisingly strong sense of rural tradition permeates almost every aspect of Baltic culture, from popular music and food to the very way people think. And where many Westerners tend to romanticise nature, people in the Baltics enjoy it in a refreshingly hands-on and non-sentimental way. The average Balt is at ease working in a state-of-the-art office in the city one day and chopping firewood out in the sticks the next.

The three countries share many natural attributes: forests with deer and boar, bogs and lakes fit for ducks, and coasts with pines and dunes that see clouds of migrating birds. These are damp lands of lichen and fungi, of mires and flower-filled meadows. But there are many distinctive characteristics, too.

ESTONIA

Situated on what is called a "boreo-nemoral" zone, Estonia is a transitional area where the coniferous Euro-Siberian taiga opens into a European zone of deciduous forest. The least populated of the three countries, it provides a truly unspoilt natural habitat.

One-fifth is covered by peat bogs, mostly in the central and eastern areas, which in spring echo with the croak of toads and frogs, and because much of the country is unsuitable for agriculture it has been spared environmental abuse. Wild, wooded meadows, found in few other countries, are particularly rich in plant life, such as orchids, and there are some 4,000 kinds of fungi.

Estonia's national flower is the cornflower, and the national bird is the swallow.

Extensive forests

Forests and woodlands cover almost half the country and nearly half the forested land belongs to the state, which is a profit-making concern that considerably facilitates conservation efforts. Timber companies today operate all year round for maximum efficiency, and

LEFT: a roe deer in the Lithuanian forest.
RIGHT: peacock butterflies are common in all three countries.

illegal logging has been a problem. In 2010, to raise state funds, some 20,000 hectares (50,000 acres) were put up for sale in small plots.

There are still vast areas of untouched forest, and primeval forests remain in Järvselja in Tartumaa County and Puruni in Ida Virumaa County, which, together with the wetland, provides a haven to all sorts of indigenous wildlife. A good indicator of the state of Estonia's forest ecosystems is the number of forest-dwelling predators, such as bears, lynx and wolves, as well as beavers, elk and deer. There are estimated to be stable numbers of all these at present, with some several hundred lynx, together with

around 100 wolves and more than 500 brown bears. Forests are also home to the flying squirrel, an animal seldom found elsewhere in Europe. Ten species of rare and protected birds include the golden eagle (250 pairs), white-tailed eagle, spotted eagle and eagle owl, as well as the rare black stork.

Long coast and many islands

The country has a long and, in many areas, dramatically beautiful coastline that covers some 3,794km (2,357 miles), most of which belongs to the more than 1,000 islands. The coast differs from the rough granite seaboard of its northern neighbour, Finland, and the sandy beaches of Latvia to the south. It changes from limestone cliffs in the north to sandy beaches and shelving coastal meadows in the west. These coastal meadows used to be widespread but today only a few are grazed; the rest have become overgrown with juniper or reed, and conservation programmes are under way to restore them.

For most of the second half of the 20th century, much of it was a restricted zone. This helped to preserve it from extensive development. Today, grey seals frequent the undisturbed shores and roughly one-fifth of the estimated 7,500 Baltic grey seals tend to keep close to the Estonian coast. During mild and ice-free winters, many give birth to their pups on the small islets.

The country is also a stopover point for Arctic waterfowl migrating along the East Atlantic Flyway. According to some estimates, up to 50 million water and coastal birds use the abundant coastal wetlands. Many stop here

---

TOP 10 NATURE SIGHTS

Lahemaa National Park, Estonia. Set beside the north coast, Lahemaa is a great place to see Estonian nature in all its rugged beauty. *www.lahemaa.ee*

Lake Peipsi, Estonia. The fifth-largest lake in Europe is by far the best for fishing. *www.turism.tartumaa.ee*

Saaremaa Island, Estonia. This natural gem abounds in unusual flora and fauna. *www.saaremaa.ee*

Gauja National Park, Latvia. Around the spectacular River Gauja there is some wonderful hiking and impressive caves linked to local folklore. *www.sigulda.lv*

Ķemeri National Park, Latvia. Part forest, part swamp, containing medicinal waters. A birdwatchers' treat. *www. kemeri.gov.lv*

Kolka, Latvia. Unique for many reasons – sublime beaches, remarkable lighthouse, great birdlife. *www.kolka.info*

Aukštaitija National Park, Lithuania. Nature trails through the many lakes and unspoilt forest. *www.anp.lt*

The Curonian Spit, Lithuania. Carved out by the wind and Baltic Sea, this is a natural miracle of pine forest and dune. *www.nerija.lt*

Trakai Historical National Park, Lithuania. Close to Vilnius, Trakai is a labyrinth of forest, lakes and villages. *www. seniejitrakai.lt*

Žuvintas Biosphere Reserve, Lithuania. A boggy area rich in wildlife, it is known as the "kingdom of birds". *www. zuvintas.lt*

In one wooded meadow in Vahenurme in Pärnumaa County, Estonia, there are 74 different species of flora per square metre.

to prepare for the long journey to their Russian Arctic breeding grounds. During the first two weeks of May, every small inlet teems with coots, grebes, ducks, geese and swans.

The biggest coastal wetland is Matsalu, a large bay surrounded by various coastal habitats. During the spring migration, more than 2 million waterfowl pass though Matsalu, primarily long-tailed and other Arctic diving ducks.

The islands, which make up nearly 10 percent of the country's total territory, really set the country apart from its otherwise similar southern neighbours. The largest of these are Saaremaa and Hiiumaa, both of which are becomingly increasingly popular tourist destinations because of their raw beauty and unchanged way of life. There are hundreds of species of moss, and recently scientists were overjoyed to discover completely new species on Hiiumaa. But many of the islands are all but inaccessible in winter when, around January, the surrounding sea freezes over for about three months.

National parks

There are four national parks in Estonia, as well as many nature reserves. Two of the most spectacular are Karula and Lahemaa National Parks. Karula National Park, near Valka in the south of Estonia, was established in 1993 to protect a unique landscape and its rich natural ecosystem. More than 70 percent of the territory is covered by forest, which varies from dry sandy pine forests to waterlogged swamp forests. This, along with many small lakes and streams, creates an ideal habitat for wildlife, including wolves, elk, otters, beavers, golden eagles and black storks.

Lahemaa *(see page 165)* is the oldest national park in Estonia and is the best developed for tourism, with a visitors' centre, well-marked trails and paths and guided tours. The park has glimmering cliffs, broadleaf primeval forests, stone fields with giant boulders, small coastal lakes and bogs, as well as charming coastal vil-

lages, farms and old German manor estates with immaculately landscaped parks.

Lakes produce whitefish, notably Lake Peipsi, and Võrtsjärv is famous for pike-perch and eel, which are prized for the table.

LATVIA

Latvians' love of nature is particularly striking for its, well . . . naturalness. And it's apparent in everything from the way many people routinely adorn their homes with fresh flowers, to the fact that many Latvian surnames are derived from the names of various trees, flowers, animals and birds. It is mainly a low-

lying plain, which is generally fertile, with lakes towards the east. More than 8 percent of the country is protected by law in four state reserves, three national parks and other protected areas.

Latvia's national flower is the oxe-eye daisy, and its national bird is the pied wagtail.

The coast

Latvia has an especially beautiful coastline, which stretches for some 494km (307 miles) along the Baltic Sea. Locals certainly make good use of the abundance of white sandy beaches during the summer, but you can always find a secluded stretch of beach for yourself if you're prepared to drive that little bit

LEFT: a brown bear at Järvsela, Estonia.
RIGHT: the national bird of Lithuania, white storks are considered harbingers of good fortune.

further on from popular tourist spots such as Jūrmala, Saulkrasti and Liepāja. In the last century the resort of Jūrmala, which is just 20km (13 miles) away from Rīga, was considered one of the most prestigious summer spots in the entire USSR.

As in Estonia, the strict coastal restrictions during Soviet times helped preserve much of the natural beauty of the coastline, and there are still countless picturesque fishing villages strewn right the way along the shores where locals sell smoked fish and other seafood on rickety stalls by the roadside.

Latvia is one of the few places in the entire Baltic Sea region where natural salmon spawning still occurs.

straightened, most large and medium-sized rivers retain their natural contours.

Many lakes provide feeding and breeding grounds for numerous bird species. Some of the most ecologically valuable of these are the shallow coastal lagoons along the Baltic coast. Places such as Lakes Pape, Liepājas, Engure, Babītes and Kaniera were cut off from the sea

Rivers and lakes

Latvia has more than 12,000 rivers, which together stretch for 38,000km (23,610 miles), as well as more than 2,000 lakes. The Latgale region, where many of these are found, is known as the "Land of the Blue Lakes". Nearly all inland waters ideally suited for swimming and fishing are pollution-free.

There are still a few beds of river pearl, a freshwater mussel requiring a pristine environment to produce its pearls, which were once collected for royalty. Much of the river water, however, originates beyond Latvia's borders, over which they have no control, and occasionally industrial pollutants get into the larger rivers. Although some rivers have had their courses

long ago and are now fresh water. Rare species of birds, such as the bearded tit, common and little bittern, corncrake, hen harrier, and little and spotted crake nest in Lake Pape and its surroundings. The lake and the nearby Nida marsh are important stopovers for bean and white-fronted goose and curlews during migration.

Forests and marshland

Forests cover some 45 percent of Latvia's territory – compared, for example, with 8 percent in Britain. Most are mixed coniferous and broadleaf, with mainly pine, spruce, birch, aspen and black alder, though oak and lime trees are especially important in Latvian life. About a quarter of Latvia's forests feature extensive areas of wetland, habitats that have been mostly destroyed in other European countries. These so-called "swamp" forests cover large areas of low-lying ground that are permanently or seasonally flooded. Many rare plant and animal species belong here. Home to more than 1,000 pairs of black storks (about 10 percent of the world's population), 500 pairs of the lesser spotted eagle, woodpeckers and many other species, these forests are a dream for birdwatchers.

The forests also have a rich supply of berries – wild strawberries, blueberries, raspberries and loganberries. The berry-picking season

otters live in the rivers. There are an estimated 200–400 wolves at large, as well as 400 lynxes. Beavers, which were hunted to extinction by the end of the 19th century, were successfully reintroduced into the country in the 20th century and now number an estimated 50,000–80,000.

Marshland makes up almost 5 percent of the country, most of which is unspoilt habitat. There are more than 20 protected plant species within this territory, and at least 15 species of bird that nest here, including the crane, golden plover, black grouse, whimbrel, merlin and peregrine. Marshes are also popular with berry-

lasts from late June until late September, the latter also being the time for gathering mushrooms, a favourite pastime – the Latvian word *sēņot* means "to go mushroom-picking". The most popular mushrooms are the edible boletus (very tasty with sour cream), orange cap boletus, chanterelles and rusulla. Best of all, the vast majority of forests, with a wealth of berries, mushrooms and hazelnuts, are free for everyone to enjoy.

Indigenous Latvian wildlife is similar to that of its Baltic neighbours. Some 4,000 Eurasian

LEFT: there are estimated to be around 400 lynx in the forests of Latvia. **ABOVE:** Konik Polski wild horses in Pape Nature Reserve, Latvia.

pickers for the cranberries, cloudberries, cowberries and bilberries that grow here.

National parks

Nearly 7 percent of Latvia is protected by law. There are five nature reserves, two national parks and 240 protected areas – nature parks, protected landscape areas, restricted areas and biosphere reserves.

Teiči State Reserve (*see page 246*) is the largest protected marsh in the Baltic and a sight well worth seeing. A raised bog covers most of the territory, but there are also 19 lakes, hollows, mineral-soil islands, fens, swamps and natural meadows. It also has the largest concentration of pre-migratory cranes in Latvia. An ancient

Russian village of Russian Old Believers (people who adhere to the Russian Orthodox Church as well as old pagan beliefs) still exists on one of the marsh islands. The marsh can only be entered in the company of a guide.

Gauja National Park *(see page 241)* is one of the most spectacular places in Latvia and is named after Latvia's longest river. For 90km (56 miles) the Gauja flows through a breathtaking valley that is the heart of the park. Nowhere else in Latvia are there so many steep banks, ravines, streams, sandstone and dolomite cliffs, and caves. Sigulda makes a good starting point.

Forests

Once entirely covered with thick forests and bogs, about a third of Lithuania is still under tree cover. Most of the forest is coniferous, but in the central and southern parts of the country, small areas of Central European deciduous forests have survived.

The forests and wetlands are home to elk, wolves, lynxes and beavers, and the edible dormouse. The rare mountain hare can be found in marshy bog lands. Birds of prey include the white-tailed eagle, osprey, honey buzzard and lesser-spotted eagle. In 1969 a breeding centre was set up for the European bison, once com-

LITHUANIA

Like its Baltic neighbours, Lithuania is predominantly flat. Its highest point is at Aukšasis, which stands an underwhelming 294 metres (964ft) above sea level. It lies on the western fringe of the East European Plain that stretches across Belarus and part of Russia. Much of the country is agricultural land, producing corn and root crops, while cattle include the indigenous Light Grey Lithuanian breed, found in the south and west of the country. As the country encompasses both coniferous and broadleaf forests, it has a mixture of habitats sustaining a rich variety of wildlife.

Rue is Lithuania's national flower and the white stork is the national bird.

ENVIRONMENTAL CONCERNS

There have been a number of threats to the purity of the Baltic States' environment, starting with the Soviet withdrawal, during which aircraft fuel and oil from marine terminals was dumped. Power plants running off oil shale in Narva give Estonia unusually high sulphur dioxide emissions, and air pollution occurs around chemical and cement industries. There is also natural erosion of arable land by wind and water. Some 70 percent of Lithuania's wetlands has been lost through land drainage for agriculture, and mineral fertilisers washed from fields into the water is a big problem. *For the environmental concerns of the Baltic Sea, see page 310.*

NATURE AND WILDLIFE ◆ 71

mon to the region, in Pasiliai Forest in the Panevėžys district. Their numbers, then diminishing, have all but disappeared.

By the water

Lithuania's glacial history can be seen in the country's abundance of rivers, lakes and wetlands. More than 800 rivers, including the 937km (582-mile) Nemunas, transform the landscape into a liquid latticework, and about 3,000 lakes cover some 1.5 percent of the country. Many of these are ideal for swimming. It's still possible to find your "own" lake, where few others go, even in the height of summer.

composed mostly of dunes and pine forests that separates the Curonian Lagoon from the Baltic Sea. This precious natural habitat has a number or rare and protected plants, as well as a distinctive insect life, including a rich diversity of butterflies, such as the Camberwell Beauty. There are also sea eagles here, and the largest colony of stalks in the country. Long-nosed seals are sometimes seen on the shore.

National parks

There are five national parks and 30 regional parks, covering around 12 percent of the country. Aukštaitija National Park *(see page 301)* was

There are some 60 different kinds of freshwater fish, including native perch, tench and sea trout, as well as introduced species such as sturgeon. Lake Žuvintas in the south is an important breeding ground and migration resting ground for many kinds of water birds. It is also one of the few breeding grounds for endangered species such as the aquatic warbler and ferruginous duck.

Although Lithuania is the largest of the Baltic states, it has the shortest coastline at just 99km (62 miles). Most of it is taken up by the Curonian Spit *(see page 320)*, a thin stretch of sand

LEFT: hunters on Hiiumaa island, Estonia.
ABOVE: as elsewhere in Europe, foxes have become common in suburban areas.

the first one, designated in 1974, and covering an area of 40,570 hectares (100,250 acres) around Ignalina, Utena and Švenčionys. The park is especially picturesque and perfectly encapsulates the lush, primeval beauty of Lithuanian nature.

The majestic Trakai National Park *(see page 284)*, which lies 25km (16 miles) from Vilnius, was designated in 1992 and embraces the historic city of Trakai, together with the forests, lakes and villages in its vicinity.

Between all the various national parks and nature reserves, the sizeable protected natural habitat of Lithuania supports a huge variety of wildlife, including elk, deer, wolves, foxes and wild boar. Bird species include ospreys, white-tailed eagles and white storks. ❏

OUTDOOR ACTIVITIES

From river rafting to sky–diving, snowboarding to Zorbing,
the long coast, sleepy rivers and lush national parks are
ideal places to get active and have some recreational fun

Rural tourism and outdoor recreation are increasingly important in the Baltic economy. Estonia, Latvia and Lithuania continue to come up with good reasons for tourists to trek beyond the capital cities for some outdoor fun. The countries' nearly untouched ecosystem is scattered with small tourism enterprises, offering activities from hot-air ballooning to river rafting and horse riding on wild mares.

Regardless of the sport, and dramatic high ground notwithstanding, the countryside has sufficiently diverse beauty to create a playground for the outdoor enthusiast – and none are more enthusiastic than the Baltic peoples themselves.

Gauja National Park

The national parks in all three countries are well equipped for outdoor activities, with hiking trails and tended waterways. Latvia's major playground, Gauja National Park, centred on the towns of Sigulda and Cēsis, is a particular magnet for outdoor adventurers. Like every state park in the Baltics, it is carved with hiking trails, observation points and camping sites, as well as historic landscapes that include castle ruins and archaeological excavation areas.

The River Gauja cuts through the park's ancient valley of sandstone and dolomite cliffs. There is water rafting, trail bungee-jumping, and a cable car for an overview of the scenery. Lacking dramatic white-water river rafting on the slow-moving Gauja is by no means danger-ous, and offers an ideal way to enjoy the park's natural splendours with the family. Tourists can rent rafts that accommodate around 10 people with an accompanying guide, as well as private canoes and boats. The Gauja is riddled with small whirlpools, which swimmers are cau-tioned about, and any skilled canoeist can work his or her way to a thrilling amount of speed on the 90km (55-mile) stretch of river.

Avid spelunkers will be able to find the largest cave in the Baltic States – Gūtmanis cave – in the centre of Gauja National Park. The cave's natural sand catacombs wind 18.8

Vučko, is open every weekend between Octo-ber and March, and there is also a summer bob-sleigh from May to October.

Water sports

During the summer months, the coast provides activities and relaxation in a variety of ways. Sailing between the mainland and Estonia's remarkable 1,520 islands is perhaps the most elegant way to enjoy the stunning coast. Visi-tors can splurge on a yacht trip to the island of Kihnu or spend a more casual day in the Bay of Pärnu watching the Baltic sunset over the boats. Or they might take a fishing trip. There is no

metres (62ft) deep, 12 metres (40ft) wide and 10 metres (33ft) high.

Sigulda's most prized recreational feature is the professional 1,420-metre (4,660ft) long bob-sleigh track. Open year-round, it allows visitors to live out their dream of participating in one of the Winter Olympics' most popular sports. In professional bobsleigh and luge training and competitions, athletes reach speeds of up to 125kph (78mph). Amateurs, however, will fly through the concrete track at a much safer speed of 80kph (50mph) under the guidance of professionals. The tourist bobsleigh, called

shortage of sailing trips along the country's 3,794km (2,357-mile) shoreline. Sea excursions are so popular, however, that booking should be made at least a few weeks in advance.

Yacht charters for both bareboat and skip-pered vessels are available at the main marinas, in Tallinn, Jūrmala and Klaipėda, but boating has not yet reached its full potential.

For those who prefer boating activities of a more sporty nature, speedboat, jet-ski and wake-board rentals are offered at most of the seaside resorts. Windsurfing is also a popular coastal activity, and the relatively safe shallow waters are a good place to learn. Water temper-atures seldom rise above 17°C (63°F) in sum-mer. Diving centres in Tallinn, Kipsala island on

LEFT: cycling along Pirita Beach, Estonia.
ABOVE: rowing on Lake Galvė, Lithuania.

the River Daugava in Rīga, and from a base in Lithuania's Kaunas offer certified courses with trained professionals as well as open-water dives. There is diving in some lakes, too, but the best place for diving is off the coast, where one can explore the Baltic Sea's deep underwater secrets, including wreck sites. The wrecks in the Baltic are of special interest, but you need a guide, as there are unexploded World War II mines and munitions here.

Extreme and airborne sports

Traditional daredevil activities include the annual ice-horse race on Lake Sartai, Lithua-

> *The first European Women's Hot-Air Balloon Championship was held in Altyas, Lithuania, in 2010.*

nia. The latest craze is for kiiking, invented by Estonian Ado Kosk, in which participants are strapped to rigid poles and swing through 360 degrees. In Rīga, you can imagine you are on the moon when you go catapult jumping.

Zorbing, dry and wet, is another newcomer, involving huge transparent balls. In Dry Zorbing the participant is strapped inside the ball

and then tumbles around, hurtling down hills at speeds of up to 56kph (35mph). In Wet Zorbing the ball has some water in it, and the participant slides about as the ball rolls around, much as in a water slide.

There is no better way to take in the patchwork countryside than from above. There are pleasure flights in Rīga, and the Kaunas Flying Club offers delta-plane flights and paragliding for recreational enjoyment. Professional lessons are provided for beginners, though flights depend on weather conditions.

Skydiving has also, as it were, taken off. Founded in 1992 at Pociunai Airfield, the Kaunas Skydiving Club is the oldest parachute club in Lithuania and one of the most popular in the Baltics. The club is open every weekend from March to October and organises more than 5,000 jumps a year. Although the majority of skydivers are familiar to the sport, the club's professional staff offer training for beginners, who can choose a static-line or tandem jump. Skydiving is on offer in Riga and Tallinn, too.

Hot-air ballooning is a less intimidating way to enjoy the landscape from the air. A tradition that goes back for years, all three countries have air-balloon festivals that bring a rainbow of floating ornaments to the skies each summer. The rides are an ideal way to enjoy a scenic evening of relaxation, with baskets comfortably carrying up to three people. For a cityscape ballooning trip visit Eurocentras in Vilnius. For a taste of rustic scenery, Nemunaitis village in the Alytus district of Lithuania is the best place to call.

Horse riding

For centuries, horse riding has been the most traditional and best-enjoyed outdoor activity. Even today, Balts treasure this age-old way of getting around that carries a trail of culture and folklore behind it. The flatlands make hacking easy and, whether it's bareback riding along the coastal dunes of Latvia or keeping to the tame wooded paths of Estonia, riding is one of the most romantic ways to enjoy the outdoors. There are numerous stables and riding clubs throughout all three countries that offer lessons for every level, and many agriturismo farms have their own horses.

Winter sports

The polar freeze that strikes northeastern Europe from mid-November, lasting until late March, has earned quite a name for Baltic winters. Yet the long snowy days serve as the perfect excuse to head to the country for some winter sports and hot mulled wine. Temperatures in all three Baltic states sink to between 0 and −15°C (32 and 5°F) during the winter. With a generous snowfall, these temperatures create ideal skiing conditions.

There are no Alpine peaks – the highest it gets in the Baltics is 318-metre (1,044ft) Suur Munamägi (Big Egg Hill) in Estonia. Yet that same country's "winter capital", Otepää, has ski

jumps and holds the World Cup Cross-Country Skiing Championship each January.

Winter sports such as skiing, snowboarding, hockey, ski-mobiling – even ice fishing – manage to keep Baltic inhabitants entertained all season long.

Golf

Golf is a 21st-century arrival in the Baltic States. The rural landscapes, with an abundance of water hazards, woodland and wild areas, offer fine opportunities for inventive courses. Clubs tend to open from April to October. In Estonia Valgaranna (White Beach) Golf in Pärnu

and the Niitväja Tallinn Golf Club are both 18 holes. The first course to open in Latvia was Ozo, just north of Rīga, in 2002. It has 16 ponds and 50 sand bunkers, and you will need to produce a handicap certificate. To the south of the city is Saliena Golf, with an 18-hole championship Club Course and a 9-hole Garden Course.

Lithuania's European Centre GC, opened in 2007, is an 18-hole championship-standard course, next to lake Girja, 20 minutes' drive from Vilnius. The 18-hole Capitals Golf Club between Vilnius and Kaunas, opened the same year, is also well located, in a rural setting with lakes and woodland.

For details of Outdoor Activities, see Travel Tips, page 362. ❑

LEFT: hot-air ballooning over Vilnius. **RIGHT:** snowboarding in Otepää, Estonia's "winter capital".

FOOD

Baltic food is fresh and wholesome, relying on the natural flavours of fish from its waterways, meat and dairy produce from its farms, a colourful array of fruit and vegetables from its gardens and juicy berries from the forests

B altic cooking today is basically pretty straightforward country fare. The plain, wholesome, unspicy dishes characteristic of all three countries – although especially Latvia and Estonia – demand little artistry, but nevertheless can be very good.

The best place to see what's in the Baltic larder is in Rīga, where, if your schedule allows, you should take an hour or two to peruse the Zeppelin hangars that house the city's massive – and extremely crowded – market. Scores of indoor stalls tout fresh and fermented dairy products: vast slabs of soft white cheese, harder yellow cheese, bottles of sour cream, yoghurt and cultivated sour milk. In another hall, high-quality fresh pork gleams pink, and many varieties of sausage and ham wait to be sampled. Smoked fish sells at one end of the market, while fresh fruit is on offer at the other.

Summer harvest

In summer, baskets are piled high with early apples and pears – small irregular specimens that are not subject to the trading controls that are all too familar in Western Europe; glass tumblers spill over with red and black berries and tiny yellow mirabelle plums. Look out for the different varieties of nuts, the dried fruit, the umbrils of caraway seed drying on the branch, huge bunches of fresh, strong, flat-leaf parsley, pots of honey, barrels of sauerkraut lined up for tasting and trays of fresh, home-made black, brown and white bread. These staple foods, which are brought in by private sellers from

the nearby countryside, are the raw materials of traditional Baltic cooking.

These ingredients are usually served at the table with very little seasoning. In the vegetable hall you may smell dill and garlic – but for flavour Latvia mostly relies on fermented milk, smoked fish and cheese, and bacon, with a sprinkling here and there of caraway seed, rather than strong herbs and spices. Onions are considered too strong to feature heavily. Lithuanian cooking, partly influenced by the Orient, is the most pungent of the three.

This hint of oriental spice in Lithuanian cooking is a result of the country's complicated political past. From the 15th century exiled

LEFT: the stalls are piled high in Rīga's huge central market. **RIGHT:** honey features regularly in local cuisine.

Crimean Tatars and refugees from the Golden Horde flocked to this powerful state to coexist with Russians, Belarussians and Poles under the leadership of the Polish/Lithuanian noble class. The results today are a half-forgotten legacy of exoticism and luxury, recipes which dare to include black pepper and nutmeg and marjoram. Spices were imported from the East; marjoram was probably brought into the country from Italy, via Catholic Poland.

With independence came a rediscovery of the richness of Estonian, Latvian and Lithuanian traditional country-style cooking. In each of the three capitals, countless traditional res-

keeps well and is an ideal accompaniment to the local beer, cheeses and pungent cured meat and fish. One type of pale rye loaf, which has a smooth, shiny, tan-coloured crust, is known as Rīga bread and is best eaten when it is fresh and sweet. (Most bakers hang a two-pronged testing fork beside their self-service shelves.)

Other Baltic speciality breads include the plain dark rye variety that is often served in hotels and which should not be judged by the dryness and sourness it exudes when left indefinitely exposed to the air. (Don't let this put you off.) Among the white breads are the robust and versatile French *baton*, not at all like

taurants have opened, typically offering heavy butter-doused Lithuanian *cepelinai* and other local dishes. However, the best local cooking can usually still be sampled in private homes.

Bread baskets

Excellent natural resources, quality farming and careful husbandry contribute to the goodness of Baltic food. The lush land provides rich harvests of grains and berries, dark forests provide the ideal environment for mushroom growth, fish populate the rivers, lakes and sea, and pig and dairy farming are important industries.

Rye bread, which has a strong rich taste, is enhanced by molasses, made from native-growing sugar beet, and caraway seed. This bread

its Gallic counterpart, and the creamy-coloured sourdough loaves that are usually home-made and well worth seeking out for their extraordinary muscular texture.

More than one Western traveller has made a meal out of bread alone, to the consternation of the locals, who cry: "But where's the sausage to go with it, or the butter?" (In the Baltics they love their meats and fats.)

Porridge and potatoes

Although porridge used to be a staple food in these parts, porridges made from cooked grain are now rarely seen on menus except on special occasions. The ancient Latvian version, called *putra*, is made of barley (or a mix of barley and potato) and typically served with a ladle of bacon fat, some smoked meat or fish, or perhaps also with milk products, as a main course. In Estonia mixed-grain porridges are sometimes served with milk. There is also a breakfast speciality that is akin to Scottish porridge: *kama*, made of ground toasted grains and raw oats, is mixed with yoghurt or milk and eaten with salt or honey. *Kama* is good for upset stomachs. There is another dish that is similar to porridge, which is made of mushy peas and then eaten with bacon fat.

The Baltic Germans introduced the potato to the Baltics at the start of the 18th century, and

> If a Lithuanian were asked to name his or her favourite dish, it would probably be something prepared with potato, particularly latkes, known in Lithuania as bulviniai blynai.

dough made from this yeast-leavened wheat, which tastes deliciously fresh.

In Latvia the array of savoury baking is highly enviable. Special treats include cheese- and meat-filled yeast-dough buns and yeast-dough horns stuffed to the brim with minced bacon. If pizza makes you think of pasta, look no further than

the whole region fell for its charms, especially the Lithuanians. Today they eat boiled potatoes with everything from yoghurt to bacon fat, and, like the Poles and the Jews, they are fans of grated potato pancakes. The same grated potato is used to make a variety of filled rissoles, such as *cepelinai*, meaning that this potassium-rich foodstuff plays a part in most daily diets. Yeast-leavened wheat dough – the foodstuff from which genuine pizza bases are made – is another staple carbohydrate here. On street corners in Tallinn you can buy slightly sweet white

LEFT: pickled herring and local mushrooms in Lithuania. ABOVE: *Grūdenis* is a thick country stew from Latvia that uses a pig's head.

Lithuania, where cooking is strongly influenced by the Russian and Polish fondness for Slavic *koldūnai* – another Baltic treat.

Fat feasts

One of the hallmarks of Baltic food is the non-prevalence of protein. Meat and fish, at least in Latvia and Estonia, are eaten in very small quantities, almost as a dressing or garnish to the bread, pasta or porridge as the focus of a meal. Rich, fatty foods, rather than lean meats, tend to prove most popular at special feasts.

Although fat features so prominently in the Baltic diet, it is interesting to note that traditional food here is rarely fried. Vegetables and carbohydrates are typically boiled first and are then covered later with fat – whether it's in the form of bacon, cheese or, quite simply, butter.

Pork is without doubt the most commonly eaten meat, though quality beef is also available, as well as game, including duck and sometimes hare. (The term pork covers salt pork, sausage and the black pudding – blood sausage – that Estonians eat every year on Christmas Day.)

In the 15th century Lithuania was highly renowned for its smoked wild boar. Domestic pig farming was later introduced by the Germans with exceptional results. This pork-production industry was so successful that smoked lean pork from the Baltics, all pink, wrinkled, juicy

and tender, is believed to have been the stuff of many a privileged Communist Party banquet. Smoked lean pork is certainly more inviting than the wedges of salted pork fat, the dietary mainstay of the labouring male peasant in the 1900s, which are still classed as a delicacy.

On commercial menus you will come across hot, fresh meat dishes more familiar to the visitor than anything mentioned so far. In many restaurants, meat cutlets, fried escalopes, meatballs and boiled and fried sausages are more often than not prepared by foreign chefs.

Fish dishes

If you like fish, you'll find there is much in the way of local delicacies to tempt you here. Local fish preparations, such as smoked saltwater salmon, pickled herring, smoked sprats and smoked eel, rank among the best fish dishes in the world. If you travel around the fishing villages, you will have the chance of sampling locally smoked fish, while around the inland lake districts you are likely to encounter fresh-

> In Tallinn, look out for bars and restaurants that have won Silver Spoon Awards from the Gastronomy Society of Estonia. These are given annually in 10 different categories.

water fish dishes, notably those using trout, pike and pike-perch.

In Latvia and Lithuania fish is often cooked in bacon fat – a rare case of frying. Russian caviar, once the pride of every restaurant menu, is becoming increasingly difficult to find and is now very expensive. More affordable are the Estonian fresh fish soups, which are made with vegetables and thickened with flour and milk.

Cold dishes

Until early in the 20th century two-thirds of traditional Baltic dishes were those for its cold table. This is something that seems to come especially into its own at breakfast, when a mix of cheese and meat, as well as vegetables and cream, is served. At other times of the day, the cold table is often supplemented with soup.

Salads are an important part of the cold table. They are usually accompanied by dressings and eaten with bread. One of the culinary highlights of a visit can be a bowl of tomatoes and cucumbers picked straight from a country garden, tossed with fresh dill and parsley and sour cream.

Sometimes strips of meat or cheese are used in the same way as raw vegetables to make composite salads for the cold table, but often these are covered in bottled flavourings. Unfortunately, they represent only a poor attempt at a quick urban cuisine adapted from the country.

Soups

Although there are old recipes in Lithuania for varieties of beetroot soup along the lines of the Russian/Ukrainian/Polish beetroot-based borchst, and for mushroom soup, this liquid dish is most typically found on the menus of cheaper eateries. Lithuanian beetroot soup has a sweet-and-sour base and is flavoured with sorrel, a rich source of iron and vitamin C.

Estonian food is generally fairly mild, and its soups are no exception. A classic Estonian soup contains milk, dried peas and buckwheat grains, and the majority of varieties of this are made with milk and vegetables, or with yoghurt and dill cucumber.

Under German influence, Latvia and Estonia used to make a sweet bread soup out of leftover fruit. Since the bread was probably sour and black the soup was closely related to the sour-sweet *ķīselis* made with summer berries. Beer soups belong to this curious category.

profusion alongside peas and cabbages and rhubarb. Somewhere near the vegetable garden you will also find apple trees and plum trees and, in an ideal world, a beehive. A guest might enjoy an inspiring summer tea made from baked sour windfall apples sweetened with clear plum jam and macaroons. Nothing is wasted.

Another crop that is increasing in importance in Latvia and Lithuania is sea buckthorn, which produces a juice full of minerals.

Cakes

At the opposite end of the spectrum from the healthy ideal of the country garden is the Baltic sweet trolley. Nowadays, cakes are generally

Garden produce

The country garden is something that is celebrated in all three states, and it cannot be stressed highly enough how vital a part it plays in Baltic culture. One of the most charming and notable poems in Lithuanian literature – one that is frequently, and many believe quite rightly, compared to Virgil's *Eclogues* – is called *The Seasons*, written by an 18th-century clergyman, Kristijonas Donelaitis. In the kitchen garden, which became popular in Donelaitis' time, the sweetest tomatoes, ridge cucumbers, courgettes, beets, kohlrabi, potatoes, swede and turnips grow in

LEFT: strawberries, just one of many forest fruits.
ABOVE: cold beetroot soup, a summer dish.

BERRIES FROM THE FORESTS

Blueberries, bilberries, cloudberries, cranberries, lingonberries, raspberries, strawberries, whortleberries... there is a wonderful kaleidoscope of berries found in the Baltic forests and bogs. You can come across these in roadside stalls, as well as in restaurants and on the dining table. Try corn pancakes with berries and yoghurt for breakfast, or as pies and tarts or flavoured ice creams. Buy them bottled or in jams in markets and shops. There are juices and country fruit wines, and gins flavoured with berries – including juniper berries, which are often used in cooking. Anyone with a garden will grow berries and currants along with their flowers.

more popular than desserts in the Baltics, and there are some excellent specialist chocolate shops. In Lithuania, look out for treecakes and honey cakes. Treecakes are made by adding dough in layers to a rotating wooden pole in front of a hot fire. The result is a cake with many age lines and fungi-like appendages clinging to its outer "bark", where dollops of egg and lemon dough have been added. Despite its peculiar appearance, it is quite delicious.

In cafés, where many varieties of shortbreads, shortcrust and flaky pastries, and eclairs are sold, you can't help noticing that Latvians and Estonians have a penchant for eating large amounts of sweet whipped cream with their cakes. Chocolate cafés are the in-thing in Rīga.

Drinks and picnics

Coffee is one dietary feature that distinguishes Russia from the Baltics: coffee is far more prevalent here. Both tea and coffee are served without milk. Mineral water is normally good-quality (note that it is not safe to drink tap water in Rīga – always buy bottled water instead).

If you are in the mood for something stronger, you'll find that the majority of bars and cafés serve beer on tap rather than in bottles. The main breweries (Kalnapilis and Utenos

> Founded in 1870, Rīga's major chocolate manufacturer, Laima, makers of chocolate boxes, candies and biscuits, offers tours of its factory. See www.laima.lv

in Lithuania, Aldaris in Latvia and Saku and A le Cocq in Estonia) all have their loyal following. The local brews are available on tap in most restaurants. The current craze in Vilnius is for live beers from the nation's microbreweries.

Herbal eau-de-vie, Rīga Black Balsam (a dark brew, which tastes like a mixture of treacle and Campari), sweet Lithuanian liqueurs, locally produced Russian vodka and sparkling wines complete the standard alcoholic line-up. You may also find expensive wines from France and less costly but decent vintages from Georgia, Hungary and Romania.

Traditional food is considered by many Balts as something they make at home, but wouldn't necessarily look for when they go out, hence its scarcity in restaurants. The best local food is therefore enjoyed in private homes or as a picnic, composed of some of the delicacies offered at a typical Baltic cold table – excellent fresh vegetables, cold meats and tasty, albeit mild cheeses. Although the fare served in long-established hotels may seem rather heavy and fatty to the diet-conscious, health-obsessed Westerner, it can work wonders for an empty stomach. More imaginative chefs are beginning to look at how to use traditional ingredients in new ways. ❑

SPECIAL OCCASIONS

Christmas Day is celebrated with pork dishes in Estonia, goose in Protestant Latvia, and fish and mushrooms in Catholic Lithuania. At midsummer – an important date in the Baltic calendar – dairy products come into their own. A special dense yellow country cheese, smoked and flavoured with caraway seeds, is traditionally produced for midsummer (Jāņi, or St John's Day) in Latvia; a similar, spicier cheese is eaten in Lithuania, where *kugelis*, the national potato dish is in every home. You can sample both varieties of cheeses in Rīga's Central Market, and you should keep an eye out for local cheeses while travelling round the country.

LEFT: Gira, a Lithuanian non-alcoholic brew made from dark rye bread.
RIGHT: honeycomb and home-made cheese.

Estonia, Latvia and Lithuania

0   50 km

0   50 miles

FINLAND

Åland
Mariehamn
Korpo
Storhandet
Parainen
Salo
Lohja
Ekenäs
Hanko

Vantaa
Espoo
Helsinki

Gulf of Finland
(Soome laht)

Narva
Jõesuu
Narva
Sillamäe

Mohni
Prangli
Aegna
Naissaare
looduspark
Naissaar
Lähemaa
rahvuspark
Kohtla-
Järve
Puhatu
looduskaitseala

BALTIC
SEA

Stockholm
Rostock
Stockholm
Rostock
Rostock, Lübeck
Copenhagen, Kiel

Väike-
Pakri
Paldiski
Osmussaar
Nova
Kärdla
Vormsi
Haapsalu
Rohuküla
Tallinn
Maardu
Kose
Purila
Kauksi
Jõhvi
Jõuga
Rakvere
Slanc
Pandivere
kõrgendik

Kõpu
poolsar
Kalana
Hiiumaa
Emmaste
Kassari
Muhu
Panga
Soela väin
Matsalu
looduskaitseala
Lihula
Vändra
E 263
E 264
A3
Čudskoe ozero
Peipsi järv
Kallaste
E 67

Vilsandi
rahvuspark
Vilsandi
Saaremaa
Viidumäe
looduskaitseala
Kuressaare
Abruka
Sõrve
poolsar
Pootsi
Pärnu
Soomaa
rahvuspark
Viljandi
Võrtsjärv
Alam-Pedja
looduskaitseala
Tartu
RUSSI
Räpina
Põlva
Pskovskoe
ozero
Psk

Kihnu
Häädemeeste
Torva
Sakala
kõrgendik
Otepää
kõrgendik
Kānepi
Võru
Pecory

Gulf of Riga
Ruhnu
Kura kurk
Irbes šaurums
Kolkasrags
Salacgrīva
Rūjiena
Burtnieks
Valga
Suur Munamägi
318
Haanja
kõrgendik
(Haanja Highland)
Abtsnes ez.

Ventspils
Šlītere
Nationalpark
Upesgrīva
Saulkrasti
Tūja
Valmiera
Strenči
E77
A2
Ostro

Pāvilosta
Ugāle
Usmas
ez.
Talsi
Engure
Gauja
Nationalpark
Cēsis
Gulbene
Vilka
Krasnogorodsk

Zlēkas
Kuldīga
Tukums
Jūrmala
Rīga
Ropaži
Sigulda
LATVIA
Gaizinkalns
312
Madona
Balvi
Ica
Lubāns

E22
A10
A2
E77
Saldus
Brocēni
Dobele
Vecumnieki
Saulspils
Baloži
Ogre
Lielvārde
Aizkraukle
Pļaviņas
Jēkabpils
Rēzekne
Ludza
Rázna
Zilupe

Liepāja
Grobiņa
A9
Zāgare
Jelgava
E67
Bauska
Jaunjelgava
A6
Līvāni
Aglona
A13
E262

Skuodas
Salantai
A11
Mažeikiai
Plateliu
ez.
Naujojo
Akmenė
Joniškis
Biržai
Pasvalys
Nereta
A6
Daugavpils
Kraslava
Verchnedvinsk

Palanga
A13
Telšiai
E272
A11
Kuršėnai
A12
E77
Pakruojis
E67
A10
Rokiškis
Kupiškis
E262
A6
Visaginas
Braslav
Mioŋ

Klaipėda
Kretinga
Gargždai
Plungė
Užventis
Šiauliai
A9
Radviliškis
E272
Panevėžys
Sventoii
Utena
Švenčianski grjady
Postavy
Hlybok

Kelmė
LITHUANIA
Anykščiai
A2
Molėtai
Aukštaitijos
nacionalinis
parkas

Neringa
Silalė
E77
A1
Raseiniai
Kėdainiai
A8
Ukmergė
E262
E272
Širvintos
Utena

Šilutė
Tauragė
A12
Viešvilės
rezervatas
Jurbarkas
Nemunas
Jonava
Kaišiadorys
Vilnius
BELARUS

Kuršskij
zaliv
Sovetsk
Neman
Šakiai
Kaunas
Kauno
marios
E85
Elektrenai
A1
Traku ist.
nacionalinis
parkas
A3
Juozapinės
293
Smarhon'
Sosenka

RUSSIA
Černjahovsk
Pregolja
Gusev
Vilkaviškis
A6
Prienai
Priena
E28
A16
A4
A15
E85
Osmjany
Maladžiecna

Kaliningrad
Ozersk
Marijampolė
A7
Alytus
Varena
Dokš

Bartoszyce
Ketrzyn
Gizycko
Suwalki
Metelys
Dzūkijos
nacionalinis
parkas
Druskininkai
Čepkeliu
rezervatas
Lida

Dobre
Miasto
POLAND
Minsk

PLACES

The principal sites in this detailed guide to
Estonia, Latvia and Lithuania are clearly cross-
referenced by number or letter to the maps

Added together, the countries of Estonia, Latvia and
Lithuania, each covering about the same area, are a little
larger than England and Wales, or the size of Washington State. They sit side by side on the eastern edge of the
Baltic Sea between Poland and the Gulf of Finland. Tallinn,
the northernmost capital, is on roughly the same latitude as
Scotland's Orkney Islands and southern Alaska. Vilnius, capital of Lithuania in the south, shares an approximate latitude
with Newcastle and Newfoundland. This means that summer
days lengthen into white nights and winter days are grey and short.

Although they have linguistic, cultural and historical differences, the
three countries share a similar landscape. The overwhelming image is one
of quiet roads and flatlands, rising in low, rolling hills towards the east, of
myriad small rivers and lakes and of forests of the tallest pines. Scattered
throughout are ancient hill forts and occasional boulders, "presents from
Scandinavia" left by retreating glaciers. Like some of the oldest trees, these
have frequently been bestowed with magical properties.

The landscape is essentially rural, with vast tracts of arable and pasture
lands, bogs and forests. Some of the remaining neoclassical manors, built
by the occupying Russians, Scandinavians, Germans and Poles, have been
converted into restaurants, hotels or cultural centres. In the cities, it is the
legacy of these conquerors and their religions that prevail, in particular
the Hansa merchants who for centuries monopolised trade. Urban development in Soviet times left the capitals' Old Towns
largely untouched and now, spruced up and inviting,
each is a Unesco World Heritage Site.

The Baltic Sea's "Amber Coast" is a wonder of endless white pristine beaches backed by dunes and pine
forests. Its spas and safe swimming beaches have made
its resorts popular for millions.

Travelling by public transport is not difficult, and a
visit to one country can easily include a day or two in
part of another.   ❏

PRECEDING PAGES: watery landscape at Aukštaitija, Lithuania; figures outside the
National Drama Theatre, Vilnius; autumn colours in Pärnu, Estonia.
TOP: Midsummer Festival. **ABOVE RIGHT:** Kõpu lighthouse, Hiiumaa island, Estonia.

ESTONIA

The smallest of the three countries has a fairytale capital, hundreds of lakes and islands, ruined castles, restored manors and relaxed coastal spa resorts

The northernmost of the Baltic States is Eesti Vabariik, the Republic of Estonia. It is also the smallest, least densely populated of the three countries. On the south side of the Gulf of Finland, its capital, Tallinn, is 85km (53 miles) from Helsinki and about 130km (80 miles) from St Petersburg. Finns have long taken advantage of Estonia's proximity and relative cheapness, making the ferry crossing in droves. Other European visitors have joined their ranks, particularly cruise-ship passengers and weekenders from the UK.

It is easy to see the attraction: Tallinn has the prettiest Old Town in the Baltics, a medieval enclave set on a hillock above its port. Within the fairytale walls and towers and beneath the Gothic spires are winding cobbled lanes leading to the old square. Beside this ensemble, a rapidly developing commercial district has redrawn the city's skyline and given locals more places to spend their new-found wealth.

Estonia has a second city in Tartu in the south, a distinguished university town that brims with student life. The historic, west-coast towns of Pärnu and Haapsalu are popular health resorts, and maintain a pace of life that's decidedly more relaxed than in the capital. A very different

scene can be found in the industrial northeast of the country, particularly in the city of Narva, which has a high ethnic Russian population and is struggling to find its place in the new European Union economy. Much of the Russian border is taken up by Lake Peipsi, the fourth-largest lake in Europe, where a settlement of Old Believers flourishes.

Beyond the urban areas, nearly 40 percent of the country is forested with pine, spruce and junipers, and inhabited by elk, brown bears and beavers. The land is mostly flat and unpopulated, dotted with around 1,500 lakes. The largest islands are Hiiumaa and Saaremaa, rural backwaters where the earliest stone churches in the Baltics can be found. ❑

PRECEDING PAGES: Orjaku jetty, Hiiumaa island. **LEFT:** Old Town Days festival in Tallinn's Town Hall Square. **TOP:** St Olav's church, Tallinn. **ABOVE LEFT:** sunset over the Baltic. **ABOVE RIGHT:** a female elk in the birch woods of central Estonia.

Estonia

0 ——— 20 km

0 ——— 20 miles

N

LÄÄNEMERI

(BALTIC SEA)

Liivi laht

(Gulf of Riga)

Rostok

Stockholm

Naissaare looduspark

Naissaar

Tallinna laht

Tallin ❶

Tahn

Väike-Pakri

Paldiski

Keila

8

Suur-Pakri

Kurkse väin

Keila

Saue

Osmussaar

Rummu

4 E67

Harj

Iood

Nova

Riisipere

Kof

Silma looduskaitseala

Turba

Alema looduskaitseala

Tahkuna looduskaitseala

Lehtma

Vormsi

Ants Laikmaa majam-muuseum (Ants Laikmaa Museum)

Risti

9

4 E67

Ra

Ristimägi (Hill of Crosses)

Kärdla

Sviby

❶❹❶❺

Palivere

Marimetsa looduskaitseala

Rapl

❷❹ Kõpu tuletorn (Kõpu Lighthouse)

Kõpu poolsar

Pihla-Kaibaldi looduskaitseala

❷❸

Haapsalu

Rohuküla

Läänemaa

Märjamaa

Kalana

Leigri looduskaitseala

Hiiumaa

Suuremõisa ❷❷

Käina

Sillä

Valo

Hiiumaa

❷❺ Kassari

Heltermaa

❶❸

Matsalu rahvuspark (Matsalu National Park)

Matsalu laht

Laikūla

Vana-Vigala

Järve

Emmaste

Soela väin

Penijõe

10

Lihula

Pärnu-Jaagup

Panga Pank

Koguva

Liiva

Muhu ★

Virtsu

Suuriku pank

Panga

Leisi

Maasi Ordulinnuse (Maasi Castle)

Kuivästu

Pärnumaa

Lavassaare

Vilsandi rahvuspark

Veere

Angla

Karja kirik (Karja Church)

❶❾

❷❶ Orissaare

Padeste Mõis

4 E67

Vilsandi

Mustjala

❶❽ Mihkli talumuuseum (Mihkli Farm Museum)

Saaremaa

Putla

❷❶

Kaali meteoriikraatrite väli (Kaali Meteoric Craters)

Lindi looduskaitseala

Pärnu ❶❶

Kihelkonna

Kaarma

Valjala

Tõstamaa

Pärnu laht

Uulu

Viki

Kärla

10

Püha

Põotsi

4

Karala

Viidumäe looduskaitseala

❶❼ **Kuressaare**

Saaremaa

Kihnu väin

Manilaid

Luitemea ika rahvuspark

Salme

Suur katel

Abruka

Kihnu

Häädemeeste

4 E67

Sõrve poolsar

Viierristi looduskaitseala

Nigula looduskaitse

Sääre

Ruhnu

Ainaži

Ventspils

Kura kurk

Salacgriva

Irbes šaurums

Kolkasrags

Mazirbe

Gipka

4

Īrbene

Ancee

Dundaga

Roja

Tūja

L A T V I A

Pope

Valdemārpils

Upesgrīva

Riga

Sankt Peterburg

Mohni

Soome laht

(Gulf of Finland)

Üst'-Luga

31 Viinistu

Bol. Kuzёmkino

26 Loksa **30** Käsmu **29**

Majakivi **27** Võsu Altja

32 Kolga mõis **Lahemaa rahvuspark** Sagadi mõis Ehalkivi

Narva Jõesuu

Palmse **28** Palmse mõis Kunda

la juga **1** Viitna Haljalai Aseri Purtse North Estonian Klint Narva

Saka Valaste Toila Sillamäe **37** **1** **Narva**

Jägala Õhepalu looduskaitseala Kiviöli Püssi **34** Kohtla-Järve E20 **38**

ije ala Kehra Kadrina **33** **Rakvere** Kohtla-kaevanduspark-muuseum (Mine Park Museum) Kohtla-Nõmme **35** Jõhvi **36** Narvskoe vodohranilišče

põllu skaitseala Aegviidu Tapa **Pandivere kõrgendik** **Lääne-Virumaa** Ida-Virumaa Slancy

se **5** Mäetaguse A3 E264 **39** Kuramäe

2 E263 A.H.Tammsaare muuseum Aravete Tamsalu Väike-Maarja Tudu Muraka looduskaitseala Jõuga Puhatu looduskaitseala Kingissepp

Järva-Jaani Simuna Iisaku

J Ä R V A M A Koeru Rakke Avinurme Kauksi Vasknarva **40** Koziov Bereg

Paide Vägeva Endla looduskaitseala Dobruči

Prandi Torma Mustvee **41** Gdov

Türi **2** E263 Raja Tiheda Pijussa

Jõgeva **Jõgevamaa** Kasepää

E S T O N I A Vanassaare A3 E264 Kallaste Spicino

Kolkja Polna

Võhma Põltsamaa

Lõhavere linnamägi Jilga-Jaani Tabivere **R U S S I A**

Suure-Janni **Alam-Pedja looduskaitseala** **2** Meerapalu Pnevo

Parika looduskaitseala Leie *Emajõgi* **Tartumaa** **Tartu** **2** Emajõgi Luunja Seredka

3 Viljandi Puhja Ülenurme Eesti Põllumajandusmuuseum (Estonian Agricultural Museum)

Kõpu **Viljandimaa** *Võrtsjärv* Nõo A3 Ahja **2** E263 Ahja ürgorg (Kiidjärve Mill) Räpina Pskovskoe ozero

Mustla Rõngu Karilatsi Põlvamaa

Sakala kõrgendik **4** Otepää *Pühajärv* **10** Põlva Võhandu ürgorg Värska

Abja-Paluoja Karksi-Nuia **Otepää kõrgendik** Kanepi

Tündre looduskaitseala Tõrva **Valgamaa** Sangaste **5** **6** A3 Piusa Koobastoku looduskaitseala

Rūjiena Antsla **9** Võru Kütiorg Piusa ürgorg Pečory

Burtnieks Valka **6** Valga **Võrumaa** Rõuge Suur Munamägi 318 Vastseliina **2** E263 Izborsk

Rencēni Vaste-Roosa **8** **Haanja Kõrgendik** (Haanja Highlands) **7** E77

Mõniste vabaõhumuuseum (Open-Air Museum) Mõniste **7** Paganamaa Misso Lavry

skains Ape A2 Kačanovo

Valmiera *Alüksnes ezers* Zaiceva

L A T V I A Lizepasts Rodovoe

264 Smiltene A2 Alüksne Liepna Mirnyj

Mežmuiža

Riga

THE MAKING OF ESTONIA

Estonians' origins were "not of Europe", according to an early traveller. Nobody could have such a thought today of this courageous member of the European Union

In the days when visitors to Estonia often arrived by sea, the first glimpse of Tallinn, the capital, made a lasting impression. Its ancient ruins and quaint houses with steeply peaked roofs, more Mediterranean than Baltic, captivated many visitors. In summer, it might have been the south of France, with early 19th-century Russians making an annual summer pilgrimage from St Petersburg. "I have seen delicate creatures," wrote an English visitor in 1841, "who at first were lifted from the carriage to the bathing-house, restored day by day, and in a fortnight's time bathing with a zest that seemed to renew all their energies."

In the evenings, "a band of military music plays, and restaurants offer ices, chocolate, etc., and you parade about and your friends join you, and you sit down and the gnats sting you; and if you don't like this, you may adjourn to the *salle de danse* close by, where the limbs so late floating listlessly on the waves now twirl round in the hurrying waltz."

Estonia had been a Russian province since 1721, and while the lot of the Estonian peas-

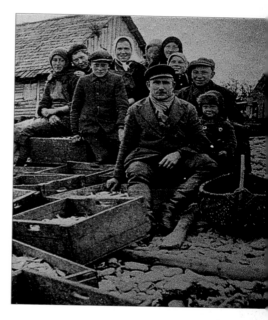

In 1988 nearly a quarter of the population of Estonia gathered in Tallinn in a mass singing demonstration against the USSR, which became known as the "Singing Revolution".

ant had been pathetic for many years (and most ethnic Estonians were peasants), tsarist rule became increasingly repressive. By the late 19th

LEFT: Saaremaa islanders, around 1920.
RIGHT: fishing village in the early 20th century.

century there were no more foreign tourists, Russians excepted, and as far as most foreigners were concerned, Estonia ceased to exist.

A curious race

A declaration of Estonian independence after World War I caught the world by surprise. Russia, torn apart by revolution, was unable to do much to counter the move. Authors of travel guides rushed in to appraise the reincarnated nation. "The broad visage of the Estonian," wrote one, as if reporting on a newly arrived specimen at a zoo, "has slanting eyes, low forehead, high cheekbones and projecting lower jaw." His conclusion was that Estonian origins were "not of Europe". Estonian independence lasted only until World War II. It then disappeared under the even heavier hand of Communist Russia and was presumed lost for all time. Rather suddenly in 1988, extraordinary reports were received in the West of a "Singing Revolution". Tens of thousands apparently spent that summer giving throaty voice to all the old Estonian songs and defiantly waving the long-hidden national flag. Within two years, although not without moments of nail-biting uncertainty, Estonia was independent again.

For all the ravages of a Soviet economic policy that had aimed at turning Estonia into an annexe of heavy industry, much of the character that delighted visitors of 150 years ago had survived. Russians were still visiting the country in droves, but for the "Old European" atmosphere and the food rather than the beaches and swimming, which were prime casualties of environmental vandalism.

As for the newly independent Estonians, they had borne the burden of the previous half-century with fortitude. The "non-European" physical features of the ethnic Estonians are a reflection of Finno-Ugric ancestry. Because of the similarities between the Estonian and Finnish languages, Estonians had been able to follow Finnish television during the Soviet era. Its terms of reference did not flatter the Soviet system.

Mixed nationalities

Estonia's frontiers have been chopped and changed over the centuries. Their present configuration makes Estonia a country of some 44,000 sq km (17,000 sq miles), small enough to be covered by a day's driving in any direction, with a population of less than 1.4 million of whom about 69 percent are ethnic Estonians. The remaining 31 percent are predominantly Russians, most of whose families were sent in to man the industries that represented Estonia's role in the Soviet economic scheme. A few people living in the eastern part of the country are the descendants of 17th-century Old Believers, a sect that fled from Russia to escape, among other things, the tax that Peter the Great imposed on the beards they wore.

An additional group are the diluted remnants of Estonia's most influential settlers, the Germans. The latter came in two guises: the first were 13th-century Teutonic Knights who arrived ostensibly as bearers of Christianity but also as migrants with an urgent need to find somewhere to live, having recently fallen on hard times in the Holy Land; these people were followed by German craftsmen and merchants who formed the burgher class that ultimately monopolised the towns and cities. To an unusual degree, Estonians have taken a back seat while others have written their history. These 13th-century Germans were not the first to arrive, and many others followed after them.

Hardy beginnings

The future Finns and Estonians were among the first tribes to drift across Europe from Asia.

RISE AND FALL OF THE MANOR

The most striking echoes of Estonia's feudal past can be found in the grand manor houses that dot the countryside. Some estates date back to the 13th century, when newly arrived Germanic lords staked out their holdings with wooden structures or fortified strongholds. In the 18th century, the manor house saw its heyday as families with the means built palatial Baroque and neoclassical complexes. Though many have been spectacularly restored, hundreds didn't survive the Soviet era. Regular rows of chestnut or birch trees flank rural roads, indicating the approach to an old manor, but often the house itself is eerily absent. *See page 194.*

Leaving the lower slopes of the Urals, they followed the river courses, subsisting mainly on fish, and clothing themselves in animal skins. They had already reached the Baltic coast when mentioned by Tacitus in the 1st century AD. "Strangely beast-like and squalidly poor, neither arms nor homes have they. Their food is herbs, their clothing skin, their bed the earth. They trust wholly to their arrows, which, for want of iron, are pointed with bone ... Heedless of men, heedless of gods, they have attained that hardest of results, the not needing so much as a wish."

There seems to have been some pushing and shoving among new arrivals on the Baltic shores,

future Danish flag. Their spirits up, they took possession of Tallinn.

Some years earlier, in 1200, around 500 heavily armed German knights had landed further south in the Gulf of Rīga with a commission to spread the word of God. They did so more efficiently than the Danes, who were themselves recent converts.

The rule of the knights

In the end, the Danes asked the Teutonic Knights to lend a hand against the Estonian pagans. The knights tackled the task with customary efficiency and declared, in 1227, that,

especially when large numbers of Slavs turned up, but eventually the future Finns, Estonians, Latvians and Lithuanians took up positions in more or less the same pattern that persists today.

The first conquerors were the Danes under Valdemar II, who arrived with what should have been an invincible armada of 1,000 ships. The Estonians resisted the invasion so fiercely that the Danes were in danger of being routed. They were rescued, so the story goes, by a red banner with a white cross floating down from heaven – the image that was to inspire the

LEFT: 15th-century Danish soldier in Tallinn.
ABOVE: Alexander Nevski defeats German crusaders in the "Battle of the Ice" on Lake Peipsi in 1242.

finally, the job had been accomplished. The knights transformed an economy, which had previously rested on primitive agriculture and products of the forest, into one of the best centres of farming and commerce of the Middle Ages. They constructed castles and founded towns everywhere, filling them with craftsmen and merchants recruited from Germany. Their social system was simple: Germans occupied the positions of noble, burgher and merchant; the Estonians were serfs.

This system survived political and religious change for seven centuries. In the year 1347, the Danish monarchy was desperate for cash. Tallinn, or Reval as it came to be known, was sold off to the efficient and prosperous knights. A large part of the commercial success of Reval and Narva, Estonia's two ports, was due to a virtual monopoly on trade to and from Russia. When Ivan III seized Narva and made it a Russian port it so alarmed the Baltic Germans that they sought the protection of Sweden. Under Gustavus Adolphus, Sweden was energetically bent on expanding its Baltic holdings, but there was no desire to tamper unnecessarily with a German infrastructure that worked so profitably. Later Swedish kings, particularly Charles XI, did interfere by taking over German-owned estates and either giving them to Swedes or, increasingly, keeping them

pieces, losing every piece of artillery Peter possessed. Charles' advisers urged him to press on to Moscow, but the young leader had other ideas. "There is no glory in winning victories over the Muscovites," he said breezily, "they can be beaten at any time."

While Charles went off in pursuit of other enemies, Peter laid the foundations of Petersburg and planned a second attack on Narva. He entrusted the command to a Scot named Ogilvie, who not only succeeded in overwhelming the garrison but decided, apparently independently, to take no prisoners, military or civilian. A terrible massacre was finally stopped by the

for themselves. The dispossessed and disgruntled who had previously turned to Sweden for protection against Russia, decided they now needed protection from Sweden. With perfect impartiality, they turned to Russia. Peter the Great readily agreed to help.

The battle for Narva

The outcome was the titanic struggle between Peter and the equally legendary Charles XII of Sweden. A Russian force 35,000 strong made for Narva, held by a much smaller Swedish garrison in the castle. Charles, who was not yet 20, hurried to its aid. He arrived with 8,000 men and, in the middle of a snow storm, plunged straight into battle. The Russians were cut to

VIEW OF THE ESTONIAN PEASANT

Early travellers were from the upper crust, and could not be expected to have much empathy with the working man. Lady Eastlake reported of the Estonian peasant, "Beyond his strict adherence to his church, we can find but little interesting in his character; nor indeed is it fair to look for any, excepting perhaps that of a servile obedience or cunning evasion, among a people so long oppressed... Provided he can have a pipe in his mouth, and lie sleeping at the bottom of his cart, while his patient wife drives the willing little rough horse... Offer him wages for his labour, and he will tell you, with the dullest bumpkin look, that if he works more he must eat more."

arrival of Peter the Great in the country. He is said to have ended the proceedings by cutting down some of the crazed attackers with his own sword. Moreover, he said, there was a perfectly good use for able-bodied Swedish prisoners: the conditions at the Petersburg building site were so bad that the workforce was dropping like flies.

Era of Russian domination

With Narva under his belt, Peter turned to Reval and its Swedish garrison. The defenders put up a great fight but ultimately they succumbed to thirst and an outbreak of plague.

happy if they could subsist on dusky bread and water".

Nothing much had changed by the middle of the 19th century. Lady Eastlake, who moved in privileged circles during her stay, kept her eyes open and provides a wonderful insight into conditions. The ruling Tsar Nicholas I was so paranoid about revolutionaries – the insurrections of 1848 were just around the corner – that police surveillance everywhere was oppressive. If nothing else, though, it kept crime figures low. Over a whole year, Lady Eastlake reported, there had been only 87 misdemeanours among Reval's 300,000 population,

The Great Northern War between Peter and Charles was far from over, however, and in the course of fighting that swept across Europe the Baltic States were utterly devastated, the horror compounded by plague. With the Peace of Nystad in 1721, Sweden finally ceded its Baltic possessions, and Estonia, for one, prepared for its first taste of Russian rule.

Like the Swedes, Peter was not inclined to upset the way the German hierarchy ran Estonia, and the Estonians continued, according to one commentator, "to live and die like beasts,

"and five of these consist merely in travelling without a passport".

Most illuminating of all, perhaps, are Lady Eastlake's observations about the cloud that hung over young men in the form of military service in the Russian Army. The conscripts were chosen by ballot, No. 1 being the unlucky number. "From the moment that the peasant of the Baltic provinces draws the fatal lot No. 1, he knows that he is a Russian, and, worse than that, a Russian soldier, and not only himself, but every son from that hour born to him; for, like the executioner's office in Germany, a soldier's life is hereditary. . . If wars and climate and sickness and hardship spare him, he returns after four-and-twenty years of service – his

LEFT: *Reval [Tallinn], South Entrance to the Gulf of Finland*, 1856. **ABOVE:** Fat Margaret Tower burns during fighting between nationalists and Bolsheviks in 1917.

language scarce remembered, his religion changed, and with not a rouble in his pocket – to seek his daily bread by his own exertions for the remainder of his life."

Impossible choices

The last years of the 19th century saw the emergence of the Young Estonians, a sign of awakening nationalism. The social order as they saw it was still dominated by the German hierarchy, but being anti-German did not make them pro-Russian. They were simply against the status quo, and for people in that mood Marxism was a very reasonable answer. The savage oppression

exile, members of a provisional Estonian government sent up a cry for independence.

Numerous fierce battles were fought over Tallinn between local Bolsheviks, who were backed by Red Guards, and the nationalist irregulars, who included schoolboys and the Tallinn fire brigade. The tide at first went in

> Our Man in Tallinn: in its original outline, English novelist Graham Greene's famous work of spy fiction, Our Man in Havana, was to have been set in Tallinn in 1938.

of the St Petersburg uprising in 1905 destroyed any sympathy for the tsar. For most Estonians, World War I presented an impossible choice between Germany and Russia when, in truth, they would rather have been fighting against both. Nevertheless, tens of thousands found themselves in tsarist uniform, their plea to form their own units under their own officers falling on deaf ears.

The Russian Revolution in 1917 simplified the choice, the more so when it was announced that an Estonian national army was to be formed. About 170,000 volunteers immediately joined up, while many Estonians preferred to join the supposedly internationalist ranks of the Bolsheviks. From their various places of

favour of the Bolsheviks and by the end of 1918 they held Narva and Tartu, and Russian comrades had advanced to within 32km (20 miles) of Tallinn. The struggle amounted to civil war, and this was fought with all the savagery associated with such a terrible event.

The tide eventually turned, although not without considerable clandestine help given to the nationalists by the British Navy that involved using captured Russian destroyers and a series of raids by torpedo boats that penetrated the naval defences with which Peter the Great had ringed the Russian Baltic ports. The final battle was at Narva, and resulted in the nationalist coalition driving some 18,000 Bolsheviks across the Russian border. One year later, with the Bolsheviks still engaged in heavy fighting elsewhere, Russia renounced sovereignty over Estonia "voluntarily and for ever".

Communists were not inclined to accept the new government. There was an attempted putsch in 1924, which resulted in street fighting in Tallinn. Numerous other disturbances were countered by increasingly authoritarian measures. In the end these amounted to dictatorship and the sad conclusion that the country was not quite ripe for parliamentary democracy.

Farms for all

Prior to the war, more than half of Estonia had belonged to 200 German-Balt families. An Agrarian Reform Law passed after independence took over all baronial and feudal estates, together with those belonging to the Church and the former Russian Crown lands. The land was redistributed and 30,000 new farms created. The lot of the previously hapless peasant was further improved by the establishment of the right to engage in trade.

Estonia was still struggling to find its feet when any gains were put in jeopardy by the secret protocol of the 1939 Nazi–Soviet Pact. Stalin and Hitler agreed that the Soviet Union would annex Estonia, Finland and Latvia, and Germany could claim Lithuania, although this was later amended to give Lithuania to Russia as well. A blatantly rigged election set the stage for an outright annexation on 6 August 1940, and almost immediately 60,000 Estonians went missing. They had been forcibly conscripted into the Soviet Army, deported to labour camps or executed.

The collapse of the Nazi–Soviet Pact naturally changed everything. German forces invaded in July 1941, meeting determined resistance in Estonia, where large numbers of Soviet troops were cut off. Estonia had only about 1,000 Jewish families, nothing like the numbers of Latvia and Lithuania, but even so 90 percent of these were murdered as Germany set about incorporating the country in the Third Reich.

By the end of the war some 70,000 Estonians had fled to the West. The population had dropped from more than 1 million pre-war to no more than 850,000. The educated classes did

not wait to find out what would happen when the German forces in Tallinn surrendered to the Red Army on 22 September 1944.

Russian invasion

Tens of thousands of those who did not flee were consigned to Soviet labour camps. The vacuum was filled by the arrival of comparable numbers of Russians with the dual purpose of manning heavy industry and completing the Russification programme begun by the tsars. There was little Estonians could do except to turn their television aerials towards Finland to see how their Finno-Ugric cousins were getting along.

At home, Soviet policies continued unabated, so that during the 1980s the proportion of Russians and other Soviet implants living in the country rose to 40 percent. With the whole of the country's industry under Moscow's remote control, no thought was given to the ecological impact of belching industrial works.

With their stars firmly attached to Moscow's wagon, Estonia's loyal Communist Party members were totally opposed to any sign of a nationalist revival in Estonia. The long-term implications of *Glasnost* and *Perestroika* were, however, not lost on them, and they took no comfort at all from the 2,000 demonstrators who summoned up enough nerve to mourn the anniversary of the Nazi–Soviet Pact in Tallinn's

LEFT: a 1930s advertisement for pork products.
RIGHT: Soviet tanks thwart a German invasion of Estonia, from *La Domenica del Corriere*, August 1941.

Hirvepark in August 1987. In this respect, the party hardliners and the large Russian minority were as one.

While members of the Estonian Heritage Society went about discreetly restoring national monuments, the radical-chic banner of environmental concern brought the independence movement to life. The first scent of this potential awakening came with the cancellation of plans for increased open-pit phosphorus mining in the northeast of the country. This was followed by demands for economic self-management and then, most extraordinarily, came the "Singing Revolution".

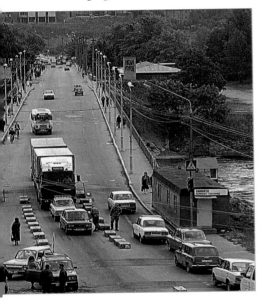

The extent to which the Estonian establishment fell into line with the new mood was revealed when the Estonian Supreme Soviet defied the USSR Supreme Soviet by endorsing the legitimacy of a declaration of sovereignty. In the end it took a military coup attempt in Moscow to push the independence movement to its final conclusion. On 20 August 1991, with Gorbachev under house arrest and Russian tank units rolling into Tallinn, Estonia formally declared its independence. There were tense moments as the world waited to see whether there would be a repetition of the events in Czechoslovakia in 1968. In the event, the dissolution of the Soviet Union happened so rapidly that Estonia moved gratefully to the sidelines.

The Baltic Tiger awakes

Their long-awaited dream of regaining independence now realised, Estonians were faced with the daunting realities of post-Soviet existence: decaying factories, triple-digit inflation and a colossal environmental clean-up bill.

It was the swift and daring economic reforms carried out during these crucial days that laid the foundation for the country's "Baltic Tiger" economic growth in the mid-1990s. Aid and advice poured in from Western governments, while so-called "foreign Estonians" – those whose families had fled the 1944 invasion and settled abroad – flocked in from Sweden, North America and Australia, bringing their expertise and investment dollars. Most notably, in June 1992, the Bank of Estonia ignored IMF warnings and launched the Eesti kroon. It became the first stable currency of the former USSR, thanks in a large part to the country's pre-World War II gold supply, which, as fortune would have it, was still kept by the Bank of England and the US Federal Reserve.

Fuelling the cautious optimism of these heady and hectic times was the prospect of ridding the Estonian territory once and for all of its many remaining Russian military forces, a job that was finally accomplished on 31 August 1994. The joy of bidding farewell to Russia's troops was dampened three weeks later by the *Estonia* ferry disaster, which claimed 852 lives and left a lasting scar on the psyche of the young nation.

Along with fast-paced economic development, and the inevitable parliamentary scandals and corruption charges that came with it, the remainder of the decade was a time of reconnection with the West. On the international political level, an unpredictable and outspoken president, Lennart Meri, who served as head of state from 1992 to 2000, supplied world leaders with enough wry commentary on East–West relations to ensure that Estonia was never far from the minds of the major power players.

It was towards the end of the decade that the "little nation that could" hit the first serious pothole on its road to recovery. An economic slowdown in 1998, brought on by a monetary crisis

LEFT: the Russian border crossing at Narva, 1992.
RIGHT: independence demonstration, Tallinn, 1990.
FAR RIGHT: Estonia is one of the most internet-savvy countries in Europe.

Finnish transmission of TV programmes from the West had a profound effect on Estonians, with Peyton Place a favourite programme of former president Lennart.

in Russia, proved to any remaining doubters that, although Estonia could still fulfil its age-old role as a trade link between Russia and Europe, it was far wiser to keep its gaze firmly fixed westwards. It came as no surprise then when, in the September 2003 referendum, 67 percent of Estonians voted to join the European Union. Indeed,

most hopeful 1990s-era reformers would never have imagined. City skylines became obscured by builders' cranes, streets were suddenly awash with luxury cars, chic cafés opened and closed according to popular whims, and foreign tourists began visiting in droves.

The party was brought to a screeching halt by the worldwide economic crisis in 2008. Barring Latvia, no nation in Europe was harder hit by the downturn. The fragility of the nation's newfound wealth, much of which had been fuelled by cheap loans, became all too clear. Double-digit GDP growth turned into double-digit decline while inflation soared to 20 percent. Even the

when the nation subsequently joined the EU – and NATO – the following year, many saw it as the final step in restoring Estonia's proper place in the family of Western European nations.

True Europeans

Membership of the EU turned out to be a mixed blessing for the small nation. As much-needed investment and development funds poured in, talent poured out, with many young, skilled professionals moving abroad in search of better opportunities. Their absence, though, did nothing to slow the breakneck pace of development that their country was experiencing. Driven mainly by a construction and real-estate boom, the economy rocketed to levels that even the

nation's famed IT sector, which had been making waves with innovations like Skype, couldn't keep the country from slipping into recession.

Some respite was provided by a reserve fund that a frugal government had put away during the fat years, but the first glimmer of recovery came after Estonia, once again defying Western advisers, refused to devalue its currency. Instead it tightened its belt enough to join the Eurozone. On 1 January 2011, the nation said goodbye to its beloved kroon, which had become a symbol of its post-independence success. Estonians traded it in for a currency which they hope will bring them even deeper into the European fold and banish any notion, among investors at least, that they are "not of Europe". ❑

FESTIVALS

Festivals are a way of life, whether music, song, folk or religious. But some are more recent dates on the calendar, such as Tallinn's Rat Race and Kuldīga's midsummer naked run

Music has long played an important part in the Baltic countries, and it was certainly crucial in the "Singing Revolution" that divorced the Baltic States from Moscow. In addition to the giant song festivals that occur every four or five years, music festivals dot the calendar. Jazz, classical and sacred music events ensure all tastes are catered for, and visitors should seek out performances in some of the many well-preserved buildings around the countries. There are large traditional folk gatherings at Võru in Estonia and at the Makslas Festival in Cēsis in Latvia. In summer, the coast sees big beach parties at Pärnu, Estonia, and in Liepāja, Latvia, where the Baltic Beach Party attracts bands from around Europe.

Festivals are not just to hear music. The June Rat Race in Tallinn, for instance, sees office workers in business suits and skirts run round the Old Town with computer keyboards and mobile phones, and Run, Run Horse is a big equestrian get-together in Sartaii, Lithuania. On the coast, there are sea festivals in Salacgrīva and other Latvian villages, and around half a million people visit the Sea Festival in Klaipėda, Lithuania, in July, which is famous for its crafts stalls, music and boating events.

Catholic Lithuania can claim the most important religious festivals, including Užgavėnis (Mardi Gras), when an effigy of winter is burnt, winter and spring join in battle, and people in Vilnius dress as witches and ghouls to see winter driven out.

Pilgrimages take place in the Catholic south of Latvia at Aglona, and at the Madonna of the Gates of Dawn in Vilnius, Lithuania.

ABOVE: at an Estonian festival dancers show off well-stitched finely emroidered skirts, sumptuous socks and elegant shoes.

BELOW: folk dancing in Lithuania's open-air museum at Rumš The three countries' outdoor museums are custodians of tradit ways of life and hold regular events.

LEFT: oak leaves are a sign that the countries are not far from their pagan past. They are worn on the night of St John and line wedding paths.

MIDSUMMER

Midsummer's Eve, 23–24 June, is a magical time in the Baltic countries. Bonfires, lit by a person with any of the variants of the given name John, burn brightly and are leapt over for luck, On Estonia's islands old boats may be sacrificed in the flames. In Lithuania wheels are raised on poles at the centre of the bonfires. There are songs, dancing and games, and plenty to eat and drink, especially beer, as people head for the country in search of their pagan roots. Historically, midsummer marked the break between the sowing and harvesting seasons. Oak and flower wreaths are worn, young women bathe their faces in the morning dew, blossoms are set adrift on lakes and rivers, and couples go in search of glow worms and the illusive fern flower, which blossoms only on Midsummer's Eve – the fact that it does not exist allows couples to linger longer in the woods. In Estonia, Jaanipäev is so light that, with night banished, the two lovers Hämarik (dusk) and Koit (dawn) finally meet for a brief kiss. In Kuldīga, Latvia, a more recent tradition is the naked run over the Venta River bridge at 3am by a few score stalwarts in no more that oak wreaths.

There is a public holiday in all three countries on 24 June, and in 2010 the Estonian government added 23 June as national holiday, to commemorate the day that German troops were driven from Estonian soil in 1919.

: a masker at énės, the carnival, ations in Lithuania, Morė, a huge effigy ter, is paraded h the streets and while Lašininis, a fat winter, is driven out apinis, who ents spring.

massed choirs are a feature of the Baltic countries. Here nds of Latvians have come together to sing a handful of the 's 1.2 million folk songs.

RIGHT: high times at the Sea Festival in Klaipėda, Lithuania's biggest event, with craft stalls, music and marine activity, inluding the international Baltic Sail rally.

TALLINN

Estonia's fairytale port city has an enchanting, historic Old Town with a cosmopolitan outlook and a village feel. Tradition goes hand-in-hand with vibrant galleries and bars

Estonia's capital is an exceptionally harmonious mix of the old and the new. Its historic Old Town, far from being a medieval museum piece, abounds in wireless internet zones and enjoys a cutting-edge club scene, while in the "new" downtown area, ancient wooden churches vie for space with gleaming glass high-rises. Its population is four times that of its next largest rival, Tartu, and though it has a cosmopolitan atmosphere, with only 410,000 inhabitants and a small city centre, Tallinn ❶ often feels like a village.

Stretched along the rim of Tallinn Bay, just across the Gulf of Finland from Helsinki and midway between St Petersburg and Stockholm, the city holds a blessed maritime position that has made it a little bit too interesting over the centuries to other nations. Danes, German knights, Swedes and Russians have each held sway. The resulting layers of cross-cultural history have given the city its unique flavour.

Neighbourhood by neighbourhood, the surroundings change dramatically. Leave the Germanic, gabled houses of the Old Town in one direction and you find yourself among swanky 1930s offices. Chose another road and you'll see narrow, leafy streets that have changed little since they were home to factory workers in the late 19th century.

A couple of tram stops along and you're met with the sort of Baroque grandeur that would fit into any Tolstoy novel. Skirting this mosaic are districts of bland, Soviet-era housing.

In other outlying areas, such as Pirita, one can escape both the city's complicated history and its urban bustle and simply enjoy beaches and forests.

The Old Town

The first place to visit is the **Old Town** (Vanalinn), perched on a low hill by the shore. Set apart from the rest

Main attractions
TOWN HALL SQUARE
ALEXANDER NEVSKY CATHEDRAL
TOOMPEA CASTLE
BASTION TUNNELS
KADRIORG PARK AND PALACE
KUMU ART MUSEUM
PIRITA CONVENT RUINS
SEAPLANE HARBOUR

PRECEDING PAGES AND LEFT: winter and summer views of Tallinn. **RIGHT:** strolling along Vana turg.

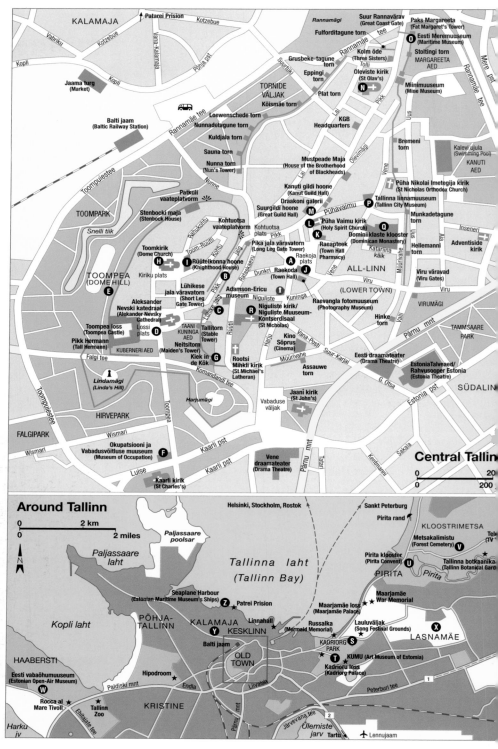

of the city by old fortification walls, this is one of the purest medieval old towns in all northern Europe. Upper Town (Toompea), site of the original Estonian fortification, crowns the hill at 48 metres (157ft) above sea level. **Lower Town** (All-linn) spills out over an inclined horseshoe below. As they developed, each acquired distinct personalities: the ecclesiastical and feudal powers lived above, the merchants and guild members below.

The only practicable way to explore the winding, rough cobbled streets is by foot, so strap on robust walking shoes and head for the spires of the medieval district. There are several ways to arrive at the Old Town. Passing through the picturesque, 16th-century **Viru Gates** (Viru väravad) in the east and heading up the highly commercial Viru Street is the most travelled path into the Old Town. As with routes from most other directions, it quickly leads to **Town Hall Square** Ⓐ (Raekoja plats). A more appropriate place to start your tour, however, is just a bit further up, on **Toompea**, the birthplace of Tallinn.

Upper Town

One of Estonia's most famous legends holds that Toompea hill in the Upper Town is the burial mound of Kalev, the giant who founded Tallinn. When Kalev died, his widow Linda, in her immense grief, carried stone after stone to cover his grave until this massive hill was formed. It's no surprise that this spot is associated with the origin of the town – it was here during pre-Christian times that the first permanent settlement in Tallinn was built. The foreign empires that ruled the northern Estonian lands all used Toompea as their power base, stationing their respective political representatives in Toompea Castle, now home to the nation's government.

Passage to Toompea from the Lower Town is provided by two scenic streets: **Pikk jalg** Ⓑ (Long leg) and **Lühike jalg** Ⓒ (Short leg), whose curious

names have given rise to a tired joke, perpetuated by generations of tour guides, that Tallinn "walks with a limp". The long, sloping Pikk jalg is thought to be the oldest street in Tallinn, dating back to Viking times. It begins under the archway of the four-sided **Long Leg Gate Tower** (Pika jala väravatorn), built in 1380, and continues a straight, steady climb upward to **Castle Square** Ⓓ (Lossi plats). The extravagant mansions high up along the cliff to the right are a good indication of the wealth and power of Toompea's gentry, while the fortified defensive wall to the left is a testament to the political tensions and ill-will between the residents of Toompea and the Hanseatic Lower Town.

Lühike jalg, a narrow, winding lane with a staircase, was historically the main pedestrian passage into Toompea. Today it's flanked on both sides by some of Tallinn's more intriguing art shops. At its top stands the **Short Leg Gate Tower** (Lühikese jala väravatorn), built in 1456. The sturdy wooden door you pass here is original and dates from the 17th century.

TIP

Though local women have become used to it, walking on Tallinn's cobblestoned streets in high heels is a recipe for disaster. Wear sturdy shoes when exploring the Old Town.

BELOW: Alexander Nevsky Cathedral.

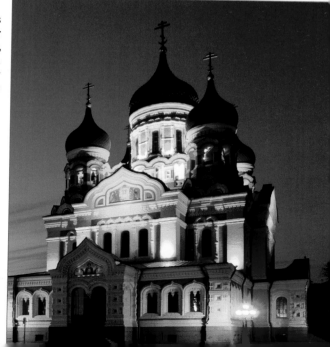

Interior of Alexander Nevsky Cathedral.

Around Castle Square

Reaching Lossi plats at the top of these streets yields the dramatic sight of the grand, onion-domed **Alexander Nevsky Cathedral** (Aleksander Nevski katedraal; daily 8am–7pm). Built from 1894 to 1900, the impressive structure now serves as the most important place of worship for Tallinn's Russian Orthodox faithful, and its interior has been beautifully restored with a massive iconostasis and several icons.

Originally, however, the church had a sinister political function. In the late 19th century, imperial Russia was carrying out an intense campaign of Russification in its outer provinces. As part of its drive to assert cultural dominance over the mainly Lutheran Germans and Estonians, the tsarist government built this towering Orthodox cathedral directly in front of the castle, in the heart of what had been one of the city's best-loved squares. The name of the church is itself very telling – Prince Alexander Nevsky was the Russian military leader whose forces famously defeated the Baltic-based German crusaders in the "Battle on Ice" on Lake Peipsi in 1242, the climax of Sergei Eisenstein's classic 1938 film *Alexander Nevsky*.

During the construction of the cathedral, a rumour circulated that builders working on the foundation had stumbled upon an iron door bearing the inscription, "Cursed be anyone who dares disturb my peace." The story with its obvious political undertones was taken by superstitious locals to be a sign that old Kalev's grave had been discovered, and that he was not at all pleased with the building project. The notion soon gained further support when cracks began to appear around the building's base.

The cathedral somehow managed to escape Kalev's wrath and, more miraculously, even survived the changing political winds of the early 20th century: after Estonia became independent in 1918, there was talk of removing the offensive structure. Reflecting popular sentiment, the writer Tuglas Friedebert declared, "It looks like a samovar and should be blown up." Plans were put on hold because the new state lacked the necessary funds for demolition.

BELOW: Toompea Castle.

ompea Castle

ext to the cathedral stands **Toom-
a Castle** (Toompea loss), historic
at of power in Estonia and home
the *Riigikogu*, Estonia's parliament.
a permanent structure, the castle
tes from 1229 when the Knights of
e Sword built a square fortress sur-
unded by a circular, stone wall. In
e 14th century this was rebuilt into
convent-style fortress with an inner
urtyard, 20-metre (65ft) high walls,
d four corner towers, three of which
e still standing. The Baroque palace
front of you was built from 1767–73
the order of Russian Empress
atherine the Great, and served as the
ministration building for the Rus-
n provincial government in Esto-
a in tsarist times. The three-storey
rliament Building in the courtyard
as built in 1922 on the foundations
the convent.

Around the castle's south side is
e peaceful **Governor's Garden**
uberneri aed). This is the best place
view another Tallinn landmark,
e 45.6-metre (150ft) **Tall Hermann**
ikk Hermann) tower dating from

1371. Tradition dictates that whichever
nation flies its flag on Tall Hermann
rules Estonia.

To see the castle's most medieval-
looking side, you can take a quick
detour down Falgi Street, which passes
south of Pikk Hermann. Only when
you reach the bottom of the hill and
look back do you begin to understand
just how daunting Toompea's defences
were. On the way down, paths on the
left lead to the small Lindamägi (Linda's Hill), topped by a small statue of
the mythical Linda, grieving widow of
Kalev. Tallinn residents adopted it during Soviet times as a kind of unsanc-
tioned memorial to the thousands of
loved ones who were deported to Siberia and never returned. Since there
would be no gravesite for these victims, relatives would lay flowers here,
at considerable risk to themselves if
they were caught.

Peaceful Toompark

The beautiful **Toompark** starts just
to the north of this spot, and circles
around the entire northwest side
of **Toompea** ⓔ. With its forested

BELOW LEFT: the
symbolic Linda
monument.
BELOW: inside the
Bastion Tunnels.

The Danish King's Garden.

BELOW RIGHT:
Lutheran Dome Church.

pathways and moat, this is one of the town's most relaxing places for a summertime stroll, and yields unforgettable views of the town's medieval walls and towers.

Invaders and fortifications

Heading straight back up Falgi Street gives the opportunity for a different kind of detour. A right turn on Toompea Street leads to the awkwardly named **Museum of Occupation and of Fight for Freedom ❻** (Okupatsiooni ja Vabadusvõitluse muuseum) at Toompea 8 (Tue–Sun 11am–6pm; charge), a high-tech and dramatic introduction to the 1940–91 period, when Estonia was occupied first by the Soviet Union, then briefly by Nazi Germany, then for another 45 years by the Soviets.

A return to the hill by the same route brings you firmly back into the medieval era. The sturdy-looking round tower on your right is **Kiek in de Kök ❼** (1475–6). Its name, which in Low German literally means "peek into the kitchen", refers to the tower's 36-metre (118ft) height. Soldiers sta-

tioned here joked that they could ͏ right down the chimneys and into ͏ kitchens of the houses below. Duri the Livonian Wars (1558–83), Ivan t Terrible's forces blew a massive h͏ in its top floor. As a memorial to t battle, six stone cannon balls were into the tower's outer wall and are s͏ visible today. Now the tower op͏ ates as a museum (May–Oct Tue–S 10.30am–6pm, Nov–Apr Tue–S 10.30am–5pm; charge) displayi the development of the town and defences.

The tower also serves as the entrar to one of the city's most popular attr͏ tions, the **Bastion Tunnels** (Bastioni Käigud; book ahead, enquire at Ki in de Kök museum or tel: 6446 68 When the Swedes were fortifying t͏ side of Toompea with earthwor and high walls in the late 1600s, th͏ included a string of hidden tunnels order to move men and ammuniti͏ where they were needed. The tunn͏ never saw use in the 17th century, b͏ found new life as World War II bon shelters, and then as Soviet bunke Now refurbished, they are open to t͏

Staggering Brits

The first budget airline into the Baltics from the UK was Ryanair, and Rīga was its chosen destination, not just because it was the centre of the three states but, said CEO Michael O'Leary, because the Latvian government had been so willing to cooperate. Estonia had not been in a rush to see planeloads of Britons arriving, and some actively opposed it, seeing the effect that budget airlines' "low expectation" travel had on destinations such as Amsterdam and Prague. Besides, it already had its share of booze-tripping Finns, who in summer arrive on more than 40 ferries a day. But Tallinn could not hold out against the additional income budget airlines would bring, and by late 2004 some 25,000 passengers a month were pouring into the new capital of stag weekends. More recently the number of Brits seen staggering along the cobblestoned streets has dropped, but the phenomenon is still noticeable in summer.

On offer in a city more suited to a honeymoon romance than blurry booze-ups are go-karting, paintballing, boar-hunting and Kalashnikov shooting by day, and strip shows and alcohol by night. Tallinn is not a large town, and some bars are easily taken over by boisterous groups, but they are not difficult to avoid. Some hotels actively discriminate against stag tours, but while bad behaviour is controlled, it is not going away. Britons have become Tallinn's new Finns.

blic. Though adults may find the
ain to "future Tallinn" silly, the exhib-
s here provide a good historical over-
ew of the city and the tunnels.

anish King's Garden

nother historic battleground is just
eps away, along the wall that leads
ack towards Lossi plats. Crossing
rough a rectangular passage in the
all brings you to the **Danish King's
arden** (Taani kuninga aed), where,
cording to legend, King Waldemar
camped when his forces were first
ying to conquer Toompea in 1219.
 was here that a red flag with a
hite cross, which became the Danes'
ational symbol, supposedly floated
ownward from the heavens, spurring
em on to victory. In reality, the bat-
e was decided by a group of Slavic
ercenaries who began attacking the
tonians from the opposite slope.
The two towers here, the small,
und **Stable Tower** (Tallitorn) and
e larger, square **Maiden's Tower**
leitsitorn), both date from the 14th
ntury. The name "Maiden's Tower"
ironic – the tower was a prison for
ostitutes. For years it operated as a
fé, and employees claimed to have
ard ghostly noises.

ome Church

th Toom-Kooli Street and Piiskopi
reet lead from Lossi plats to Kiriku
ats (Church Square) and the majestic
ome Church ❽ (Toomkirik; Tue–
n 9am–6pm), the prime Lutheran
urch of Estonia, established just
ter the Danes arrived in Toompea in
19. When you step into the church,
u will probably find yourself stand-
g on the burial slab of Otto Johann
uve, also known as "Tallinn's Don
an". The hopeless playboy asked to
 buried in this spot so that people
tering the church would step on
m, and by doing so wash away his
ns. The church's Baroque interior
 dominated by a huge collection
 coats of arms. These tradition-
ly accompanied the casket during

funeral processions, and were later
kept in the church as a memorial.
Along the northern wall, opposite the
entrance, are the lavish tombs of some
eminent historic personages, including Pontus de la Gardie, French-born
head of Swedish forces during the
Livonian Wars; A.J. von Krusenstern,
a Baltic German explorer who in 1886
became the first mariner to circum-
navigate the globe under the Russian
flag; and Admiral Sir Samuel Greig of
Fife (1735–88), commander of
Russia's Baltic Fleet and reputed
lover of Catherine the Great.

Just outside the church is the green,
two-storeyed, neo-Renaissance **Knighthood House ❶** (Rüütelkonna hoone),
a grand structure with a distinguished
history. Built in the late 1840s, it originally served as a meeting hall for the
Knighthood, a guild-like organisation
that united Toompea's noble families.
It now hosts cultural events.

Kohtu Street to the right of Knighthood House leads down past some
impressive houses once owned by
Toompea's noble elite. The street soon
ends at the **Kohtu Street viewing**

TIP

Street finder: *tänav*
means street, *väljak/
plats* is square, *puiestee*
is avenue, *mantee
(mnt)* is road.

BELOW: Patkuli
viewing platform.

platform (Kohtuotsa vaateplatvorm), from where there is a spectacular view of the red-tiled roofs of the medieval Lower Town, as well as the modern city and port beyond the town walls. The nearby **Patkuli viewing platform** (Patkuli vaateplatvorm) can be reached by turning right on Toom-Rüutli, then left at the end of that street onto a nearly hidden passage. This platform looks over the northern section of the Lower Town and gives an excellent view of St Olav's Church *(see page 123)*, the town wall and several of its towers. From the Patkuli viewing platform you can head straight down Rahukohtu Street to continue touring Toompea, or make your way down the Patkuli Steps and into the Lower Town.

The Lower Town

In medieval times, the area now called the Lower Town (All-linn) was the Hanseatic city of Tallinn (or Reval, as it was then known), a busy trading city of international stature. In 1248 it was granted autonomous status and from then on had its own government, local laws, social institutions and defence forces. More importantly, it was t[h]e domain of merchants and artisa[ns,] labourers and servants, all of who[m] would have contributed to the gene[ral] bustle of commerce as they went abo[ut] their daily routines.

For at least seven centuries, the soci[al] and cultural heart of Tallinn has be[en] **Town Hall Square** (Raekoja plats), t[he] attractive open area at the centre of t[he] Old Town. Even now the square acts [as] the chief gathering place for the [city's] residents. In spring and summer i[t is] invariably covered in café tables, a[nd] in winter there is a Christmas Mark[et].

Presiding over the square is t[he] **Town Hall ❶** (Raekoda; July–A[ug] Mon–Sat 10am–4pm; charge). Histor[ic] records indicate that another town h[all] occupied this spot as early as 132[-] but the present late-Gothic structu[re] was completed in 1404. **Old Thom[as]** (Vana Toomas), the soldier-shape[d] weather vane on the spire, has be[en] watching over the city since 1530 a[nd] has become a symbol of the town. T[he] Baroque spire and the fanciful, drago[n-] shaped drainpipes are from 1627. Vi[si-] tors in July and August should not p[ass]

an opportunity to see the interior, with its vaulted ceilings and wood-carved benches. Summer visitors can also climb the 64-metre (210ft) **Town Hall Tower** (Raekoja torn; May–Aug daily 11am–6pm; charge) for spectacular views of the Old Town.

Across the square from the Town Hall stands the **Town Hall Pharmacy** (Raeapteek), one of the oldest continuously running pharmacies in Europe. Records first mention it in 1422, but it may have been established decades earlier. From 1580 to 1911 it was managed by 10 generations of the same family. Some of the useful preparations sold here in centuries past included minced bat, burnt bees, snakeskin and powdered unicorn horn. These days the same cures are sold here as in any modern pharmacy, but there is a small exhibition room (Tue–Sat 10am–6pm; free) displaying archaic equipment and medicines.

Holy Spirit Church

Just a few paces from the square through the Saiakang (white bread) passage stands the **Holy Spirit Church** (Püha Vaimu kirik; May–Sept Mon–Sat 10am–4pm, Oct–Apr Mon–Fri 10am–2pm; charge). In the 13th century it operated an almshouse tending to the city's sick, elderly and poor. Unlike other churches, the Holy Spirit Church's congregation was made up of Tallinn's lower class and included ethnic Estonians. It was here that the first sermons in the Estonian language were given after the Reformation, and in 1535 the church's pastor, Johann Koell, translated and published what's thought to be the first book in Estonian. The building was completed in the 1360s, but its spire has been replaced numerous times following devastating fires, the last one in 2002.

The most eye-catching addition to the church is the large blue-and-gold clock near the main doorway. Created by well-known Tallinn woodcarver Christian Ackermann in the late 17th-century, it is Tallinn's oldest – and by far most captivating – public timepiece. The church's interior is every bit as awe-inspiring, particularly the altar, commissioned from renowned Lübeck sculptor and painter Bernt Notke in

Tallinn's oldest clock, on the Holy Spirit Church.

BELOW: Inside the Town Hall.

Creepy Tales

The tradition of sharing ghost stories in Tallinn goes back centuries and, if local legends are to be believed, just about every building in the Old Town has a resident spook. Even former prime minister Mart Laar can sometimes be seen giving VIP visitors ghost tours of this part of the city.

Of all the city's legends, the best known is that of "The Devil's Wedding" that supposedly took place at Rataskaevu 16. In the tale, a landlord, in desperate need of cash, unwittingly takes up the Devil's offer to rent out a room for his wedding party.

Later, stories arose about mysterious party noises from the flat. Adding to the intrigue today is a false window at the top of the house, which is in fact painted on the facade.

1483. Figures of the Virgin Mary with Child, Apostles and saints, all painted in bright, clear blue, red and gold, stand at the centre of the cupboard-type altarpiece.

Pikk Street curiosities

Holy Spirit Church is on the corner of Pikk (Long) Street, which leads to the northern edge of the Old Town. This once-busy artery connected the port to the town's marketplace. The grand-looking building at Pikk 17, opposite the Holy Spirit Church, is the **Great Guild Hall** (Suurgildi hoone), which served as a meeting place for Tallinn's Great Guild, a wealthy association of merchants that wielded considerable influence over town affairs. The hall is now used by a branch of the **Estonian History Museum** (Eesti Ajaloomuuseum; May–Aug daily 11am–6pm, Sept–Apr Thur–Tue 11am–6pm; charge), which chronicles the nation's developments up to the 18th century.

Architectural oddities along Pikk Street include the eccentric, Art Nouveau facade of the **Dragon Gallery** (Draakoni galerii) at No. 18, with seahorse-tailed serpents and Egyptian slaves. Next to it is the Tudor-style **Kanut Guild Hall** (Kanuti gildi hoone), with statues representing St Canute (Canute IV of Denmark martyred in 1086) and the founder of Protestantism, Martin Luther. High up, across the street from the Kanut Guild Hall, a man wearing a monocle gazes down. Popular legend says that a jealous wife installed it to break her husband's habit of spying on young women as they practised ballet in the upper floors of the Guild Hall.

At Pikk 26 is the eye-catching **House of the Brotherhood of Blackheads** (Mustpeade maja; daily 10am–7pm; free). The exquisite Renaissance facade is from 1597, and its beautiful carved wooden door, one of the most recognised architectural elements in Tallinn, was installed in 1640.

A careful observer will notice something eerie about the building at Pikk 59. Its cellar windows are completely bricked over – this was the **KGB Headquarters** during the Soviet period. The placard on the front of the building reads: "This building housed the headquarters of the organ of repression of the Soviet occupational power. Here began the road to suffering for thousands of Estonians."

St Olav's Church

Just a few paces further along is Tallinn's largest medieval structure, the enormous **St Olav's Church** (Oleviste kirik). The church was first mentioned in historic records in 1267 and originally served a Scandinavian merchants' camp that occupied the end of Pikk Street. An absurdly tall 159-metre (522ft) Gothic-style pavilion steeple was built on the top of the tower in 1500, making St Olav's the tallest building in the world at the time. Numerous bolts of lightning hit the steeple through the centuries, and twice, once in 1625 and again in 1820, the church was burnt to the ground. The steeple you now see was installed

ter the first fire, and is 124 metres 07ft) tall, 25 metres (82ft) shorter an the original. In spring and sumer, able-bodied visitors can make the gorous climb to the top of the tower Apr–Oct daily 10am–6pm; charge) for ectacular views.

Humbler in size than the church it just as awe-inspiring are **The hree Sisters** (Kolm õde) at Pikk 71. his magnificently restored ensemble three brightly painted 15th-cenry terrace houses are a favourite for notographers and now serve as the emises for a luxury hotel. Their less ectacular counterparts, **The Three rothers**, are located around the cor-er on Lai Street.

Museum in the tower

kk Street ends at the **Great Coast ate** (Suur Rannavärav) and its famous th-century **Fat Margaret's Tower** aks Margareeta). With a diameter 25 metres (82ft) and walls up to 5 etres (17ft) thick, the cannon tower as a formidable part of the town's fences. It's now occupied by the tonian Maritime Museum **O** (Eesti

meremuuseum; Wed–Sun 10am–6pm; charge). Four floors present an extensive look at the nation's seafaring history from Neolithic times to the present. Heading back to the square via nearby Vene Street brings you past a well-restored medieval house at No. 17, which contains the **Tallinn City Museum O** (Tallinna linnamuuseum; Mar–Oct Wed–Mon 10.30am–6pm, Nov–Feb Wed–Mon 10.30am–5pm; charge). This is by far the city's most modern and engaging history museum, chronicling Tallinn's development from its founding until today.

Latin Quarter

Further up Vene Street is the area that came to be called the "Latin Quarter". In medieval times it was the domain of the powerful **Dominican Monastery O** (Dominiiklaste klooster; 15 May–30 Sept daily 9.30am–6pm, museum at Müürivahe 33 open 15 May –30 Sept daily 10am–5pm; charge). Known as **St Catherine's Monastery**, it was founded here in 1246 by the Dominican Order, and played a key role in the town's religious affairs. The

The memorial to the victims of the Estonia ferry disaster, located outside the Old Town close to the Great Coast Gate.

BELOW: The Three Sisters.

Brightly painted doorway on one of the Old Town's numerous medieval buildings.

BELOW: St Catherine's Passage.

Reformation movement in 1525 closed it down, and in 1531 the abandoned complex was ravaged by fire. Though not all of the building remains, the monastery's beautiful courtyard and ancient corridors still give an impression of monastic life in medieval times. The corridors display a collection of medieval stonemasonry salvaged from elsewhere in the Old Town.

A separate museum, round the corner at Müürivahe 33, gives access to the monastery's inner chambers, which exhibit additional stone carvings, as well as archaeological finds from the monastery grounds.

Just south of the monastery, the narrow **St Catherine's Passage** (Katariina käik) that connects Vene and Müürivahe streets is absolutely not to be missed. One side of the picturesque passage displays some intriguing – if somewhat eerie – stone burial slabs that were removed from the former St Catherine's Church, directly behind them, during renovation. The lane leads to Tallinn's famous **Knit Market**, a section of the town wall where elderly ladies sell traditional woollen

creations. From here, the **Viru Gates** are just a few steps away.

Needle-Eye Gate memorial

A walk down Harju Street, a few metres from Town Hall Square, reveals a very different aspect of the city's history: the devastation of World War II. About halfway down the street a terraced park sits in a strangely empty block. This is where several buildings, including a hotel and a cinema, once stood. On 9 March 1944, with Nazi Germany still occupying Estonia, the Soviet Air Force bombed Tallinn, destroying entire neighbourhoods and leaving 20,000 homeless.

In 2008, when the block was being landscaped, planners restored one of the narrow lanes that ran between the houses on the west side of Harju. **Needle-Eye Gate**, as it was called, had remained buried since the war and now serves as a memorial to the bombing. Glass panels allow visitors to peer into the cellars adjacent to the street, while a video display shows documentary footage of the area's history.

The **Church of St Nicholas** ⓡ (Nigu

liste kirik) that lords over Harju Street was also destroyed in the 1944 raid, but it was reconstructed from 1956 to 1984. Dedicated to the patron saint of merchants and artisans, it was founded by a group of German settlers who had set up a trading yard here in the early 13th century. This was the only church in the Lower Town that wasn't ransacked during the Reformation fervour of 1524, thanks to its head of congregation who kept the mobs out by pouring molten lead into the door locks.

The church now serves a purely secular function, operating as the **Niguliste Museum and Concert Hall** (Wed–Sun 10am–5pm; charge), which showcases religious art from Estonia and abroad. It has the distinction of housing Estonia's most famous work of art, 15th-century artist Bernt Notke's mural *Dance of Death* (see page 4), a macabre masterpiece depicting people from various walks of life dancing with skeletons. Other treasures in the museum include awe-inspiring altars from the 16th and 17th centuries, a collection of Renaissance and Baroque chandeliers, and several curious 14th–17th-century tombstones.

Harju Street ends at **Freedom Square** (Vabaduse väljak). After serving for decades as a parking lot (much to the dismay of patriotic Estonians), the square was refurbished in 2009 and now serves as a prime public space. At its head stands the Freedom Monument, which commemorates Estonia's 1918–20 War of Independence and continues to raise controversy due to its high cost and construction flaws.

Around Tallinn Bay

The Old Town is the tourists' favourite part of Tallinn, but at weekends the locals wander in the parks on the east side of Tallinn Bay. The best-loved of these is **Kadriorg ⑤**, a name synonymous with affluence, nature and, most of all, tranquillity. Kadriorg Park was laid out between 1718 and 1725 by the Italian architect Niccolò Michetti under the orders of Peter the Great, who named it in honour of his wife, Catherine. Most of it remains a wooded, informal park, planted with lime, oak, ash, birch and chestnut trees and punctuated by open fields. Among

SHOP

St Catherine's Passage (Katariina käik), a narrow lane lined with craft studios, is worth a visit for shoppers and browsers. Enter through the archway just past Vene 12.

BELOW: Tallinn harbour.

Kadriorg Palace's impressive main hall.

the more developed exceptions are the large rectangular Swan Pond with fountains and a beautiful white gazebo which provide a fittingly romantic introduction to the park.

The jewel in the Kadriorg's crown is without a doubt the lavish, Baroque **Kadriorg Palace ❶** (Kadrioru loss) that Peter had built in 1718. The palace is a stunning monument to imperial extravagance. In particular, its two-storey main hall, decorated in rich stucco work and grandiose ceiling paintings, is considered one of the best examples of Baroque design in all of northern Europe. Equally impressive is the manicured, 18th-century-style flower garden, with erupting fountains.

As the building is itself a masterpiece, it's appropriate that it houses one of the nation's top art museums. The **Kadriorg Art Museum** (May–Sept Tue–Sun 10am–5pm; Oct–Apr Wed–Sun 10am–5pm, charge) is the main home for the Art Museum of Estonia's foreign collection. While here, those interested in art should also visit the **Mikkel Museum** (Wed–

Sun 11am–5pm; charge), just acro the street in what used to be the p ace's kitchen house. Exquisite wor include Flemish and Dutch paintin Italian engravings, Chinese porcela and etchings by Rembrandt.

A quick walk up the hill from t museums will take you to the **Pre dential Residence** (1938) with c emonial guards, and then to a sm cottage, now a museum, where Pe stayed during visits while the pala was under construction.

Kumu Art Museum

The road ends at Estonia's largest a most complete art museum, the **Kun** (May–Sept Tue–Sun 11am–6pm, Oc Apr Wed–Sun 11am–6pm; charg Opened in 2006, this sprawlin modern complex serves as the ma building of the Art Museum of Est nia. Works produced by the natior artistic heroes of the 19th and 20 centuries make up the permanent c lection, while temporary exhibitio focus primarily on contemporary a The facility itself, designed by Finni architect Pekka Vapaavuori, is a fas

BELOW: Kadriorg Palace and Art Museum.

nating, multi-functional maze of copper, limestone and glass that certainly deserves exploration.

Along the coastal path

The path from Kadriorg Palace to the sea leads to the angel-like *Russalka memorial*, built to commemorate 177 men lost when the Russian warship *Russalka* (Mermaid) sank en route from Tallinn to Helsinki in 1893. The dramatic monument is now a popular spot for Russian wedding couples to honour the tradition of laying flowers. The wreck, incidentally, was discovered by Estonian researchers in 2003.

Opposite the monument, slightly further along the coast is the entrance to the **Song Festival Grounds** (Lauluväljak), scene of Estonia's "Singing Revolution". The Song Festival Arena, with a distinctive, curving roof, was built in 1960 and is Tallinn's largest outdoor stage.

Further north along the coast is the **Maarjamäe Palace** (Maarjamäe loss), a grand, pseudo-Gothic manor built by Count Orlov-Davidov in 1874. First used as a summer home, the "palace"

changed hands several times, serving as a Dutch consul's residence, a prestigious hotel, an aviation school and a Soviet army barracks. It now houses the branch of the **Estonian History Museum** (Eesti Ajaloomuuseum; Wed–Sun 10am–5pm; charge) that chronicles developments in the 19th and 20th centuries.

Just beyond is the site of the sprawling **Maarjamäe War Memorial**, an overbearing, cement-filled park that could have only been born of the Soviet 1960s and 70s.

Pirita district

Pirita Tee, a pleasant place to stroll beside the sea, leads on to the Pirita district, home to the city's most popular beach. It is also the site of the Olympic Yachting Centre, which was built for the sailing events of the 1980 Olympic Games in Moscow and is still used by locals. **Pirita Convent** ⓤ (Pirita klooster; June–Aug daily 9am–7pm, Apr–May & Sept–Oct daily 10am–6pm, Nov–Mar daily noon–4pm; charge) lies over the River Pirita and across the road. It was built in 1407–36

In summer you can take a boat Pirita harbour to the nearest islands of Aegna (40 min) and Naissaar (1hr) where there's a nature reserve and small railway.

BELOW: Kumu, the Art Museum of Estonia.

KIDS

Check out events at the Estonian Open-Air Museum, such as egg-painting at Easter, spring farm days in May, bonfires, swing songs and dancing on St John's Eve in June, an autumn fair in September and old-time festivities in the Christmas Village in mid-December (www. evm.ee/keel/eng/).

for the Swedish-based St Bridget's order of nuns and in its time was one of the two largest buildings in Tallinn (the Dominican Monastery was the other). The convent was destroyed in 1577 during the Livonian Wars but the 35-metre (115ft) high western facade with an arched portal of flagstones is still quite beautiful, and the shell of the rest of the main church is intact. Peasants continued to live on the site for a considerable time after its destruction, and their gravestones are visible in its front yard.

The Balts are fond of their cemeteries, and some say that the **Forest Cemetery** **V** (Metsakalmistu) at Kloostrimetsa, down the road from Pirita, is the most beautiful place in all of Tallinn. It looks almost like a national park, with graves running up and down small hills under a deep forest of fir trees. In 1933, the writer Eduard Vilde was the first to be buried here, and most of Estonia's stars have since followed suit, including the singer Georg Ots (1920–75), the poet Lydia Koidula (1843–86), Konstantin Päts, Estonia's first president (1874–1956),

and Lennart Meri, president of Estonia from 1992 to 2001.

Just to the east the space-age **Teletorn** (TV Tower; charge) dominates the skyline; 314 metres (1,030ft) in height, it offers unforgettable views of the city and surrounding ports from its observation deck and restaurant at the 170-metre (558ft) level. A few metres from the tower's base is the **Tallinn Botanical Garden** (Tallinna botaanikaaed; May–Aug daily 11am–6pm Sept–Apr daily 11am–4pm; charge) covering 123 hectares (304 acres) of the Pirita Valley with its beautiful gardens and nature trails.

On the western side of Tallinn and within easy reach of the city is the **Estonian Open-Air Museum** **W** (Vabaõhumuuseum; late Apr–Sep daily 10am–8pm, Oct–early Apr daily 10am–5pm; charge). Situated at Rocca al Mare on the Kakumäe Peninsula overlooking the sea near some of the most exclusive property in town, the museum contains more than 72 buildings, brought here from all over the country, showing how life has typically been lived in rural Estonia.

Suburban reality

To understand Tallinn fully, you must venture off into one of the residential neighbourhoods. Not far from the Forest Cemetery is **Lasnamäe** **X** an enormous concrete sea of nearly identical buildings with virtually no landscaping, which was the source of great controversy during the Soviet years. Begun in the late 1970s, it was nicknamed the "suburb of Leningrad" because the housing authorities repeatedly installed new immigrants from Russia, no matter how long locals had been on the waiting list. It is now more than 70 percent Russian.

Artistic Kalamaja

A very different sort of residential area lies just beyond the walls of the Old Town, in the direction of the train station. This is the **Kalamaja** **Y** district a neighbourhood that has only recently

BELOW: tradition survives in Vabaõhumuuseum, the open-air museum.

become appreciated for its architectural value and bohemian charm.

Developed in the late 19th and early 20th centuries when a new rail connection from St Petersburg sparked an industrial boom, Kalamaja became the home of thousands of newly arrived factory workers from the countryside. A hotchpotch of wooden apartment houses sprouted up along the streets. Fire and rot meant that many of these homes didn't survive the Soviet era or turbulent 1990s, but the better houses were bought up and refurbished.

Now Kalamaja has become the address of choice for artists and other young professionals, while edgy galleries are increasingly moving in. The attraction is easy to see: the stylish, colourfully painted houses lend the area a rustic charm that's impossible to find in most other areas of the city.

Market and museum ships

There are other draws for visitors as well, starting with the busy **Jaama Turg** market at the back of the train station. Selling everything from apples to tombstones, it provides a glimpse of Estonian reality that's absent from most tourist brochures.

A long stroll down Vana-Kalamaja will bring you past the area's picturesque streets to the gates of **Patarei Prison** (June–Aug Wed–Sun noon–5.15pm; charge). Originally a fortress built in 1840, it was used to house inmates throughout the Soviet period. Because Patarei has been left almost untouched since the last inmate departed in 2004, visitors are able to get an accurate impression of Soviet prison life in all its grimness as they wander its dank halls.

Just along the coast from here is Tallinn's old **Seaplane Harbour**, which is home to the Estonian Maritime Museum's **Museum Ships** ❷ (Wed–Sun 10am – 6pm; charge). In addition to a minesweeper and a patrol boat, the collection includes Europe's largest steam-powered ice-breaker, dating from 1914, and the *Lembit* submarine, built in Britain in 1938. From its decks you can peer across at the Old Town's skyline and imagine what a tempting prize Tallinn would have been to any seafaring invaders. ❑

An ornate wooden house in the Kalamaja district.

BELOW LEFT: a typical Kalamaja doorway.
BELOW: Patarei Prison.

TARTU AND THE SOUTH

The brains of the country are nurtured in Tartu, the university town in the "real" Estonia of the south, where there are lakes, historic sights and the country's "winter capital", Otepää

People often call southern Estonia the "real" Estonia. This is where ties to the land go back countless generations, the dialect is deep Finno-Ugric, and the locals have kept up a tradition of hospitality and generosity. The region is split roughly between the undulating Sakala, Otepää and Haanja highlands. Each has its own "metropolitan" focus – Viljandi, Otepää and Võru – but these cities have a rural feel. For the most part, industrial activity is secondary or subordinate to agriculture.

Tartu, city of learning

The largest city in the southern half of Estonia, with around 103,000 residents, is **Tartu ❷**, 187km (116 miles) southeast of Tallinn. Just as many say the south is the real Estonia, many call Tartu its real capital. At the very least, Tartu is the intellectual capital. Roughly a quarter of its population is made up of students, attending one of the city's 6 institutions of higher learning. Chief among these is Tartu University, founded in 1632, which was a powerhouse for Estonian (as well as Latvian) intellectuals during their National Awakening. It has endured as the main seat of higher education in the humanities and currently has around 18,000 students.

Tartu was first recorded in 1030 as a stronghold built by Grand Duke Yaro-

slav of Kiev. The city has been razed on several occasions since – by Estonians in 1061, Germans in 1224, the Great Northern War in 1708 and by fire in 1775 – and most buildings in the Old Town date from the 18th century.

The city has developed in a north–south fashion along the River Emajõgi, with most of the main university buildings sprinkled on the northern end where the Old Town lies. This district is immediately distinguishable by the wide, cobbled Raekoja plats (Town Hall Square), anchored by a pinkish

Main attractions
TARTU
VILJANDI
OTEPÄÄ HIGHLANDS
PÜHAJÄRV OAK
MÕNISTE OPEN-AIR MUSEUM
HAANJA HIGHLANDS
VÕRU

LEFT: Tartu Town Hall. **RIGHT:** statue of the kissing students.

TIP

St Anthony's Guild, on Lutsu 3 near St John's Church, is a collection of craft studios where visitors can watch artists at work. Concerts are held in its courtyard in summer.

neoclassical **Town Hall**  (Raekoda) at its head, from 1798. The grey clock tower rising from the middle of its roof was added in the 19th century to help the students be on time for classes.

In front of the Town Hall stands a fountain with a kissing couple under an umbrella. The statue, a symbol of Tartu's student population, was designed by the Estonian artist Mati Karmin in 1999 and quickly became a meeting point.

Along the northern side of the square is an unbroken row of pastel-coloured buildings greatly responsible for Tartu's reputation as the neoclassical prima donna of Estonia. The most noticeable is the **"Leaning House"** (1793) at No. 18. Erected on the old city wall and partly on marshland that later dried up, it leans markedly to the left. Inside is the **Kivisilla Art Gallery** (Kivisilla pildigalerii; Wed–Sat noon–6pm, Sun 11am–6pm; charge), with a collection that centres on the Pallas Higher Art School that ran in Tartu from 1919 to 1940.

At the foot of the square is the **Arched Bridge** (Kaarsild), which replaced the 18th-century Stone Bridge destroyed in 1944. Taking a daring walk over the bridge's top rail has become a time-honoured student tradition.

Tartu Ülikooli peahoone, the university's main building, lies just a couple of blocks north from the Town Hall, at 18 Ulikooli Street, a stately oasis in the cramped and crumbling side streets of the Old Town. Pale yellow with six white columns, the University Building is the most impressive neoclassical structure in Estonia. Completed in 1809, it was designed by the architect Johann Krause. Visiting its **Art Museum** (Kunstimuuseum; Mon–Fri 11am–5pm; charge) will allow you to take a peek at its impressive concert hall, classical statuary replicas, and a lock-up, where students were incarcerated for such infractions of conduct as duelling or insulting cloakroom attendants.

Further north on Jaani Street is the 14th-century brick Gothic **St John's Church** (Janni kirik). The renovation of the interior, which lasted for decades, was completed in 2005. On the exterior you can admire hundreds of tiny terracotta sculptures. The 15 faces above its pointed portal represent the Last Judgement.

BELOW: the Leaning House.

Central Tartu

0 — 200 m
0 — 200 yds

SUPPILINN

TARTU ULIKOOLI BOTAANIKAAED (BOTANIC GARDENS)

Tartu I innamuuseum (Tartu City Museum)

TÄHTVERE

Janni kirik (St John's)

Hill of Kissing

Tartu Ülikooli ajaloo muuseum (Tartu University History Museum)

Tartu Ülikooli peahoone

Kunstimuuseum (Art Museum)

Kivisilla Pildigalerii (Kivisilla Art Gallery)

Kaarsild (Arched Bridge)

Toomkirik (Cathedral)

TOOMEMÄGI (TOOME HILL)

Raekoda (Town Hall)

Inglisild (Angel's Bridge)

Kuradisild (Devil's Bridge)

Tähetorn (Observatory)

Turuhoone (Market Hall)

Vallikraavi

ENM (Estonian National Museum)

Teater Vanemuine

KGB kongide muuseum (KGB Cells Museum)

University Library

Pauluse kirik (St Paul's)

KARLOVA

South of Town Hall Square

The neoclassical rule is further broken on the south side of Town Hall Square. First along Vabaduse Street is the grim, brown **Market Hall** (1937). The bus station stands on the next block, and then the **Outdoor Market**, which is devoted half to foodstuffs and half to dry goods. The riverbank is dominated by modern glass high-rises. A short walk down the road is the **Aura Keskus**, a recreation centre with indoor swimming pools and water slides. Across the road on Riia Street is another set of modern buildings, comprising the Tartu Department Store and the Hansakeskus (Hansa Centre) with the Pallas Hotel on its fourth floor.

A short walk uphill from here, at Riia 15b, brings you to the **KGB Cells Museum ❸** (KGB kongide muuseum; Tue–Sat 11am–4pm; charge). Built into what was the local NKVD/KGB in the 1940s and 50s, the museum covers themes of repression and the Estonian resistance movement.

The **Vanemuine Theatre** (1977), at Vanemuise 6, and adjacent **University Library** (1980), at W. Struve Street 1, are later touches. Both are white and functional, but the library is distinguished by the students perpetually gathered on its wide fountain-clad plaza for a quick smoke. Three streets to the northwest is the **Estonian National Museum** (ENM; Kuperjanovi 9; Tue–Sun 11am–6pm) with the country's most important permanent folklore collection.

Toome Hill and Park

It is a short, pleasant walk from here to **Toome Hill** (Toomemägi), the hilly park that dominates the Old Town. In the southern side of the park stands the early 19th-century **Observatory ❸** (Tähetorn), which once had the world's largest refracting telescope. From the west entrance on Vällikraavi Street, turn up under the grey Kuradisild (1913) or **Devil's Bridge**. This is named after a Professor Mannteuffel from Germany who, in the late 19th century, introduced Estonia to the use of rubber gloves in surgical operations, but whose name resembles the German "man-devil". You will find yourself between the University Internal Hospital (1808) and the University

Town Hall detail.

BELOW: statuary in Tartu's Art Museum.

The Name Game

Tartu residents possess a wry sense of wit that comes out in their penchant for nicknaming local buildings, particularly the newer, somewhat incongruous structures that have cropped up here since 2000.

The modern, glass Emajõgi Business Centre that stands adjacent to the market is locally known as "the flask" for its flat shape, and for similar reasons, the spiralling construction behind it is referred to as "the snail". The small ensemble of bank branches on the corner of Ülikooli and Vallikraavi has been sarcastically dubbed "Wall Street", while the oversized, cubical Kaubamaja department store nearby is jokingly called "Tallinn University" by students taking a jab at what they see as the ridiculous materialism of the capital.

BELOW: Tartu's part-ruined cathedral.

Maternity Hospital (1838). Straight ahead is the ochre **Angel's Bridge** (Inglisild), also named as a result of a linguistic confusion: **Toomemägi Park** was laid out in English style and the locals confused the words "English" and "angel".

Toomemägi is strewn with statues of people connected with Tartu University. In spring biology students traditionally wash the pensive head of Karl Ernst von Baer – a professor linked to Darwin – with champagne. The monument to the writer Kristjan Jaak Peterson – the first Estonian national to enter the university – is shown erect with a stick in his hand because he is said to have walked the 250 km (155 miles) from Rīga to Tartu. The "Romantic Corner" of the park lies to the left from the statue of Baer. It consists of a stone mound called the Hill of Kissing, to the top of which bridegrooms must carry their new wives, a low Bridge of Sighing with a well-worn cement bench, and a Sacrificial Stone where the lovelorn can leave a prayer to the ancient gods.

Sacred stones are found all over Estonia; people used to gather round them on a Thursday full moon, and leave (non-bloody) sacrifices. Tartu students have continued this ritual by burning their notebooks here at midnight on the Thursday before their exams.

Toom Cathedral

The monumental ruins of the **Toom Cathedral D** (Toomkirik), which gives the hill its name, loom above this part of the park. Begun in the 13th century, this was once the largest brick Gothic church in the Baltic countries, but the majority of it was destroyed in the Livonian Wars (1558–83). The broken wings of 10 flying buttresses give an idea of its former grandeur. While the project to shore up the ruins continues, summer visitors can pay to climb its two renovated towers.

The huge choir on the church's eastern end was completely restored in the early 1800s under the direction of Krause. For a time it served as the university library, but it now contains the **Tartu University History Museum** (Tartu Ülikooli ajaloo muuseum; Wed–Sun 11am–5pm; charge). On each floor are exhibitions of the history of the university, from its opening in 1632 in honour of the Swedish King Gustavus Adolphus to the present day. A lovely white Baroque hall on the second floor is a public concert room with walls lined by cases of antique biological species.

A trip across the Arched Bridge leads to **Tartu City Museum E** (Tartu linnamuuseum; Tue–Sun 11am–6pm; charge) at 23 Narva Road. Housed in a late 18th-century mansion, this relatively new museum covers the entire history of the town.

Tartu's districts

Tartu is divided into different districts each with its own name. Lai Street separates the Old Town from **Suppilinn** or Soup Town, so called because its streets are called after soup ingredients such as Bean and Potato. The industrial area south of the Old Town is the **Ropka district**, and the attractive **Karlova district** has cut-corner wooden

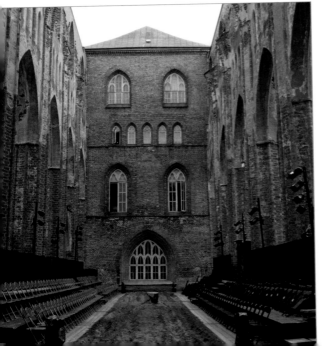

houses built during the Estonian Republic as boarding houses. The area of stately homes behind Toomemägi Park – and very popular with university professors – is the **Tähtvere district**, where some of the architecture was inspired by the Bauhaus movement. Just beyond here are the Song Festival Grounds (Laulava) where the first Baltic gathering was held in 1869. Today the stadium, with a canopy built in 1994, can hold 10,000 singers.

Architectural sights

Some of the most curious buildings in Tartu are ordinary houses. The weathered house at 65 Marta Street, beside the wooded park in which the beautifully restored **Karlova Manor** stands, for example, is a marvel of wood and stone edging work.

At Riia 27, **St Paul's Church** (Pauluse kirik, 1919) was designed by the Finnish architect Eliel Saarinen. Created in red brick with a square tower, it looks a bit like a fire station. Another architectural curiosity is the constructivist **Tammekann Villa**, built by Finnish architect Alvar Aalto in 1932 on Kreutzwaldi 6.

West of Tartu

The small city of **Viljandi** ❸, 77km (48 miles) west on main road 92, clings to the slopes of a primeval valley plumbed by Lake Viljandi. Now the capital of the Sakala upland, with about 21,000 inhabitants, the site has been settled since AD 1000, but the Old Town is tiny; one small grid between Tallinna and Tartu streets and the Castle Park (Lossipark). Its appeal is its lakeland setting and the ruined castle perched on a series of hills above the water, but it is perhaps better known among Estonians for the Viljandi Folk Music Festival, held each summer.

A good place to start a tour of the town is the **Museum of Viljandi** (Viljandi muuseum; Wed–Sun 10am–5pm; charge) at Kindral Laidoneri Square 10, in the Old Town. This square used to be the marketplace, and its central fountain covers the town well. The museum is downstairs in Viljandi's third-oldest building, originally a pharmacist's shop (1779–80), and contains a model of the former castle. It also houses many painstakingly decorated old objects of daily use, such as tankards and horse yokes, as well as exhibitions covering Viljandi county's late 19th-century history and the period of Estonia's first independence (1918–40).

The 18th-century **Town Hall** (Raekoda) stands on nearby Linnu Street. The neighbouring **Old Water Tower** (Vana veetorn; May–Sept Wed–Sun 10am–5pm; charge), dates from 1911 and has been refurbished.

The entrance to Lossipark is just down Lossi Street, over a long wooden footbridge. Begun in 1223, the **Order Fortress of Viljandi** (Viljandi ordulinnus) is presumed to have been the largest fortress in the Baltics, designed to stretch over three adjacent hills, with its only entrance on the first hill, occupied by servants. The second fold, once split between servants and horses, is now a field edged with bits of old wall. If you climb (carefully) up on the stone

Dancers in Viljandi.

BELOW: street bookstall.

A performance in Tartu's Vanemuine theatre.

BELOW: the start of the Tartu cross-country ski marathon.

by the edge, you will get a great view over a long and narrow lake. The third hill supported the castle, the church and the prison. This final section has more ruins than the other two, and they stand out starkly against the sky.

A bright red-and-white suspension bridge (Rippsild) leads from this end of the castle grounds into the rest of the park. Built in 1879, the 50-metre (164ft) bridge was brought to the town from Rīga in 1931 by a German count whose favourite daughter, the story goes, had persisted in racing her horse across it.

The 15th-century church of the former Franciscan monastery, **St John's Church** (Janni kirik), has its own wooden footbridge, at the head of Lossipark just off Pikk Street. It is used primarily for concerts. The town's main Lutheran church, St Paul's (Pauluse kirik, 1863–6), lies outside the park across Vaksali Road. Red brick with stone inlay, it has an industrial-age Gothic veneer.

By the lake's shore Viljandi has a different feel – it is considerably sportier, happier and younger. At one end are tennis courts and a town stadium, and

there is also an athletes' hotel. Boa and pedalos can be rented from th pier beside the restaurant. It is adv able to row out to the centre if yo want to jump in because the botto of the lake is so muddy.

Otepää, the Winter Capital

Estonia's entire southern region is dc ted with pretty lakes, many of whic are swimmable (though it is alwa best to check with a local). The lar est, at 270 sq km (105 sq miles), Võrtsjärv. It is, however, only 6 metr (20ft) at its deepest. The lakes Otepää in the **Otepää Highlands** he make this cosy town not just one Estonia's most popular winter resor but also a gracious rest spot during th summer months.

Otepää ❹ is a short drive southwe from Tartu, but in its tranquillity could be a million miles away fro the city. Its population of around 4,5(doubles in winter. Tourism has becon a mainstay of the economy in Estonia "Winter Capital", and resort faciliti include a ski jump, cross-country s paths, three downhill skiing centre

a beach and hotels. The town's biggest events are the World Cup Cross-Country Skiing Championship, which attracts around 10,000 participants each January, the 60km (37-mile) Tartu Marathon involving 2,000–3,000 skiers in February, and an ice-fishing contest.

The town and its surroundings have been designated a "protected area". Building above three storeys is forbidden, salt cannot be used against ice on the roads, and motorboating on Otepää's lakes and hunting and camping in its woods are restricted, though "bloodless" hunting – with a camera – is always allowed.

The town clusters up against these woods, and the centre has a pleasantly closed-in feeling, accentuated by a narrow triangular central park. The Tourist Information Centre is based nearby, at the bus station at 1 Tartu Street. The oldest building in town is **Otepää church**. Opened in 1608, it was built by Estonian peasants so they wouldn't have to attend the church of the German population. The folklorist Jakob Hurt was its first Estonian pastor (1872–80). The current steeple was added in 1860 and is 52 metres (168ft) high.

When the Estonian Students Co-perative was forbidden from consecrating its flag in Tartu in 1884, they defiantly brought it to the Otepää church. Their trek is honoured in the tiny **Estonian Flag Museum** (Eesti Lipu muuseum; summer) in the nearby rectory. Stone reliefs on the church's front doors that depicted this momentous nationalistic event were destroyed by the Soviets, but the locals replaced them with bronze casts in 1990. The "Monument to the 54" in front of the church, dedicated to the soldiers from Otepää who died in the War of Independence, was also blown up by the Soviets – once in the 1950s, and again in the 1980s – but each time it was replaced by the local people.

Linnamägi, former site of a 10–11th-century wooden stronghold and a bishop's 13th-century stone castle, is a small tree-covered hill a short walk south from the church past a municipal garden. The first level of the hill is marked with a large stone monument dated 1116, the year when Otepää first appears in the records. Locals use this spot for their midsummer celebrations. The excavated ruins of the castle stand on the shelf above. The expansive vista from here makes it easy to imagine why ancient warriors fought for the site.

Pühajärv Oak

In ancient times Estonians gathered under oaks whenever they had to make important decisions. One of the most famous oaks is a couple of kilometres outside the centre of Otepää. Standing wide and noble between a cow pasture, vegetable patch and Pühajärv lake, the **Pühajärv Oak** is 22 metres (72ft) tall. Five people linking arms can reach around it. Its popular name is the War Tree (Sõjatamm), because of its part in independence history. In 1841, a local German landlord tried to force the Estonian peasants on his land to use heavier equipment than they felt their horses could draw. They refused, which resulted in a battle beneath the

BELOW: orienteering at Otepää.

oak. The peasants lost, but their act became a legend of Estonian solidarity. Incidentally, the biggest and oldest tree in the country, the Tamme-Lauri Oak, is located in Urvaste about 15km (10 miles) south of the town. It dates from 1326, and has a circumference of 8.25 metres (27ft).

Neitsijärv, or Virgin's Lake, which you pass on the way from the town to the War Tree, derives its name from the Middle Ages when the *droit de seigneur* meant that brides had to spend their first married night in the bed of the Pühajärv landlord. One young girl left her wedding for the manor and never appeared. In the morning, they found her bridal dress beside this lake, where she had drowned herself.

Pühajärv, the largest of the lakes in the area, literally means "Holy Lake". The public beach here is a well-maintained "Blue-Flag"-quality beach, and boats can be rented out. Soviet dissidents Andrei Sakarov and Alexander Solzhenitsyn both used to spend quiet weeks by Lake Püha and, if you ask, locals will show you where the prime minister of Estonia during the Soviet

era kept his holiday home. He alone was allowed to use a motorboat here. His home is now a guesthouse owned by Tartu University.

The southern border

About 20km (13 miles) south from here is **Sangaste loss** ❺ (Sangaste Castle; June–Aug daily 10am–6pm, Sept–May daily 10am–4pm; charge) built in 1874–81 for Count Friedrich Georg Magnus von Berg as a small-scale copy of Windsor Castle in England. It is a particularly incongruous looking orange-brick mansion set back amid acres of agricultural plains. The manor was seized in the 1930s and most of the family fled to Finland. Sangaste has passed through many hands since, even housing hay and a tractor in its octagonal, multi-vaulted ballroom after World War II. In the 1970s, it was used as a Young Pioneers' Camp. Today it is a hotel and a conference centre.

Wide pastureland separates Sangaste from **Valga** ❻, the southernmost city in Estonia, whose main claim to fame is that it straddles the border with Latvia where it becomes Valka. When both countries became independent in 1918, the new border divided streets and in some cases, even houses. After brief respite during Soviet times, border posts went up again in the early 1990s, and down again in 2007 when both countries adopted the Schengen accords. Many non-Estonians live here and unlike other southern towns it industrially developed.

If you edge southeast along the border for about 45km (30 miles), you will reach one of Estonia's largest forests. The **Mõniste Open-Air Museum** ❼ (Mõniste vabaõhumuuseum; May–Sept daily 10am–5pm, Oct–Apr Mon–Fri 10am–2pm; charge) here contains a reconstruction of a 19th-century southern Estonian farmhouse. Between Mõniste and Võru is the peaceful hamlet of **Rõuge** ❽. A picture of southern harmony, Rõuge curls in around seven clear lakes. One, called Rõuge Suurjä

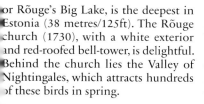

or Rõuge's Big Lake, is the deepest in Estonia (38 metres/125ft). The Rõuge church (1730), with a white exterior and red-roofed bell-tower, is delightful. Behind the church lies the Valley of Nightingales, which attracts hundreds of these birds in spring.

Hannja Highlands

To the east lie the **Haanja Highlands**. Haanja is slightly higher than the Otepää and Sakala uplands and its forests are deeper, but it has also been widely tamed by potato fields and pastureland. Its summit is **Suur-Munamägi**, or Big Egg Hill, due east of Rõuge. The highest peak in Estonia, reaching 318 metres (1,044ft) above sea level, it has a 35-metre (115ft) observation tower on its summit, and the result is a view that is truly heavenly. On the clearest days, you can see all the way to Russia and Latvia.

It may also be possible to glimpse the ruins of **Vastseliina Castle**. To reach it, head east towards the "new" Vastseliina village, whose cultural centre is in an 18th-century manor house. The "old" village, called Vana-Vestseliina, was built in the 14th century around the castle, but not much is left of either. The red-and-beige brick castle has been reduced to two towers and one section of wall, lost in an overgrown section of field. The 19th-century Vana-Vastseliina coach stop, where a tsar once stayed, has been turned into a restaurant.

The folds of Haanja were created during the Ice Age, and the landscape is smooth and unending. Gentle pastures are edged by lone farmhouses and tiny lakes that appear then fade. The most popular place for fishing is **Verijärv**, or Blood Lake, a bit closer to Võru and filled with perch and pike. Large and picturesque, at the base of another steep, forested valley, it got its name because a servant supposedly once drove a cruel lord of the manor into its waters.

Võru ❾, the urban centre for the Haanja Highlands, sprawls around the biggest lake in the town, Tamula järv. Along with agriculture, Võru depends on forestry, furniture-making and dairy production. The population is about 16,000 and the local dialect, Võru-Seto, which is spoken by the

TIP

Rõuge makes a good base for exploring southern Estonia. Ask at the tourist office in Tindi village (tel: 785 9245) for farm and rural accommodation.

BELOW: ice-fishing on Lake Pühajärv.

southern Estonians from Võrumaa and Setuma, was recently declared a separate language.

The town was officially established in 1784, and both the small yellow Orthodox church and St Catherine's Church (Katariina kirik) were built soon after. The most famous 18th-century structure in Võru is the **Friedrich Reinhold Kreutzwald Memorial Museum** (F.R. Kreutzwaldi memoriaalmuuseum; Apr–Sept Wed–Sun 10am–6pm, Oct–Mar Wed–Sun 10am–5pm; charge) on Kreutzwald Street 31. This is where the Estonian writer and doctor lived for most of his life. Kreutzwald was born in the Rakvere region in 1803 and studied in Tartu from 1826 to 1833. However, he spent the next 44 years practising medicine in Võru where he compiled *Kalevipoeg*, the Estonian national epic.

The museum is divided between three houses. The first is where the small home of Kreutzwald's Estonian mother stood; she could not bear to live in the same house as Kreutzwald's wife, Maria, who was from a wealthy German family in Tartu. This house

has an exhibition of his life and many publications. His own home has been kept as it was when he lived there and it includes portraits of the family, who ironically, spoke only German at home. On the walls of the low building at the back of the yard are interpretations of *Kalevipoeg* from a panorama of artists, including some of Estonia's best known, such as Erik Haamer, Jur Arrak and Kristjan Raud.

Kreutzwald Park runs towards the lake and a statue of Kreutzwald. The **Võru County Museum** (Võruma muuseum; Apr–Sept Wed–Sun 10am–6pm, Oct–Mar Wed–Sun 10am–5pm charge) stands at the start of the park. Exhibits range from the area's 5,000-year-old settlement to life in the 20th century. Art and handicraft displays change every month.

Return route to Tartu

The drive from Võru back up to Tartu gradually becomes less hilly, but the forests remain. Main road 2 is the most direct route, but the 64, an older road is a more leisurely option. Just beyond **Põlva ⑩** on the right is the impressive **Kiidjärve Mill**. Constructed in 19 and trimmed with orange brick, it the largest functioning watermill in Europe. The **Põlva Peasant Culture Museum** (Põlva Talurahvamuuseum 15 May–30 Sept daily 9am–6pm charge) lies on the other side of the Tartu road, in the village of Karila just beyond **Kiidjärve**. It has an old schoolhouse that is still set for lesson a windmill and a garden designed be a map of the region.

Outside Tartu, 7km (5 miles) from the city centre on the Võru road, the well-presented **Estonian Agricultural Museum** (Eesti Põllumajandus muuseum; Apr–Oct daily Tue–Su 10am–6pm, 16 Sept–14 May da 10am–4pm; charge). Fittingly, the surrounding landscape is anchored by flung farms, many of which have been renovated. It is a sign that the south ploughing on, refusing to be shaken the north's vagaries.

E-stonia

From inventing Skype to becoming a world leader in e-government, Estonia has firmly embraced the information age

One of the first things visitors notice on arrival in Estonia is the overwhelming presence of all things high-tech. Everyone, from small children to senior citizens, appears to be linked, as if umbilically, to a mobile phone. And in cafés and bars, locals are busy tapping on hand-held devices or scrutinising their laptops, surfing the internet via a wireless connection.

These outward signs are just the tip of a technological iceberg. Over the past few years, Estonia has become enamoured – some would say obsessed – with the idea of remodelling itself into an information society. The result is that new technologies, particularly those involving internet and mobile phones, have worked their way into every aspect of life, from farming to dating to buying soda at vending machines. Locals take these innovations in their stride, pointing out that this is, after all, the country that invented Skype.

Internet a universal right

Estonia has a high-tech history. In Soviet times this was where advanced software programming was developed, for espionage and space programmes, and Tallinn was a major centre for developing artificial intelligence. After independence, a "Tiger Leap" programme was introduced, to push the nation ahead by using computer technology in every field, and connecting every school to the internet. In February 2000, Estonia declared internet access a "constitutional right", and six months later, the government became the first in the world to convert cabinet meetings to paperless sessions, saving £200,000 a year in photocopying costs. A more recent programme has trained more than 100,000 adults, mostly retired people and blue-collar workers, in how to use the internet.

The mobile phone is almost universal here, and is used for far more than just talking. Nearly all customers paying for parking in central Tallinn are doing so by SMS text message, and other text-message systems are being widely used for every-thing from buying bus tickets to checking bank balances to getting weather reports. Most Estonians are regular internet users, and nearly all connections are broadband. There are over 1,100 Wi-fi "hot-spots" around the country, allowing laptop users high-speed net access in cafés, pubs, hotels, city squares, beaches, trains and inter-city buses.

Wireless connections are spreading broadband into rural areas where ADSL and cable connections don't reach. Farmers have been using the internet to track cow herds, and if rural dwellers don't have computers, they can look for official blue signs with the "@" symbol pointing to a place to log on.

One card does all

A smart ID card, which can serve as a passport within the EU, is doing away with both money and paperwork. It can be used on public transport and for filing taxes. Estonia is continually innovating, and a responsive public means that the country is often used by foreign companies as a test market for new technologies.

Linnar Viik, the Tallinn-born guru behind Tiger Leap, once told *Forbes* magazine: "People like to say, don't touch things that work. But Estonians like to look behind the thing and wonder whether there's anything we can change about it. In Estonia you might say, if it works, you can break it." ❑

LEFT: a member of the highly mobile society.

THE WEST COAST

Estonia's west coast is famous for its spa resorts of Pärnu and Haapsalu, its ghostly castles, and the abundant flowers and birdlife in the Sooma and Matsalu National Parks

The spas of Estonia's western shore used to be favoured by Russian tsars, and even under Soviet rule Russians flocked here for their summer holidays. Today they attract Western – and in particular Finnish – visitors.

Estonia's prime spa resort, **Pärnu ⓫**, one of the few places outside Tallinn where people traditionally know how to deal with a tourist. Known as Estonia's "Summer Capital", the town of 44,000 inhabitants is 130km (80 miles) due south of Tallinn on the E67.

Pärnu "old" and "new"

The city's revival began in the 1990s when the majestic Rannahotell (1937) overlooking the beach was refurbished, and the Art Nouveau gem, the Ammende Villa, reopened, both buildings restoring touches of pre-war elegance to the beach area. More recently, the Hotell St Peterburg has added some 19th-century class to the mix, and the modern Tervise Paradiis health resort has made a loud splash with its gigantic, indoor water park.

The long beachfront and numerous parks are restorative places to stroll, and the Old Town is ripe with structural curiosities. Younger Estonians particularly like Pärnu; throughout the summer the bars and cafés are popping, and the cultural calendar is packed with concerts and festivals.

The city proper, first noted in 1251, is divided by the River Pärnu. Rather confusingly, the Old Town lies on the south bank within what the locals refer to as the "new" city. The "old" city, north of the river, is where the majority of newer buildings are located. The reason for this is linked to Pärnu's complex history. During the 14th century, the area where the Old Town stands was occupied by a castle and fortification. But when the Swedes took power in 1617, they began to build across the river instead. The castle fell into decay

Main attractions
PÄRNU
KIHNU ISLAND
SOOMAA NATIONAL PARK
MATSALU NATIONAL PARK
HAAPSALU
ANTS LAIKMAA MUSEUM

LEFT: kite-flying on the beach at Pärnu.
RIGHT: Pärnu's Tallinn Gate.

TIP

The David Oistrakh Festival is a highlight of the summer season in Pärnu. It takes place in the town's new five-storey concert hall every July. Masterclasses by Estonian conductor Neeme Järvi are part of the festival.

and was finally destroyed during the Great Northern War (1700–21). This made the section on the north bank the oldest part of the city when, in subsequent centuries, development began to spill back over to the former castle area. This "old city" was, however, flattened during World War II, putting the area with the oldest buildings, or the "old town", back on the south side of the river.

Pärnu's Old Town

Touring Pärnu's Old Town is far less complicated. For one thing, it isn't very large. Visiting would take only a couple of hours, if so many of the most eye-catching buildings didn't also contain enticing bars and cafés. Its main street, the pedestrianised Rüütli Street, runs nearly the entire length of the Old Town, and is by far the city's most active. Smaller cross-streets, however, provide some of the town's more interesting architectural finds.

Pühavaimu Street, running through the Old Town's centre, is one example. First on the block is a delicate yellow building (1670), fronted by an impos-

ing balcony that bears four small lions' heads. Squeezed in next to it is an odd red- and mustard-coloured house (1877) that mixes everything from Corinthian columns to a flowery grey trim. It in turn merges into a green Baroque structure (1674) trimmed with courtly white and crowned with an old street lamp. The nearby **Almshouse** (Seegimaja), at Hospidali 1, dates from the 1600s. The grand, peaked edifice was built in 1658 and now operates as a restaurant.

Generally, the Old Town isn't so old: most buildings date from the 19th century. But it does have two intact 18th-century churches, which are perhaps most remarkable for their physical proximity but absolute disparity. **St Catherine's Church** (Ekateriina kirik, 1765–68) is a weird Orthodox conglomeration of knobs and ledges, with green roofing and unevenly soaring spires. The interior is almost lunatic in its iconography; silver shield-like icons crown the white walls. Meanwhile, the red and-white Lutheran church, **St Elisabeth's Church** (Eliisabeti kirik, 1747) at Nikolai 22 a few blocks away, is austere by comparison, but nonetheless impres-

BELOW: Pärnu Town Hall and, in the distance, the spires of St Catherine's Church.

e. Its charming interior and acoustics
ve made it a much-used venue for
assical music performances.

Medieval walls

here are two remnants of the original
th-century fortifications. One is the
ed Tower (Punane Torn), saved dur-
g the Swedish era to house prisoners.
cked down a small alley off Hom-
iku Street, it is easy to miss, particu-
ly since, contrary to its name, it is
oloured a gleaming white. The other
ece of the ancient walls is the Tallinn
ate (Tallinna Väravad). Grey and
hite with tall green doors, it some-
nes doubles as a café in summer.
Passing through the gate, you find
urself on a lovely, long, tree-lined
alk beside a finger of the River Pärnu
rled inwards to create a duck-filled
nd. This is the beginning of the lush
rks that surround the sanatoria in a
ther awesome silence.

Mud treatment

he sanatoria offer a wide variety of
eatments, from aromatic massages
the more traditional mud baths

for muscle and joint aches. Though
no longer considered a cure-all, mud
has been a mainstay of Pärnu's resort
industry since the 19th century. The
most striking symbol of this activity is the Pärnu Mud Baths (Pärnu
Mudaravila), housed in a neoclassical
building (1926) at the end of Supeluse
Street. Now used primarily as a cultural
centre, it no longer provides treatment,
having long since handed over the task
to more modern equivalents nearby.

The elaborate, mint-coloured Beach
Salon (Pärnu Kuursaal), next door at
Mere Avenue 22, functions as a gigantic tavern, as well as a cultural centre
with a bandstand behind it. Its front
pavilion, facing the beach, has a picturesque fountain and a row of ornamen-
tal wicker arches, festooned with vines
each summer.

These two buildings stand by the
northwest edge of Pärnu Beach, beginning with the Women's Beach, where
only women and small children are
allowed so that they can sunbathe nude
in peace. You can walk for miles from
here along the tree-lined promenade
that parallels the beach; continuing

*The elegant Scandic
Rannahotell in
Pärnu was designed
by the Estonian
Functionalist
architects Olev
Siinmaa and Anton
Soans. Pause over a
drink on its front
terrace and check out
its style.*

BELOW: Pärnu
Mud Baths.

Haabja are the traditional boats, hollowed out of single tree trunks, on Soomaa National Park's waterways. They are available for hire, as are kayaks and canoes.

BELOW: Tori farmyard.

north brings you through a collection of modern sculptures and finally fields of dank, waving reed, while a turn south leads to the more crowded sections of waterfront, ad hoc cafés, the Functionalist-style **Beach House** (Rannahoone) and a mini-golf course.

The Old Town has its own walks, the most famous of which is the triangular **Lydia Koidula Park**. The poet Koidula (1843–86) was born in a village outside Pärnu. She lived in the city from the age of seven until, at 20, she moved with her family to Tartu. Many consider Koidula's collection of verse, *The Nightingale of Emajõgi*, to be the foremost work of Estonia's period of National Awakening, and the pen-name Koidula, given to her by a fellow artist, means literally "singer of the dawn". Her real maiden name was Jannsen, and the modest wooden schoolhouse where her family lived is on Jannseni 37. The house itself is now the **Lydia Koidula Memorial Museum** (June–Aug Tue–Sun 10am–6pm, Sept–May Tue–Sun 10am–5pm; charge), but for those who don't speak Estonian it is a bit dull since the con-

tents are mostly cases of her poe books and writings.

The **Pärnu Museum** (Tue–Sat 10a 6pm; charge), on the other hand surprisingly rewarding. Located i dim, Soviet-style building, its outw appearance is dreary, but the artefa within are worth a look. Archaeolo cal finds date from as early as 80 BC. A 13th-century woman's costur a 16th-century Gothic chalice a embossed-leather Bible, and 19th-c tury furniture are also on display.

Pärnu's islets

A far more vivid glimpse of Eston past can be found on Kihnu a Manilaid, two small islands off Pärn coast. In summer, both can be reach by ferry from Munalaid harbour at t northwestern tip of Pärnu Bay.

Kihnu, the larger of the two, unique in Estonia as its isolation I preserved a way of life that has lo since vanished on the mainland. F centuries, while the men were aw at sea, the women were tasked wi running the island's day-to-day affai Nowadays, among Kihnu's 600 re

dents, it is they who carefully guard the islanders' cultural heritage, still wearing the same style of vivid woollen skirts as their grandmothers and great-grandmothers, and ensuring that traditional handicrafts, dances, games and music remain an integral part of everyday life. It is telling that the Kihnu wedding has been proclaimed a Unesco Masterpiece of the Oral and Intangible Heritage of Humanity.

At just 16.4 sq km (6.3 sq miles), Kihnu is small enough to navigate by bicycle – these can be rented at the harbour on arrival. There are four villages: Lemsi, Linaküla, Rootsiküla and Sääre. A 19th-century schoolhouse in Linaküla houses the freshly updated **Kihnu Museum** (May–Aug daily 10am–4pm, Sept Tue–Sat 10am–2pm, Oct–Apr Tue–Fri 10am–2pm; charge), which hosts exhibits on the island's history. Evidence suggests that seal-hunters set foot on Kihnu around 3,000 years ago, while records of permanent habitation first appeared in the early 16th century. Opposite the museum stands a church where the island's legendary 19th-century sea captain, Kihnu Jõnn,

immortalised in film and theatre, is buried.

The scenic coastline is dotted with giant boulders and fronted by islets, which are important bird habitats. A lighthouse, dating to 1864, stands at the island's southern tip.

Kihnu's little sister, **Manilaid**, known as Manija by the locals, is a far quieter affair. Its area is a mere 1.9 sq km (0.7 sq miles) and its population is just over 40. The island remained uninhabited until 1933, when families from the then overcrowded Kihnu settled here. Manilaid's one tourist farm attracts birdwatchers and visitors seeking a true sense of isolation.

National parks

From Pärnu, a side-trip north to the **Soomaa National Park** ⑫ (Soomaa rahvuspark) provides a look at a landscape that's little seen elsewhere in Europe. At the end of route 59 through **Tori** and **Jõesuu**, signs direct drivers into the heart of the 371-sq km (143-sq mile) nature reserve. Soomaa literally means "land of bogs", and while the area is known for its floodplains and

The Medieval Days festival in Parnu.

BELOW: floating sauna at Karuskose, Soomaa National Park.

Haapsalu wooden houses.

wildlife, its unique feature is its mysterious and often misty bogs – clear areas with peaty land, low trees and small ponds – a scene that doesn't look like it belongs on our planet. They can only be reached by carefully walking over specially built plank pathways. Soomaa's **Visitors' Centre** in Tõramaa (May–Sept Tue–Sun 10am–6pm, Oct–Apr Tue–Sat 10am–4pm) provides trail maps. Early June, when flowers are in bloom, is the best time to visit. In late June–August, mosquito repellent is a must.

Route 60 northwest from Pärnu leads to the small town of **Lihula**, which has a huge, Soviet-built cultural centre, a plaster-and-stone Orthodox church and a point-spired Lutheran church. Just 3km (2 miles) north from Lihula, the village of **Penijõe** is the gateway to the **Matsalu National Park ⑬** (Matsalu rahvuspark). Matsalu Bay has a range of habitats including reed beds, water meadows, hay meadows and coastal pastures. It was already noted for its birdlife back in 1870. Among the species found here today are avocet, sandwich tern, mute

swan, greylag goose and bittern. There are also some white-tailed eagles. The reserve was formed from 39,700 hectares (98,000 acres) of the bay area in 1957. It can be visited by car or, since water covers some 26,300 hectares (65,000 acres) of this same area, by boat. Boat excursions of the rivers and the bay can be arranged though the **Matsalu Nature Centre** in Penijõe (15 Apr–30 Sept Mon– Fri 9am–5pm, Sat–Sun 10am–6pm, 1 Oct–14 Apr Mon–Fri only), located in a restored 17th-century manor house.

Haapsalu and Matsalu Bay

Matsalu Bay (Matsula laht) lies in the southern part of the coastal district of Läänemaa. One of the flattest sections of the already rather flat Estonia, it is also low in arable land, but the overall impression is certainly pastoral. The main town is **Haapsalu ⑭** which has close to 10,500 inhabitant. A large military base and fishery were established here under the Soviets, and although the entire district has been under either Russian or Soviet control since 1710 (except for the 20 years o

BELOW: Haapsalu Castle.

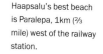

the republic), many locals identify with the Swedes, who ruled over them from 1581 to 1710. It was under the Russians, however, that Haapsalu became a spa of great repute and that many of its fanciest buildings were constructed.

The town originally centred around the **Haapsalu Episcopal Castle** (Haapsalu piiskopilinnus), which dates from 1279. Little of the castle remains, but its courtyard has become a favourite spot for picnics and concerts, and technological additions mean that visitors hear sound effects emanating from various corners. In summer, the castle doubles as a museum (May and Sept daily 10am–4pm, June–Aug daily 10am–6pm; charge) chronicling the town's history, and its watchtower is open to the public.

The best-preserved part of the castle is the Romano-Gothic cathedral, one of only three functioning cathedrals in Estonia. Single-naved and towerless, it was built to double-up as a fortress, and its immense facade looks stubbornly impenetrable. Inside, the tall white walls and high-vaulted ceiling are almost bare. In a side chapel is a baptismal font from 1634, with Adam, Eve and the serpent etched into its bowl – a vivid reminder of original sin to be washed away. Against its wall leans a sad wooden sculpture of a woman holding a child; a memorial to the people from Läänemaa deported to Siberia. The box beneath it, marked "1949–1989", contains Siberian soil. Directly above it is the window of the White Lady, focus of a Haapsalu legend (see box opposite).

In front of the castle entrance is the large square that used to house the town market, and to the west is the place that served as the Swedish Market (Roosti turu). It now encloses a pleasant café, open in summer. On the square's east side is the **Läänemaa County Museum** (May–Sept Tue–Sat 11am–6pm, Oct–Apr Tue–Sat 11am–6pm; charge), within what used to be the Town Hall. Many of the artefacts come from the castle, and there are

exhibitions about Haapsalu's days as a summer resort.

Across the street from the Läänemaa Museum, **Ilon's Wonderland** (May–Sept daily 10am–6pm, Oct–Apr Tue–Sat 11am–4pm; charge) shows off the works of one of Haapsalu's most famous residents, Ilon Wikland, illustrator of Astrid Lindgren's Pippi Longstocking books. Ilon was born in Haapsalu and, although she fled with her family to Sweden at the age of 14, she has depicted the town and the small house on Rüütli Street beside the Adventist church where her father was minister in many drawings.

The town has also been rich in handicraft artists, and the "Haapsalu Shawl", created of such fine wool that it can be drawn through a ring, is known throughout Estonia. A couple of shops specialise in local crafts, and one particular shop/museum near the Swedish Market allows visitors to try their own hand at craftmaking.

African Beach

Just a couple of streets to the north is the seaside **Promenade** (Promenaadi).

TIP

Haapsalu's best beach is Paralepa, 1km (⅔ mile) west of the railway station.

BELOW: Haapsalu.

One of many old locomotives on display at the Estonian Railway Museum.

BELOW: the Estonian Railway Museum occupies the Emperor's Salon at Haapsalu station.

Here you can see the ghosts of Haapsalu's spa days by walking down to the "African Beach", so called because locals sunning themselves here, covered with the town's famous curative mud, were said to resemble dark-skinned Africans. Additionally, in the early 20th century there used to be, along with little bathing houses, statues of wild animals set in the water. Although the water isn't safe for swimming any more, locals are still fond of strolling the path alongside it.

Tchaikovsky Bench

The restored **Resort Hall** (Haapsalu kuursaal), built in the 1900s, is an historic delight with green-painted timber, lacy cut-out porticoes and surrounding rose garden. For generations, concerts have been held in the bandstand beside it. Of interest here are a sundial and steps by the artist R. Haavamägi, who was born in Haapsalu, and the Tchaikovsky Bench. The Russian composer used to favour Haapsalu for his holidays and even used a motif from a traditional Estonian song his 6th Symphony. The bench is dec rated with the composer's likeness ar at the press of a button, it plays sor notes from the 6th. This is the sp where he came every evening to wat the sun set. The Tchaikovsky Festival one of a number of music festivals he here during the summer.

Continuing further down Sadan Road from this point will bring you the **Estonian-Swedish Museum** (Ra narootsi muuseum; May–Aug Tue–S 10am–6pm, Sept–Apr Tue–Sat 11an 4pm; charge), where the history of t local seafaring Swedish communi comes to light. Swedes settled alo Estonia's coasts and islands as early Viking times, and maintained a cultu separate from the Estonians. Nearl the Haapsalu Yacht Club continu to thrive, but has been upstaged by **Grand Holm Marina**, which has be built to cater for the summer Bal yacht crowd, a few metres away.

Town activity has moved away fro the castle and beach down the lengt Posti Street. However, if you wand the quaint backstreets or the curio

nd creepy overgrown **Old Town Graveyard** – which lies on Posti Street opposite the very comfortable Haapsalu Hotel – you will find it easy to understand the appeal that Haapsalu as held for artists.

tation fit for a tsar

rom Posti Street, Jaama Street leads ff to the right. At its end is the splenid railway station, built in 1905 to eceive Tsar Nicholas II on his summer oliday. After years of neglect, it was pruced up for the town's 725th annirsary celebrations in 2004. A number f antique locomotives are on display n the tracks, and the station's Empere's Salon houses a small branch of he **Estonian Railway Museum** (Eesti audteemuuseum; Wed–Sun 10am– pm; charge). Further on, paths lead hrough a park, ending at the reedy, alm Paralepa Beach.

ainter's home

Heading out of town back towards allinn will take you past the home of nts Laikmaa, an influential early 20th-entury Estonian painter. Laikmaa was an eccentric, and the home he designed for himself, which has been turned into the **Ants Laikmaa Museum ⑮** (May–Sept Tue–Sat 10am–6pm, Oct–Apr Tues–Sat 11am–4pm; charge) is a peculiar blend of red-and-white piping with a steep moss-covered roof that has to be seen to be believed. A small sign points towards a bumpy road leading through the woods. The house at its end, in a large yard, was begun in 1923 and was changed in design so many times that it was never finished during Laikmaa's lifetime. Laikmaa was immensely popular in Haapsalu. He was known for known for his handsome moustaches, for using carriages long after the advent of the car, and for appearing in costume when the mood struck him. He was also the host of many unusual house parties.

From here Tallinn is about an hour's drive northeast. If you feel that you have not yet truly experienced the sea, head west. At **Rohuküla**, 8km (5 miles) away, you can catch a ferry to the islands of **Vormsi** or **Hiiumaa** *(see page 159)*, where the water is clean and tourists are few and far between.   ❑

Medieval Days festival in Haapsalu.

BELOW: west coast reflections.

THE ISLANDS

Saaremaa and Hiiumaa, the two largest islands off Estonia's west coast, are idyllic rural retreats of windmills, fishing boats and farmhouse bed-and-breakfasts

Most of the 1,500 or so islands off the coast of Estonia are mere hiccups, but two are so sizeable that island acreage ultimately accounts for some 10 percent of Estonia's total land territory. These larger islands, Saaremaa and Hiiumaa, are perhaps the most unspoilt and attractive corners of the country. Their pristine condition is due partly to the Soviet occupation. Clustered off the western shore, these islands were, rightly, considered likely points of escape to the West and were therefore kept for the most part incommunicado from the rest of the Soviet Union. At the same time, since they were clearly impractical for any industrial projects, they were spared the scars of heavy development. As a result, both islands are now prime destinations for Estonians in search of a bucolic, summer getaway, as well as for Finns, many of whom come to take advantage of Saaremaa's golf courses and luxury spas, or own summer houses on the islands.

Distinct way of life

Finnish pensioners were by no means the first of Estonia's neighbours to have territorial designs on Saaremaa and Hiiumaa. In the 13th century the islands were divided between the Oesel-Wiek (Saare-Lääne) bishopric and the Livonian Order. Three centuries later,

Saaremaa (Oesel) reverted to Denmark while Sweden took Hiiumaa. In 1645, Saaremaa was also assigned to the Swedes, and from then on they were destined to share Estonia's fate. Somehow, the islanders stubbornly retained a distinct way of life. They also began to stockpile impressive monuments left behind by the parade of conquering egos. The 13th-century churches and 18th-century manor houses that decorate their shores have now been mostly repaired, and have become mainstays of the islands' tourism industry. There are

Main attractions
MUHU
KURESSAARE CASTLE
ANGLA WINDMILLS
HILL OF CROSSES
KÕPU LIGHTHOUSE
KASSARI ISLAND

LEFT: perfect boating waters.
RIGHT: Saaremaa windmill-keeper.

BELOW: monument at Kuressaare relating to the local legend of the giants Piret and Suur-Toll (Toell the Great).

some delightful farm bed-and-breakfasts from which to choose, too.

MUHU ISLAND

To reach Saaremaa, the largest of all the Estonian islands, it is necessary first to cross **Muhu** ⑯, where the ferry from **Virtsu** on the mainland docks. Estonia's third-largest island, Muhu is only 201 sq km (78 sq miles) and, along with about 500 smaller islands, belongs to the greater Saaremaa County. Muhu does not hold nearly as many attractions as its larger neighbour, but it does have sights worth stopping to see.

The most commercial of these is unquestionably **Pädeste mõis** (Pädeste Manor). The estate, which dates from the 16th century, was once the home of the Baltic-German Buxhoveden family. Its Tudor-style main building (1875) is now being restored, and the beautifully decorated outbuildings have been turned into a luxury guesthouse and exclusive gourmet restaurant – reputed to be one of the best in the Baltics.

More down-to-earth sightseeing can be found in the village of **Koguva**, where the outdoor **Muhu Museum**

(15 May–15 Sept daily 10am–6pm, 16 Sept–14 May Tue–Sat 10am–5pm; charge) is located. The area nearby is thought to have been settled in the late Iron Age, but this still-inhabited fishing village was first documented in 1532. Of the 105 buildings that remain, parts of three date from the early and mid-18th century, making it the oldest preserved conglomerate of peasant architecture on the islands. A stroll through the village, with its thatched roofs, moss-covered rock walls and windmill, evokes images of a much quieter age.

Koguva is not far from the causeway that leads to Saaremaa. It is a beautiful road, and terribly romantic. The water on either side is filled by a beckoning green carpet of swaying reeds. In spring, it changes to white as thousands of swans come here to mate.

SAAREMAA ISLAND

Saaremaa is, at some 2,668 sq km (1,030 sq miles), a spacious, quiet and unassuming place. Much of its land has been cultivated, and the simple island roads are laced with field after field of

livestock and wheat, interrupted only by patches of thick forest. Industry is at a minimum and, with the exception of those involved in tourism, those inhabitants who aren't at work on the land tend to be connected to the sea.

Kuressaare's gems

There is only one town of real consequence, **Kuressaare** ⑰, on the south side of the island, where 15,000 of Saaremaa County's 35,000 inhabitants live. Kuressaare is said to have been particularly popular with party officials during the Soviet regime, and it certainly is extremely handsome.

Most of the buildings in the centre are gems of late 18th- and early 19th-century neoclassicism, with pretty wooden houses and gardens mixed in beside them. Side streets reveal an ancient hand-pump for water or a freshly painted home with a paint-can tied proudly to its wooden gate. On Kaevu Street, an old windmill has been transformed into the unabashedly touristy Veski bar and restaurant.

Activity focuses around the triangular plaza where Tallinna Street turns into Lossi Street. At this junction are the market, the administrative halls and, after 9pm, the main spot for local youths to see and be seen. The yellow **Town Hall** (Raekoja, 1654–70) lies along the hypotenuse of this triangle, its entrance protected by stone lions. A peek inside is a good idea, as the building houses art exhibitions as well as the town's Tourist Information Centre.

To the left of the Town Hall stands an 18th-century fire station of burnt-brown wood. Opposite it is the **Weigh House** (Vaekoda), with a stepped gable. Dating from 1663, the Weigh House is now a popular café and pub, and encloses one side of the tiny Market Square. Here, in addition to jars of gooseberries in season you will find a range of distinctively patterned, hand-made woollen sweaters and mittens for sale, and items carved from the island's fragrant juniper wood. Sometimes there will also be a table or two

piled high with slippery black mounds of the expensive Saaremaa speciality, eel.

A second, smaller square lies a few steps down Lossi Street. This has the County Seat and a monument for the fallen in the War of Liberation. It is actually the third such monument erected here; twice the Soviets tore it down only for the locals to reconstruct it.

Continuing down Lossi will take you past the **Apostolic Orthodox St Nicholas Church** (Nikolai kirik, 1790). Its fancy front gate tied with large silver-painted bows is unmistakable, and its white exterior is topped with rounded green spires. The interior echoes this colour scheme, and treads between neoclassical and Byzantine styles.

Episcopal Castle

Kuressaare's main tourist attraction and its *raison d'être* is at the end of the street. The **Kuressaare Episcopal Castle** (Kuressaare piiskopiliinus) was built as the Bishop of Oesel-Wiek's foothold on Saaremaa, and first recorded in

Colourful traditional costume at an island festival.

BELOW: Kuressaare's 14th-century castle.

1384. It is the only entirely preserved medieval stone castle in all of the Baltic nations. Ringed by a large and beautiful public park, a moat and imposing bastions erected during the mid-17th century, the castle is in the unyielding, geometric, late-Gothic style, made of white-grey dolomite quarried in Saaremaa. Each corner is crowned by a tower with an orange turret, and at the heart of the castle is a tiny, symmetrical courtyard. From the courtyard, stone steps lead down to basement rooms and up to a narrow, vaulted cloister. The former refectory lies on the west, and to the north are the austere former living quarters of the bishop.

Ten elaborate wooden epitaphs from the 17th century represent coats of arms of noblemen in Saaremaa and their individual occupations. One has oars, another tools, a third stags and arrows. Climbing the towers is worthwhile but requires fortitude; the watchtower in the southeast corner of the convent building is connected by a drawbridge suspended 9 metres (30ft) above the ground, and the defence tower is honeycombed with stone stairways. Some of the castle's upper rooms house the **Saaremaa Museum** (May–Aug daily 10am–6pm, Sept–Apr Wed–Sun 11am–6pm; charge). This rich collection traces the inhabitants of Saaremaa from the 4th millennium BC and has a number of fascinating woodcarvings, including its pride and joy, the late 16th-century *Coronation of St Mary* attributed to Lübeck artist Henning van der Heide, and the oldest preserved wooden sculpture in Estonia: *Seated Madonna with the Infant* (1280–90). Other sections of the museum encompass the late-Tsarist and pre-World War II period, as well as the island's natural history.

Down to the beach

From the castle, it is a pleasant walk down to the small, newly built yacht harbour. Nearby is Kuressaare's popular public beach. More secluded bathing can be found just a few minutes south of the town at the Mandjala-Järve beach.

Other spots to visit in Kuressaare include the restored Kuursaal (Resort Club), a grand, ornate, wooden rec-

BELOW: Vilsandi
Lighthouse.

ation hall built for tourists in 1861. stands not far from the castle. At llimaa 7 is the **Aaviks' Memorial useum** (Aavikute majamuuseum; ed–Sun 11am–6pm; charge), a tiny, d-fashioned house that was once me to a renowned linguist, Johans Aavik (1880–1973), and his cousin osep Aavik (1899–1989), a musician d composer.

aaremaa island road trip

avelling to **Kihelkonna** in the west, d following the coast up to Leisi in e north, then back south to Kuresare will take you into **Vilsandi ational Park** (Vilsandi rahvuspark), hich encompasses Vilsandi and 150 her offshore islets. Many of Saareaa's interesting sites will be passed the way. First stop is the **Mihkli rm Museum ⑱** (Mihkli talumuuum; 15 Apr–30 Sept Wed–Sun 10am– m; charge) near the town of Viki. though small, this open-air museum ows exactly what a typical farm in estern Saaremaa is like. The main velling house (1834) stands with the her buildings in a circle enclosing a

yard and a little flower garden. Most of the roofs are covered with reed, and the walls are of dolomite or wood. Original objects from the farmstead include household equipment with the Mihkli family emblem.

Turning at Kihelkonna north towards **Mustjala**, you will first catch a glimpse of the pointed red bell-tower of the medieval Kihelkonna church and then the ancient, weathered-grey Pidula watermill. From here it is a short drive to the **Panga Scarp** (Panga pank). This steep limestone outcrop is one of the highest points on the island and one of the loveliest. The water below is almost olive green, but so clear you can easily make out the thousands of pebbles that line the sea floor. In the distance, the horizon stretches blue and endlessly, except for the tiny shadow of Hiiumaa island. In summer the sound of crickets fills the air.

Unsurprisingly, this very magical place has played a central role in island superstitions. In pre-Christian times, locals would throw one baby boy, born the winter before, off the cliff into the water every spring; this was an offering

The waters around the islands are rich in fish.

BELOW: a Kaali meteor crater.

to the sea god with the prayer that he send back a lot of fish. In later times, they threw a ram instead, and even up to the 1930s, there are records of barrels of the island's famous beer being poured over the cliff's edge to ensure a good catch. Island brides have continued the tradition of "scarp pitching" to this day: on the eve of their wedding they often write their maiden name on a piece of paper, put it into a bottle and throw it off the cliff.

Turning east takes you to **Leisi**, an attractive rural town, from where the road heads south and in a few miles reaches the **Angla Windmills** (Angla tuulikud). In the mid-19th century, there were about 800 windmills on Saaremaa, and the windmill has become the most recognised symbol of the island. Only a small proportion of the original windmills have survived, but at Angla five remain, sticking up suddenly on a slight swell amid windswept wheat fields.

BELOW RIGHT:
Kaarma church
sculptures.

Medieval churches

Nestled behind a moss-covered stone wall on a sloping lawn across from

fields of cattle 2km (1¼ miles) fro here is one of Saaremaa's greatest tre ures: the 14th-century **Karja chur** ⓳. Saaremaa is packed with some the earliest churches in the Baltics, b no other has such marvellous sto sculptures still intact. These sculptu tell a thousand tales *(see box below)*.

If you head south again, turni right at the Liiva-Putla fork, you w reach the hamlet of **Kaarma**, site another medieval church. Work beg on Kaarma church in the latter half the 13th century, but it was rearrang over subsequent centuries and is str ingly large. Its artefacts are more vari than those of Karja. The christeni stone, for example, dates from the 13 century, the wooden "Joseph" suppo ing the pulpit is from around 14. and the elaborate Renaissance p pit was finished in 1645. Restorati work has exposed fragments of ea mural painting. Other 13th- and 14 century churches in the area worth v iting include Valjala church and Pü church situated east of Kuressaare. T latter most clearly shows how the churches were built not just to be re

Stories on the Church Walls

A relief on the first left buttress upon entering Karja church (Karja kirik) depicts village life. A woman listens to another with a pig on her back, symbolising gossip, while the man beside her has a rose behind his ear, representing silence. This is on the northern and thus colder side of the church, the side where the women sat because they were considered to be stronger.

St Catherine of Alexandria, to whom the church is dedicated, is carved into the northern arch before the altar. This 14th-century beauty, the legend goes, was wooed by King Maxentius of Egypt who was already married. She refused him and, enraged, he had her arrested and torn to pieces. The sculpture shows her with Maxentius' wife on her left, clinging to her skirt, St Peter on her right and the evil king crushed beneath her feet. Directly opposite is St Nicholas, the protector of seamen, and on his left are three village girls who were too poor to marry until he became their benefactor.

Painted on the ceiling above the altar is a table of Christian and pagan marks: the Star of Bethlehem and the symbol of Unity, both drawn with endless lines; the three-legged symbol of the sun; the "leg" devil; and two pentagons, symbols of gloom, which locals point out were also symbols of the Soviet Union.

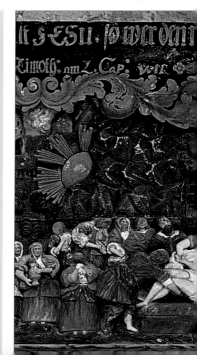

ous centres but also to serve as defen-
ve strongholds.

If you turn left at the Liiva-Putla
ork, you reach a much older land-
aark, the **Kaali meteoric craters ⍟**
Kaali meteoriidikraatrite väli). These
re not particularly beautiful – the
rgest one is referred to as Lake Kaali
nd looks like a big opaque green pud-
le – but it is remarkable to think that
ne bowl surrounding it was carved out
y part of a 1,000-ton meteor that hit
ne earth here nearly 3,000 years ago.
ight smaller craters, made from other
ips of the meteor, dot the woods sur-
ounding it. There is a large visitors'
entre and a guesthouse.

Iaasi fortress

nally, before leaving Saaremaa, a stop
the **Maasi Order castle ruins ⍟**
Maasi ordulinnuse varemed), 4km
½ miles) north of **Orissaare** on the
rissaare–Leisi road, rounds out the
ory of the island's medieval strug-
es. The Maasi fortress was in many
nses Kuressaare Castle's less fortu-
ate sister. Established by the Livo-
an Order in the 14th century, it was
meant to defend the island's eastern
side. Denmark took possession when it
purchased this part of Saaremaa in the
1560s, but more than once the fortress
was taken over by attacking Swedes
and used against the Danes. To prevent
a repeat of this tactic, King Frederik of
Denmark ordered it destroyed in 1576.
Today, some exterior walls are still visible, and the newly excavated vaults
have been restored to make it possible
for visitors to enter.

HIIUMAA ISLAND

For natural beauty, **Hiiumaa Island** is
perhaps more rewarding than Saaremaa. At 989 sq km (382 sq miles), it is
Estonia's second-largest island, but has
only 10,000 inhabitants, 3,600 of them
in the capital of Kärdla on the north
coast. There is virtually no settlement
in its heart, where there is a peat moor
and swamp, and almost all agriculture
focuses on the southern and western
edge. Some yet to be cultivated areas
in the south contain another natural
oddity, "wooded meadows", and the rest
of the island is overwhelmed by pines
and junipers. A road rings the island,

*Karja Katariina
church. The islands'
medieval churches
keep their doors open
for visitors in the
summer months. If
closed, a caretaker can
usually be found
nearby who will let
you in with a big
iron key.*

BELOW: the Angla
Windmills,
Saaremaa.

BELOW:
Kõrgessaare, one of Hiiumaa's stately manor houses.

conveniently passing its most interesting sights, but there are so few cars on it that inhabitants typically drive on either the left or right according to whim.

Fishing is the most important industry, although the coast is notoriously treacherous to approach because of the shallow waters of endless shoals and rocks. This means that you have to walk out quite a way over pebbles simply to get your stomach wet, but don't let this deter you from taking a swim in the clean, peaceful waters.

Historic Suuremõisa

The eastern harbour of **Heltermaa** has been slightly dug out, and it is here that the ferry arrives from the mainland, from **Rohuküla** by Haapsalu. Just inland is the historical hamlet of **Suuremõisa ㉒**. Hiiumaa once had around 25 stately manor houses, but most have either been destroyed or have irreparably deteriorated. The Suuremõisa manor is one exception. Built by a Swedish family called Stenbock in 1772, then bought by O.R.L. von Ungern-Sternberg – for decades Hiiumaa's richest and most powerful

landowner – this manor still has i main building, stable-master's hom and stables, outbuildings and cellar and expansive front and back lawn Under the trees there are graveston for the family's much-feared gua dogs. Inside the main building are rooms, some with original painted ce ings and ceramic fireplaces. A prima school and an agricultural school a housed here, but in summer the buil ing is open to tourists.

Just down the road is the attracti **Pühalepa Church**. Built of timber the mid-13th century, then replace with stone in 1770, its tall white be tower, topped by a hexagonal brow roof, has been extended three tim since then. Turned into a cellar by th Soviets, the church resumed servic on Christmas Eve 1990.

On its south side stands a rath squat white chapel containing th tomb of Ebba Margarethe Gräf Stenbock, Suuremõisa manor's fir owner. On its north side, strewn am alders, are a tumble of other old grav Around the northeast corner is a l set in the church wall; this is the sp

through which the priest used to hand out bread to the poor and needy. A few feet down the gravel road to the north, away from the main road, brings you to the **Contract Stones**, otherwise known as "Hiiumaa's Stonehenge". The origin of this large pile of boulders, which were evidently brought here by hand, is unclear. One popular theory is that before going out to sea local sailors would bring a heavy stone to this spot, and by doing so make an agreement with God to ensure a good voyage and a safe return.

Back up the coast in the main town of **Kärdla** is the Rannapaargu Café. To reach it, you must walk down Lubaahju Street past yet another Hiiumaa peculiarity, the giant swing. Found in villages all over the island, the swings are particularly busy on Midsummer's eve. A new holiday centre is another place for summer activity in Kärdla, offering horse riding, and a spot where visitors can catch trout and have them prepared on the spot. The **Hiiumaa Museum** (Mon–Fri 10am–5pm; charge) is housed in Kärdla's 19th-century Pikk maja (Long House).

Hill of Crosses

Outside town, 5 km (3 miles) west on the road to the **Kõpu Peninsula**, is a more sombre attraction, the **Hill of Crosses ㉓** (Ristimägi). Like many Estonian coastal areas, Hiiumaa was populated for centuries by a large group of Swedes, who, by a time-honoured arrangement with the Swedish Crown, were given a special status as freemen. In 1781 Stenbock, with the help of Russian Empress Catherine the Great, arranged for 1,000 of Hiiumaa's Swedes from the village of Reigi to be stripped of their land and rights, and forcibly resettled in Ukraine. Their last church service was held on this hill. According to legend, a local farmer marked the spot with a small, wooden cross. Later, a tradition was established that each new visitor would add his own cross made from sticks found on the ground. The site is now eerily covered with thousands of crosses.

Some of Hiiumaa's most interesting structures are the lighthouses that twinkle along the shore. The most remarkable is the **Kõpu Lighthouse ㉔** (Kõpu tuletorn; 1 May–15 Sept

Hiiumaa's Kõpu Lighthouse.

BELOW: a Hiiumaa guesthouse owner with smoked fish.

Map on page 96

At the end of the Saaretirp headland nothing remains but a needle point and a large heap of stones: if you find a pebble with a hole in it, make a wish and place it on the pile, and your wish may come true.

daily 10am–8pm; charge), halfway out along the thickly forested Kõpu Peninsula, on the windswept western wing of the island. This soaring four-cornered and red-crested white lighthouse looks like a cross between a space rocket and a pyramid. First lit in 1531, it is considered to be the oldest continuously operating lighthouse in the world.

KASSARI ISLAND

Understandably, many of Estonia's best-known artists and writers keep summer retreats on Hiiumaa; conductor Eri Klas, for example, has his on Kõpu. But the most popular spot for summer cottages is **Kassari** ㉕, just southwest of Heltermaa. Kassari is one of between 200 and 400 islands (depending on the water level) that cling to the coast of Hiiumaa. It curves in so close to the shore by the town of Käina that it has been incorporated into the larger island with two short bridges. The bay between them, Käinu Bay, is rich in sea mud that attracts birds, including golden eagles and other rare species. You may even see an eagle or two flying over

the road. These birds, in turn – along with the island breezes and the sea – are responsible for the richness of flora all over Hiiumaa.

In fact, the island has about 975 different species of plants, some of them, such as the orchids, also quite rare. Kassari, however, is richest in junipers whose berries and bark might be called the island staple. Its uses include the wood for butter knives that keep butter from turning rancid; the branches for sauna switches to perk up the kidneys; the berries for a vodka spice, a source of vitamin C; and for medicinal purposes. This scraggy dark bush has even been fashioned into furniture.

Junipers crowd the pebbly projection of **Saaretirp** with special determination. This mile-long promontory is a favourite place to picnic or ponder. The island's sheltered position makes the water warm, and beside it the apples crop early. The last owner of the former Kassari manor house, Baron Edvard Stackelberg, had an especially large orchard, though neither it nor his home still remains. But the small servants' house directly opposite where it stood is in good shape and houses a branch of the Hiiumaa Museum. The exhibition contains a huge light reflector from the 19th-century Tahkuna lighthouse, maps of island history and traditional fishing tools.

Ancient chapels

Down one more pebble-laden lane is the **Kassari chapel**, the only stone chapel surviving in Estonia with a roof of thatched reed. Carefully restored in 1990, it is illuminated by a simple central candelabra and candles on each blue-coloured pew.

One final church to note back on Hiiumaa island, just inland from Kassari, is the **Käina church** (Käina kirik), built between 1492 and 15... Although it was heavily bombed during World War II, it is still a very moving spot. The wind rushes through the limestone shell and over the old tombs that are set directly into its floor.

BELOW: island cottage. **RIGHT:** Kassari chapel.

EAST OF TALLINN

Two of Estonia's important wildlife regions lie to the east of the capital: Lahemaa National Park and Lake Peipsi, the fifth-largest lake in Europe. Beyond them rises industrial Narva

East from Tallinn on the E20, the Narva Highway, the capital's industrial sprawl gives way to a scene more typical of the country – vast, flat stretches of road flanked on both sides by forests and ponds. About an hour's drive from the capital, this road becomes the southern border of **Lahemaa National Park** (Lahemaa rahvuspark), a truly peaceful and intriguing area of the country close enough to Tallinn to make it a practical day trip. More than 75 percent of the 72,500-hectare (180,000-acre) park is woodland, and the population is fewer than 20 per square kilometre. There are remains of ancient settlements, freshwater lakes, wetlands, a few farms, fishing villages and four manor houses. Sheltered bays dip between craggy promontories that jut into the Gulf of Finland. It is an important wildlife area with deer, elk and bear, and during the migration season, for special species such as the black stork. Plant life abounds, and among the 650 documented varieties is the rare arctic bramble.

Loksa ㉖ and **Võsu** ㉗ are the park's two main towns. They are the best stopping points for food shops and cash machines, though neither are of intrinsic interest. Loksa is much the larger, with a cargo port, and a mainly Russian population. It is easy to make

trips around the park from either town, but one can just as easily use the E20 itself as a starting point.

Palmse Manor

The turn-off at **Viitna** leads north, to Lahemaa's most famous landmark, the striking **Palmse Manor** ㉘ (Palmse mõis; May–Sept daily 10am–7pm, Oct–Apr daily 10am–4pm; charge). The beautiful house and grounds are a testament of 18th-century aristocracy, but this land's history goes back much further. In 1286, a group of nuns from

LEFT: the ballroom at Palmse Manor. **RIGHT:** the Manor dates from the 18th century.

the Cistercian Order of St Michael in Tallinn were given the land by the King of Denmark. The pond they built here for their fish farm is still in use. In 1673, the Von der Pahlen family, Baltic-German nobles, bought the estate, and in 1730 built the manor house. It was rebuilt in 1782, and was their home until Estonia's first independence in 1918, when the property was nationalised.

After World War II, the manor served as a Soviet Pioneer camp and fell into disrepair. Renovation lasted between 1972 and 1985, and today the estate is a perfect period piece, filled with Empire furniture. Visitors are welcome to stroll the grounds, where they'll find a peaceful swan pond, landscaped gardens and a café.

During the warmer months (May–Oct), one of the outbuildings flanking the manor's front courtyard displays an altogether different kind of history – it houses a coach and car museum exhibiting antique bicycles and buggies, early 20th-century European roadsters and an enormous Zil-111 limousine used by Nikita Khrushchev. Across

the courtyard is the **Lahemaa Visitor Centre** (15 May–15 Sept daily 9am–7pm, 15 Apr–14 May and 16 Sept–15 Oct daily 9am–6pm, 16 Oct–14 Apr Mon–Fri 9am–5pm). Here you'll find information in English on the park's sights and nature walks, and more importantly, detailed maps – a necessity in this area of small, confusingly marked roads.

A turn from Palmse to the northwest leads to another impressive German estate, **Sagadi Manor** (May–Sept daily 10am–6pm; charge). It was built in 1749 and renovated at the end of that century in a classical style. Like Palmse Manor, it has been decorated to reflect 18th-century elegance. One of the renovated outbuildings is a hotel and restaurant, another is a museum of forestry. A stroll behind the house leads to a pond and swathes of lawn where interesting and often bizarre modern wooden sculptures are on display.

Seaside Altja

Most of Lahemaa's other attractions can be found to the north, in the form of several tiny seaside hamlets that do

the area's four rocky peninsulas. One of these gems is **Altja** ㉙, a wonderful example of a timeless Estonian fishing village. The old, thatched-roofed wooden buildings were restored in the 1970s, and the village has since become a popular local tourist spot. You'll find a 19th-century inn, a traditional village swing and several paths along the coast. The headland is dotted with attractive sheds for storing fishing gear.

Another coastal village, **Käsmu** ㉚, is much less typical. This is called "captains' village" because of the lavish houses that sea captains built here, giving it a decidedly affluent look. A drive through the village reveals some of the most unusual and beautiful residential property in Estonia. There is a slightly dark side to all this beauty, however. The village's original economic prosperity is linked to its residents' salt-smuggling activities in the 19th century. In the 1920s, when Finland imposed the prohibition of alcohol, the economic focus here shifted to alcohol-smuggling. Käsmu is now also known for its **Maritime Museum** (free), housed in what was a school of

navigation in the late 19th and early 20th centuries. The musty and somewhat jumbled museum displays a collection of sailing artefacts, as well as works by local artists and a few Saku beer bottles from a century ago.

Viinistu Art Museum

Like Käsmu, the tiny village of **Viinistu** ㉛, north of Loksa, also made a good share of money from smuggling alcohol, but what puts it on the map nowadays is something else entirely – art. This village of just 150 is home to the **Viinistu Art Museum** (Viinistu kunstimuuseum; 15 June–Aug daily 11am–6pm, Sept–14 June Wed–Sun 11am–6pm; charge), which has the largest private art collection in the country, with between 200 and 300 19th- and 20th-century Estonian paintings on display, easily rivalling the state-owned museums in Tallinn.

The reason the collection is here is that former resident Jaan Manitski fled as a child with his family to Sweden during World War II. After making his fortune as financial adviser to the famous pop group ABBA, he returned

Most villages in Estonia once had wooden swings like the one in Altja. They were social gathering places for young people.

BELOW: restored wooden buildings, Altja.

Viinistu Art Museum, founded by the former manager of the pop group ABBA.

to Viinistu, eventually converting the town's Soviet-era fish collective into this art and cultural centre. The village has a modern guesthouse and restaurant, as well as a respectable, old-fashioned tavern. The road that leads through the village ends in a small trail that follows its rocky coastline. Offshore, **Mohni island**, an uninhabited nature reserve, is visible.

On the western side of the park another manor, **Kolga mõis** ㉜, remains unrestored due to a lack of funds. The graceful 18th-century building is a cliché of a crumbling pile, with falling plaster, peeling wallpaper and a cracked exterior. Until recently a small hotel and restaurant had been operating on the premises, but their future remains unclear. Rejoining the E20, one can either head back west to the modernity of Tallinn, or turn east, towards the Russian border and what was Estonia's heavy industrial zone during Soviet times.

Industrial Estonia

BELOW: Rakvere Castle.

If Estonia were a jigsaw puzzle, the northeast corner would be the one piece that didn't fit. Ida-Viru County, which straddles the main transport routes leading to Narva at the Russian border, is the heavily industrialised region of Estonia. It is rich in energy-producing oil shale and supplies more than 90 percent of the nation's electricity. During the Soviet period, thousands of ethnic Russians were settled in the region to work its plants and mines, and small villages suddenly became factory towns filled with rows and rows of apartment blocks. When Soviet industry collapsed, this area was hardest hit. Most jobs here disappeared, leaving decaying buildings, environmental hazards and a population of mainly ethnic Russians whose role in the newly independent Estonia was far from clear.

So many years later, the situation has been slow to improve. The area's economy still lags far behind that of the rest of the nation, and the eyesores of the last century – dilapidated buildings and enormous hills of mining waste – line the roads. For this reason Estonians from other areas have written off the northeast as not worth visit-

ing. But it is for this same reason that many foreigners find it fascinating. It offers the chance to see a side of Estonia ignored by most guidebooks, and to glimpse the Soviet past without a Russian visa. It also has its own medieval castles, natural beauty and some sights that aren't found anywhere else in Estonia.

Castles of the north

The E20 leads into the area from the direction of Tallinn. Before reaching the heart of Ida-Viru County, it passes some points worth mentioning. One of these is **Rakvere** ㉝, the country's seventh-largest city, located at the midpoint between Tallinn and Narva. For Estonians, the name Rakvere is always associated with the town's meat-processing plant, but its main attraction for tourists is **Rakvere Castle** (Rakvere linnus; May–Sept daily 11am–7pm; charge).

The castle was built in 1253 on the site of a wooden one that was destroyed during the Livonian Wars. For better or worse, it is the most commercially developed of Estonia's castles. It not only has the obligatory historical displays in its interior, but also features such crowd-pleasing amenities as a tavern, wine cellar and a medieval torture and horror chamber. In summer, its front courtyard has a number of smithies, a petting zoo, archery range and other activities. Other sights in Rakvere include the ruins of a Franciscan monastery dating from 1515 and several charming streets of late 19th-century buildings.

The much smaller castle at **Purtse** ㉞ (May–Sept Tue–Sun 10am–6pm) is another medieval sight worth seeing. It easily missed, as it stands several hundred metres away from the highway in the middle of several other buildings. The red-roofed edifice dates from 1533, the Swedish period, when Purtse was a free port. Although the castle was partially destroyed during the Great Northern War (1700–21), it was inhabited until 1938, and fell into disrepair.

Now restored, it serves as a concert hall and exhibition centre.

Hands-on at Kohtla mine

Kohtla-Järve ㉟, the heart of Estonia's mining region, is further east. Though by population it is Estonia's fourth-largest city, it has a decidedly sleepy, residential feel, and other than a large monument to miners, it has virtually no points of interest.

The area's real gem, by far one of Estonia's most fascinating museums, lies instead 10km (6 miles) south of here in the village of **Kohtla-Nõmme**. The short drive past forlorn, abandoned houses and emaciated cockerels leads to the **Kohtla Mine Park Museum** (Kohtla kaevanduspark-muuseum; Mon–Fri 10am–5pm, Sat–Sun 11am–3pm; charge). Opened in 1937, the Kohtla mine was one of a dozen shale mines that operated in Ida-Viru County during Soviet times, and grew to encompass around 60km (37 miles) of tunnels. After it closed in 2001, about 1.5km (1 mile) of it was turned into this hands-on "underground museum". Visitors are given

A sign shows the way to the wine cellar at Rakvere Castle.

BELOW: this statue, built to mark Rakvere's 700th anniversary, recalls the fact that the town was once known as Tarvaspää – literally "Bull's Head".

Elk alert.

hard hats, electric lamps and overalls before descending into the tunnels. The tour guides, all former mine workers, demonstrate the gigantic digging and clearing machines, give children rides on the tiny train that once carried miners to their stations, and let guests put a few holes in the rock with a large mining drill. The museum has become a popular attraction, so pre-booking by phone is required (tel: 3 324 017).

Commercial Jõhvi

The road reconnects with the E20 at **Jõhvi ㊱**, the administrative centre of Ida-Viru County. Many Estonians wryly refer to this town of 12,000 as "the real border of Estonia", since it is the last where the majority are Estonian-speakers, and all towns to the east of it have a decidedly more Russian feel. Apart from Narva, Jõhvi certainly has more commercial activity than anywhere else in the county, but it also has its historic sites, such as the charming green-topped **Orthodox Church of the Epiphany** (Issanda Ristimise kirik). It was built in 1895, and Alexy II, Patriarch of Moscow and all of Russia from 1990 to 2008, was the rector here in the 1950s.

Jõhvi's more impressive church however, is St Michael's (Mihkli kirik in the centre of town. Built in 1364, i served as a church and fortress unti it was destroyed in the Livonian War in the 16th century. Its present form comes from a 1728–32 reconstruction Inside is the **Jõhvi Fortified Church Museum** (Jõhvi kindluskiriku muu seum; Tue–Sat 11am–4pm; charge which outlines the church's histor and displays archaeological finds from the location. The 30-minute CD tour i available in English.

More than anything, Jõhvi is regional hub. From here, roads lea in several directions and into very di ferent types of territory. To the nort lies some truly spectacular scener The coastline from **Toila** to **Ontik** and **Saka** is made up of dramatic hig cliffs, rising up to 56 metres (184ft) ou of the sea. This natural monument a symbol of Estonia, and is referred t as the **North Estonian Klint**. It is th edge of the vast limestone plateau o which this region sits. The waterfall i

BELOW: Valaste waterfall.

laste is Estonia's highest at 26 metres
5ft), but is somewhat artificial in that
was created by diverted water.

Toila is home to the picturesque **Oru
irk**. The large regional park contains
ore than 200 different plants, as well
nature walks and a pebble beach.
1e land is on the former property
a German baron who had a manor
use built here in 1899. Estonia's first
esident used the house as a holiday
treat, but it was destroyed in 1943.
1e park remains, and many of the
iths pass through manicured gardens
id statuary.

talinist Sillamäe

ist from Jõhvi is **Sillamäe 37**, an
triguing, Soviet-era relic that should
t be passed up. The entire town is
perfect museum piece of Stalinist-
yle architecture. Though there was
village here as far back as 1502, Sil-
mäe really came into being during
e Soviet period, when it was a centre
r mining and processing uranium.
1e town, which retains its look of a
andiose, planned city from the early
50s, was a secret military area, popu-

lated exclusively by Russians and not
marked on local maps.

Its main street, Kesk, cuts through
the small town centre, where nicely
trimmed gardens, a town hall and a
community centre are accented with
an unmistakably Socialist-Realist statue
of a bare-chested man holding an atom
aloft. A grand formation of steps leads
to the park-like Mere Avenue, and then
towards the seaside promenades. A
block west, at Majakovski 18a, is the **Sillamäe Museum** (May–Sept Mon–Fri
10am–6pm, Oct–Apr Tue–Sat 10am–
6pm; charge) where, among the various minerals and Soviet banners on
display, is a recreated apartment from
the 1950s.

On the border

The E20 reaches the Russian border
at **Narva 38**. With just under 66,000
inhabitants, it is Estonia's third-largest
city, and its least Estonian. Nearly 96
percent of its inhabitants are Russian-
speakers. Here more than anywhere in
Estonia, questions of citizenship and of
the role of minorities in the Estonian
republic become acute. Many residents

*In Soviet times
workers digging
radioactive materials
out of Sillamäe's
mines were allowed
to retire in their 40s,
given the hazardous
nature of their work.
Most, however, didn't
live more than five
years beyond
retirement.*

BELOW: Narva
Castle.

Language Politics

Given Narva's 95 percent ethnic Russian population, one might assume that
theirs is the only language to be heard in
the city. The truth, however, isn't so black
and white. While attempts to enforce the
use of Estonian in instances where it's
legally required have certainly met with
some resistance here, as have reforms
forcing Russian high schools to teach
mainly in Estonian, many in the younger
generation have fully embraced the state
language.

For some it's a matter of principle, for
others, no doubt, more a practicality –
certainly being bilingual is an advantage
in today's job market. In any case, a
visitor to Narva shouldn't be surprised
when a local, after finishing a conversation
in Russian, turns to address them in
perfect Estonian.

*On the short road
from Narva to
Narva-Jõesuu stands
a restored T-34 tank,
which supposedly
marks the place
where Soviet forces
broke through
German lines in
1944.*

feel that they are neither part of Estonia nor Russia, living in a kind of no-man's land.

Indeed, the border itself is the city's most striking feature. **Ivangorod Castle** and **Narva Castle** stand facing one another across the River Narva like sentries guarding their respective lands. The **"Friendship Bridge"** stretches across the river between them, with EU flags on one side and Russian flags on the other. Ignoring geopolitical concerns, locals casually stroll across to the Russian side for cheaper grocery shopping. Western visitors wishing to follow them will need a Russian visa, something that takes several days and considerable expense to procure.

The city was first mentioned in 1240 when it was listed in census records compiled by the Danes, who built Fort Narva. They sold the castle, along with the rest of northern Estonia, to the Teutonic Order in 1346. In 1492, the year the Russians finally repelled the Mongols, Tsar Ivan III built a fort at Ivangorod on "his" side of the river.

Narva flourished in the Swedish period, taking over Tallinn's position as

the primary trading port between Russia and the rest of Europe. It continued to flourish under tsarist rule as well. By the late 19th century Narva was an industrial giant and a major seaport. Its largest company, Kreenholm Textile Manufacturing, employed more than 10,000 people in its factories: Estonia's first strike was organised here in 1872.

During the first republic Narva remained part of Estonia. The city was affected by economic depression during the 1920s and 1930s, and suffered terribly during World War II. On 17 August 1941 the Germans entered Narva and when, in July 1944, they were finally driven out, 98 percent of the city had been destroyed. After the war, the Russians set about rebuilding the town. Two electric plants that were subsequently constructed now produce most of Estonia's energy.

Narva's bastion

Almost nothing remains of Narva's Old Town, which is filled with block apartments. The **Town Hall**, built by the Swedes, was one of the few buildings that survived the war, but is now in

rious state of neglect. Narva Castle, to
e right of the bridge, is the city's only
al tourist attraction. Narva's statue of
nin stands in the grounds of the cas-
e; it is hidden on the left-hand side
the compound, symbolically facing
st across the river towards Russia.
ie walls around the fort are walkable,
d photographers should note that
the late afternoon the southwest
rner bastion offers superb views
both forts. Inside its multi-storey
wer, the **Narva Museum** (Wed–Sun
am–6pm; charge) displays artefacts
m the town's history, as well as
hibitions on Estonian history and
odern art. Of particular interest are
e photos of Narva's Old Town taken
fore the war.

The 15km (9-mile) drive north along
e river leads to **Narva-Jõesuu**, a
pular beach resort town in the 19th
ntury. It is trying, with very limited
ccess, to recapture some of its past
ory, despite intrusive factory smoke-
icks and other post-Soviet debris.
ie town is still filled with early 20th-
ntury gingerbread houses, and one
the most colourful is just off Ranna

Street. The Orthodox Church, created
from rough-hewn logs, is a gem. Two
spa resorts operate here in summer.

South to Tartu

Backtracking to Jõhvi, the final spoke
of the Ida-Viru County hub leads south,
through an area where nature and spir-
ituality replace the noise of human
development. Highway 3 provides
the quickest access to Tartu 132km
(82 miles) away, but a small detour
on Highway 33 leads to **Kuremäe** 39,
home of the striking Orthodox **Convent of Pühtitsa** (Kuremäe jumalaema
uinumise nunnaklooster; daily 10am–
6pm; charge), the only Eastern Orthodox nunnery in the Baltic States.

Approaching Kuremäe, the green
domes of the Pühtitsa Cathedral
beckon through a forest of oak and
pine. Pühtitsa is Estonian for "holy
place", and indeed the convent is built
on a site that has been sacred since the
16th century, when a peasant saw a
vision of the Virgin Mary on the top
of a hill. An icon was found beneath
an ancient oak tree near the same spot,
and the icon of the Assumption of the

Orthodox priest, Kuremäe

BELOW: outside the communal dining hall, Kuremäe nunnery.

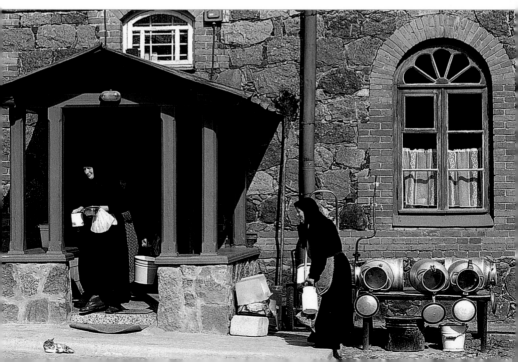

Map on
page 96

Mother of God is still the convent's most prized possession, surrounded by precious gems and mounted on a pillar to the right of the cathedral altar.

The first nun was sent to Pühtitsa in 1888 to establish the convent, and the complex of buildings, circled by a high granite wall, was designed by Mikail Preobrazhensky, a professor at the St Petersburg Academy of Arts. The five-domed, three-aisle Cathedral of the Assumption, which can accommodate up to 1,200 worshippers, was finished in 1910. There are five other churches in the complex, including a small one just outside the main walls, which is used for funeral services. Today there are more than 100 nuns in residence. Some 24 hectares (60 acres) of the 75-hectare (187-acre) property are farmed. Cash is raised from the sale of icons and other religious items made by the nuns, who also give tours from 9am to 4pm daily for a fee. At other times, visitors are welcome to explore on their own.

From Kuremäe either take a road that links up with Highway 3 at **Jõuga** to continue south, or extend the detour to historic **Vasknarva** ⓐ, at the Russian border. The town was founded the 12th century as a way-station the trade route linking the principalities of Novorod and Pskov with Tar and Tallinn. All that remains of Livonian fort are two broken walls.

Lake Peipsi

Either route leads to the shore of **Lal Peipsi** (Peipsi järv), where there are fests of tall conifers and white beach of bleached oyster shells. There a occasional fishing villages strung alor the water's edge, their attractive cla board houses painted a variety of ce ours, each fronted by banks of vibra flowers and backed by greenhous which are used to extend the sho growing season.

Mustvee ⓐ, 65km (40 miles) nor of Tartu, is Lake Peipsi's largest tow and the centre of Estonia's commu nity of Old Believers. These are Ru sians who fled to Estonia in the 17 century to avoid religious persecutic *(see page 44)*, and they have since dev oped their own distinct culture ar traditions. There are approximate 15,000 Old Believers in Estonia tod. most of them living here along th shore of lake.

The town itself has two church and several incongruous mode apartment blocks. Just south of Mu tvee, the 7km (4-mile) village stre that connects **Kükita**, **Raja**, **Tihe** and **Kasepää** is perhaps more indic tive of the Old Believer culture. It lined with two-storey houses, mc with small towers or balconies. Eve one of these houses should traditio ally have an icon inside and a spade the yard. The Old Believers Museu in **Kolkja** will provide more insig into the history and practices of th group, but visits must be pre-arrange by someone who speaks Russian Estonian (tel: 53 922 444).

From Raja, the highway to Tar leads away from the lake and the real of Russian village life, and back in 21st-century Estonia.

LATVIA

Sandwiched between the two other countries,
Latvia has the largest capital city, superb Art
Nouveau architecture and a great
recreational national park

The main highway of the Baltics is the 1,030-km (640-mile) River Daugava, which starts in Russia and arrives, via Belarus, in the south of Latvia near Daugavpils. German crusaders arrived near the river's estuary at a place they called Rīga, and made it their base for the conquest of the Baltic peoples and the expansion of Hansa trade.

Today, Rīga is the most exciting city in the Baltics. It is rich with the architecture of the medieval merchants, who built and funded gabled homes and storehouses. In the expanded late 19th- and early 20th-century city there are exquisite Art Nouveau buildings, many designed by Mikhail Eisenstein, father of the filmmaker Sergei Eisenstein, who was born here. Nearly a million of the country's 2.3 million population live in Rīga, and there is no other city in the country approaching its size. It also has the most exciting market in the Baltics and one of the most popular seaside resorts at nearby Jūrmala.

Second to the Daugava is the River Gauja, which is the centre of a fine national park north of Rīga. To the east are the more remote blue lakelands of Latgale, a Catholic stronghold and place of pilgrimage where you can find excellent local pottery. To the west is Kurzeme, the former

domaine of the Duchy of Courland, where you can explore the well-preserved medieval towns of Liepāja and Ventspils on the Baltic coast and, inland, Kuldīga. To the south is Zemgale, home to the nation's most stunning Baroque treasure, the Rastrelli-designed palace at Rundāle.

The soul of Latvia and the Latvians is not in buildings but in the countryside among its magic oaks and ancient hill forts. People are happiest spending a weekend on the family farmstead tending vegetable gardens, singing songs and drinking beer by a bonfire or just relaxing in a steamy sauna. In a country with countless rivers and lakes and almost 500km (300 miles) of pristine beaches, it is not difficult to imagine why Latvians prefer nature to urban living. ❏

PRECEDING PAGES: forest at Slītere National Park; midsummer bike ride.
LEFT: folk dancers in the Old Town of Rīga. **TOP:** strudels in a Ventspils café.
ABOVE LEFT: a white stork. **ABOVE RIGHT:** art nouveau detail, Rīga.

Latvia

0   20 km
0   20 miles

N

Stockholm
Karala   Saaremaa   Kuressaare
Salme
Abruka
Sörve
poolsan
Sääre

Kihnu väin   Pootsi
Manila

Kihnu   Hääde

Kura kurk
Irbes Šaurums
Ruhnu

BALTIJAS JŪRA
(BALTIC SEA)

Aina

44 Salacgrīv

Nynashamm,
Karlshamn

Rostok

Lübeck,
Travemunde

Kolka **16**
Mazirbe
17
Slītere
nacionālais
parks

Gipka
Roja
15
Dundaga
Kaltane

Staldzene
Ande

Irbene

Nogale   Upesgrīva

Rīgas Jūras Līcis
(Gulf of Riga)

T
Du

Ventspils **18**
Pope
Leči
V e n t s p i l s
Ugāle **12**
Piltene
10
Zlēkas
11
Usma-
sz.
Užava
Venta

Valdemārpils
Mērsrags

Talsi   **14**
Igene   Bērzciems
Engure   Abragciems
Lauciene   Engure
Engure
dabas
parks

43 Saulk

T a l s u
Uģma
Stende
 Renda
Abava
Sabile **9**
Kandava

A10

Milzkalne
Ragaciems   *Vecaki*
Lapmežciems
Jūrmala   Berģi
Rīga
A10   Rum
Babīte ✈ **1**

Jūrkalne
Edole
Alsunga
Kuldīga **8**
Kabile
Pūces
Zemīte
Zante

Jaunmoku
pils
34
Tukums
33

Kuldīgas

Pāvilosta

Durbe

Liepājas
Aizpute
13
Skrunda
A9
Durbe
Druva
Broceni
35 Jaunpils
Saldus
Dobele

T u k u m a
Kalnciems
Olaine

Baloži
Ķekava

A7
Brankas
Āne
Līvbērzes
36 **Jelgava**
Jelgavas
Iecava

L   **A**   **T**

Liepāja
19
Grobiņa
Dubeni

S a l d u s
D o b e l e s
Auce
Bēne
Tērvete

Nakotne
E77   A8   Mežotne

B a u s

Embūte
Priekule
Vaiņode   Pikeliai
Ezere
Naujojo
Akmenė
Žagarė

Eleja
37
Rundāle   Bau

A12

Liepāja
Dunika
Nīca
Barta
Skuodas
Mosēdis
Seda
Ylakiai
Mažeikiai
Viekšniai
Venta
Venta

Papes
dabas parks
Rucava

Pampāļi

Joniškis

Žeimelis
Vaškai
Linkuva   Pasva

Pakruojis
Joniškelis
Pumpēnai
Smilgiai

Šeduva

L   **I**   **T**
Panev

A9

Baisogala

Krekenava

Around Rīga

0   5 km
0   5 miles

Rīgas Jūras
Līcis

Daugava
Kalngale
L.
Baltezers
Baltezers
Gauja
A 2
E 77

J ū r m a l a
Lapmežciems
Bigauņciems
Vaivari   Asari
Bulduri
Dzintari
Pumpuri   Majori
Dubulti
6

Mežaparks
Brāļu kapi
(Cemetery of Heroes) ★
Ķīšezers
Rīgas kinostudija
(Film Studios)
4
Rīgas motormuzejs
(Motor Museum)
Brīvdabas muzejs
(Open-Air
Ethnographic
Museum)
3

2

Kēmeri
Kēmeri
7
nacionālais
parks
Sloka
Spunciems
Celmi

Melluži
Babītes ezers
Skulte ✈
A 10
A 9
Mārupe
Jaunmārupe
Rasas

Rīga

Ūlbroka   A 4
Rumbula
Saurieši
Plavniekkalns
5 Salaspils

Tīreli
Tiraine   A 7
Gaismas
Kekava
E 77
A 5
A 6
Baloži
Daugava

Nevēžis
Kēd

Krakēs

Šeduva

THE MAKING OF LATVIA

The Baltic States' first woman president was elected in a
country shaped by Hansa traders, Russian maritime
ambition and warring neighbours

When Latvian independence was self-proclaimed in 1918, the country had to be assembled like a jigsaw puzzle out of territory inhabited by Lettish-speakers. This amounted to the southern half of what had previously been Livonia together with Latgale and the Duchy of Courland.

To complicate matters, the city of Rīga, Latvia's capital, had hitherto been for all practical purposes an independent city-state with an overwhelmingly foreign population. It was a German city from the day the crusaders landed, and it had remained a predominantly German city of Hanse merchants through all the vagaries of Polish, Swedish and Russian rule. The Latvians managed to restore themselves to a majority

Between the World Wars, Latvians comprised 75 percent of the population, but under Soviet annexation the combined effect of mass deportations and Russian immigration reduced the Latvian majority to 52 percent by 1989.

between World Wars I and II, but independence was then snuffed out by Soviet annexation.

Against the backdrop of massive impending change in eastern Europe and the Soviet Union, Latvians knew they were in a private race against time. It had been the Kremlin's intention all along to obliterate the 1918 frontiers so that Latvia, like Estonia and Lithuania,

LEFT: Rīga port by an unknown artist, from the second half of the 17th century.

RIGHT: figure from the banner of the first all-Latvian song festival, held in 1873.

was in effect an unbroken extension of Russia itself. The struggle which ensued was a replay of events leading up to World War I, the reincarnation of the land of the Latvians.

Crusaders' arrival

Curious events had led to the arrival of the German crusaders in 1200. Almost 1,000 years after Christianity had been adopted as the official religion in Armenia and then Rome, it had still not reached the eastern shores of the Baltic, and there was rather a rush among the Pope and various Christian princes to make up for lost time. To this end, a number of missionary monks were dispatched. Meinhard of Bremen established a colony at Ikšķile, 25km (15 miles) upstream from present-day Rīga in 1180 and persuaded Latvians to be baptised in the river in such numbers that he was made a bishop. The test came when he informed his converts that the price of salvation was the payment of a tithe. They not only abandoned the faith en masse but put the bishop in fear of his life. He implored Pope Clement III to send help, but died before any was forthcoming. His successor, Bishop Bertold, called for a holy crusade in the Baltics, but met his end on the tip of a pagan spear.

The Pope had other problems. The crusade in the Holy Land had gone disastrously wrong

and large numbers of crusaders, expelled from their strongholds, were homeless. Led by Bishop Albert (Albrecht von Buxhoevden), they were dispatched to the Daugava where they went about their business with Teutonic efficiency. "All the places and roads were red with blood," wrote a chronicler of the Knights of the Sword.

Almost at once, Rīga had a defensive wall, a fortress and at least one church. By 1211, Bishop Albert was ready to start building a cathedral. Word was sent to the Pope that the Daugava mission had been accomplished and that a contingent of knights was being sent north – to Estonia – where the Danes were experiencing similar difficulties with truculent pagans.

The Knights of the Sword were in due course amalgamated with other orders; these came to be known collectively as the Teutonic Order. Having discharged their divine duties, they tackled the secular task of creating a city-state for themselves with immense zeal. They imported fellow Germans not merely to build the city and port but also to organise the region's agriculture. The Latvians were excluded from the process except as labourers.

Looking to Lithuania

The military power of the Teutonic Order was eclipsed in the 15th century, but by then the German economic and landowning oligarchy was thoroughly entrenched in Latvia. It was safe as long as Russia was kept out of contention by the Mongol Empire. With the demise of the latter, however, an alarming threat materialised in the person of Ivan the Terrible. The only recourse was to seek the protection of Poland-Lithuania, and there was a price to be paid. Lutheranism had made inroads in Latvia under the German influence and Poland was uncompromisingly Catholic. The Jesuits were to be given a licence to bring Latvians back into the fold.

The way the Jesuits went about their task revived memories of the Teutonic Order, and this was coupled with a rigid Polish feudal order that was harder on the peasants than anything previously experienced. The country was sharply divided on the desirability of Polish protection. Rīga profited enormously by being elevated to the role of Poland's principal port, so the merchants had no reason to complain.

The landed gentry and the peasants, however, were paying the price, and they became

THE HANSA CONNECTION

Rīga's wealth in the late Middle Ages was in part due to its joining, in 1282, the Hanseatic League, Europe's first free-trade organisation. The league was started by German merchants' societies *(Hanse)* to protect the herring trade in Lübeck and its vital salt suppliers in Hamburg. The alliance soon developed into a powerful one of more than 150 port-cities that came to control the shipping of fish, flax, fur, grain, honey and timber from Russia and the Baltics, and cloth and other goods manufactured by Flemish and English guilds. Rīga had exclusive rights to transport goods along the Daugava, and Livonia had its own Hanseatic diet or parliament.

increasingly desperate for protection against the protectors. Protestant Sweden seemed the most likely candidate. The resulting Swedish-Polish war saw the Swedes repulsed, but Latvia was left a wreck.

Gustavus Adolphus tried to topple the ruling order again 20 years later, and this time a Poland much weakened by events elsewhere

> The Swedish–Polish War was followed by the bitter winter of 1601 in which 40,000 Latvian peasants died from cold and hunger.

A duke's empire

Though Protestant, the Kettlers had been friends of the English Stuart kings and Jacob (James) had been named after his godfather, James I. He had been a great shipbuilder, and at Ventspils he built an impressive navy, turning out 24 men-of-war for France and 62 for Britain. With unbounded ambition he acquired territory for the duchy in the Gambia and Tobago.

The duchy brought a degree of stability to the south of the country. In the north there had been few tears when the Jesuits were sent packing by the Swedes. Historians consider this period of Scandinavian rule, which brought

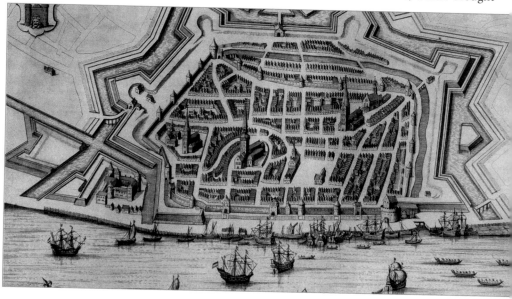

succumbed. The Swedes rebuilt Rīga Castle, added barracks outside the Swedish Gate and built castles on the River Daugava. Poland remained in charge of Latgale in the east and, in the south and west, the Duchy of Courland.

In 1561 this small slice of Latvia had been awarded to Gotthard Kettler, the last Grand Master of the Teutonic Order, who, fearful of Russian incursions on his land in the north, had submitted to Poland, and had been granted a degree of independence. Its importance grew under Duke Jacob, who became a prince of the Holy Roman Empire.

LEFT: a knight of the Livonian Order.
ABOVE: copperplate engraving of Rīga, 1638.

with it unprecedented construction of schools and hospitals, the implementation of a code of laws and the translation and publication of the Bible in Latvian, a golden age. The barons, however, were horrified when their estates were expropriated and given to the Swedish aristocracy. Hoping to be third time lucky, they looked again for a more sympathetic protector: their choice this time was Russia.

The Great Northern War

The Great Northern War of Sweden versus Russia, which began in 1699, was a titanic struggle that swept across the entire breadth of Europe. In and around Latvia, the Swedish Crown sought to finance the war by taking 80 percent of the estates, dispossessing both the Swedish barons, who had only just been given them, as well as the remaining Germans. These lands were squeezed for all they were worth and reached the point where they were providing the Swedish Crown with more revenue than all other sources put together.

Peter the Great's ally Augustus II, the odious Elector of Saxony, launched an invasion of Livonia in 1700 that got as far as Rīga before it was halted. Peter the Great was called on for help, but his forces were tied down at Narva in Estonia. In the event, the Russians were defeated at Narva and the victorious Charles turned his attention

by a Protestant pastor in Latvia before marrying a Swedish army officer. The marriage had failed and Martha was pursuing other interests among the Russian nobility.

Menshikov loyally relinquished the lovely Martha and she became Peter's mistress. On embracing the Orthodox faith, she changed her name to Catherine and after eight years of companionship he married her. Peter changed the law to allow him personally to crown her Empress in 1724. On Peter's death, Catherine was proclaimed empress in her own right. The accession to the Russian throne of a Latvian peasant was all the more extraordinary because

to Augustus. The Elector of Saxony was in no position to resist, and he surrendered.

Servant girl becomes empress

Sweden was not destined to hold on to Latvia or its neighbours for much longer. Peter the Great's ultimate victory in his duel with Charles XII opened the way to realising his dream of Russian control of the eastern Baltic. By then he had another, purely personal, interest in the region. Some years earlier, he had been struck by a woman called Martha who had arrived at court on the arm of first one and then another of his ministers, the second being Prince Menshikov. She was a servant, the daughter of a Lithuanian peasant, who had been employed

there was practically no social or economic mobility in Latvia: ethnic Latvians weren't even allowed to own property in their own capital. Martha's change of name and religion is an indication of the way in which ambitious Latvians had to leave behind the indigenous culture in order to break out of a rigidly tiered system. The result was that the Latvian language and everything that went with it was pushed further and further into rural backwaters.

Balts at the Russian court

Catherine I died after a reign of only two years, but the Latvian connection with the Russian Crown was renewed when Peter's niece Anna acceded to the throne. While Catherine was undoubtedly fast, Anna was downright debauched. More to the point, she was the dowager Duchess of Courland, and she brought German Balts from Jelgava, Rīga and elsewhere to the Russian court en masse. Jelgava, then called Mitau, was the capital of Courland. Anna's father-in-law was Duke Jacob's son, and he had introduced French opera and ballet into its social milieu. Anna granted the first Russian constitution in Jelgava in 1731, but it was her chamberlain and lover, Ernst Johann Biron, who has left the greatest mark. An opportunist and a scoundrel, he became the Duke of Courland after Anna's husband died and was

an excruciating death. There was a repetition in 1840, with the peasants directing their fury at the Lutheran Church.

Four centuries after the demise of the Teutonic Order, the Latvian establishment was still dominated by German aristocrats and burghers.

> Empress Anna's lover, the Duke of Courland, managed to find enough money to bring in Bartolomeo Rastrelli, the future architect of St Petersburg's Winter Palace, to construct the sumptuous palace at Rundāle.

a power behind the throne. He was responsible for sending some 20,000 to Siberia.

The German Balts in Russia's courts used their influence to restore the port of Rīga after the depredations of the Russo-Swedish Wars. This care did not extend to other parts of the country. It was said that, Rīga apart, Latvia was ruled by wolves for a century afterwards.

Neglect and ghastly conditions led, in 1802, to a peasant uprising led by "Poor Conrad" who, reflecting the revolutionary mood in France, was called "the Lettish Bonaparte". The revolt was put down ruthlessly and Poor Conrad died

LEFT: Town Hall Square, Rīga, by K.T. Fechhelm, 1819.
ABOVE: festivities on Midsummer's Eve, 1842.

The country had subsequently been ruled by Poland, Sweden and Russia, but the old German system had somehow endured despite efforts to dislodge it. To rebellious 19th-century peasants, the Lutheran Church was a symbol of German domination. The Russian Orthodox Church hastened to exploit anti-Lutheran feelings. The Orthodox catechism was translated into Latvian and given away free in large numbers. German landowners retaliated by refusing to make any more land available for Orthodox churches. German–Russian rivalry took on a life of its own, and the role of the German Balts sparked a furious row between Tsar Alexander III and Bismarck. Lutheran pastors were locked up or sent to Siberia, and as many as 30,000 of their flock were formally advised that they were henceforth Orthodox.

The Latvian peasant derived some benefits as the region was drawn into the Russian economic sphere to counteract German influence. The Russian railways were extended to the Baltic coast, and Rīga handled a large share of Russia's trade. At the same time there was a remarkable sprouting of literary activity in Latvian. Rich Germans held on to their positions, but the lower rungs had to make room for Latvians. All of this increased Latvian political awareness, but satisfaction at overcoming the old German obstacles did not make organisa-

tions like the New Latvians pro-Russian. Political sympathies on the workshop floor in Rīga were more inclined towards Karl Marx.

The Baltic Revolution

The Baltic Revolution of 1905, which coincided with the St Petersburg uprising, was aimed with equal venom at everything German and Russian. Order was restored in Rīga only by the intervention of the Imperial Guard. The tsar had no qualms about letting the outraged German barons take their revenge, and when they had done so he rewarded them with concessions, such as granting permission to reopen five German schools. One way or another, the German element clung on, and at the onset of

World War I, the population of Rīga was still at least 50 percent Baltic-German.

The wounds of the rebellion had not yet healed when World War I broke out. The country was at first occupied by a defensive Russian Army. In 1915 the Latvians were permitted to raise a national army. When the Russians withdrew in confusion after the Bolshevik revolution, the Latvians put up a spirited defence of Rīga against the advancing Germans at the cost of some 32,000 casualties. When the Germans took Riga, it was not the prize that they were hoping for. The port was inactive, the machinery having been shipped to Russia.

A secret national organisation bent on Latvian independence was formed within the first months of German occupation and was in contact with refugees in Russia and exiles who had fled after the 1905 rebellion. The Allied victory in November 1918 simplified matters. A state council simply proclaimed independence and offered citizenship to all residents apart from Bolsheviks and German Unionists. The fly in the ointment was that 45,000 German troops still occupied Rīga. When they withdrew, the Bolsheviks arrived and there was no organised force to stop them. They declared Latvia a Soviet republic. The situation was rescued by Estonia, which drove the Bolsheviks off its soil and then crossed the border to help the Latvians do likewise.

Independent Latvia was in a sorry state. The population was a third below pre-war levels, industrial output was virtually nil, and many children had never been to school. A land-reform programme expropriated the German baronial estates and redistributed them in parcels to Latvian peasants.

Agrarian reform was supplemented by a takeover of industry and commerce, or what was left of them. The Latvian language was of course given official status, and there was a general revival of Latvian culture. Perhaps the most significant statistics were the changing population ratios. By 1939, Latvians enjoyed one of the highest standards of living in Europe and were once again in a commanding majority in the country, as high as 75 percent.

The Nazi–Soviet pact

Progress came to a jarring halt in 1940. The Bolsheviks undertaking to respect the independence of the Baltic States "voluntarily and for ever" vanished with the Nazi–Soviet Pact of 1939. A Soviet invasion was followed by annexation. The Nazi–Soviet Pact was short-lived, and in June 1941 the German Army drove out the Soviet forces. Latvia, together with Estonia and Lithuania, was made part of Hitler's Ostland. The consequences for Latvia's 100,000 Jews were horrific: 90 percent were murdered.

Rīga was reconquered by the Soviet Army on 8 August 1944, and with that the NKVD set about restoring order in its customary manner. An estimated 320,000 people out of a population of just 2 million were deported to the east; most never returned. Tens of thousands more

Kārlis Ulmanis, President of Latvia in the 1930s, was arrested by the Soviets in 1940. He probably died in Turkmenistan, but his remains have not been found.

fled westwards only to be forced to work in German factories under daily bombardment by the Allies. Active guerrilla resistance to the Soviet regime continued until as late as 1951, but little news of it leaked out to the West.

More executions and deportations followed in the purge of so-called bourgeois nationalists in 1949–53, and all the time Russians were surging in ostensibly to man the industrial machinery of the Five-Year Plans. Khrushchev purged 2,000 influential locals who raised their voices in protest, replacing them either with Russians or so-called *Latovichi*, Russians who purported to be Latvians on the strength of a few years' residence in the country. Notorious *Latovichi* such as Arvīds Pelše and Augusts Voss rigorously enforced Russification policies. Even folk singing was driven underground. Signs of a revival surfaced in the 1980s. It began with the unobtrusive restoration of derelict churches and the odd historical monument. Poets and folk groups also performed discreetly.

The principal catalyst that brought protest out into the open was the green movement. Environmental concern served as cover for the formation of nationalist pressure groups, and before very long the underground press was

addressing such taboo subjects as the activities of the secret police and human-rights violations. The breakthrough occurred in 1986, when public protest managed to stop the construction of a hydroelectric scheme on the River Daugava.

With this victory in hand, and a softer line on public protest coming from Moscow, the resistance movement grew. The National Independence Movement of Latvia (NIML), founded in June 1988, maintained that the illegal annexation of 1940 invalidated the Soviet regime. A census taken in 1989 revealed that Latvians were on the brink of becoming a minority in their own country – they represented a mere

52 percent of the total population, around 30 percent in Rīga. The Russian minority rallied in opposition, forming an organisation known as Interfront.

Return of the republic

The Soviet Union eventually collapsed so quickly and so passively that it is all too easy to forget how bravely Latvians demanded "total political and economic independence" and, specifically, a free market economy and a multi-party political system. Nor will Latvia forget the five killed by Soviets at the Ministry of the Interior in January 1991, nor the freezing cold nights on makeshift barricades against Soviet tanks in Old Rīga. Elections gave the

---

LEFT: traditional "Lettish" costume, 1920s.
RIGHT: Krišjānis Valdemārs *(second left)* and other key figures of Latvia's National Awakening.

nationalists a two-thirds majority, and the country was renamed the "Republic of Latvia".

The regaining of independence in 1991 was the first step in a sequence of events that would reunite Latvia with the rest of Europe. In 1994 Latvians celebrated the final withdrawal of Russian troops with the demolition of a Cold War radar station in Skrunda. Cultural life returned to the sovereign nation, and a free market economy struggled with bank crises and privatisation scandals, often involving politicians and prominent members of society, but eventually experienced unparalleled, and necessary growth. The question of citizenship for Russian residents has largely been resolved, but not without acrimony. Parliament also experienced growing pains, with the collapse of 11 governments in nearly as many years. But in June 1999, Vaira Vīķe-Freiberga was elected president by the *saeima*, the first woman head of state in the post-Communist world (*see box below*). She was

> Philippe Halsman was born in Rīga in 1906 and lived in the building on Kaļķu Street that now houses a T.G.I. Friday's restaurant. A friend of Einstein and Dalí, his photographs graced the magazine covers of Time and Life.

in place in time to steer the country through negotiations to join both NATO and the European Union in 2004.

After EU membership the economy soared, with annual GDP growth reaching 11 percent, and a property boom attracted unprecedented foreign investment to the country. But the populist government ignored the warnings of economists and did nothing to put out the fires of runaway inflation and an overheating economy. A real-estate bubble financed by the loose lending policies of both local and Scandinavian banks fuelled this impending disaster. The ripple effect of the Lehman Brothers collapse in 2008 became a tsunami in Latvia that left the nation's economy in ruins.

Unlike more prudent Estonia, Latvia spent its windfall tax revenues recklessly and put no money aside for a rainy day. It also decided to bail out the nation's largest privately owned bank, Parex Banka, with taxpayers' money, infuriating the local populace. The IMF and EU agreed to loan Latvia €7.5 billion. A peaceful anti-government demonstration on Cathedral Square in early 2009 ended in a riot by drunken hooligans. The coalition government collapsed and the opposition New Age Party took the reins, making tough decisions to save what was left of the economy. Government employee salaries were slashed by nearly half as unemployment soared to over 20 percent. Although the situation has begun to improve, an election in late 2010 will set the country on its next course. ❏

THE FIRST WOMAN PRESIDENT

Born in Rīga in 1937, Vaira Vīķe-Freiberga fled the country with her family ahead of the invading Soviet Army, arriving in Germany where she spent much of her childhood in a displaced-persons' camp. The family emigrated to Canada where she gained her bachelor's and master's degrees in psychology and a PhD in experimental psychology. In 1998, repatriated to Latvia, she became director of the Latvian Institute and a year later was elected Latvia's president. Intelligent and erudite, Freiberga speaks five languages. Since leaving office she has become a member of, among other organisations, the European Council of Tolerance and Reconciliation.

LEFT: Vaira Vīķe-Freiberga.
RIGHT: empty streets in a Soviet-built suburb of Rīga as independence dawned in 1991.

MANOR HOUSES AND CASTLES

There are hundreds of manor houses scattered throughout all three countries, but it is only recently that work has begun to restore them

Architecturally, the manor houses of Estonia, Latvia and Lithuania come in a mix of styles, from Baroque to neoclassical, neo-Gothic to neo-Renaissance, reflecting the tastes of successive owners, foreign influences and passing whims. They are also reminders of feudal times under foreign occupation: these were the homes of the landowning Danish, Swedish and German aristocracy, of merchants, Russian counts and governors on whom much of the population, long enslaved, had to depend.

A number were destroyed in the first Russian revolution of 1905, a peasants' revolt against the landowners. After confiscation during the first independence, many houses were left without the resources to keep them standing. Little respect was given to their finery under the Soviets, who turned them into collective farms, schools and medical or social institutions, while in the 1990s the newly independent nations looked on them as vestiges of an occupation force. But within a dozen years, a realisation had begun to grow that some of these buildings played an inherent part in the nations' stories, and should be cared for and preserved.

In Estonia, 200 manor houses are now under state control, half of them in daily use; in Latvia they are increasingly being converted into country-house hotels, like Rumene Manor in Courland, which has been refurbished by the architect Zaiga Gaile, Latvia's former first lady. In Lithuania, where the Manor House Preservation Programme was introduced in 2003, a number are being transformed into museums which explain their history and purpose. In some cases attempts are being made to revive stables and farmwork and, should you imagine yourself living in splendour, you will find some manors are for sale.

ABOVE: Kukšu muiža in Lativa is a fine example of a restored manor house. Now a 13-bedroom hotel, the riverside building has met thick cellar walls and dates from the 16th century. It fell into disrepair under the Soviets when it was used as a collective farm

LEFT: a figure from Turaida, Latvia's largest and most visited castle. The brick fortress dates from 1214 and was restored in the mid-20th century.

CASTLES

Each Baltic capital rose around a medieval castle, which came with the crusading Orders and the proselytising Church, whose timber strongholds across the country were soon replaced by sturdier stone. The various power struggles that went on for centuries ensured that they remained fortified, though many today are no more than weed-covered ruins, while others have been incorporated into domestic estates. Notable is the stronghold of the Bishop of Saare-Lääne (Oesel-Wiek) at Haapsalu, in Estonia, which contains the Cathedral of St Nicholas, and his Episcopal Castle at Kuressaare on Saaremaa island, the only complete medieval fortress in the Baltics.

Cēsis, in Latvia, is the place to go to feel the crusading Livonian Brothers of the Sword, who built their headquarters here. Their castle looks romantic, despite damage during the Great Northern War.

Most distinctive are the red-brick Gothic castles. Without stone, they lack carvings, but there was no choice in areas with nothing to quarry and only bricks to bake. Adornments had to be made in the form of wooden balconies, jetties and balustrades. In this style are Turaide, built in 1214 under Archbishop Albert, the founder of Rīga, and, in Lithuania, Kaunas Castle and the magnificent island castle of Trakai, rebuilt from ruins during the 20th century.

Greatest of the northern European Gothic red-brick castles is Malbork (Marienburgas in Lithuanian), now in Poland, and headquarters of the Association of Castles and Museums Around the Baltic Sea.

Above: Cēsis castle, headquarters of the Livonian Brothers of the Sword, is one of Latvia's top sites.

Below: Vana-Vastseliina Castle in Estonia dates from the 14th century and, like many castles, it was destroyed in the Great Northern War

LEFT: neoclassical Veliuona Manor in the historic Lithuanian town of the same name was designed by Mykolas Zaleckis and completed in [...]. It is one of the largest wooden buildings in the region and it houses a local museum of archaeology and ethnography.

[...] the interior of Kukšu muiža, whose restoration was helped by [...] of furnishings compiled in 1855. Wallpaper was removed to [...] late 18th-century wall paintings in four of the rooms.

RĪGA

The largest of the three countries' cities is the most diverse. Set beside the wide River Daugava, Rīga has a Unesco-status Old Town with Art Nouveau buildings and a massive Central Market

Rīga

With a population of nearly a million, **Rīga ❶** is the largest and most cosmopolitan city in the Baltic States. It almost seems too big for the country it occupies: roughly a third of the nation lives in the Latvian capital. Spread either side of the River Daugava, the city lies some 8km (5 miles) from the great sagging dip of Rīga Bay, and for some 3,000 years these warm waters have provided both a gateway and an outlet for the continental heartlands. Like Tallinn in Estonia, its skyline is an impressive collection of towers and spires. Expertly manicured parks, a meandering canal that once served as a moat and tree-lined boulevards separate the Old Town from the sprawling "new" city. Rīga's status as a Unesco World Heritage Site is more than evident in its medieval churches, guild halls and winding cobblestoned streets, as well as in its ornately decorated Art Nouveau buildings, many of which have been lovingly restored to their original 19th- and early 20th-century grandeur.

A final blessing for Rīga's citizens and an ever-growing number of foreign visitors is Jūrmala, the lovely sandy beach just a half-hour's drive from the city centre (*see page 215*). This collection of seaside residential towns spread out over 20km (12 miles) has

been favoured by generations of holidaymakers from its beginnings as a 19th-century spa to its heyday as a fashionable haunt in the 1930s and later the premier destination for rest and relaxation in the Soviet Union.

The Old Town

Rīga is not a difficult town to get around, and nearly everything of merit can be reached on foot. The dead-straight Brīvības iela (Freedom Street), is the main artery of the city and leads directly to the **Freedom Monument ❹**

Main attractions
OLD TOWN
OCCUPATION MUSEUM
CHURCH OF ST PETER
MENTZENDORFF HOUSE
RĪGA CATHEDRAL
RĪGA CASTLE
MUSEUM OF THE HISTORY OF RĪGA
   AND NAVIGATION
RĪGA ART NOUVEAU MUSEUM
CENTRAL MARKET

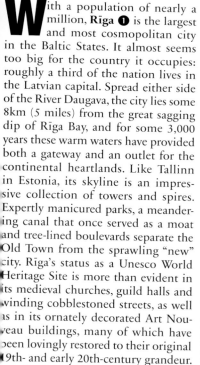

PREVIOUS PAGES: House of Blackheads.
LEFT: birds'-eye view of the old town.
RIGHT: strolling the city.

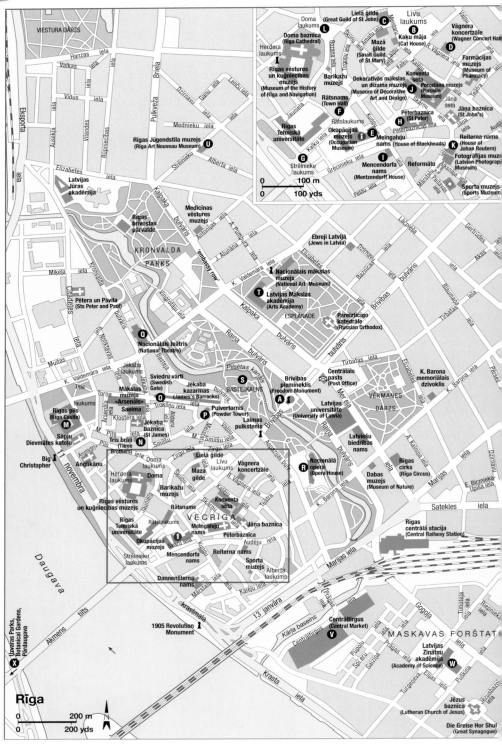

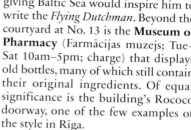

(Brīvības piemineklis, *see page 209*), the perfect place to begin a tour of Old Rīga – known locally as Vecrīga.

Walk down Kaļķu iela (Lime Street) to **Livu Square ⑥** (Līvu laukums), named after the now nearly extinct Finno-Ugric people who founded a fishing village here long before Germans or even Latvians arrived on the scene. Today the square is the city's liveliest, populated by buskers and souvenir touts and hundreds of locals and tourists taking advantage of the fantastic views provided from a large concentration of summer beer gardens.

On the opposite side of the square is the yellow **Cat House** (Kaķu māja), whose two felines perched on top of its towers caused quite a stir nearly 100 years ago. Local lore has it that the owner of the building was engaged in a dispute with the powerful Great Guild across the street. To show what he thought of them, he turned the cats around so that their backsides faced his foes. The dispute was later settled and the cats were returned to their original positions where they remain to this day.

The Great and Small Guilds

The city's two guild halls are on the west side of the square. Traditionally only Germans were allowed to belong to the **Great Guild of St John ⑥** (Lielā ģilde), a merchants' guild founded in 1384. The building was last redesigned in 1866 by the city architect J.D. Felsko and today it is the home of the Latvian Symphony Orchestra. The **Small Guild of St Mary** (Mazā ģilde) was for artisans and was started in the mid-14th century. Both functioned until the 1860s, but they were not finally dissolved until the 1930s.

To the left of the guild halls, on Richard Wagner Street is the **Wagner Concert Hall ⑦** (Vāgnera koncertzāle), the concert hall named after the illustrious German composer, who conducted in the building for two years before he fled to avoid his creditors. The clandestine journey on the stormy, unfor-

giving Baltic Sea would inspire him to write the *Flying Dutchman*. Beyond the courtyard at No. 13 is the **Museum of Pharmacy** (Farmācijas muzejs; Tue–Sat 10am–5pm; charge) that displays old bottles, many of which still contain their original ingredients. Of equal significance is the building's Rococo doorway, one of the few examples of the style in Rīga.

Town Hall Square

Continue walking up Kaļķu iela until you reach the next square. Rātslaukums encapsulates all of Latvia's history and in its centre stands the **House of Blackheads ⑤** (Melngalvju nams; Tue–Sun 11am–5pm; charge). This historic gem was heavily damaged during World War II. The remains were destroyed by the Soviets after the war, but the Dutch Renaissance guild house was rebuilt with private donations and opened in time for the city's 800th anniversary in 2001. The building also houses a **Tourist Information Centre**. Founded in the 13th century, the brotherhood organised the city's social life and the house became a meeting

TIP

Rīga's Tourist Information Centre in the Town Hall Square is open daily 10am–7pm. There are also information kiosks at the airport, main rail and bus stations. See www.rigatourism.com

BELOW: statue of Roland outside the House of Blackheads.

Mentzendorff House.

BELOW: the soaring
nave of St Peter's.

place for bachelor merchants arriving from abroad. One of the community's patron saints was St Mauritius, who was black and gave the brotherhood its name. The historic **Town Hall ⑥** (Rātsnams) opposite, also recently rebuilt, is the seat of local government. A third floor was added to the original architectural plan, as well as a modern wing behind the building.

Occupation Museum

Next to the Blackhead Brotherhood house is an ugly black building, the former Museum of the Latvian Red Riflemen, home to the excellent and chilling **Occupation Museum** (Okupācijas muzejs; 11am–5pm, closed Mon in winter; free). The museum retraces Latvia's plight under the Nazi and Soviet occupations from 1940 to 1991, with explanations in English, German and Russian. The moving exhibit depicts the life of Latvians deported to Siberia and those who fought the Soviets in the forests. The museum is important for anybody interested in recent Latvian history. In front of the Occupation Museum,

facing Akmens Bridge is **Latvian Riflemen Square ⑥** (Strēlnieku laukums), with a red granite Monument to the Latvian Riflemen in its centre. This controversial landmark was once dedicated to the riflemen who joined the Bolsheviks after the revolution. In a time of dramatically changing fortunes, the Latvian Riflemen split, some remaining true to the tsar, others joining the Latvian freedom fighters and still others swearing allegiance to the Reds. Some of the last gained respect as the bodyguards of Lenin and infamy as the executioners of the Romanov family in 1918.

Church with a view

Facing the rebuilt Blackheads' house is the elegant steeple of the **Church of St Peter ⑪** (Pēterbaznīca; Tue–Sun 10am–6pm; charge). A lift glides heavenwards to a viewing platform 72 metres (236ft) up in the 122-metre (380ft) steeple. The first church here, made of wood, was built by the city's craftsmen in 1209. Two centuries later it was rebuilt in stone. In 1709, 15 years after the steeple was completed,

city fell to the Russians and Peter the Great took a special delight in climbing to the top of the tower, then the tallest wooden structure in Europe. Then it was struck by lightning in 1721, he personally helped to put out the fire.

Mentzendorff House

At the corner of the square, at Grēcinieku Street 18, is the half-timbered **Mentzendorff House ①** (Mencendorfa nams; Wed–Sun 10am–5pm; charge), which offers a good idea of what life was like in a prosperous German's home in the 17th–18th century, though the building itself dates back to the 16th century. Among its former owners was Andreas Helm, head of the Small Guild, and Rheinhold Schlevgt, master of the Order of the Blackheads, who established a pharmacist's in the premises. Its restored interior has *trompe-l'œil* wall decoration and painted ceilings inspired by Jean-Antoine Watteau. The rooms have been furnished with period pieces from the Museum of the History of Rīga and Navigation.

St George's and St John's

Facing St Peter's on the north side are two other important churches. **St George's** now houses the **Museum of Decorative Art and Design ①** (Dekoratīvās mākslas un dizaina muzejs; Tue–Sun 11am–5pm; charge), and it should be visited if only to see the building's interior. This was the original church in the city, founded by the crusading Bishop Albert of Bremen in 1204 as a chapel for the Sword-Bearer's Order. It stood beside the castle complex which launched the first crusades against the Baltic people. Rebuilt after a rebellion in 1297, it was the first stone building in the city and it remains one of the few examples of Romanesque. It has not been used as a church since the Reformation, when it was turned into a storehouse.

Next to St George's is **Jāņa Sēta**, a small square abutting part of the old red-brick city wall, on the other side of which is the red-bricked **St John's** (Jāņa baznīca; Tue–Sun 11am–6pm; free), which is distinguished by a steeply stepped Gothic pediment. The church started life in 1234 as the chapel

BELOW LEFT: the Monument to the Latvian Riflemen.
BELOW: St John's Courtyard.

Chimney sweeps claim to have the oldest guild in Rīga, and you may still see them, wearing top hats and white gloves. Rub their brass buttons for good luck.

of a Dominican abbey. In 1330 it was enlarged and its buttresses became the dividing walls of the new side altars. It was taken from the Dominicans during the Reformation, and in 1582 a divine service in Latvian was held here for the first time. On the south wall, facing St Peter's, is a grille covering a cross-shaped window behind which two monks were cemented up during the building of the church, and for the rest of their short lives they were fed through the small gap.

Opposite the entrance to the courtyard is the **Statue of the Bremen Town Musicians** from the Grimm fairy tale. It was a gift from the city of Bremen, home of Bishop Albert, founder of Rīga. Sandwiched between the two churches is Ecke's Convent, which once belonged to the mayor of Rīga. In 1596, after allegations of embezzlement circulated around town, Ecke was forgiven after donating his lavish home to an Order of nuns that cared for widows who could no longer support themselves. It currently houses a teashop and small hotel. Behind the building is a further courtyard,

BELOW RIGHT:
Dome church with St Peter's.

Konventa Sēta, which is now hom to an upmarket hotel, dozens of shop and cafés as well as the **Rīga Porc lain Museum** (Rīgas porcelāna mu ejs; Tue–Sun 11am–6pm; charge). medieval architecture has been lo ingly restored, making it difficult imagine that this complex of hous once supported a convent that looke after the city's poor.

Baroque mansions

Head southeast to the corner of Audē iela (Weavers' Street) and Mārstaļu ie and look out for the **House of Joha Reutern 𝕂** (Reiterna nams) whe exhibitions are often held. It was buil by this rich German merchant in 168 during the Swedish occupation, an beneath the roof is a frieze showir the Swedish lion devouring the Ru sian bear. At No. 21 is another Baroqu mansion, which was built in 1696 f Reutern's son-in-law, a burgher name Dannenstern. Both have fine doorwa by the local stonemason Hans Schmi sel, who was responsible for the han some if rather out of place portal c St Peter's Church.

The Burning of Rīga

For nearly 100 years before Peter I's arrival, the city had been under the control of the Swedes, who had rebuilt its castle, the flag-topped citadel to the north just by Vanšu Bridge. Rīga had been the largest city in their empire, bigger even than Stockholm.

After the Swedes had been driven out in a nine-month siege by Peter's Russian army, the city was in no great shape, and two-thirds of the population had died. Among them were many Latvians who were barred from living within the city walls. Since the arrival of the German crusaders and the construction of the city in stone, the Latvians had been relegated to the lands beyond the city walls, and to Pārdaugava on the river's far bank, where they lived in buildings that had to be built out of wood. Each time the city was threatened, as it had been by the Russians, they had to burn their property and accept the protection of the city walls.

The eighth and last time this happened was in 1812 when an eagle-eyed watchman on St Peter's belfry spotted a distant cloud of dust heralding the French invasion. Four churches, 705 houses, 35 public buildings and hundreds of acres of vegetable plots were torched before it became clear the dust was caused by a herd of cows. Napoleon crossed Latvia via a different route.

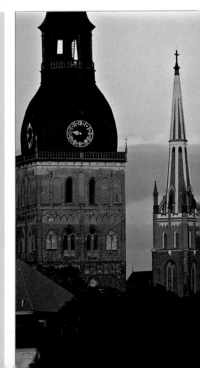

Nearby is the **Latvian Photography Museum** (Latvijas fotogrāfijas muzejs; Wed–Sun 11am–5pm; charge), which has a collection of late 19th-century photographs of rural landscapes as well as some impressive pictures from World War I. A highlight of the museum is the Minox spy camera produced in Latvia just prior to the war and later manufactured by the famous German firm Leica.

Just past the museum on the left is Peitavas Street, where a **Jewish synagogue** has been beautifully restored. The only Jewish place of worship in Rīga that survived the Nazi occupation of Latvia, it was spared for fear that a blaze might spread to other nearby buildings. It is open to visitors, and services are held here every Saturday.

Cathedral and square

All streets in the Old Town lead to **Cathedral Square ❶** (Doma laukums), the cobbled focal point of the Old City, where tourists pose for photos in front of the largest church in the Baltics and then spend far too much money for a drink at a beer garden with a view. **Rīga Cathedral** (Doma baznīca; Sat–Tue, Thur 9am–6pm, Wed, Fri 9am–5pm, winter daily 10am–5pm; charge), or St Mary's, is a magnificent red-brick structure, with a gable like a Hanseatic merchant's house and a bulbous dome of northern Gothic solemnity. Steps lead down to the north door because the city's constant rebuilding has meant the ground level has actually risen over the years.

The cathedral was begun by Bishop Albert just after St George's, in 1211, and he is buried in the crypt. The plaques, tombs and headstones decorating the interior show just how German the city remained, no matter who owned it. Especially notable is the 6,768-pipe organ, which was, at the time of its completion in 1884, one of the world's largest. It was such a grand project that the tsar himself donated money to the cause and Franz Liszt composed music for its inauguration.

The cloister gardens are surrounded by a 118-metre (387ft) vaulted gallery (Sat–Tue, Thur 9am–6pm, Wed, Fri 9am–5pm, winter daily 10am–5pm), one of the most outstanding examples

BELOW: Cathedral Square.

of north European medieval construction work, which also houses hundreds of pieces of local history including tombstones, the original Dome cockerel and a huge stone head thought to be an ancient pagan idol.

Next door, with its entrance at Palasta Street 4, the **Museum of the History of Rīga and Navigation** (Rīgas vēstures un kuģniecības muzejs; daily 10am–5pm; charge) is an eclectic collection of historical items and memorabilia, and does not have too much to do with the sea. Its scope is very wide and it is one of the best museums in the city, reflecting the wealth of its merchants. It was the first public museum in the Baltics when it opened in 1773 and it was based on the collection of Nicolaus von Himsel, a medical practitioner who had died nine years earlier at the age of 35.

Renaissance style

Pils iela (Castle Street) leads off Cathedral Square in front of an elegant, green 19th-century Venetian Renaissance building. At the time of writing it was being renovated to house the Foreign Art Museum presently at Rīga Castle.

In the corner of Anglikāņu Street off Castle Street is a smart brown Renaissance-style building, which belongs to the **Danish Embassy**. It was built as the British Club for expatriates, merchants and sundry travellers (Napoleon called Rīga "a suburb of London"), and every brick and detail of the Anglican church behind it was brought from Britain, including a shipload of earth to provide the foundations. Women were allowed in the club once a year.

Rīga Castle

Pils Street arrives at **Rīga Castle** Ⓜ (Rīgas pils), which the Swedes redesigned in 1652. The first castle was built here in 1330 by the Livonian Order, who later decamped to Cēsis. In 1481, in one of many internecine wars within the city, it was razed by the townspeople, but the Livonian Order returned to besiege the town 34 years later, eventually prevailing and forcing the locals to rebuild it. Today it houses two museums of interest: **History of Latvia** (Latvijas vēstures muzejs; Tue–

Sun 11am–5pm; charge) and **Foreign Art** (Ārzemju mākslas muzejs; Tue–Sun 11am–5pm; charge).

The Three Brothers

Opposite the castle, Mazā Pils Street dives into the narrow lanes of the Old Town again. The most attractive group of buildings here are the three buildings known as **The Three Brothers** (Trīs brāļi). These are the oldest residences in the city, merchants' homes of almost doll's-house proportions dating from the 15th century. They have been colourfully restored, and they show how the families would live on the lower floors while leaving the upper areas for storage. One of them is home to the city's small **Museum of Architecture** (Arhitektūras muzejs; Mon–Fri 9am–5pm; free).

Nearby is the red-brick **St James'** (Jēkaba baznīca; daily 9am–7pm; free), the principal Catholic church. Its 73-metre (240ft) thin green spire, topped by a gold cockerel, is one of the three sky-pricking steeples that shape the city's skyline. In 1522 it became the first church in Latvia to hold a Lutheran service, but 60 years later, when the Polish King Stephen Bathory took the city for a brief spell, it was handed to the Catholics, who have kept faith here ever since. In front of it is the peach-coloured residence of the archbishop, and on the north side is the parliament building on Jēkaba Street which was blockaded against Soviet attack in 1991. One of the original cement barricades erected to protect the building is displayed in front of the church.

Swedish Gate

Turn right along Trokšņu Street, leading directly to the charming **Swedish Gate**  (Zviedru vārti). Built in 1698, this is the only gate left in the city walls, and through it the condemned were led to their fate. The executioner lived in the apartment next to the gate; he would place a red rose on his window ledge on any morning he had to perform. The street on the far side of the gate is lined by the yellow **James' Barracks** (Jēkaba kazarmas), erected for the occupying Swedes. Turn right up Torņa Street past the old houses

Jacob's Barracks.

BELOW LEFT: the Powder Tower.
BELOW: the Swedish Gate.

Art Nouveau

Rīga experienced great affluence as Art Nouveau became fashionable, and the city is littered with examples of this flamboyant style

Art Nouveau, the architectural style that brings such an unexpectedly decadent air to Rīga's streets, celebrated the triumph of the bourgeoisie at the end of the 19th and beginning of the 20th century. In highly developed Rīga more than in any Russian city, the new urban middle classes found prosperity.

A new wave of architects jumped at the task of designing residential blocks, academies, schools, department stores, libraries, banks, restaurants and factories. The result is that nearly one in three buildings in Rīga – some 40 percent of the boulevard city that grew up in the 1900s – is in Art Nouveau or Jugendstil.

Eisenstein's ornamentation

Rīga hosted a mixture of new, often decorative approaches to building. The residential houses in Alberta Street, built by civil engineer Mikhail Osipovich Eisenstein, father of the great Russian filmmaker, are saturated in finishing details. Inside the entrance to 2a Alberta Street the exterior decoration evolves into a turquoise hall of columns, embroidered with leaves and curves.

Eisenstein's "decoratively eclectic Art Nouveau", a staggering synthesis of rationality and ornament, is shared by other contemporary Rīga architects, including the Baltic Germans Friedrich Scheffel, Heinrich Scheel and Reinhold Schmaeling. All studied in St Petersburg, where Art Nouveau flourished. The entrance hall to Scheel and Sheffel's residential block with shops at 8 Smilšu Street shows a characteristic affinity with the Arts and Crafts movement. That thread takes the curious visitor back to one of Rīga's most important architects, the Baltic German Wilhelm Bockslaff. Bockslaff built the graceful Stock Exchange (1905), on Kalpaka Boulevard. Since 1919 the building has housed the Latvian Art Academy. Its pastel-coloured ceiling, embroidered after the style of William Morris, is a treasury of stained glass, and the whole building is a fine monument to the eclecticism of Art Nouveau.

Houses, shops and banks on Brīvības Street and nearby Ģertrūdes and A. Čaka streets employ the perpendicular to express the solidity and the excitement of town life. Architects of this so-called "rational" Art Nouveau from the mid-1900s include Latvians Jānis Alksnis, Eižens Laube, Paul Mandelstamm and Konstantīns Pēkšēns.

Latvia's romantic style

Laube, Mandelstamm, Pēkšēns and Aleksandrs Vanags all graduated from Rīga Polytechnical Institute, which encouraged them to develop a specific Latvian style. A general heaviness, in some cases as if the building had been poured out of a mould, in others as if it were a test-run for different building materials, including stucco, wood, stone, brick and plaster, characterises this National Romanticism. It incorporated stylised ethnographic ornaments, and the natural materials used in an urban setting, together with tapered window recesses and steep roofs, suggested a continued link with rural life.

The individual features of scores of these buildings, testaments to high-spirited urban living, make a walk around Rīga a joy. But Art Nouveau isn't just evident on the buildings' facades. A visit to the Rīga Art Nouveau Museum on Alberta Street is an absolute must to see how furniture, flatware and even plumbing fixtures were embellished in this style. www.jugendstils.riga.lv ❏

LEFT: dramatic figures in Elizabetes Street.

built against the red-brick city wall that has been partially restored. At the end of the street is Pulvertornis, the **Powder Tower ℗**, the last of 18 city towers. Its round red-brick walls and concave, conical roof, topping 26 metres (85ft), are reminiscent of Lübeck, queen of the Hansa cities. The **Latvian Museum of War** (Kara muzejs; Wed–Sun 10am–5pm; free) is housed inside.

Around the parks

To say that the Old City is an island is rather fanciful, but it is entirely surrounded by water. The old moat that encircles it on the landward side is now a small canal running through a series of attractive parks from the ferry terminal in the north on the far side of the castle, to the railway station and market in the south. To the north, on Kr Valdemāra Street, is the **National Theatre ℚ** (Nacionālais teātris). To the south, between Brīvības and Kr Barona Street, is the fine 19th-century **Opera House ℝ** (Nacionālā opera), formerly known as the German Theatre, which has been lovingly renovated with private donations.

In the park just to the north of Brīvības is **Bastejkalns ⓢ**, the high spot of the city and not much more than a hiccup with little waterfalls and pleasant summer terraces by the canal. Five inscribed stones nearby commemorate the film cameramen and policemen killed here during the Soviet attack in January 1991.

The rallying point for the nation is the **Freedom Monument** (Brīvības pieminēklis) on Brīvības, the elegant lady designed by K. Zāle in 1935. Locally known as Milda, she holds aloft three golden stars representing the three regions of Latvia: Kurzeme, Vidzeme and Latgale. An honour guard keeps watch over Milda while Latvians lay flowers at her feet, an act that once held the prospect of a one-way ticket to Siberia. The sentries are ceremoniously replaced on the hour from 9am to 6pm. Beyond the monument on the left is the **Russian Orthodox Church**

(Pareizticīgo katedrāle), which was gutted by the Soviets for use as a planetarium.

The Esplanade park behind it leads to the 19th-century **Arts Academy ⓣ** (Latvijas Mākslas akadēmija) and the **National Art Museum** (Nacionālais mākslas muzejs; Mon–Fri 11am–6pm, Sat–Sun noon–5pm; charge). It has a permanent exhibition of paintings by 18th-century Baltic Germans and the Latvian masters Rozentāls, Annuss, Valters, Padegs and Liberts, and frescoes by the nation's most revered artist, Vilhelms Purvītis. Outside is a statue of Janis Rozentāls (see page 210).

Just off the park on Skolas is **Jews in Latvia** (Ebreji Latvijā; Sun–Thur noon–5pm; charge), a museum dedicated to the achievements and history of the Latvian Jewish community.

Art Nouveau facades

Elizabetes iela at the top of the park should be followed for a while to appreciate its Art Nouveau and National Romanticism buildings (see

The National Art Museum.

BELOW: an art nouveau facade featuring Pan, mythical birds, a lion and other motifs.

Janis Rozentāls, self-portrait, 1900.

feature, page 208). Nos 10a, 10b and 33 were designed by Mikhail Eisenstein, father of Rīga's most famous filmmaker, Sergei Eisenstein, director of the 1925 epic *Battleship Potemkin*. But most of his work can be seen in Alberta iela to the northwest (second right and first left after Kr Valdemāra), where he was responsible for nearly all the houses on the right side plus No. 13 opposite. After years of neglect during the Soviet era, many of the buildings have been renovated. At the end of the street is Strēlnieku iela, with another Eisenstein masterpiece at 4a, which has his typical bright blue touch.

Museum of Art Nouveau

On the corner of Alberta iela and Strēlnieku iela was the house that the Latvian architect Konstantīns Pēkšēns built for himself. The **Rīga Art Nouveau Museum** ⓤ (Rīgas Jūgendstila muzejs; Tue–Sun 10am–6pm; charge) is located on the ground floor and is intended to look like the original apartment designed by Pēkšēns, who lived there. All seven rooms, including

BELOW: Academy of Science in the Moscow district.

the bathroom and kitchen, contain Art Nouveau fixtures and furniture. Two other famous people lived here: the artist Janis Rozentāls (1866–1916) and the writer Rūdolfs Blaumanis (1863–1908). The **Rozentāls and Blaumanis Museum** (Jaņa Rozentāla un Rūdolfa Blaumaņa muzejs; Wed–Sun 11am–6pm; charge) is located on the top floor. The flat is filled with household effects and Rozentāls' paintings of early 20th-century Rīga, his family and friends and their holidays in Finland.

At the southwesterly end of Elizabetes on Merķeļa iela is the **Museum of Nature** (Dabas muzejs; Wed–Sat 10am–5pm, Sun 10am–4pm; charge), which displays all manner of objects from rare fossils to freaks of nature preserved in glass jars.

Central Market

Beyond the railway station are the five 20-metre (66ft) high Zeppelin hangars, built by the Germans in Vainode, southwestern Latvia, in World War I and brought here in the 1920s to house the **Central Market** ⓥ (Centrāltirgus) – one of the real wonders of Rīga.

The city's market had for three and a half centuries been sited beside the Daugava and even then it was one of the largest in the Baltic region. It must still be a contender for the title of Europe's largest market, with more than 3,000 vendors. It is built over a large underground storage system, and each hangar has its speciality: meat, dairy products, vegetables and seafood. Cream is sold in plastic bags, there are barrels of sauerkraut, fancy cakes, pickled garlic, dried herbs and mushrooms, smoked fish and whole stalls selling nothing but tins of sardines.

Beyond the pavilions, the old flea market spreads across acres of pavement. Open every day, it is at its busiest on Friday and Saturday.

Moscow district

The market is at the edge of the **Moscow district** (Maskavas forštate, known locally as "Little Moscow" here for centuries, ethnic Russians ave lived. Among the oldest of its ommunities are the Old Believers ho settled here after fleeing from e late 17th-century religious perse- tion in Russia. The area was also a brant centre for Jewish life in Rīga, tinguished under the Nazis. Unlike e orderly German-influenced streets d manicured parks of the city centre, e Moscow district always had a wild reak and character of its own. Its 9th-century wooden houses and Art ouveau buildings have yet to benefit om the city's growing prosperity.

In the middle of it is the squat, rown, Empire State replica belong- g to the **Academy of Science** W Zinātņu akadēmija), and just beyond, Jēzusbaznīcas Street, is a fascinating ctagonal wooden **Lutheran Church f Jesus** (Jēzus baznīca), built in 1822 om solid, wide boards. At the end of e street are the ruins of the **Great ynagogue** (Die Greise Hor Shul), hich was burnt to the ground on 4 ly 1941 with dozens of Jews inside.

The Moscow district is typified by lapidated 19th-century wooden buildings, Soviet concrete monstrosi- ties and post-independence prosperity that has run amok in the form of shiny glass car dealerships and shopping malls. But some things never change, and among them is the only gold dome in the city peeking out from the skyline in a clump of lime trees. Named after its principal benefactor, the businessman Alexei Grebenschikov, **Grebenščikova baznīca** is the place of worship for the Old Believers. The church now has the largest parish of the faith in the world, with a congrega- tion of approximately 25,000.

The left bank

On the opposite bank, across Stone Bridge (Akmens tilts) from the Old Town, is the attractive suburb of **Pārdaugava**, which has many wood- built houses. From here there is a good view of the Old City skyline.

Victory Park (**Uzvaras Parks**) has a Soviet victory monument and is popular with Russians. Near the park is a railway museum, and about a mile from the bridge are the **Botanical Gardens** X, with a palm house. ❏

BELOW: Central Market.

AROUND RĪGA

Just a short bus or train ride from the centre of Rīga are a number of places in which to have fun, from the Open-Air Ethnographic Museum to the city's seaside playground at Jūrmala

Main attractions
LAKE ĶĪŠEZERS
RĪGA ZOO
OPEN-AIR ETHNOGRAPHIC
  MUSEUM
MOTOR MUSEUM
SALASPILS MEMORIAL PARK
JŪRMALA
ĶEMERI NATIONAL PARK

BELOW: Lake Ķīšezers.

While high society in London and Berlin was thinking only about green spaces to live in, Rīga's wealthy elite were already designing **Mežaparks ❷** (Forest Park), one of Europe's first garden cities. Tired of the overcrowding and squalor of the city proper, prosperous Germans created this place, known then as Kaiser Park, beside **Lake Ķīšezers** to the north, where only summer cottages and entertainment facilities were permitted. Neglected during the Soviet era, many of the impressive Art Nou-veau properties have been renovated, and the park is once again inhabited by the cream of local society, its property commanding some of the highest prices in the country.

The park is also home to **Rīga Zoo** (Zooloģiskais dārzs; May–Oct 10am–7pm, winter until 5pm; charge), which has brown and polar bears and is well worth a visit, and the **Song Festival Stadium** (Lielā estrāde), which can accommodate 10,000 singers and 25,000 spectators. They gather every five years for a major festival as they

have done since 1873. A small beach on the lake is a popular destination for swimmers and sunbathers.

Aktīvās Atpūtas Centrs (Pāvu iela; tel: 2955 4155) on Lake Ķīšezers is an activity centre where you can hire bicycles and roller blades, and go boating, jet-skiing, windsurfing, water-skiing and parasailing. "Ice boating" was first held on Lake Ķīšezers in 1926, and it was here that the Rīga Yacht Club devised the rules for the sport.

Open-Air Museum

Perhaps of greatest general appeal is the **Open-Air Ethnographic Museum** ❸ (Brīvdabas muzejs; daily 10am–5pm; charge), 10km (6 miles) northeast along Brīvības Street. More than 100 buildings are set out in 100 hectares (250 acres) of woodland beside Lake Jugla. The idea for the museum arose in the wake of the desolation of the countryside after World War I, and work began on it in 1924.

The most impressive building is the 18th-century Lutheran church (Usmas baznīca) just to the left of the entrance. The whole building, including its fig-urative woodcarvings, was made with axes. There is a special, highly decorated seat beside the altar for the local German landlord, and the front pews were reserved for imported German workers. Attending church was obligatory for all workers at that time, and those caught skiving were put in the stocks or the pillory exhibited outside. Before the 19th-century organ was installed, the only music would have been an accompanying drum.

The museum display is divided into Latvia's ancient regions and it shows the contrasts between the rich Kurzeme farmers and those of poorer Latgale. Farmsteads were built for the family unit, which usually meant three generations. Costumed figures populate the village, and a blacksmith, potter and spoon-maker often perform. There are occasional folk gatherings here, and a major crafts fair is held on the first weekend in June – it's very entertaining and should not be missed.

Film and Motor Museums

In the same direction is the Motor Museum, about 5km (3 miles) from

TIP

For both the zoo and for Lake Ķīšezers, take tram No. 11 from Barona iela to the Mežaparks stop.

BELOW: the Open-Air Ethnographic Museum.

Film maker Juris Podnieks (1950–92), a watchful eye in a changing world.

BELOW: Jūrmala villa.

the centre of town along Brīvības iela. Šmerļa Street leads down to it from Brīvības, passing by the city's **Film Studios ④** (Rīgas kinostudija), which operate an open-door policy. Since 1940 the studios have produced mainly documentary films, and its protégés included Juris Podnieks. His 1989 film about the Soviet Union, *Hello, Do You Hear Us?*, which won the Prix d'Italia, included extraordinary footage of the Chernobyl disaster. This is also a great place to rent costumes and film props.

Just beyond the film studios, the street forks right into Sergeja Eizenšteina Street, where the glistening facade of the **Motor Museum** (Rīgas motormuzejs; daily 10am–6pm; charge) stands out like a brand new Rolls-Royce radiator grille. Rīga has been a key player in motor manufacturing in eastern Europe: its Russo-Balt factory, for example, presented Russia with its first car and tank. However, the fruits of its labours are rather poorly represented in this museum. The high spots are waxwork figures of the famous with their vehicles: Stalin in his 7.3-tonne bullet-proof car which

had hydraulic glass windows 8cm (3in) thick; the writer Maxim Gorky with his 1934 Lincoln; Foreign Minister Molotov's Rolls-Royce Wraith; USSR President Leonid Brezhnev at the moment of impact when he crashed his 1966 Rolls-Royce, together with the subsequent press cuttings saying that his non-appearance was due to a "sudden bad cold".

A stroll in the cemeteries

Just to the south are the great cemeteries of the city (take tram No.11 from Barona iela in the centre of Rīga), which are highly regarded by Latvians who use them almost like parks: the **Cemetery of Heroes** (Brāļu kapi) for the casualties of World War I and the War of Independence (1915–20), **Raiņa Cemetery** (Raiņa kapi) for the great and the good of Latvian literature, and the old **Forest Cemetery** (Meža kapi), final resting place of heads of state as well as common folk.

Although overgrown and neglected, the Russian **Pokrov Cemetery** (Pokrova kapi) is also worth a look. The epitaphs on its ageing headstones

hronicle the life of tsarist-era bureaurats, while at the far end, near Sencu
la, is the final resting place of fallen
oviet soldiers, marked by an enornous gold-painted concrete statue of
marching Red Army infantryman
olding aloft a flag bearing the hamner and sickle of the USSR. You can
lso take a look at the Orthodox chapel
n the middle of the grounds.

The **Great Cemetery** (Lielie kapi)
located nearby and includes the
emains of large crypts of prominent
iga families dating back to the late
8th century. The graves of the revered
atvian folk-song collector Krisjanis
arons, whose likeness can be seen
n 100 lat banknotes, and the equally
mportant educator and National
wakening icon Krisjanis Valdemars
an be found here.

alaspils

he A6 follows the right bank of the
iver Daugava for 16km (10 miles)
outheast to **Salaspils ❺**, where the
ivonian Order built its first palace, in
ne 14th century, and in 1412 signed an
mportant agreement with the Bishop
f Rīga, establishing shared rule over
ne capital. On this site in 1605 the
wedes suffered a crushing defeat by
ne Poles. But Salaspils is destined to
o down in the history books primaly as the site of a nightmarish World
/ar II concentration camp where
3,000 died.

A 40-hectare (100-acre) **memorial
ark** was opened in 1967, centred
n a long, sloping concrete building
nscribed: "The earth moans beyond
his gate." On the far side are half a
ozen monumental statues and a
engthy, low black box where wreaths
re placed. It emits a continuous and
erie ticking noise, supposed to repesent a beating heart. The sites of the
ormer barracks are marked, and an
nscribed stone indicates the place of
ne gallows. There were 7,000 children
illed among the Latvians, Belarusians,
oles, Czechs, Austrians, Dutch and
ermans who died here. On the oppo-

site side of the highway is a memorial
to 47,000 Soviet prisoners of war who
perished under the Nazis.

Jūrmala

The word *jūrmala* in Latvian simply
means seaside, and this is the name
given to the Baltics' most famous resort,
extending west from **Lielupe**. **Jūrmala
❻** has long been the playground of
Rīga, from its 19th-century spa days to
its heyday in the 1930s. Peggie Benton,
an English diplomat's wife, was in Rīga
at the outbreak of World War II, and
like many people from the city rented
a villa at Jūrmala for the summer. "The
Latvians kept up the delightful Russian
custom of bathing naked," she wrote in
Baltic Countdown. "One soon learned
not to worry and got used to strolling
up to a policeman, tightly buttoned
into his uniform, to ask how much
longer until the red flag went up and
we had to put our clothes on again."

During the Soviet era Jūrmala
became *the* destination for holidaymakers from across the USSR, and ugly
concrete hotels began to overshadow
the quaint European atmosphere

TIP

At the end of July
Jūrmala hosts the New
Wave international pop
singers' competition,
which attracts wealthy
Russian-speakers from
across the former USSR
and turns the resort into
an expensive mini-
Moscow for one week.
In 2010 Chelsea
football club owner
Roman Abramovich
attended the event
having arrived in his
115-metre (377ft)
yacht, one of the world's
largest.

BELOW: the beach
at Jūrmala.

At the start of the 19th century a local forester named Ķemeris discovered the health-giving properties of the sulphur springs, peat and mud found in the area, and built simple baths and huts to encourage people to visit what later became the resort that bears his name.

BELOW: a variety of ships off Jūrmala.

which attracted so many people here.

Today, Jūrmala is still a favourite for Russian tourists, and although many of the buildings have been restored or renovated, a slightly Soviet atmosphere, and mentality, remains. This frustrates locals and fascinates tourists.

Not actually a proper city, rather a collection of small seaside towns, Jūrmala stretches along a narrow strip of land, pressed against the beach by the River Lielupe, which follows the coast for about 8km (5 miles) before emptying itself into Rīga Bay just west of the mouth of the Daugava.

The main beaches at Majori and Dubulti have both been awarded Blue Flags guaranteeing water purity and a variety of services such as changing stations, toilets, fresh water for rinsing off and emergency medical support, not to mention seaside bars and cafés. On a typical summer day you can expect the beaches to be packed and to see football and volleyball games as well as the occasional woman in nothing more than a bikini and high heels using the beach as her personal catwalk. Topless sunbathing is fairly common, but nude beaches are rare. The spas around town are yet another reason to visit.

Majori and Dubulti

A casual stroll down the main pedestrian street of Jomas iela in **Majori** will afford every visitor with countless opportunities to eat, drink and shop. At the end of the street is the **Antique Automobile Exhibit** (Seno spēkratu izstāde; May–Sept 11am–6pm; free), which displays classic vehicles from the early to mid-20th century.

The cultural high point of Majori is the **Rainis and Aspazija Summer Cottage** (Raiņa un Aspazijas memoriālā vasarnīca; Wed–Sun 11am–6pm; charge), an attractive wooden house once lived in by the poet, playwright and journalist Jānis Rainis in a street called J. Pliekšāna iela, which was Rainis' real name. He lived here during his last three years, from 1926 to 1929, and a museum preserves his effects, which include more than 7,000 books in 11 languages. In fact, he usually rented out the large house to holidaymakers, opting to live and work in

ne smaller house next door where he ased to complain about the noise from is tenants' gramophone. His wife, the oet and writer Aspazija, is also commemorated at the house.

There is an abundance of seaside ntertainment all along this coast, but ast strolling round brings rewarding ghts such as the renovated Lutheran hurch in **Dubulti** (Dubultu luterāņu aznīca), whose towering steeple can e seen from a great distance, and the right-blue wooden Orthodox church earby. Jūrmala is also home to dozens f spa hotels that offer mud baths and ther health treatments often used by German and Finnish pensioners. The rban centres provide top-notch restaurants and nightlife as well as excelnt examples of wooden Art Nouveau uildings. To the east, in Bulduri, is he **Līvu Water Park** – with dozens of vater slides and pools, both indoors nd out – not to mention a popular oolside bar, saunas and hot tubs.

Getting to Jūrmala

nyone driving to Jūrmala, or even hrough it, needs to buy a permit for the day from the roadside offices on its outskirts. Most people take the trains, which leave Rīga station roughly every 20 minutes, or the cheaper minibuses that depart from the terminal across the street from the train station.

There are a dozen train stops to choose from between Lielupe and **Ķemeri ➐**, a spa town set back from the sea. In its heyday the grand Ķemeri Hotel had a cosmopolitan air, hosting international chess championships and social events, and although it is scheduled to reopen in the near future its renovation has been plagued by construction problems and legal battles.

Majori is the central stop, with cafés, restaurants, souvenir shops and an outdoor concert hall, all within easy reach of the railway station.

Vecaki beach

Although not as popular with tourists as Jūrmala, the beach at **Vecaki**, 20km (12 miles) north of Riga, is a Latvian favourite with a few beachside bars and beach volleyball courts as far as the eye can see. Take a Carnikava-bound train (40 minutes) from Central Station. ❑

Much of the land close to the Latvian coast lies on poorly drained soil, and the forest cover is broken by numerous small lakes and bogs.

LEFT: fanciful wooden villa near Jūrmala beach.

Nature Hikes in Ķemeri National Park

Without its grand 1930s Art Deco hotel to attract upmarket tourists, gamblers and spa-goers, the old resort of Ķemeri, just west of Jūrmala, has become something of a backwater. The town itself owes its existence to the park's sulphur springs and the curative properties of the mud. These days Ķemeri attracts more nature-lovers than spa-goers, as it is the perfect starting point for a hike through the Ķemeri National Park (Ķemeru nacionālais parks).

Founded in 1997, this 380-sq km (147-sq mile) park is only a short distance from the sea. Made up of wetlands, swamps, raised bogs, forests and lakes, it is the perfect breeding ground for rare and not so rare species of flora and fauna. More than 250 species of birds, including endangered black storks, sea eagles and white-backed woodpeckers, inhabit the park, as well as mammals such as wolves, lynx, elk and deer. Of the 900 plant species, 86 are protected, including two types of wild orchids.

The park offers a variety of different nature trails with bird-watching platforms and several kilometres of wooden boardwalks over the swampy terrain. The park service provides an information centre at the Meža māja (May–Oct Wed–Sun 10am–5pm) in the centre of the town where you can ask about specific routes through the park. Some boardwalks may be closed due to renovation.

KURZEME: THE WEST COAST

To the west of Jūrmala lies a rural area of "blue" cows and amber-washed beaches that was once owned by the powerful dukes of Courland

Kurzeme is the westernmost region of Latvia, a healthy agricultural area half-surrounded by sea. It was once known as Courland (Kurland in German), named after the Kurši, the amber-rich seafaring people who dominated the coast before the arrival of the German crusaders. Not unlike their contemporaries, the Vikings, the Kurši often supplemented their incomes by sailing across the sea to Sweden, and even as far as Denmark, to wreak havoc on local populations, stealing everything that was worth taking. Several of their exploits are mentioned in Scandinavian sagas.

In 1561, after the break-up of Livonia, Courland came into its own. It became a duchy under the sovereignty of Poland, and included the region of Zemgale (formerly Semigallia) to the south of Rīga, plus a small corner of modern Lithuania.

Powerful dukes

Courland's dukes enjoyed a degree of independence, building castles for themselves and Lutheran churches for the people. Many became rich and powerful, notably Jacob Kettler (1642–82), who went empire-building and collected a couple of outposts, one in the Gambia, West Africa, the other the Caribbean island of Tobago. Kettler amassed his fortune largely from the

pines that grow exceptionally tall and straight. The most impressive forests are in the Slītere National Park (Slīteres Nacionālais parks; *see page 224*) and along the sandy coastal region, which was once below the sea. Trees grow to around 35 metres (110ft), and some of them are up to 500 years old.

Kurzeme's thriving shipbuilding and trading activities were conducted at the two important ice-free ports of Ventspils and Liepāja, which have once again become major trading hubs, rivalling even Rīga. The coast around

Main attractions
KULDĪGA
PEDVĀLE OUTDOOR ART MUSEUM
UGĀLE CHURCH
DUNDAGA ESTATE
SLĪTERE NATIONAL PARK
VENTSPILS
LIEPĀGA
PAPE NATURE PARK

EFT: Courland countryside.
RIGHT: Kuldīga.

The bad woman in Zlēku church.

Kurzeme is a continuous white sandy beach, from just north of the major Lithuanian resort of Palanga up to the Kolka Peninsula and down to the fishing village of Mērsrags and Lake Engure in the Bay of Rīga. Beyond this is Jūrmala, Latvia's riviera *(see page 215)*, and Zemgale *(see page 235)*.

For 45 years, until 1991, most of this coast was used by the military and was therefore inaccessible; today, even in the heat of summer, much of it remains completely deserted save the occasional kite-flyer or windsurfer. Between the coastal lowland in the west and Rīga Bay in the northeast, towns, villages, churches and estates are tucked in the valleys and wooded corners of a landscape that rolls between rivers and hills. Kuldīga and Talsi are the principal inland provincial towns.

Kuldīga

The town of **Kuldīga** ❽ is 160km (100 miles) west of Rīga, and is a good centre for exploring the region. A castle was first built here in 1242, and in 1561 the town, known then as Goldingen, was made the capital of Courland by the first duke, Gotthard Kettler. The castle was built beside the River Venta, which was navigable all the way to Ventspils and the sea.

The city declined after the Great Northern War (1700–21) and the castle was reduced to little more than a ruin: only a park and an engraved stone marking its location remain. The churches are worth exploring: **St Anne's** (Sv Annas baznīca) has an impressive neo-Gothic spire, **St Catherine's Lutheran Church** (Sv Katrīnas luterāņu baznīca) has a fine wooden altar and pulpit from 1660, and there is a grand view over the town from the top of its 25-metre (85ft) tower. The **Holy Trinity Catholic Church** (Sv Trīsvienības katoļu baznīca) in Raiņa Street also has an impressive altar, which was donated by Tsar Alexander I in 1820.

Part of the town's charm is derived from the Alekšupīte, a tributary to the River Venta, which runs by a mill and between wooden houses that date from the 17th century. Most of the old, red-tile roofed buildings are centred around the square overlooked by the

19th-century town hall, but the main pedestrian street today is Liepājas, which runs from Raiņa Street a few roads back. With a wooden building that looks as if it might be a Wild West saloon, this street leads to the main modern square, dominated by two Soviet-style buildings housing a hotel and supermarket – practically the only eyesores in an otherwise charming medieval town.

At the 19th-century brick bridge over the Venta you can see the Ventas rumba, Europe's widest waterfall, extending the 110-metre (360ft) width of the river. In the park overlooking the river is the **Kuldīga Museum** (Kuldīgas novada muzejs; Tue–Sun 9am–5pm; charge), whose building is more interesting than its exhibits. It served as part of the Russian pavilion at the 1900 World's Fair in Paris and was bought by a wealthy businessman who had it shipped to Kuldīga as a gift to his fiancée.

Roma villages and vineyards

A pleasant drive leads northeast of Kuldīga, to Sabile and Kandava, towards Tukums. These villages are known for their Roma population. Vīna kalns (Wine Hill), in **Sabile ⑨**, features in the *Guinness Book of Records* as the most northerly place in Europe where vines are grown. The town has one of the region's few surviving synagogues, which is now an arts centre. On the other side of the river is the **Pedvāle Outdoor Art Museum**, created in 1992 on a former baronial estate (Pedvāles brīvdabas mākslas muzejs; daily May–Oct 10am–6pm, Nov–Apr 10am–4pm; charge). Visitors can explore 150 hectares (370 acres) of rolling hills covered in sculptures and modern art on a grand scale and can even book a room at the museum's guesthouse.

Kandava has a pleasant Old Town, but only a fortification wall and powder tower remain of its original castle. It does, however, have the old-est fieldstone bridge in Latvia. Due south of Kandava at **Zante** you'll find the **Kurzeme Fortress Museum** (Kurzemes cietokšņa muzejs; Wed–Sun 10am–5pm; charge), where you can explore restored trenches, bunkers and military machinery, including a Soviet tank and aeroplane, from the two World Wars.

Between Kuldīga and Ventspils is the small town of **Piltene ⑩**, the seat of a bishopric that retained its independence from 1234 to 1583. The remains of its castle of the Livonian Order lie behind the church, built in 1792.

Zlēkas

Danish craftsmen were imported via Piltene, and art historians detect their hand on the robust folk carvings of the altars and pulpits of local churches. But the principal carvings at Piltene, which have not survived, were by the 18th-century master carvers from Ventspils, Nicolas Soeffren the Older and Younger, ship carvers who turned their skills to church work.

Among other local churches with fine carving is **Zlēkas ⑪**, between

BELOW: the pulpit in Ugāle church.

A native Courland "blue" cow.

Piltene and Kuldīga. This is the largest church in Courland and it has a fine black-and-gold Baroque pulpit and altar which were carved by local craftsmen. Its confessional dating to the late 16th century is the oldest in Latvia. At **Ēdole**, on the opposite side of the main Ventspils road and about 20km (12 miles) northwest of Kuldīga, there is a church that dates from the 17th century. It also has a restored 13th-century castle (Ēdoles pils).

Ugāle church

One of the most interesting churches is at **Ugāle** ⑫, directly north of Kuldīga on the road between Tukums and Ventspils. Built in 1694, its organ was installed four years later, making it the oldest in the Baltic. Is has 28 stops, including the only surviving Baroque register. It was built by Cornelius Rhaneus from Kuldīga.

The beautiful, unpainted limewood carvings by Michael Markwart from Ventspils include stars that once revolved and angels' wings designed to flap. The neighbouring village of Usma is the origin of the 18th-century Lutheran church in Rīga's Open-Air Ethnographic Museum, and its location on the shore of Lake Usma makes it an excellent destination for water sports including fishing and sailing.

Aizpute

After Courland's incorporation into Russia in 1795, the small town of **Aizpute** ⑬, about 130km (80 miles) to the south, earned the nickname "Klein Danzig" because nearly two-thirds of the population were Jews. The town makes a pleasant stop, and has a church dating back to 1254 and castle ruins from the same period. A more recent castle built entirely from stacked firewood is its latest tourist attraction.

Around Talsi

The region northeast of Kuldīga is **Talsi** ⑭, centred on the market town of the same name. Like a painting on a chocolate box, it is a pretty, tranquil idyll tucked under hills beside a large pond. Not surprisingly, it has long been an artists' haunt. In its cobbled streets is a small local museum and a Lutheran church, whose pastor Karl

BELOW: smalltown Kuldīga.

menda was an accomplished musi-
an and a friend of Beethoven.

North of Talsi is a series of former
rge country-house estates. The pal-
e at **Nogale** (Nogales pils) is a par-
:ularly good example. It was built in
880 for Baron von Firks as a summer
sidence and hunting lodge, and from
20 to 1980 it was a school. It has now
een restored and is once again pri-
:ely owned. The two-storey neoclas-
:al building overlooks a lake and 70
:ctares (170 acres) of parkland.

The neighbouring village to the west
Valdemārpils, where the main estate
now a school. It takes its name from
rišjānis Valdemārs, one of the leading
ghts of the National Awakening, who
as born in nearby **Cīruļi** in 1825. He
:came enchanted by the sea near here
Roja and went on to found Latvia's
st seamen's school at Ainaži, right up
the Estonian border.

Outside his country manor in
aldemārpils is one of the oldest elm
:es in the country and the biggest in
e Baltics, a huge and crippled beast
at once served as a pagan holy site for
orship and sacrifice.

Dundaga estate

The largest estate in the whole of the
Baltics was **Dundaga ⑮**, the northernmost village of any size on this cape.
In the 18th century the castle's lands
stretched for 700 sq km (270 sq miles),
and today some attempts are being
made to restore some of its former
glory. The crozier and sword, symbols
of the Church and the Sword Bearers,
are inscribed on its entranceway, and
the main door inside the courtyard is
guarded by a statue of a bishop and a
crusader. The estate belonged to the
bishops of Courland, the last of whom
was Herzog of Holstein, brother of
Germany's Frederich II.

Today the building houses two
schools and a tourist information
centre, and is used as a venue for local
events and concerts.

The local church (Dundagas baznīca),
which is dated 1766, has woodcarvings
by Soeffren and an altar painting
by Latvia's great 20th-century artist,
Janis Rozentāls. Memorials to several
members of the Osten-Sachens family
are scattered in the church grounds,
but the most notable memorial

*A gateway at
Dundaga.*

BELOW: the
distinctive
memorial to Arvīds
Blūmentāls, the
original "Crocodile
Dundee".

The radio-telescope at Irbene, between Kolka and Ventspils, with a 32-metre (105ft) dish, is sometimes open to the public.

(Krokodils), located on the north side of Dundaga, is dedicated to local boy Arvīds Blūmentāls, who emigrated to Australia and, after hunting 10,000 crocodiles, served as the prototype for the character "Crocodile Dundee".

Secret coast of the Livs

On the Rīga Bay side of the cape, the road from Jūrmala continues through pine trees of extraordinary stature, which have provided masts for many ships throughout the ages. Dozens of sleepy fishing villages, which were completely isolated during the Soviet era, dot the coast. Even today, one has the feeling that not much has changed here save a rejuvenation of traditional summer sea festivals.

All around this peninsula, which encircles the carefully controlled **Slītere National Park** (Slīteres nacionālais parks), there is scarcely any sign of life. The reserve is an important wildlife area caring for a number of endangered plants, and supporting the busiest birdlife in the region; in April some 60,000 migrating birds congregate here. It also provides a habitat for

RIGHT: forest at Slītere National Park.

swamp turtle and natterjack among other species. A Landscape Protection Zone has been organised to conserve the forest landscape and biologic diversity along the sea coast, while allowing visitors to enjoy the area **Kolka** ⑯ is the main centre for information about the park.

At the top of the peninsula, just beyond Kolka, is a point where the waters of Rīga Bay meet the Baltic Sea. The marked line where the seas meet runs out past the half-washed away lighthouse to the horizon, and when the wind blows, the waters are whipped up into a great crashing wall Kolka is also home to the **Liv Centre** which is part Liv history museum, part information centre (Kolkas līvu centre Mon–Fri 9am–4pm; free), where you can learn about the proud people that once populated the coastline.

Continuing down the western, Baltic side of the coast are a further series of former fishing communities. Typical is **Mazirbe** ⑰, where farmlands stretch back from the dunes of the bleached sand, which is strewn with small cockle and mussel shells. If you're lucky you

Hotels, Politics and Rock 'n' Roll

For centuries Liepāja, or Libau as it was known, was dominated by Germans, Poles, Russians and, of course, Latvians, but today the biggest influence on the city appears to be Danish. In fact, one Danish rock musician in particular is leaving a lasting mark. Louis Fontaine, born Steen Lorenz, first visited the city in the 1990s as part of a European tour for his rock band and fell in love with the place. Eventually, he moved to the city, opening up Latvia's first boutique hotel, the Fontaine Hotel, as well as the Fontaine Palace, a 24-hour rock club.

As Fontaine's business interests grew, he came into contact with what he deemed corruption in local politics and became a vocal opponent of the city's mayor. He later ran for office on an anti-corruption platform, claiming that if he were elected there would be a "new sheriff in town". He even created a music video for his campaign in which he was dressed as a cowboy with a ten-gallon hat, a six-shooter in one hand and a bottle of Jim Beam bourbon in the other.

Fontaine was elected to the city council, but did not replace the incumbent mayor. Today he owns restaurants, clubs, bars, hotels, a spa and a travel agency in Liepāja. He also organises the annual Fontaine Festival on the Promenade in August, featuring acts from both home and abroad.

ight even find a chunk of amber. white wooden hall built with help om Estonia serves as a meeting place r the last of the Liv community.

entspils

he heyday for **Ventspils** ⑱ was under ike Jacob, who launched his ships r the Caribbean and West Africa om here. But, after his death, Vent ils went into decline and following e plague of 1710 was reduced to st seven families. It enjoyed a cul al renaissance during the years of dependence, and after World War the Soviet Union built it up as an dustrial centre. In the 1990s Russian trodollars made the tiny town the althiest in Latvia, and its manicured rks, tidy streets and renovated build gs are a testament to this prosperity. e pipeline has dried up in the wake worsening relations between the o countries, and the city now sur es on revenues from oil tankers at portside terminal.

Ventspils' charming historical centre tiny and can easily be explored on ot. The town's most striking attrac n is the restored **Livonian Order stle** (Ventspils pils) dating back 1290, which houses the **Ventspils useum** (Ventspils muzejs; Tue–Sun am–5pm; charge) and a medieval taurant. Behind the castle is the omenade on the bank of the River nta where visitors can watch ships ssing by or, in the summer, take a ort cruise from the east end. The th-century Baroque **Town Hall** is o worth a visit, as well as **St Nicho- ' Church**, built in 1835 on the oppo e side of the square.

Sunbathers can take advantage of the y's Blue Flag beach, and a few hours 1 be whiled away at the **Seaside Out- or Ethnographic Museum** (Piejūras vdabas muzejs; May–Oct Wed–Sun am–6pm; charge), where the main raction is a working narrow-gauge lway. Nineteenth-century houses and hing boats hundreds of years old are o on display.

Liepāja

The other significant port on this coast is **Liepāja** ⑲, 130km (80 miles) south of Ventspils, with almost twice its population (85,000). Liepāja is a centre of metal-smelting and was a major Soviet military base with submarine pens. Known throughout the nation as the city where the wind is born, Liepāja was Latvia's Gdansk, where the first organised grass-roots opposition to Soviet rule began in the 1980s.

The city is also a major cultural centre, claiming some of the nation's best musicians and artists as its own. While it's often hard to find a live act in Rīga, rock bands perform nearly every night at "Latvia's 1st Rock Café", in Liepāja city centre.

There's plenty to see and do in Liepāja. Start in the Old Town at the 18th-century **Trinity Lutheran Church** (Sv Trīsvienības luterāņu baznīca), built in 1758, with an unusual Baroque facade and elaborate Rococo interior. Its most impressive asset is its organ dating from the same period which, until 1912, was one of the world's largest, with 7,000 pipes

Liepāja's Rock Café.

BELOW: wooden stocks at Ventspils Castle.

Awaiting sentence at Liepāja Old Prison.

and 131 registers. Head down Lielā iela to Rožu laukums, the main square, designed in 1911 with more than 500 rose bushes, giving it its name. Walk down Zivju (Fish) Street for a look at 17th-century warehouses and wooden homes with red-tiled roofs. To the left, on the corner of Kungu and Bāriņu streets, is the old **Liepāja Hotel**, where Peter the Great once slept. Ironically, across the street is another historic home where the Russian tsar's adversary, Charles XII, King of Sweden, supposedly spent the night. At the end of Zivju Street is **St Anne's Lutheran Church** (Sv Annas luterāņu baznīca), Liepāja's oldest place of worship, dating to the early 16th century, with a beautiful altar carved by Nicolas Soeffren.

The **Liepāja Museum** (Liepājas muzejs; Thur–Sun 10am–6pm; charge), located in a fine 19th-century house on Kūrmājas prospkets, is also worth a visit. The street ends at the Blue Flag beach, one of only three in Latvia, where a monument to mariners lost at sea was erected in 1977. Just south of the bronze statue are the main beach, seaside park and concert hall.

A night in the cells

North of the canal separating the O from the New City is the fascinati **Karosta** or military naval base bu in 1893 by Tsar Alexander III. It was city unto itself, with its own housin schools and churches, but now is l tle more than a collection of emp administrative and apartment buil ings and military barracks. The on building that seems to have wit stood the test of time is the colourf **St Nicholas' Orthodox Church** (Nikolāja pareizticīgo katedrāle). T **Old Prison** (Karostas cietums) is n a museum, and the years of sufferin have supposedly left their mark the building as it is purported to haunted. Daring visitors and scept of the supernatural can participate "Behind Bars", a theatrical performan where tourists are locked up in ce overnight. This can be arranged at t tourist information centre. Just nor of the city, ruined fortifications slow recede into the sea, creating an eer beautiful landscape.

Breeding ground

To the south of Liepāja, the immac late beach continues its drift towar distant Lithuania, passing eroded san banks and dunes on the coast befo crossing the border and arriving at t large resort of Palanga *(see page 319)*

Birdwatchers and nature-love who might have enjoyed the Slīte National Park should also stop at t **Pape Nature Park** (Papes dabas par at **Rucava**, the last town before t Lithuanian border. With money fro the World Wildlife Fund, the pristi seaside breeding ground for birds a other animals has been preserved. W cattle and horses that have been reint duced in this thriving ecosystem al inhabit Lake Pape and its surroundi swamps. A bird-watching tower h been erected and several miles of h ing trails have been created to make t park accessible. Accommodation c also be arranged at the Rucava tour information centre.

LATGALE

Ceramics, glassware and local produce are the rewards for exploring this land of myriad lakes, gentle uplands, outposts of Old Believers and a deep Catholic faith

Latvia's easternmost region is "The Land of the Blue Lakes". A mass of deciduous trees makes it not just bluer, but greener, too. It is the poorest and the most remote of the regions. Its people, who speak a dialect some regard as a separate language, have larger families and are more gregarious. They sometimes like to think of themselves as the Irish of Latvia. If there is any festival or gathering here it will be lively. Traditionally, the people of Latgale had homesteads adjoining each other, rather than isolated country homes as in the rest of Latvia. They continue their established crafts, especially ceramics, making big, chunky jugs and candelabra which are thickly glazed and seen everywhere.

Rubbing up against Russia, Belarus and Lithuania, Latgale's geography has given it a different history, too. While Kurzeme and Zemgale were being recruited to the Lutheran cause by the dukes of Courland, the Swedes in Rīga and Vidzeme were banishing practising Catholics, and many of them came to Latgale, where Catholic Poland held sway. They left their mark in the baroque Jesuit style of their grand churches: St Peter's in Daugavpils, St Ludwig in Krāslava, the Holy Cross of Pasiene and the huge white country church at Aglona, where Catholics from all over Europe gather in their thou-

sands on the Feast of the Assumption. Among these slightly distant lands is Daugavpils, Latvia's second-largest city, tucked in the far southeast 224km (140 miles) from Rīga, and the best part of a day's train ride away.

Plaviņas to Līvāni

The town of **Plaviņas** ⑳ is the last on the A6 from Rīga before Latgale. Here the River Daugava spreads out like a vast mirror in the summer, and in winter it is the place to see the collision of huge ice sheets. Just beyond

Main attractions
OPEN-AIR ETHNOGRAPHIC MUSEUM, JĒKABPILS
ST PETER'S CHURCH, DAUGAVPILS
STS BORIS AND GLEB CHURCH, DAUGAVPILS
KRĀSLAVA MANOR
LAKE DRĪDZIS
AGLONA
LUDZA CASTLE RUINS
PASIENE CHURCH

LEFT: Assumption Day procession in Aglona.
RIGHT: bee-keeper.

Fearing imprisonment or execution after the failure of the 1905 revolution, the playwright and political activist Jānis Rainis fled to Lugano, Switzerland, where he wrote many of his most famous works. He returned to Latvia in 1920 and became a member of parliament.

Pļaviņas the road follows the Daugava upriver to **Jēkabpils** ㉑, named after the Courland duke. Beside the road on this north bank is **Krustpils Castle** (Krustpils pils), built in 1237. Once a fortress of the Livonian Order, it came into the possession of the Korf family in the 16th century and remained their property until it was seized by the Latvian government in 1921 as part of the land reforms and used as a military base. It is now home to the **Jēkabpils Museum** (Jēkabpils muzejs; Mon–Fri 9am–6pm, Sat & Sun 10am–5pm; charge).

The town of Jēkabpils, marked by the dome of a **Russian Orthodox church** (Sv Gara pareizticīgo baznīca) of 1887, lies on the far bank of the river. It was a main river staging post for logging and the fur trade and had a settlement of Old Believers. It is famous as the birthplace of Jānis Rainis (1865–1929), the most important literary figure of the National Awakening. His father was an estate overseer and he built Tadenava, the house where Jānis was born. The building is now the **Rainis Museum** (Raiņa muzejs; May–Oct Wed–Sun 10am–5pm; charge), containing the family's household items. Of all local attractions, the **Open-Air Ethnographic Museum** (Sēļu sēta; May–Nov Mon–Fri 10am–6pm, Sat–Sun 10am–5pm; charge), displaying old farm buildings and antiquated agricultural contraptions, is the most interesting.

Līvāni ㉒, the next town upstream, is known for its excellent blown-glass art, some of which was used as decoration in the Olympic village in Athens, produced at the now defunct Līvānu stiklu fabrika. Call ahead for a tour of the **Glass Museum** (tel: 6538 1855).

Daugavpils

Daugavpils ㉓, near the Lithuanian and Belarus borders, is at a crossroads between the Baltic and Black Sea routes, and the road and railway from Warsaw to Moscow. This former capital of the Duchy of Pārdaugava, known as "Polish Livonia", has a sprinkling of 18th–19th-century mansions and the odd bright splash of Art Nouveau. The city has been attracting "foreigners" for many centuries, from the Old

BELOW: a country road near Daugavpils.

Believers, the sect exiled from Moscow in the 18th century, to others just coming to this relatively prosperous town to find work. Many left, too, including Markus Rothkowitz, who went to the USA in 1903 at the age of 10 and became the painter Mark Rothko. It is an industrial town, and Russification under the Soviets was intense. Prior to World War II one-third of the 40,000 population was Russian or Polish. Now there are 106,000 inhabitants, only a small percentage of whom are Latvian. The industries that the Soviets built up – textiles, bicycle manufacture and locomotive repair sheds – have suffered economically, but its importance as a service and transportation hub has grown.

St Peter's Church

The stunning white Catholic church of **St Peter's** (Sv Pētera katoļu baznīca) is perhaps the most striking attraction in the centre, apart from a series of bars and cafés on the city's busy pedestrian street of restored 19th-century apartment blocks named after the Latvian capital. This mid-18th-century former

monastery building is an example of a fortress church and its twin-towered facade is a mark of the Jesuit Baroque which was brought in from Lithuania. It is a basilica with three naves, the middle one rising to an impressive tunnel vault. At the end of the street by the river is the **Daugavpils Museum** (Daugavpils novadpētniecības un mākslas muzejs; Tue–Sat 10am–6pm; charge), which is worth a quick stop.

Sts Boris and Gleb Church

The three most impressive structures in Daugavpils are located outside the centre. Follow the main street next to the river across the train tracks to see two beautiful churches: the 10 onion domes of the Orthodox **Sts Boris and Gleb Church** (Sv Borisa un Gļeba pareizticīgo katedrāle), built in 1904, are only outdone by the blue pastel colour of its facade, and the Catholic church (Dievmātes katoļu baznīca) across the street looks like a smaller copy of the basilica at Aglona *(see page 232)*. Daugavpils' pride and joy is the huge red-brick **fortress** (Daugavpils cietoksnis; closed for renovations), the

Russian Orthodox Church, Jēkabpils.

BELOW: Sts Boris and Gleb church, Daugavpils.

Ceramics in Latgale

In 1990 four potters from Latgale created the Pūdnīku skūla (Potters' School), an organisation that promotes the art of making traditional ceramics without the aid of modern technology. They wanted to preserve this almost extinct centuries-old artform for future generations.

Aivars Ušpelis, a bearded man with dreadlocks and tattoos, who looks more like a Hell's Angel than an iconic potter, is one of the movement's founders. He has revived the art of creating "smoked" clay pots, vases, plates and candelabra that are black in colour and lack the glazing popular in modern ceramics. The Potters' School organises demonstrations and exhibitions around the country. For a demonstration or to buy some of his ceramics, call Mr Ušpelis, tel: 2946 6372, or contact his colleagues at www.turisms.latgale.lv.

Prepared for a cold winter.

BELOW: a procession at Aglonas Basilica during the Feast of the Assumption.

only example of this type of architecture to have survived in the Baltics.

Some 45km (30 miles) east of Daugavpils is the town of **Krāslava** ㉔, and in its centre is Krāslavas pilsmuiža, one of the finest examples of an 18th-century Polish manor house, which has suffered much over the years and is currently closed to the public, although a tour can be arranged via the Krāslava information centre, www.kraslava.lv. It has a distinguished church, **St Ludwig's** (Sv Ludviķa baznīca), completed in 1767 in Baroque style.

Lakeland region

Rolling lands of rivers and lakes spread north from Krāslava, towards Rēzekne, Latgale's capital. Just above Krāslava, lying next to the Hill of the Sun, (Sauleskalns), is **Drīdzis** ㉕, probably the most beautiful and certainly the deepest of Latvia's lakes at 65 metres (213ft). **Ežezers** ㉖ (hedgehog) lake, full of little islands, is to the northeast and nearby is Velnezers (the devil's lake) whose crystal-clear blue waters are so unusual that for centuries locals have claimed that it has mysterious

properties, thus earning its dubious name. **Rāzna** ㉗ just south of Rēzekne, is the country's second-largest lake at 56 sq km (21 sq miles), and there are plenty of local houses to rent as well as some campsites. Northwest of Rēzekne is Latvia's largest lake, **Lubāns** ㉘ but much of its 82 sq km (32 sq miles) is hardly more than marshland making Rāzna all the more impressive.

Aglona pilgrims

Northeast of Daugavpils, down stony tracks on the east side of the road to Rēzekne, is the village of **Aglona** ㉙, which is much too small for its grand Baroque church (Aglonas bazilika) to which thousands of pilgrims make their way on the Feast of the Assumption (15 August) each year, on foot, by gypsy cart, car and charabanc.

The object of their veneration is a picture of the Virgin Mary, kept behind the altar, which is said to have healing powers. The picture is reported to have been presented by Manuel Palaeologus to Lithuania's Vytautas, who gained favour with the Byzantine emperor when he brought Benedictine monks

to the country. In 1700 the picture was copied and either the copy or the original, depending on which camp you follow, remained in Lithuania while the other came here to Aglona the year that the church was founded. Money came from Jeta-Justine Sastodicka, a local Polish aristocrat, whose portrait hangs on the present basilica's west wall. The church was built to accommodate Dominicans from Lithuania whom Sastodicka invited to teach, heal and convert.

This is the second church on the site. The first one, made of wood, burnt down in 1787 and a two-towered Italianate creation rose up around the original organ, which was saved. A monastery and cloister are attached to the church; Dominicans lived here for 150 years until the tsar forbade people from becoming involved in the church.

In 1992, when a visit by the Pope to Aglona was announced, five Lithuanian-trained Latvian novices took up residence, while the grounds in front of the church were completely levelled to pave the way, literally, for the hullabaloo of a papal visit.

Rēzekne

Although modern and rather unprepossessing, **Rēzekne** ❸, 60km (38 miles) north of Daugavpils, is a relaxed place and a good centre for exploration. Its population of 35,500 is about one-third that of Daugavpils, but Rēzekne is the capital of Latgale.

The **Regional Museum** (Latgales kultūrvēstures muzejs; Tue–Fri 10am–5pm, Sat 10am–4pm; charge) is just up from the trio of churches in the main street, and has a nostalgic look at the town as it used to be before it was largely destroyed in World War II. The statue in the middle of the road, *Latgales Māra*, which symbolises the liberation of Latgale from the Bolsheviks in 1920, was destroyed twice by the Soviets in 1940 and 1950, but was erected for the third time on this spot in 1992. Rēzekne is one of many ceramics centres in the region, and typ-

ical pottery makes an attractive souvenir from shops and workshops in and around the town.

On a steep hill overlooking the city you'll find a lonely stone arch, practically all that remains of an ancient castle (Rēzeknes pilsdrupas).

Some 25km (15 miles) southeast of Rēzekne is **Ludza** ❸, one of the most attractive towns in the country and home to one of the most picturesque **castle ruins** (Ludzas pilsdrupas). Perched upon a hill overlooking two lakes, a three-storey brick wall marks the place where the largest fortress in Latgale protected Teutonic crusaders since the 14th century. A museum has local ceramics and finds from the 10th century onwards.

From Ludza the road goes east to Russia at Zilupe. To the south is the fourth of Latgale's great Catholic churches, **Pasiene church** ❸ (Pasienes katoļu baznīca). An echo of the church at Daugavpils, it's a twin-towered wedding cake built in 1761, 67 years after a Dominican mission was founded. From here there is a magnificent view across the plains of Russia. ❏

BELOW: the ruined castle at Ludza.

ZEMGALE

Latvia's smallest region stretches from Rīga Bay south through fertile plains that have produced a number of glittering palaces, most notably Rastrelli's Rundāle

The region of Zemgale was for a time linked with Courland, and from Lithuania in the south to Lake Engure, halfway along the west side of Rīga Bay, it borders the modern region of Kurzeme. Skirting Rīga, it then slips below the River Daugava and slides along the length of the Lithuanian border, tailing away to the far southeast. Apart from the northerly area around Tukums, most of Zemgale is characterised by a dead flat, fertile plain, part of the central lowlands that in places actually sink below sea level. This is the breadbasket of Latvia.

The main river is the Lielupe, which flows through the ancient towns of Bauska and Jelgava, Zemgale's capital, which the dukes of Courland and Semigallia made their home. There are a number of large 18th- and 19th-century estates in the region, but this was the frontline in World War I, and many were burnt by the retreating Russian Army. One exception is the palace at Rundāle, near Bauska, which has been magnificently restored and is now the finest in the Baltics. All of these places are within easy striking distance of Rīga.

West to Tukums

The region of Tukums lies to the west of Rīga and Jūrmala, and is a steppingstone into Kurzeme and the Baltic coast. Heading west from the capital,

the A10/E22 passes through scenes of World War I conflict, notably at Ložmetējkalns, site of the "Christmas battles", heroic attacks by the Latvian Riflemen on a strong German position in late 1916/early 1917.

Tukums ㉝ is the first town of any size on this road. It has a castle mound and was originally a Liv settlement. It has a pleasant old centre, and a tradition of weaving, which is carried on in an artisan's workshop on Tidaholmas iela (Tue–Sat 10–5pm; charge). In Harmonijas Street is the art museum which

Main attractions
TUKUMS
JAUNMOKU PILS HUNTING LODGE
ENGURE LAKE AND NATURE
  RESERVE
JAUNPILS MANORIAL CASTLE
JELGAVA HISTORY AND ART
  MUSEUM
RUNDĀLE PALACE
BAUSKA CASTLE RUINS

LEFT AND RIGHT: Rundāle Palace, built between 1736 and 1768.

has a collection of works by the most important 20th-century Latvian artists, including Rozentāls. The Lutheran church dates from 1670.

To the south of the town is the 17th-century **Durbe Castle** (Durbes pils; Tue–Sat 10am–5pm, Sun 11am–4pm; charge), set in a park with a collection of textiles and agricultural implements. Another manor house, to the north of Tukums, is **Milzkalne**, on the highest spot in the region with a view over Rīga Bay, and is home to Šlokenbeka Castle. It was built as an estate in the 15th century, and its buildings were erected in a square formation and surrounded by walls to serve as a fortress. It is the only example of this type of medieval architecture left in the Baltics. An odd museum dedicated to road-building in Latvia with exhibits of antique machinery is located inside (May–Oct Tue–Fri 9am–4pm, Sat & Sun 10am–3pm, Nov–Apr Mon–Fri 9am–4pm; free).

A few miles past Tukums on the Ventspils road is **Jaunmoku pils** ❸, a renovated hunting lodge. It was built in 1901 by Wilhelm Bockslaff, who designed the Art Academy building in

Rīga for George Armitstead, one-time mayor of the capital. Its most striking features are its ceramic stoves, built by the firm of Celms & Bēms, especially one imprinted with old postcards of Rīga from the city's 700th anniversary celebrations in 1901. On the first floor is the **Museum of Hunting and Forestry** (daily 9am–5pm; charge), which includes a collection of around 40 different animal horns from all over the world. The lodge provides facilities for hunters' holidays in the area.

A short distance southwest is the own of Kukšu, with a prime example of a manor house: the **Kukšu Muiža**, now functioning as a hotel following a lengthy restoration. *See accommodation, page 341.*

Coastal communities

From **Lapmežciems** to **Bērzciems**, most of the communities on the coast have names ending with *-ciems*, meaning village. Their attractive farm buildings stand near the sea and lurk in the wood. The **Engure Lake and Nature Reserve** lies beyond the thatched church tower roof at the little port of

Engure. This beautiful body of water stretches along the coastline separated from the sea only by a narrow strip of land. Some 50,000 birds visit this extensive (18km/12-mile), shallow lake every year, and nearly 170 different species inhabit the reserve.

South of Tukums, on the road to Dobele, is **Jaunpils** 35, a village with a lakeside manorial castle and church dating back to the 16th century. This was the estate of one Baron Reke, whose coat of arms is hung over the church altar. Visitors can also spend the night at the castle for a pittance and dine at the medieval tavern where all dishes are made in accordance with an 18th-century recipe book loosely translated as *How to Cook for Nobility*. Dobele's chief claim to fame is a ruined castle of the Livonian Order.

Jelgava, the dukes' town

South of Rīga, the only town of any size is **Jelgava** 36. Though you would not know it to look at it, Jelgava is a historic town, formerly called Mitau, that once rivalled Rīga. The history of the town, and of the 11 dukes of Cour-land and Semigallia, who were friends of the Russian Romanovs and influential at court in St Petersburg, is laid out in the **History and Art Museum** (Wed–Sun 10am–5pm; charge). This is housed in the Academia Petrina, built for Duke Peter von Biron in 1775 and once an important educational and scientific centre. It lies just behind the landmark tower of the ruined **Holy Trinity Church**. Exhibits include gold and silver ducats minted here and a waxwork of Duke Jacob. Also in the old part of town is **St Ann's Church**, from 1619, which has an altar painting by Janis Rozentāls.

The wide, slow Lielupe, which slips north into Rīga Bay, has always carried river traffic. Past the bridge on the right is the Rastrelli-designed **Jelgava Palace**, a large and solid Italianate building on the site of the town's original castle (1265). Since 1957 this three-storey, brick-red and cream building set around a square has housed an agricultural college. It is an impersonal resting place for the dukes of Courland and Semigallia, but their tombs are worth a look (daily May–Oct 9am–5pm; charge).

Kukšu Muiža, now a luxurious hotel.

BELOW: re-enacting the past at Jaunpils.

Frederick-Wilhelm, the penultimate of the Kettler dynasty of dukes, altered the family's fortunes when he married Ivan V's daughter Anna Ivanova, in St Petersburg in 1710. The 17-year-old newlyweds had just started back to the young duke's palace in Jelgava when he became ill and died. Reluctantly, Anna was obliged to continue her life in Jelgava. Bored and confined in what to her must have seemed something of a backwater of wooden homes and flat farmlands, she began an affair with Ernst Johann Biron, an ambitious Courlander on the palace staff. In 1727 Anna became Empress Anne of Russia, peopling her court with German Balts and making Biron a count.

Rundāle Palace

Within nine years of Biron becoming a count, he was wealthy enough to employ Bartolomeo Rastrelli (1700–71), the architect who later built St Petersburg's Hermitage or Winter Palace, to design a manor for himself at Rundāle, to the south of Jelgava, which he at first called Ruhental, meaning Peaceful Valley in German.

Rundāle Palace ❸⑦ (daily 10am–6pm charge) is an imposing, well-restored palace of 138 rooms, approached through a grand drive flanked by twin semicircular stables. At the height of its construction between 1736 and 1768 it employed 1,500 labourers and artisans. Work on the building and grounds, some of which still have to be restored, was interrupted first in 1738, after Biron had achieved his ambition of becoming Duke of Courland and diverted Rastrelli into turning Jelgava Castle into Jelgava Palace. The second interruption was more serious when, after becoming regent of Russia for a year following the empress's death, Biron was banished to Siberia for 23 years.

In the 19th century it was used by the tsarist governors, and the new government took it over in 1920, restoring its war damage. Rundāle has been under reconstruction since 1972. Its stairways, galleries, landings, rooms and halls are gracious and well decorated. The wall paintings are by the Italians Francesco Martini and Carlo Zucchi and the exquisite decorative moulding is by Michael Graff from

Berlin. His oval Porcelain Study is particularly striking. On the ground floor there is a collection of period furniture and ornaments.

The finest rooms are upstairs, where some interesting Dutch, Flemish and Spanish paintings from the 17th and 18th centuries are hung. The dukes' throne stood in the Gold Hall, which is matched in magnificence by the White Hall or ballroom, where the intricate stucco work includes a delicate heron's nest on the ceiling.

Mežotne Manor

Rundāle was the apogee of the fusion of German and Russian society which came together and flourished in the region in the 18th and 19th centuries. A number of important manors were built in this accessible area. The one at **Mežotne**, on the River Lielupe a few kilometres northeast of Rundāle, which was given by Tsar Paul I to his children's governess, Charlotte von Lieven, in 1797, has been restored and is now an elegant hotel and conference centre. One of the grandest houses otherwise was at **Eleja**, due south of Jelgava on the main road to Vilnius, but it is now just a forlorn ruin.

Tērvete writer's museum

The flatlands of Zemgale were originally inhabited by the Semigallians, who in the 13th century produced one of the greatest Latvian leaders, Viesturs. The centre of his domains was to the west of Rundāle in **Tērvete**, but the tribe was pushed south by the German crusaders who built a castle on the site of their stronghold, some of which still remains. Nearby is the **Meža Ainavu Park**, which has a museum called **Sprīdīši** dedicated to one of Latvia's most respected writers, Anna Brigadere, who lived here from 1922 to 1933 (May–Oct Wed–Sun 10am–5pm; charge).

Her most famous creation was Sprīdītis, an impish character who overcomes great obstacles to gain the heart of the woman he loves. The park has a vast selection of foreign and domestic trees, wooden sculptures of characters from many of Brigadere's literary works and castle ruins. A number of walking trails begin in the town.

Bauska

To the east of Rundāle is **Bauska**. On arrival there is a car park just beyond the bridge over the River Mūsa. The river shortly converges with the Mēmele, helping to form half a moat for the Livonian Order's castle, which was not rebuilt after its destruction in the Great Northern War. The huge red-brick ruins at the confluence of the two rivers are among Latvia's largest and most picturesque. Climb the tower for a good view from the top or explore the renovated duke's residence.

Every September the castle puts on an arts festival with a medieval theme. There is a small museum in the castle, and another in the town, where there is also a synagogue.

From Bauska the road leads directly north back to Rīga, past **Iecava**, which is best known for its large egg factory, fine Lutheran church from 1641 and neighbouring cemetery. ❑

Mežotne Manor's grand interior.

BELOW: Good Friday procession at Bauska castle ruins.

VIDZEME

The River Gauja runs through the rural heartlands of eastern Latvia to make Gauja National Park the country's great outdoor leisure area, centred on Sigulda and Cēsis, while quiet villages harbour the country's folkloric and literary heritage

ying to the east of Rīga, Vidzeme is the largest of the country's four regions. In the north it stretches om the Bay of Rīga all along the tonian border, and in the south it s beside the right bank of the Dau- va from the capital to the eastern gion of Latgale. Beside the river's nks, there are castles and remains ancient settlements, pointers to a owerful past.

At the heart of the region is another ver route which, though less exalted, just as ancient and rather more guiling. This is the River Gauja, hich runs through a deep gorge at e centre of the **Gauja National rk** (Gaujas nacionālais parks). It Latvia's showcase rural attraction, h in wildlife, full of prehistoric hill rts and containing one of the most portant archaeological sites. They ll it "Little Switzerland", and have stalled a bobsleigh run, but "little" the key word. The Baltics' second- ghest point is in Vidzeme: it is just 2 metres (1,025ft).

auja National Park

uja National Park begins at **Sigulda** , 50km (30 miles) northeast of Rīga, d is an easy day trip from the capital the A2 or by public transport. From gulda the park extends north through sis to Valmiera. Sigulda and Cēsis

are the main centres for information about activities and excursions such as walking, biking and boating, par- ticularly canoeing on the River Gauja, which is a popular way to appreciate the park.

The park covers around 900 sq km (350 sq miles) along more than 100km (60 miles) of river, and is divided into sections with varying degrees of access. All boating activity is popular on the river, and organised parties embark in inflatables for overnight camps, taking three days to travel from Valmiera to

Main attractions
GAUJA NATIONAL PARK
SIGULDA
UNGURMUIŽA WALL PAINTINGS
CĒSIS
ĀRAIŠI ARCHAEOLOGICAL SITE
ALŪKSNE
LAKE ALAUKSTA

FT: Turaida castle.
GHT: Cēsis.

Sigulda. Logging on the river ended when the area was designated a national park in 1973.

There is something rather sedate about Sigulda. It is a pristine and airy little town which hides its affluent past beneath a film of cleanliness. It became popular during the National Awakening as a place where Latvians from Rīga could discover their rural roots. It has more recently become a winter sports centre, with a bobsleigh run and ski slopes on the far side of the railway crossing.

Sigulda Castle (Siguldas pilsdrupas) is through the town on the left. Deeply moated and once incorporating a convent, it was built by the Crusaders' Order of Sword Bearers, who came here as soon as they arrived in Latvia in 1207. They used large boulders and stuck them together with mortar mixed with eggs and honey. Today, it is a crumbled ruin with an open-air concert hall in its midst. The attractive country house beside it is the modern "castle" (Siguldas pils), built in 1878. It now houses the city council and an upmarket restaurant. Artists

and writers of the Awakening used t come for inspiration, and Rozentā and other painters used to like hikin up to Gleznotāju kalns, Painters' Hil just to the east, which has one of th best views over the Gauja (walk fro the car park on the far side of the ol castle). Kronvaldu Atis (1837–75), teacher of Latvian, is remembered by statue outside the new castle, and som of the stained glass produced durin his lifetime is still in situ in what now a sanatorium.

Līgatne nature trails

One of the best places to see wildli and natural scenery, with possibiliti of sighting at least a deer, is just nort of Sigulda in **Līgatne**. There are als some rare plants here, such as Lady Slipper orchids, *Linnaea borealis* an woodland tulips, and in spring it is ca peted with lily-of-the-valley. Turn le to Līgatne through **Augšlīgatne** on th Sigulda to Cēsis main road, turning le again just before the river, where the are two parking spots and day ticke to the parks can be bought. Natu trails are mapped out, and a ferry tak

Kaupo and the Christians

The church at Krimulda, a 20km (12-mile) drive north from Sigulda, was erected in 1205 and is the oldest working house of worship in Latvia. At the time, a Liv tribe ruled by a chieftain named Kaupo populated the area. Unlike many of his contemporaries, Kaupo decided to embrace the new Christian faith brought by the German crusaders and even travelled to Rome, where he met Pope Innocent III. The Pope recognised him as the Christian ruler of the Livs and sent him back to Turaida with 100 pieces of gold, with which he began construction of the church.

Although the Livs weren't happy with the new arrangement, Kaupo remained loyal to his new religion and the crusaders until his death in 1217 at the Battle of Viljandi in present-day Estonia. He is said to be buried either somewhere within the church or in a nearby wood where a memorial has now been erected in his honour.

It will never be known whether or not Kaupo was a true believer or just a shrewd ruler who wanted a strong ally against neighbouring Latvian and Estonian tribes. Today you can visit the beautiful little church any time of the day or night, explore nearby nature trails and caves, or take a look at the 18th-century wooden Minister's House on the opposite bank of the stream.

ars over the river. From Sigulda there re two ways across the Gauja. The oad goes over a bridge, and every 30 minutes a cable car swings alongside it, 0 metres (135ft) above the river, taking 4/2 minutes to cover the 1km (²⁄₃-mile) istance. On the far side, the road falls way to the right to reach the side of ie river, where day tickets to the park an be bought in the car park.

ūtmanis' Cave

he banks of the Gauja are character- ed by red sandstone cliffs and caves, ie deepest of which is **Gūtmanis' ave ㊴** (Gūtmaņa ala), found oppo- te the car park. Scratched by graffiti 1ore than 300 years old, the cave is 19 1etres (62ft) deep and the fresh spring ater that wore it away still bubbles 1to it, tasting strongly of iron. The cave named after a healer called Gūtmanis ho first used the water as a cure.

Some 10 minutes' walk further up 1e road is **Turaida Castle** (Turaidas ils; 10am–6pm, until 5pm in win- r; charge), a fort of red bricks and a 1ngle round tower, which breaks up 1rough the forest heights. This is all

that remained after lightning ignited the castle's gunpowder store in the 17th century.

In the language of the ancient Livs who first settled this valley, Tura- ida means "the Garden of the Gods". Inside the castle there is a gallery and a small museum charting its history. On the path to the castle are a wooden Lutheran church (1750), the oldest in Vidzeme, and a few yards away, beneath a large elm tree, a black marble slab marks the grave of Maija, the Turaida Rose (Turaidas Roze), a young woman murdered in 1620.

Detour to Bīriņi

From Turaida the road continues to **Inciems**, where it meets up with the road to Valmiera. Time allowing, a pleasant detour on the P9 to **Bīriņi** is also recommended. The 19th-century neo-Gothic manor house at Bīriņi (Bīriņu pils) is surrounded by a beau- tiful park with a lake and a charming tavern – a perfect place for lunch.

Back on the A3, the next small town along this road is **Straupe**, where there is something familiar about the

The forbidding bulk of Turaida Castle.

BELOW: bobsleigh track at Sigulda.

Horse-drawn transport in Cēsis.

old castle (Lielstraupes pils), dating from 1263. The square tower, which rises in a dark dome and lantern, and the scrolled and stepped gable of the building below, are reminiscent of the cathedral in Rīga. The castle is in a pleasant setting beside a large pond near the River Brasla, and today it is used as a clinic for rehabilitating substance abusers.

In the grounds are a bell-tower and a Lutheran church that has some interesting 17th-century painted panels. Tombstones and tablets mark the passing of generations of the von Rosen family, owners of the castle and fierce protectors of the German Baltic way of life. The present generation is scattered, though some have helped in its restoration. It has an organ made in Rīga in 1856 by the firm of Martin, and the acoustics make it a good recital venue.

Another German monument is nearby at **Ungurmuiža** ❹ (Tue–Sun 10am–6pm; charge), on the way to Cēsis. This belonged to the von Campenhausens who had it built in 1751. It is the only existing wooden

Baroque building of this period left in Latvia, and although it has been pillaged many times over the years, its fantastic 18th-century wall paintings on the second floor have been restored to their former glory. A park surrounds the building and many ancient trees can be seen here.

Cēsis

Surrounded by nature trails, **Cēsis** ❹ is a major centre of leisure activities in both summer and winter. A pleasant, wide-open town, it was a popular cultural centre during both the National Awakening and first independence. Its attractive yellow-and-white, two- and three-storey buildings date back several centuries, and a Lutheran church, **St John's** (Sv Jāņa baznīca) was started in 1281. There are several hotels and good places to eat, but don't leave without tasting the local Cēsu beer from northern Europe's oldest brewery (Cēsu alus darītava) which has been in operation since 1590. Once produced in the castle brewing operations have moved a few streets away to Aldaru laukums or Beer Square.

Cēsis was a walled town and a member of the Hanseatic League, and it history is well documented in the **Cēsis Museum of History and Ar** (Cēsu vēstures un mākslas muzejs daily 10am–6pm; charge), which occupies the Medieval Castle, Cesis Mano the New Castle and Coach House. Th castle is a chalky-white fortified con vent that served as a power base for th Livonian Order.

Cēsis also has the distinction c being the birthplace of the Latvia flag. At the end of the 13th century, a ancient chieftain was killed in battl and was laid out on a white sheet. H blood stained the sides, leaving a whit stripe in the middle.

Āraiši archaeological finds

The locality was inhabited by Balt Finns until the Letgallians move in around the 6th century, and it h notice a reconstructed wooden fortress (Uldevena pils; Apr–Oct Thur–Sun 10am–7pm; charge) on the right side of the road. Inside you can see how ancient Latvian tribes once lived, and it's also a great place for a picnic by the river. Just outside the city centre you can visit the **Andrējs Pumpurs Museum**, where the writer once lived (Andrēja Pumpura muzejs; Tue–Sun 10am–5pm; charge). There is an old church and the ruins of a 13th-century castle located in the same park overlooking the river.

Before the A6/E22 meanders into the Latgale region, it is worth noting the 13th-century crusader castle at **Koknese** ㊾, which was once perched high on a hill above the river, but is now at the water's edge. Following the river downstream past a white Lutheran church set on a wide sweep in the river, the road comes to the ruins of the two-storey castle (Kokneses pilsdrupas) where the Pērse meets the Daugava.

Madona to Alūksne

Madona ㊿ to the north is the next town of any size, a quiet spot with a renovated inn from the 16th-century Swedish days. Just north of Madona is **Cesvaine** (51). Its impressive late 19th-century "castle" (Cesvaines pils), a mix of neo-Gothic with an Art Nouveau interior, was the hunting lodge of Baron Adolf von Wolf, who had no fewer than 99 estates in the Baltics. The castle was badly damaged in a fire in 2002 but has since been restored to is former glory and now houses a school, museum and tourist information centre.

West of Madona is **Gaiziņkalns**, the highest hill in Latvia, 312 metres (1,025ft). You can climb up to its summit for a 360-degree view of the lakes, pastureland and acres of deep green forest, not to mention an ugly new privately owned recreation area.

North of Cesvaine is **Gulbene** (52), where a manor house with a fine portico lies in ruins: bullet holes still pepper its facade. In 1944 the Germans blew up the church tower before the advancing Russians to deprive them of a viewing platform: it fell on the church, destroying the roof. Beside it is the only statue of Martin Luther in the Baltics.

A white stork on its chimney-top nest. Numbers have decreased, but the birds are still a relatively common sight in Latvia during the spring and summer.

BELOW LEFT: the old train from Gulbene to Alūksne. **BELOW:** Orthodox church at Gulbene.

A rape field adds a splash of yellow to the Vidzeme countryside.

From Gulbene a narrow-gauge railway runs up to the attractive town of **Alūksne** 🈷, which is centred on a ruined 14th-century Livonian castle (Livonijas ordeņa pils) on a lake. It sits on an island reached across a small wooden bridge and is devoted today to sports activities. A granite rotunda was built on top of the site of an ancient Letgallian fort on the southwestern shore of the lake by the Nietinghoff family to honour the dead of the Great Northern War.

One of the town's main claims to fame is that its pastor Ernst Glück adopted Martha Skavronska, the daughter of a Lithuanian grave-digger. She went on to marry Peter the Great and become Catherine I of Russia.

Glück also produced the first Latvian translation of the Bible, in 1689, and a copy of it, one of only a dozen left in the world, is kept along with many others in the **Bible Museum** (Ernsta Glika Bībeles muzejs; Pils 25a). The earliest Latvian religious tract, *God's Word*, dates from 1654, and a copy is also in the museum. When Glück first arrived in Alūksne, he lived in the castle, but he later moved to a single-storey wooden manse behind the Lutheran church, and his plantation of oaks is still standing.

Literary trail

Between these eastern towns and the Gauja National Park, a number of Latvian literary figures, who play such an important part in the country's nationhood, are remembered in a pastoral setting that can have changed little since they knew it more than 100 years ago. Beneath shady trees are several wooden barns, cottage gardens full of flowers and small platforms for the delivery vehicles to collect and return the milk churns.

Beside **Lake Alauksta** 🈴 is the **Skalbe Museum** (Kārļa Skalbes memoriālais muzejs; May–Oct Wed–Sun 10am–5pm; charge), which contains local painted furniture. Kārlis Skalbe (1879–1945), a writer of fairy tales, died in Sweden where he had fled the Soviet invasion. His remains were returned in 1992 and buried beneath a stone overlooking the lake.

The museum (Brāļu Kaudzīšu memoriālais muzejs; May–Oct Wed–Sun 10am–5pm; charge) at the nearby village of **Vecpiebalga** 🈵 celebrates the Kaudzītes brothers, Reinis and Matīss, who jointly wrote Latvia's first major novel, *The Time of the Land Surveyors* (1879). Much of the house, Kalna Kaibēni, was designed by the brothers, and the lathe used by Rainis is one of the earliest surviving in the country. A granary and sauna are part of the well-preserved home. Not far away is a museum dedicated to the composer Emīls Dārziņš, with an exhibition of writers and composers who have emigrated (Emīla Dārziņa muzejs; May–Oct Wed–Sun 10am–5pm; charge).

At **Ērgļi** 🈶 there is a museum (Rūdolfa Blaumaņa memoriālais muzejs; May–Oct Tue–Sun 10am–5pm; charge) where the playwright Rūdolfs Blaumanis was born. **Indrāni**, nearby, is the setting of one of his most famous plays.

BELOW: the Lutheran church at Alūksne.
RIGHT: Straupe.

LITHUANIA

The southernmost Baltic state, bordering Poland, Belarus and the Russian exclave of Kaliningrad, has a Baroque capital and a fabulous sandy coast

The people of Lithuania are predominantly Catholic, an impossible fact to miss. Vilnius, the capital, owes its Baroque flavour to the Jesuits who built its university as well as its many splendid churches. Outside the capital, the astonishing Hill of Crosses, just north of Šiauliai, is the biggest testament to the country's faith.

These shrines are an extension of a pagan tradition of wood-carving, seen everywhere, from the Witches' Hill on the Curonian Spit to the monuments commemorating the victims of the crimes committed during the Soviet occupation. Sometimes the recent tragic past doesn't seem so far away. Some will always think of Vilnius as the Jerusalem of Lithuania, a once-vibrant Jewish community and centre of Yiddish publishing wiped out during the Holocaust.

In spite of their Catholicism, the ethnic Lithuanians were the last people in Europe to convert to Christianity. At the height of its history the Grand Duchy of Lithuania famously stretched from the Baltic to the Black Sea. Such grandeur can be glimpsed at the dukes' castle at Trakai.

Vilnius today is a lively capital with a nightlife to rival many cities in the West. The country's second city, Kaunas, is where you'll find some of the best museums, including one devoted to Lithuania's towering artistic figure, M.K. Čiurlionis.

The River Neris, which connects Vilnius with Kaunas, runs down to a lagoon where it is separated from the Baltic Sea by the Curonian Spit. This exceptional sandbar of small fishing villages stretches south into the old region of Königsberg, now the Russian exclave of Kaliningrad. Further north, Klaipėda, Lithuania's third city, is the centre of coastal activities and as different to its two bigger relations as can be.

Add to this a rural landscape that's barely changed in the last century and the result is one of the most endearing and mystifying countries in Europe. ❏

PRECEDING PAGES: traditional farm labour; Trakai, the island castle stronghold of the dukes of the Grand Duchy. **LEFT:** a good day's catch. **TOP:** Zemaitija National Park. **ABOVE LEFT:** colourful wooden houses. **ABOVE RIGHT:** the Lithuanian coast has no shortage of long sandy beaches.

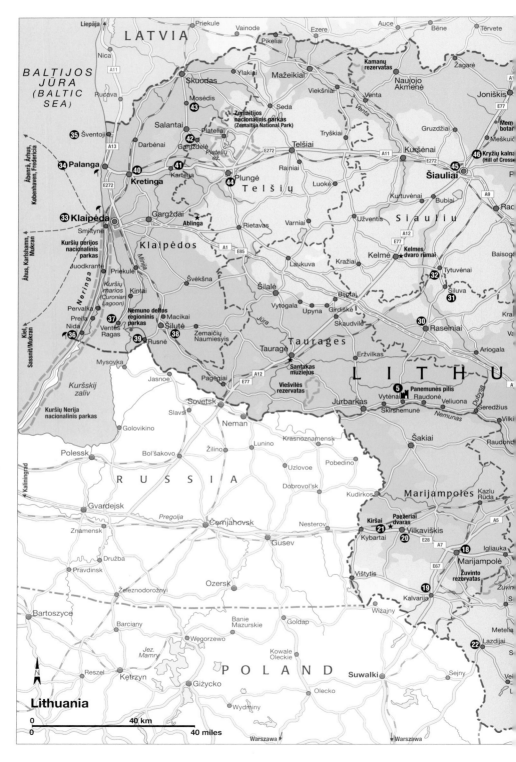

Lithuania

0   40 km

0   40 miles

THE MAKING OF LITHUANIA

One of Europe's most devout Catholic countries, Lithuania did not at first take willingly to the baptismal font, nor to the succession of foreign powers that left their mark on this proud nation before it finally won independence

The story of modern Lithuania could easily begin in 1385 with the unhappy tale of the 11-year-old Princess Jadwiga of Poland (c. 1373–99), who was due to marry young Wilhelm von Habsburg. The wedding was to take place in Kraków, then capital of Poland. The festivities were in full swing when, unexpectedly, a delegation of Lithuanian nobles arrived and went into urgent conference with their Polish counterparts. The outcome was that the archbishop headed for the castle with unsettling news for little Jadwiga. The wedding was called off and she was going to marry another man instead.

For the Polish nobility, if not for Jadwiga, the proposal just put forward by the Lithuanian delegation made more sense than her marrying a Habsburg. A conjugal union between Poland and Lithuania would create a force capable of seeing off the Teutonic Knights who were grabbing ever more of the Baltic lands. Jadwiga must have seen things differently; at least the

Eagle-eyed visitors to Lithuania will soon spot its rich ethnic history. Look around and you'll see bricks, drain covers and the like illustrated in a beguiling array of former rulers' languages.

Habsburgs were Christians. The Lithuanian Grand Prince she was now supposed to marry was a pagan. The Lithuanians had resisted every attempt to convert them to Christianity. Moreover, Prince Jogaila was three times her age and

LEFT: Logging on the River Nemunas in the mid-20th century. **RIGHT:** Grand Duke Vytautus.

it was known that he had already murdered a number of close relatives. Jadwiga watched helplessly as the castellan of Kraków entered the castle, seized the downcast von Habsburg and banished him from the kingdom.

For his part, Jogaila had no more love for the Poles than he did for their religion. The Lithuanians were proud to be pagans. Jogaila had distinguished antecedents including Mindaugas, the first to unite the peoples of Lithuania in 1230. In 1251 Mindaugas was baptised into Christianity and on 6 July 1253 he was crowned King of Lithuania. Both Christianity and the idea of the king didn't really take; Mindaugas was the only crowned King of Lithuania and, though baptised, his adherence to Christianity was minimal at best. Most of the country remained pagan.

Founder of Vilnius

The next strong leader to emerge was Gediminas (1316–41), the founder of the Gediminaičai, or as it was later called the Jogailaičiai (Jogaiłłian) dynasty that ruled Lithuania and Poland for the next 250 years. He founded Vilnius, where he built his hilltop castle overlooking the Neris and Vilnel (or Vilnia) Rivers. Though he remained pagan he brought in Dominican and Franciscan teachers and he also encouraged the

> *The Order of the Lithuanian Grand Duke Gediminas, reinstituted after independence, has been awarded to Olympic boss Antonio Samaranch, philanthropist George Soros and musician Mstislav Rostropovich.*

to make some territorial concessions to Poland and release all Polish prisoners and slaves.

On 15 February 1386, Jogaila bowed his head for a splash of baptismal water, assumed the Christian name Ladislaus (the Poles afterwards called him Władysław-Jagiełło), and three

immigration of artists and craftsmen. By the time he died, Gediminas had so successfully fought against the Tatars of the east that the Lithuanian Empire reached down to the Black Sea. In the west, the coast around Klaipėda (Memel in German) had been seized by knights of the Livonian Order in 1225. Before the orders merged, however, they also had to fight the Teutonic Knights of the southern lands that became Prussia, as well as Lithuania's dukes.

Poland was very much Rome's champion, and the marriage of Jadwiga and Jogaila was not agreed without conditions. First Jogaila would have to become a Christian. Second, he would have to convert his empire to Christianity. The terms of the marriage also required Lithuania

days later he married an unhappy Jadwiga. The following month they assumed the crowns of both Poland and Lithuania. The marriage, alas, did not have a fairy-tale ending. Jadwiga hated her husband from beginning to end and sought consolation in burying herself in good works for the poor. She died leaving her fortune to the educational establishment in Kraków, which later became the Jagiełłonian University.

King Ladislaus V – Jogaila's full title – fulfilled one of his contractual obligations by going straight to Vilnius and smashing Perkūnas' statue. What followed was the usual fusion of old pagan beliefs and newfangled Christianity. Perkūnas' mother was transformed into the Lithuanian Madonna. A bishop was appointed, and mass baptisms were organised at which converts were presented with a white smock and given a Christian name.

Last of the great rulers

The new king's previous position as Grand Prince of Lithuania per se was given to his cousin Vytautas (Witold, c.1350–1430), another grandson of Gediminas, who was the last of the great Lithuanian rulers. He built the impressive red-brick island castle at Trakai after the nearby castle of his father, Kęstutis, had been attacked once too often by the German crusaders. He drove back the Turks and mustered a

the position of both King of Poland and Grand Duke of Lithuania. The union was solidified by two sets of "Lithuanian Statutes" and finally written down in constitutional form agreed in 1569 at the Union of Lublin. The two countries were to share a king and a two-tiered government, but Lithuania kept a separate administration and its name.

Although Lithuania was territorially the larger of the two partners, Poland exerted the greater cultural influence. The Lithuanian nobility were Polonised and spoke Latin at court and Polish at other times. For the other social strata, the effects of the union were more

bodyguard of Turkic Karaites whose descendants live by the castle today. In 1410 he and Jogaila decisively defeated the German crusaders at Grunwald/Tannenberg (Žalgiris), and under Vytautas' rule the Grand Duchy became one of the largest states in Europe, occupying Belarus and Ukraine. Even with shared privileges, the rivalry between the Polish and Lithuanian nobilities see-sawed for many years. The union was considerably strengthened by Jogaila's son Casimir (by a later wife), who held

LEFT: *The Battle of Tannenberg*, 1410, when the Teutonic Knights were vanquished. **ABOVE:** *The Union of Lublin* confirms the Polish-Lithuanian pact in 1569. Both paintings are by Jan Matejko (1838–93).

PAVLOVO RESPUBLIKA

A bizarre testament to the country's historical reputation as a land of tolerance, the Pavlovo Respublika was a fully independent "state" of several farmsteads, existing from 1769 until 1795. The brainchild of the Polish priest Paweł Brzostowski (1739–1827), the republic had its own president, printed its own money, had its own flag and was recognised by the last Polish-Lithuanian parliament before the country was absorbed into the Russian Empire. The ruins of the 18th-century building that served as the republic's headquarters can be visited by those with a taste for the quirky past. Find it on route 3937, 30km (19 miles) southeast of Vilnius.

painfully felt. The Polish social order was rigorously imposed throughout the joint empire. Unlike the nobility, the Lithuanian bourgeoisie did not assume the status of their Polish counterparts. They were summarily demoted, disenfranchised and lost the right to own land.

The Lithuanian peasant had even more reason to rue the Polish takeover. "Common cruelty was an established feature of social life," argues the historian Norman Davies. "Faced with the congenital idleness, drunkenness and pilfering of the peasantry, the nobleman frequently replied with ferocious impositions and punishments. The lash and the knout were the accepted symbols of noble authority. The serfs were beaten for leaving the estate without permission, for brawls and misdemeanours, and for non-observance of religious practices. A dungeon, together with chains, shackles, stocks, hooks and instruments of torture, were part of the regular inventory."

Shared history with Poland

The history of Lithuania right up to the partition of the union by Prussia, Russia and Austria at the end of the 18th century is therefore tied to Poland's. Lithuania's separate identity had grown progressively weaker, and the parti-

NAPOLEON'S GRAND FROZEN ARMY

The northern Žirmūnai suburb of Vilnius was the focal point of historical fanfare in early 2001 when workers from a building development stumbled on a mass grave. At first, the remains were thought to be victims of the Soviet regime. A second trench with nearly 20,000 skeletons was unearthed a few months later, revealing coins and army uniform fragments that made it clear these were soldiers from Napoleon's Grande Armée.

In June 1812 the soldiers had marched through Vilnius on their way to Moscow. Welcomed as liberators from the Russian occupation, they were embraced by the city's residents. However, on their defeated trail back to Paris from Moscow five months later, the remaining half-starved and sickly soldiers arrived when the city's temperature was –30°C (–22°F). The army of nearly half a million – the largest ever raised in Europe – had been reduced to 40,000. That winter in the freezing city a further 30,000 died. As the corpses littered the streets, residents did not know how to dispose of them.

When Russian forces reoccupied the city, the corpses were placed in the thawed ground of trenches the French soldiers had dug on their advance to Moscow, hoping for the first major confrontation with the Russians. They had dug their own graves. The bones were placed in a mass grave in Antakalnis Cemetery, where they have been commemorated with a statue.

tions made matters worse. Little Lithuania or Lithuania Minor, which included Königsberg (modern-day Kaliningrad) and the coast, was given to Prussia; Russia took the rest. Tsar Alexander I toyed with the idea of reconstituting the Grand Duchy – with himself as Grand Duke – but was prevented from pursuing his idea by Napoleon's invasion. Welcomed as a liberator, Bonaparte was given the keys of Vilnius on his march with his 500,000-strong Grande Armée towards his 1812 defeat in Moscow.

To begin with, it was the Lithuanian nobility and educated classes who fretted under the Russian yoke. They joined the Polish uprising of 1831, and paid dearly. Next time round, about 30 years later, it was a stirring among the peasants, which the Russian government quelled with reforms giving peasants the right to hold up to 50 hectares (120 acres) of land each. This satisfied some of them, but others were firmly under the thumb of the Roman Catholic clergy and could not accept with good grace anything on offer from Orthodox Russia. The Russian administration responded by decreeing that only Orthodox subjects were to be employed by the state, even in the most menial capacity.

Russification

From 1864 onwards, the tsars did their utmost to Russify their Lithuanian holdings, and it was the declared policy of Muraviev, the Russian governor, to eradicate the traces of ancient Lithuania once and for all. That generally took the form of imposing Russian Orthodoxy. Non-Orthodox nobles were not allowed to buy property. They were permitted to rent it, but only for 12 years. Peasants could not buy land without a "certificate of patriotism", for which one of the qualifications was that they were Orthodox. An otherwise qualified landowner could lose his privileges simply by taking a non-Orthodox wife. Land for Jews was out of the question.

The programme of Russification reached its extreme in education. The university was closed down and only Russians were admitted to schools above elementary level. The use of the Lithuanian language was banned for all official purposes, and the Latin alphabet, in which

Lithuanian was written, was also prohibited. It became a punishable offence to have a prayer book that was written in Latin characters.

The Russian revolution of 1905 gave the Lithuanians a chance to reclaim some of their dignity, if not their independence. Resolutions were passed demanding the creation of an autonomous state with a *seimas*, or National Assembly, with Vilnius as the capital. Threatened with a campaign of passive resistance, concessions were made such as the reintroduction of the Lithuanian language in schools. National literature sprouted with amazing rapidity, but the great symbolic victory was that Vilnius,

effectively part of Poland for five centuries, was restored as the Lithuanian capital. Just as it seemed that the country might be freed of its shackles, World War I broke out.

Driven out of East Prussia, the Russian Army rampaged through Lithuania, burning, plundering and taking away all Lithuanian men of military age. The German troops in pursuit were received almost as liberators, but it was quickly apparent that Germany also considered Lithuania a source of cheap labour. The various claims submitted to the conference by a Lithuanian delegation were made to look irrelevant as the Russian revolutionary war, not to mention the activities of a renegade German force under General Bermondt, overflowed into

LEFT: Napoleon's *Grande Armée* crosses the Nemunas at Kaunas, 1815, at the start of his Russian campaign.
RIGHT: 1920s illustration of wolves attacking a woman and child in Lithuania.

Lithuania. A combined force of Estonians, Poles and Lithuanians managed to repel a Bolshevik invasion, but while they were thus engaged the Polish Army marched into Vilnius and was able to hold the capital. This takeover was in direct violation of the 1920 Suwałki Treaty signed by both Polish and Lithuanian governments. Polish forces held on to it even as the Bolsheviks swept towards Warsaw. In the end they surrendered it to the Bolsheviks rather than to Lithuania, and Kaunas became the interim capital. It was a small compensation when Lithuania reclaimed Klaipėda (Memel) and the coast from Germany in 1923.

under the terms of the secret Nazi–Soviet Pact. "Whether you agree or not is irrelevant," Molotov told the Lithuanian government, "because the Red Army is going in tomorrow anyway." The invading troops had an approved government trailing in their wake. The existing parties were dissolved, and those leaders who had not already fled were sent to Siberia.

The Soviet propaganda machine then went into action. The previous government, it said, was "indifferent to the real interests of the people, has led the country into an impasse in the fields of both domestic and foreign policy. The vital interests of the Lithuanian people have

The possession of Vilnius (Wilno in Polish) bedevilled relations between Poland and Lithuania. The city was undoubtedly the ancient capital of the Lithuanian state, but over the course of 500 years it had become overwhelmingly Polish in every other respect. In 1910 a controversial Russian census broke down the population as 97,800 Poles, 75,500 Jews and only 2,200 Lithuanians. The argument centred on the issue of whether language determines nationality. After five centuries of Polonisation and Russification, the Lithuanian language tended to be spoken only in rural areas and among peasants. The national revival did not take off until the first quarter of the 20th century. The Red Army occupied Lithuania in 1940

been sacrificed to the mercenary interests of a handful of exploiters and rich people. The only thing left to working people in the towns and in the country has been unemployment, insecurity, hunger, indigence and national oppression." The majority of the Lithuanians steadfastly denounced the Soviet annexation as illegal.

The first Soviet deportations of Lithuanians began in June 1940. Soon after, Lithuania, together with Latvia and Estonia, was occupied by the Germans. The 150,000 or so Jews in Lithuania all but vanished in Hitler's grim Final Solution, as Germans and Lithuanians set about the systematic murder of the Lithuanian Jewish population. Lithuania lost another 200,000 people to Stalin's deportation orders.

Soviet tanks roll in

When the three Baltic States moved almost in unison out of Soviet control in the late 1980s the lead in Lithuania was taken by Sąjūdis, a breakaway movement sanctioned by the Kremlin. Its objective was full independence. There was no need to consult the Soviet Union, it said

> In 1948 future President Valdas Adamkus won two gold and two silver medals in the track and field events of the "Olympic Games of the Enslaved Nations".

cheekily, because no one had ever recognised the 1940 annexation. This was too provocative even for the easygoing Soviet leader Mikhail Gorbachev and, on the day that the parliament voted for unilateral independence, Soviet tanks drew up outside. Despite the freezing temperatures, thousands found themselves on the streets. There were shootings at the TV tower in Vilnius where 14 were killed and 700 injured.

In July 1991 seven border guards were killed in Medininkai, in the south of the country, by Soviet special forces. But on 21 August Soviet troops began to leave the country and the statue of Lenin in Lukiškiū Square was torn down. By September all three Baltic countries had been admitted into the UN. Kaunas-born Vytautas Landsbergis (*b.*1932), a doctor of music and author of a number of books on Lithuanian artists and musicians, served as de facto head of state until 1992, when elections for the presidency took place.

An independent state

Through the hardship of the 1990s, self-esteem began to return, Pope John Paul II paid a visit almost as soon as he could, in September 1993, clearly delighted once more to be united with such a faithful congregation who were busily looking for funds to restore their churches. In Vilnius hard work was rewarded in the granting of Unesco World Heritage status to the Old Town.

The economy slowed at the end of the 1990s, following Russia's crisis, but recovered in the

LEFT: the Jewish quarter of Vilnius before World War II.
RIGHT: President Valdas Adamkus casts his vote after the scandal that ousted his predecessor in 2003.

first decade of the 21st century. Lithuania's own crisis struck in 2003 when Rolandas Paksas, a populist president, was impeached for corruption involving the awarding of Lithuanian citizenship to a rich Russian financial backer and gaining him the distinction of being the first political leader in Europe to have been judicially removed from office.

A former president, Kaunas-born Valdas Adamkus, who had had a career with the Environmental Protection Agency in the US, was re-elected in time to preside over Lithuania's admission into the EU and NATO in 2004. Relations with its neighbours were beginning

to normalise, too, with agreements reached with Moscow about Russian citizens travelling across the country to reach the Russian exclave of Kaliningrad.

The year 2009 was a milestone. Celebrating 1,000 years since the word Lithuania was first used in written texts, it was also one of the toughest after independence. Vilnius was awarded the title of European Capital of Culture just in time for the national airline to go bust and the global economy to nosedive, meaning the city never received the visitors it badly needed. On 12 July Dalia Grybauskaitė was elected the country's first female president, setting the tone on austerity measures to come by taking only half her salary. ❏

VILNIUS

A beautiful city, both ancient and modern, Lithuania's capital is renowned for its Baroque churches and an Old Town that is both a delight and an education to explore

Lithuania's capital lies rather inconveniently in the far southeastern corner of the country only a couple of dozen kilometres from Belarus. Vilnius ❶ grew up on a hill beside the River Neris, near the point where it is met by the smaller River Vilnel. It was a stronghold against first the Teutonic Knights and then a Tatar invasion that never came.

The Neris flows westwards towards Kaunas, Lithuania's capital during the period in the 20th century when Vilnius and the surrounding area was annexed by Poland. For 17 years the two countries were not on speaking terms. Poland and Lithuania had been joined by marriage in 1386. In 1795 Vilnius was swallowed into the Russian Empire, and as Russification followed Polonisation many churches the Jesuits had built, evolving a local Baroque style, were given over to the Russian Orthodox belief.

Heritage site

In spite of many decades of neglect, Vilnius has one of the largest Old Towns in eastern Europe, bristling with the confident and robust Gothic, Baroque and Renaissance towers of churches that seem too large and too numerous for the half a million population. In 1994 the Old Town was designated a Unesco World Heritage Site, ensuring that the maintenance and upkeep of these churches, along with the streets, is considered an important aspect of the city's budget.

About half the population is Lithuanian, while smaller percentages of Poles (18.7 percent), Russians (14 percent), Belarusians (4 percent) along with others comprise the majority of the city's various ethnic groups.

Before World War II Vilnius was one of the great Jewish cities of Europe,

Main attractions
CATHEDRAL
OLD TOWN
ST ANNE'S CHURCH
UŽUPIS
MADONNA OF THE GATES OF DAW
MUSEUM OF THE HOLOCAUST
NATIONAL ART GALLERY
ANTAKALNIS CEMETERY

PRECEDING PAGES: the museum of wooden sculpture, Rokiškis. **LEFT:** high-rises in the Šnipiskes area. **RIGHT:** the view from Gediminas Hill.

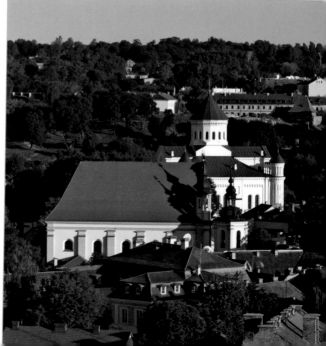

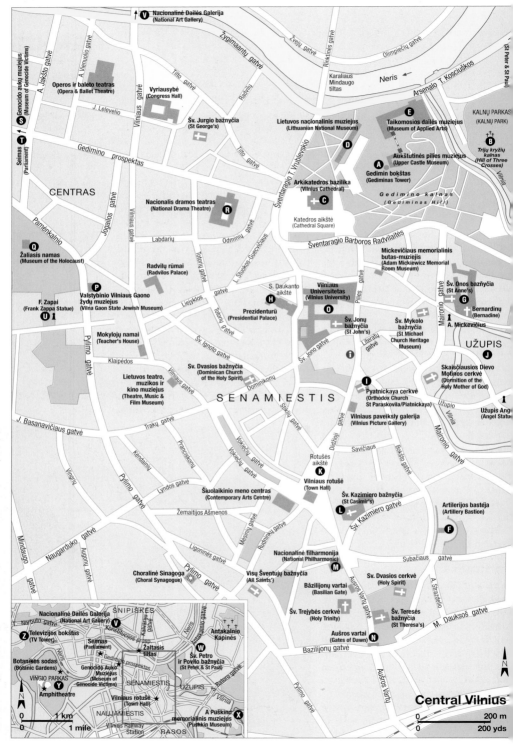

Central Vilnius

V Nacionalinė Dailės Galerija
(National Art Gallery)

Žygimantų gatvė

Rinkinės gatvė

Žvejų gatvė

Olimpiečių gatvė

(St Peter & St Paul)

Neris

Karaliaus
Mindaugo
tiltas

Arsenalo T. Kosciuškos

Operos ir baleto teatras
(Opera & Ballet Theatre)

Vyriausybė
(Congress Hall)

Vilniaus gatvė

A. Vienuolio gatvė

Tilto gatvė

Radvilų

A. Jakšto gatvė

J. Lelevelio

E Taikomosios dailės muziejus
(Museum of Applied Arts)

KALNŲ PARKAS
(KALNŲ PARK)

S Genocido aukų muziejus
(Museum of Genocide Victims)

Gedimino prospektas

Šv. Jurgio bažnyčia
(St George's)

Lietuvos nacionalinis muziejus
(Lithuanian National Museum)

D

Aukštutinės pilies muziejus
(Upper Castle Museum)

B Trijų kryžių
kalnas
(Hill of Three
Crosses)

T Seimas
(Parliament)

CENTRAS

Panerio

Jogailos gatvė

Vilniaus gatvė

Nacionalinis dramos teatras
(National Drama Theatre)

R

Labdarių

Odminių gatvė

Sventaragio T. Vrublevsko

A Gedimin bokštas
(Gediminas Tower)

Arkikatedros bazilika
(Vilnius Cathedral)

C

Katedros aikštė
(Cathedral Square)

Gedimino kalnas
(Gediminas Hill)

Vilnia

O Žaliasis namas
(Museum of the Holocaust)

Radvilų rūmai
(Radvilos Palace)

Totorių gatvė

Šventaragio Barboros Radvilaitės

Mickevičiaus memorialinis
butas-muziejis
(Adam Mickiewicz Memorial
Room Museum)

P Valstybinio Vilniaus Gaono
žydų muziejus
(Vilna Gaon State Jewish Museum)

F. Zapai
(Frank Zappa Statue)
U 1

Liejyklos

Š. Daukanto
aikštė

H

Vilniaus
Universitetas
(Vilnius University)

O

Šv. Onos bažnyčia
(St Anne's)
G

Bernardinų
(Bernadine)

A. Mickevičius

Totorių gatvė

Prezidentūrų
(Presidential Palace)

Pilies gatvė

Šv. Jonų
bažnyčia
(St John's)

Šv. Mykolo
bažnyčia
(St Michael
Church Heritage
Museum)

UŽUPIS

J

Mokyklų namai
(Teacher's House)

Klaipėdos

Pylimo gatvė

Šv. Ignoto gatvė

Šv. Jono gatvė

Literatų gatvė

Skaisčiausios Dievo
Motinos cerkvė
(Dormition of the
Holy Mother of God)

Lietuvos teatro,
muzikos ir
kino muziejus
(Theatre, Music &
Film Museum)

Šv. Dvasios bažnyčia
(Dominican Church
of the Holy Spirit)

Dominikonų

SENAMIESTIS

i

I

Pyatnickaya cerkvė
(Orthodox Church
St Paraskovila/Piatnickaya)

Užupio

Maironio gatvė

Užupis Angel
(Angel Statue)
1

J. Basanavičiaus gatvė

Kedainių

Pranciškonų

Vokiečių gatvė

Vilniaus gatvė

Šiklų gatvė

Dietžių gatvė

Vilniaus paveikslų galerija
(Vilnius Picture Gallery)

Savičiaus

Bokšto gatvė

Vingrių

Pylimo gatvė

Lyndos gatvė

Trakų gatvė

Žemaitijos Ašmenos

Mėsinių gatvė

Vokiečių gatvė

Rotušės
aikštė

K

Vilniaus rotušė
(Town Hall)

Šv. Kazimiero bažnyčia
(St Casimir's)
L

Šv. Kazimiero gatvė

Artilerijos bastėja
(Artillery Bastion)
F

Mindaugo gatvė

Naugarduko gatvė

Auguno gatvė

Ligoninės gatvė

Rudninkų gatvė

Šiuolaikinio meno centras
(Contemporary Arts Centre)

Subačiaus gatvė

Choralinė Sinagoga
(Choral Synagogue)

Pylimo gatvė

Visų Šventųjų bažnyčia
(All Saints')

Nacionalinė filharmonija
(National Philharmonic)

M

Bazilijonų vartai
(Basilian Gate)

Aušros Vartų gatvė

Šv. Dvasios cerkvė
(Holy Spirit)

Šv. Trejybės cerkvė
(Holy Trinity)

Šv. Teresės
bažnyčia
(St Theresa's)

Aušros vartai
(Gates of Dawn)
N

Bazilijonų gatvė

M. Daukšos gatvė

Strazdelio

Pylimo gatvė

Aušros Vartų

Batoro gatvė

N

Central Vilnius

0 _____ 200 m
0 _____ 200 yds

ŠNIPIŠKĖS

Nacionalinė Dailės Galerija
(National Art Gallery)
V

Z Televizijos bokštas
(TV Tower)

Narbuto gatvė

Konstitucijos prosp.

Antakalnio gatvė

Neris

Antakalnio
Kapinės

Seimas
(Parliament)

Žaltasis
tiltas

Gedimino prospektas

W Šv. Petro
ir Povilo bažnyčia
(St Peter & St Paul)

Botanikos sodas
(Botanic Gardens)

VINGIO PARKAS

Y Amphitheatre

Genocido Aukų
Muziejus
(Museum of
Genocide Victims)

SENAMIESTIS

UŽUPIS

Vilnia

N

0 _____ 1 km
0 _____ 1 mile

NAUJAMIESTIS

Vilniaus rotušė
(Town Hall)

A Puškino
memorialinis muziejus
(Pushkin Museum)
X

Vilnius Railway
Station

RASOS

and a centre of Yiddish publishing. New streets and buildings in its centre mark the site of their ghetto: some 150,000 of its inhabitants were killed by the Nazis and their Lithuanian henchmen.

Besides the variety of churches, the city's historical legacy can be viewed in a very hands-on and real way by visits to the 16th-century Gates of Dawn, with an icon believed to work miracles, and to the former KGB and Gestapo headquarters, which is now a museum. Most pleasure is to be had from inspecting the churches and simply walking the cobbled streets. These are brightened by antiques shops, restaurants, bars and cafés. There are several outstanding restaurants. The beer bars that in summer tend to bloom on the city's streets and the cavernous cellars that become the city's pulse in colder months are also an important aspect of Vilnius' charm.

Castle Hill starting point

The best place to start a tour of the city is from the top of the **Gediminas Tower** Ⓐ (Gedimino bokštas) on **Castle Hill** (Gedimino kalnas), overlooking the red-tiled roofs and the church towers of the Old Town, the Cathedral, the administrative buildings along the main avenue, Gedimino prospektas and the modern business and shopping centres on the right bank of the Neris, stretching to the Television Tower in the Karoliniškės district and beyond.

The castle on Castle Hill, the oldest settlement of Vilnius, was built by Grand Duke Gediminas (Giedymin, c.1275–1341) at the confluence of the Neris and Vilnelė Rivers. It was to this spot that he invited merchants, artisans and friars from various Hanseatic towns. According to legend, Gediminas dreamed of a powerful iron wolf howling from a hill at the mouth of the Vilnelė, a dream which signified that at this spot a magnificent fort and town would arise.

All that remains are the ruins of the southern part and the western defence tower, Gediminas Tower, which

houses the **Upper Castle Museum** (Aukštutinės pilies muziejus; daily 10am–5pm; charge). The restored 14th-century, three-storey octagonal brick tower houses a small exhibit of archaeological findings and the history of the castle, which is one of the symbols of Lithuania's independence. The independence movement scored its first victory when the old Lithuanian yellow, green and red tricolour was raised on the observation platform on 7 October 1988.

On the nearby **Hill of Three Crosses** Ⓑ (Trijų kryžių kalnas) are the symbols of Lithuanian mourning and hope, which were rebuilt and unveiled on 14 June 1989. The first crosses were erected on the hill in the 17th century in memory of martyred Franciscan monks. During Stalin's time they were removed and buried. The crosses standing today are reproductions of the originals.

At the foot of Castle Hill lies the recently completed **Royal Palace** (Valdovų rūmai), a replica of the original 15th-century building demolished by the Russians at the start of the 19th

TIP

Visiting the top of Castle Hill is a must, although the walk can be tiring for many. A relatively new funicular-type vehicle now operates for 3Lt each way. Find it in a hidden courtyard west of the Museum of Applied Arts.

BELOW: Gediminas Tower.

century and currently open only for special events and exhibitions.

The Cathedral

The settlement's original church, which became the **Cathedral** ⒞ (Arkikatedros bazilika), was built in the 13th century by the order of King Mindaugas. After his death the church reverted to its original use as a pagan shrine until the structure was recommissioned in 1387 by Grand Duke Jogaila (Jagiełło). The structure then became a symbol of Lithuania's conversion to Catholicism. It occupied the northern part of the castle complex and it was rebuilt 11 times.

The present white neoclassical building by Laurynas Stuoka-Gucevičius (Wawrzyniec Gucewicz, 1753–98) dates from 1777–1801, when it was given its dominating portico of six Doric columns topped with the imposing renovated statues of Sts Helen, Stanislaus and Casimir, supposed symbols of Russia, Poland and Lithuania. The facade has large Baroque statues depicting Abraham, Moses and the four Evangelists. The interior has three naves of equal height divided by two rows of massive pillars. The main altar is classical, and there are several interesting chapels on the right, especially the Baroque chapel of St Casimir (1623–36), which now contains the mausoleum of Kings Alexander and Ladislaus IV. As the patron saint of Lithuania, Casimir is believed to have had miracle-working powers, hence the ex-votos, the silver body parts left by the faithful as a prayer for the release from some particular ailment.

Also of interest is the Cathedral Crypt, which serves as the final resting place for many of the country's leaders, noblemen and archbishops. In 1985 a fresco was found along the crypt's wall. It is believed to have been painted at the end of the 14th century, making it the country's oldest wall painting.

In the Soviet era the Cathedral served as a picture gallery. As a symbol of national revival, it was the first church to be reconsecrated, on 5 February 198_. The 52-metre (170ft) **belfry**, which stands to the front and to the right of the Cathedral, was originally part of the city's defence walls. Although closed

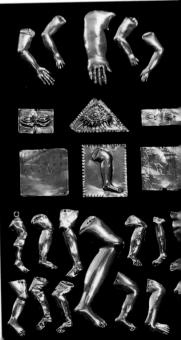

visitors, it is a distinctive landmark and a good meeting point.

Walk away from the Cathedral towards the Neris to find the **Lithuanian National Museum** ❶ (Lietuvos nacionalinis muziejus; Tue–Sat 10am–5pm, Sun 10am–3pm, Monday closed; charge), the country's biggest museum. Founded in 1855, closed by the tsarist authorities and reopened in 1968, the exhibits therein illustrate the history of the people of Lithuania from the Stone Age to 1945. There are costumes, farming and fishing equipment and recreated interiors of houses from different regions along with weapons and armour. In front of the museum sits a statue of King Mindaugas (Mendog, c.1200–63), unveiled on the 750th anniversary of his coronation on 6 July 2003.

Further round the hill on the right at No. 2 Arsenalo is the **Museum of Applied Arts** ❷ (Taikomosios dailės muziejus; Tue–Sat 11am–6pm, Sun 11am–4pm, Mon closed; charge). The museum has a number of changing exhibitions as well as a permanent collection of paintings and folk pieces, for the most part focusing on wooden sculptures and other Christian art.

The Old Town

Covering 269 hectares (665 acres), Vilnius' **Old Town** (Senamiestis) is one of the largest in eastern Europe. The main artery running through the medieval city was Pilies gatvė (Castle Street, or just plain Pilies), which begins at the southeast corner of Katedros aikštė (Cathedral Square) and runs into Didžioji gatvė (Great Street), past Town Hall Square and on into Aušros vartų and the Gates of Dawn, the only remaining gates of the town fortifications built against the Tatar invasions in the early 16th century. Only a few parts of the town wall remain in Bokšto, the street with the **Artillery Bastion** ❻ (Artilerijos bastėja; Bokšto 20), which is currently closed to the public for long-term renovation work.

On cobblestoned Pilies lie numerous historical buildings, and from the balcony at No. 26, Lithuania's independence was declared in 1918. The building is now the **Signatories' House** (Signatarų Namai; Tue–Sat

Legend has it that a dragon, the Vilnius Basilisk, lived in the Artillery Bastion (above). He turned people to stone with his gaze until he saw his own reflection in a mirror.

BELOW: Vilnius Cathedral and belfry.

Constitution Wall, Užupis.

10am–5pm, closed Sun, Mon; free), which houses a small museum dedicated to the events that can be visited only as part of a guided tour. It is well worth venturing into the side streets and courtyards for a glimpse of the 19th-century city. There are a number of antiques shops, cafés and cellar bars tucked away down these quiet lanes.

St Anne's Church

Bernardinų, at the northern end of Pilies, leads to **St Anne's Church** **G** (Šv Onos bažnyčia; Maironio 10), one of the best examples of Gothic architecture in Lithuania. Its western facade is patterned with 33 different varieties of bricks, making it amazingly graceful and harmonious. The chapel was built in the 16th century during the reign of the Jagiełłonian king Žygimantas Augustas (1520–72). The church has no foundations; it rests on alder logs. The original interior was destroyed by fires and is of minor interest. Napoleon Bonaparte is said to have been so enraptured by St Anne's that he exclaimed his desire to bring the church back to France in the palm of his hand and set it down next to Notre-Dame.

Napoleon stayed in Vilnius on the way to and from Moscow during his ill-fated campaign of 1812, at the Bishop's Palace in Daukantas aikštė, behind the university, which is now the **Presidential Palace** **H**. The French writer Stendhal was in charge of food and provisions, and it was in Vilnius, he said, that he learned to drink like a Russian. The euphoria that greeted the Grande Armée's arrival evaporated on their retreat when the city was plundered by the starving troops. In early 2001, workers from a housing development in the north of the city stumbled on a mass grave of about 30,000 Napoleonic soldiers (*see pages 262 and 282*). Some of their bones now lie in a communal grave at Antakalnis Cemetery.

The palace was built for merchants in the 16th century and redesigned at the end of the 18th century by Laurynas Stuoka-Gucevičius, whose monument stands in front of the nearby 16th-century **Church of the Holy Cross** (Šv Kryžiaus bažnyčia). In tsarist times it was the residence of the governor general, and under the Soviets it was the Palace of the Art Workers. Today it is the official residence of the President of Lithuania.

Next to St Anne's is the **Bernardine Church and Monastery** (Bernardinų Bažnyčia ir Vienuolynas); the order came here from Poland in 1469. It has a Gothic roof and a Baroque belfry, and being built on the edge of the town it was fortified with gun ports. The nearby statue represents the Polish-Lithuanian writer Adomas Mickevičius (Adam Mickiewicz, 1798–1859), born in Lithuania and educated at Vilnius University, who wrote the epic *Pan Tadeusz* about Lithuanian society.

Facing St Anne's is the former **St Michael's Church** (Šv Mykolo bašnyčia), built between 1594 and 162. in the style of the Lublin Renaissance as a family mausoleum for Leona

BELOW: Bernardine Monastery.

Sapiega, Chancellor of Lithuania. The building now houses the **Church Heritage Museum** (Bažnytinio paveldo muziejus; Tue–Sat 11am–6pm, closed Sun, Mon; charge), opened in 2009 and containing a wealth of exhibits charting the rise of the Catholic Church in the country.

The many churches in the Old Town are signs of Vilnius' geographical situation on the border of Catholicism and Orthodoxy. The **Orthodox Church of Paraskovila Piatnickaya** ❶ (Pyatnickaya cerkvė) on Didžioji Street was constructed for the first wife of Grand Duke Algirdas in the 14th century, and Peter the Great reputedly baptised Alexander Pushkin's great-grandfather here. Further up the street, the **Orthodox Church of the Holy Mother of God** belonged to Algirdas' second wife.

Užupis

Opposite St Anne's on the far side of the small River Vilnelė lies **Užupis** ❶, the first suburb outside the fortified city walls. This slightly scruffy but up-and-coming district, once dubbed the Montmartre of Vilnius because of its arty population, has designated itself as the independent Republic of Užupis (Užupio Respublika). On 1 April, the appropriate day of their declared independence, border patrols are set up and passports must be shown to their fake policemen. Their antics have been tolerated to such an extent that the Lithuanian Ministry of Foreign Affairs has opened up diplomatic relations with them. The area is as fun-loving as its residents. The tongue-in-cheek Užupis Constitution can be seen in Paupio Street and is translated into English and several other languages.

Explore the main workshop and art gallery of the republic, the **Užupis Gallery** (Užupio galerija; Užupio 2; Tue–Fri 11am–7pm, Sun 11am–3pm, closed Mon), which also houses a gift shop where unique Užupis souvenirs can be bought. A brightly painted crumbling ruin of a building, the gallery is hard to miss. Outside find sculptures on the riverbank and in the river itself, while the internal gallery space is given over to all manner of media, from children's finger-painting

EAT

Take a break from sightseeing at the lively Užupis Café (Užupio kavinė; Mon–Thur 10am–11pm, Fri–Sun 10am–midnight), located among the sculptures dotted around the riverbank.

BELOW: Town Hall Square.

The Madonna of the Gates of Dawn.

BELOW: rector's room at the university.
BELOW RIGHT: the Gates of Dawn.

to experimental photography. The **Angel statue** at the intersection of Užupio and Malūnų is a symbol of the republic. The area is known for its traditional arts, and several working galleries of jewellery, ceramics and other crafts can be found here.

Town Hall Square

Town Hall Square Ⓚ (Rotušės aikštė) was the political, cultural and economic centre of Vilnius. The original 15th-century **Town Hall** (Rotušė) didn't survive, and the present one, which was designed by Laurynas Stuoka-Gucevičius, the architect of the city's Cathedral, was completed in 1799. In the 19th century it was frequently used for cultural events, and in 1845 it became the first town theatre.

Past the Town Hall Square up Didžioji lies **St Casimir's Church** Ⓛ (Šv Kazimiero bažnyčia), the oldest Baroque church in Vilnius, built in 1604–15 and named after the patron saint of Lithuania. The saint was the son of Casimir IV of Poland; the crown on the church roof represents his royal connections. The church has long been

an object of persecution. Under the tsars it was converted into the Orthodox Church of St Nicholas and the crown of St Casimir was replaced by an onion dome; during World War I the occupying Germans turned it into a Protestant church, and the Soviets subsequently made it the Museum of Atheism and History of Religion. St Casimir's reopened for public worship in 1989 and has been magnificently restored to its original splendour.

Didžioji Street leads into Ausros vartų. The **National Philharmonic** Ⓜ (Nacionalinė filharmonija), built in 1902, is at No. 5. This is one of the city's main music venues, with both a concert hall and chamber music hall, where the national orchestra and choir regularly perform,

Gates of Dawn

The street rises to the only remaining city gate, the **Gates of Dawn** Ⓝ (Aušros vartai; Ostra Brama in Polish). In 1671 Carmelite nuns from neighbouring St Theresa's built a chapel above the gates to house a holy image of the Virgin Mary, said to have mirac-

ulous powers. Its artist is unknown and it has been encased in gold and silver by local goldsmiths, leaving only the head and hands uncovered. The chapel's interior was refurbished in the neoclassical style in 1829, and from the street below pilgrims can be seen singing and praying in front of the Virgin. Thousands of votive offerings decorate the walls, and many pilgrims of both the Catholic and Orthodox faiths come to pray, queuing up on the stairs installed in the 18th century to connect the chapel to the adjacent **Church of St Theresa** (Šv Teresės bažnyčia). Mass is held in Polish and Lithuanian.

On the way up to the Gates of Dawn, in the courtyard of the only Russian monastery to operate during the Soviet era, stands Vilnius' most important Orthodox church, the **Church of the Holy Spirit** (Stačiatikių Šventosios Dvasios cerkvė). It was built in the 17th century to serve the Russian Orthodox community, and it bears similarities to Catholic architecture. Before the altar stands a glass case containing the well-preserved bodies of Saints Anthony, Ivan and Eustachius, martyred in 1347 because of their faith, at the behest of Grand Duke Algirdas. The three saints are clothed in white during the Christmas period, black during Lent and red on all other occasions. However, on 26 June the bodies, believed to have healing powers, are left naked.

Vilnius University

A tour of the Old Town should include a visit to **Vilnius University** ❾ (Vilniaus Universitetas), founded in 1570 by the Jesuits and one of the most important centres of the Counter-Reformation. For almost 200 years the Jesuits' college was the source of enlightenment, science and culture. It was closed under the tsarist regime in the 19th century. Today, some 21,000 students study at its 12 faculties. The four-storey building with an observatory tower dates back to 1569 and its windows are Rococo. The library contains nearly 5 million volumes, making it the richest collection of Lithuanian books, as well as 180,000 manuscripts from the 13–16th century. Soon after it was founded, it became one of the best-known libraries in eastern Europe.

TIP

Street finder:
gatvė means street,
aikštė is square,
prospektas is avenue,
kelias is road.

BELOW: view from the university tower.

> *Courage illuminated the old world with light.*
>
> Virgil, quoted in the Observatory

At Universiteto No. 7 there is a map, and on the north side of the building stands a small door where visitors are required to pay an admission fee. There are 13 courtyards in the grounds. The first is named after the poet and humanist Motiejus Kazimieras Sarbievijus (Maciej Kazimierz Sarbiewski, 1595–1640). Most of the building's interior is currently off limits to visitors, although the splendid courtyards remain open to the public.

Adjacent to the university is St John's Church (Švs Jonų bažnyčia), named after St John the Baptist and St John the Evangelist. It was built in 1427, but its present Baroque look is from restoration work from 1737. Its 68-metre (223ft) bell-tower is the tallest structure in the Old Town. During the Soviet occupation the church was used as a Museum of Scientific Thought. Today the working parish church has kept some flavour of its former incarnation, as exhibits, including a 1613 map of the country along with some scientific books from the 14th century, can be found within its six chapels. The church also

functions as a regular concert venue.

Opposite the church is a passageway leading to the Observatory Courtyard and the university's **Observatory**, founded in 1753, when it ranked third in importance in Europe after those at Greenwich, London, and the Sorbonne, Paris. The top of the facade is crowned with the signs of the zodiac. Further on, in Daukanto Courtyard, the offices of the **Yiddish Studies Institute** are helpful to walk-in visitors who are investigating their Jewish past in Lithuania or surrounding countries.

The "Jerusalem of Lithuania"

An essential part of pre-war Vilnius was its massive Jewish population, which made up nearly half of the city. Today little remains of the Jerusalem of Lithuania, as Vilnius was once called. The Great Synagogue and the Schulhoyf, the traditional centre of Jewish culture around today's Vokiečių, Žydų and Antokolskio streets, suffered heavy damage during the Holocaust. The ruins of the synagogue, which dated back to 1661, remained for some year

BELOW: Choral Synagogue.

before the Soviet authorities decided to blow up what was left to make way for a kindergarten and a basketball court, and despite the small present-day congregation, there continue to be proposals to see it rebuilt. The only remaining synagogue for the small surviving Jewish community is the **Choral Synagogue** (Choralinė Sinagoga) at Pylimo 39.

Museum of the Holocaust

The **Vilna Gaon Jewish State Museum of Lithuania** ℗ (Valstybinio Vilniaus Gaono žydų muziejus; Pylimo 4; Sun–Thur 10am–4pm, closed Fri, Sat; charge) is named after the city's most famous rabbinical scholar, the Gaon of Vilnius (1720-1797). The museum has two other branches. The **Tolerance Centre** (Tolerancijos Centras, Naugarduko 10; Mon–Thur 10am–6pm, Fri 9am–4pm, Sun 10am–4pm, closed Sat; charge), has several worthwhile exhibitions, while the **Museum of the Holocaust** ℚ, also called the Green House (Žaliasis namas; Pamėnkalnio 12; Mon–Thur 9am–5pm, Fri 9am–4pm; charge) was started by Holocaust survivors. The

most important Jewish-related museum in the country, the Green House was due to reopen in October 2010, after extensive renovation work aimed at removing all traces of the original exhibits and replacing them with a more sanitised version of the events that took place in Lithuania between 1941 and 1944.

In front of the museum stands a monument to Chiune Sugihara, Japanese consul in Kaunas from 1939–40. He and his colleagues helped save 6,000 Jews by issuing them with papers to leave the country.

Around Pylimo Street

The western section of the Old Town is hemmed in by Pylimo gatvė, but dominated by Vokiečių gatvė (German Street), especially in summer when it is lined with outdoor cafés. The street is one of the oldest in the city. Its name comes from the large numbers of German traders who erected most of its buildings. Most on the east side have been rebuilt since being destroyed in

Monument to the wartime Japanese consul Chiune Sugihara, who helped many Jews escape.

LEFT: the Great Synagogue in 1944.

Jewish Extinction

A centre of Jewish culture that produced the artist Chaim Soutine and violinist Jascha Heifitz, Vilnius once had 100 or so synagogues and prayer houses stretching from Gaono to Pylimo Streets and Trakų to Rūdninkų Streets, which were, with the exception of one, destroyed during the Holocaust.

In 1941 some 50,000 Jews were herded into two ghettos. The Small Ghetto around Stiklių Street lasted from 9 June to 29 October before its 15,000 inhabitants were liquidated. The bigger ghetto, established on 6 September around Žemaitijos and Rūdninkų Streets, was liquidated two years later. Today, at Rūdninkų 18, a map showing the outlines of these two Jewish ghettos can be seen.

Most of the 50,000 Jews were killed in Paneriai (Ponar), 10km (6 miles) southeast of Vilnius off the A16/E28 on Road 106. There is also a small museum, but working hours are erratic, especially in the cooler months, so it is best to arrange an appointment (tel: 86 808 12 78).

The Yiddish Studies Institute in Vilnius University is the first of its kind in post-Holocaust eastern Europe and it organises popular Yiddish-language summer courses. The students and professors in the office welcome anybody who wants to find out more about their Jewish past in Lithuania (www.judaicvilnius.com).

Cells in the former KGB building.

World War II. The wide pedestrian pavement flanked by narrow lanes of traffic going in opposite directions makes it a prime outdoor seating spot in the warmer months. At the southern end of the street at Vokiečių 2 is the **Contemporary Arts Centre** (Šiuolaikinio meno centras; Tues–Sun noon–8pm; charge) with changing contemporary exhibits, except for the Fluxus room, where there are numerous works by the 1960s Fluxus Movement, the best known of whom is the late John Lennon's paramour, Yoko Ono.

Celebrating art and music

Along Vilniaus Street stands the Radvilos family palace (known in Polish as the Radziwiłł), all that remains of the city estate of a local noble family. Part of it functions as the **Radvilos Palace Museum** (Radvilų rūmai; Tue–Sat 11am–6pm, Sun noon–5pm; charge), where close to 200 of their family portraits are on display along with a small collection of foreign fine art. Further along the street is the **Theatre, Music and Film Museum** (Lietuvos teatro, muzikos ir kino muziejus; Tue–Sun 11am–6pm, Sat 11am–4pm; charge) with the emphasis on the history of theatre and music in the country. There are lovely music boxes from the early 1800s, pianolas and harmoniums, theatrical costumes and set designs, with a minimal nod to cinema. Downstairs is also an exhibition space with the occasional superb show. Entrance to both is at the back of the building.

Inside the **Teacher's House** (Mokytojų namai; Vilniaus 39) is one of the finest art galleries in the city, **Vartai** (Tue–Fri noon–6pm, Sat noon–4pm). Founded in 1991, it never seems to have an empty piece of wall space. Expect thought-provoking work that centres around the schools of Naïve and Surrealist art. The courtyard plays host to a large outdoor bar, Vasaros Terasa (Summer Terrace), during the summer, popular with the local clubbing set.

New Vilnius

New Vilnius unfolds along the central pedestrianised avenue **Gedimino prospektas**, opposite the Cathedral. This is where most of the administrative buildings are situated, and it is the main shopping area in the city centre. There are a number of striking new buildings as well as old ones in the street, including Neringa restaurant, at No. 23, once a meeting place for the city's intellectuals and decorated with magnificent Socialist–Realist murals of the coast dating from 1959. The National Drama Theatre ⓡ (Nacionalinis dramos teatras) at No. 4 has black-robed, gold-faced muses symbolising Drama, Tragedy and Comedy on its facade. Its repertoire is principally the classics, in Lithuanian.

The former KGB and Gestapo headquarters opposite Lukiškių Square was transformed into the misleadingly named **Museum of Genocide Victims** ⓢ (Genocido aukų muziejus

BELOW: bike rental.

Tue–Sat 10am–6pm, Sun 10am–5pm; charge). This is a shrine to the victims of Soviet tyranny, and the "genocide" in question refers to Lithuanians, whose population actually increased during the Soviet occupation. The fact is that the museum overlooks the other mass murder directed from the building between 1941 and 1944, against the country's Jewish population.

The 1.5km (1-mile) long avenue ends at the modern **Parliament** ➊ (Seimas) building, which was surrounded by barricades for several months after the Soviets attempted to storm the building in 1991. Some of the great concrete blocks and graffiti that regularly featured here have been preserved.

Vilnius has shed most of its blatant Soviet symbols. The statues of Stalin, Lenin and Kapsukas, a local Communist leader, are now sited with all other Lithuanian Soviet monuments in the tiny village of Grūtas near Druskininkai *(see page 309)*. However, close to Gedimino, at the far northern end of Vilniaus on the **Green Bridge** (Žaliasis tiltas) over the River Neris, stand four Soviet-era statues of sturdy peasants and factory workers dating from 1952.

Another statue to note is the bust of **Frank Zappa** ➍ (1940–93), at Kalinausko 1, hidden away behind the polyclinic building. Made in the mid-1990s, the bust is the work of the local sculptor Konstantinas Bogdanas, who is known for his many Soviet-era statues. Oddly enough, the deceased American rock musician had no connection whatsoever with Lithuania, and in 2010 a new cast of the statue was donated to Zappa's native Baltimore.

Outside the Old Town

A welcome addition to the city is the **National Art Gallery** ➒ (Nacionalinė Dailės Galerija; Konstitucijos 22; tel: 219 5960; Tue, Wed, Fri–Sat noon–7pm, Thur 1–8pm, Sun noon–5pm, closed Mon; charge), which lies just over the river close to the Radisson Blu Hotel Lietuva. Opened in 2009, it mounts a constantly changing series of superb exhibitions from home and abroad.

One church outside the Old Town worth making the effort to reach is the **Church of Sts Peter and Paul** ➐ (Šv

Frank Zappa memorial.

BELOW LEFT: figures outside the National Drama Theatre.
BELOW: shopping mall by the Green Bridge.

The black granite tomb in Rasos Cemetery contains the heart of Polish hero Józef Piłsudski.

Petro ir Povilo bažnyčia; Antakalnio 1). Commissioned in 1668 by Mykolas Kazimieras Pacas (Michał Kazimierz Pac, 1624-1682), a local military commander, it is the best example of Baroque architecture in the city. Pac's tombstone, inscribed *Hic jacet peccator* ("Here lies a sinner"), is embedded in the wall to the right of the entrance. Despite a plain facade, the Baroque interior is breathtaking, with more than 2,000 undecorated stuccoed figures crowding the vaults, representing mythological, biblical and battle scenes. The boat-shaped chandelier is also spectacular.

Cemeteries to the fallen

Beyond this church to the northeast of the city is the **Antakalnis Cemetery** (Antakalnio kapinės; Karių Kapų 11), which symbolises Vilnius' complicated and bloody history. In the Soldiers' Cemetery German, Polish, Russian, Lithuanian and even Turkish soldiers lie in the same soil. In a clearing at the back four giant Soviet granite soldiers stand next to a hall of fame where the dignitaries of Soviet Lithuania are bur-

ied, while 1,700 skeletons from Napoleon's Grande Armée are in a nearby mass grave *(see page 262)*. In the centre of the cemetery lie the graves of the seven border guards and the civilians killed beside the TV Tower during the fight for independence by the same Soviet Army *(see page 283)*.

Some 5km (3 miles) north of the centre over the Green Bridge and along Kalvarijų gatvė is **Verkiai Palace** (Verkių rūmai; Žaliųjų Ežerų 49), a singular neoclassical manor house now used by the scientific community. The surrounding gardens and forest are a lovely place to relax.

The other major cemetery is to the southeast of the city. **Rasos Cemetery** (Rasų kapinės; intersection of Rasų and Sukilėlių), founded in 1801, is known as the "Pantheon of the Famous". Prominent politicians, academics (Joachim Lelewel), poets (Ludvik Kondratowicz) and painters (Pranciškus Smuglevičius, 1745–1807) are among those buried here. Of particular interest are the graves of the artist and composer Mikalojus Konstantinas Čiurlionis (1875–1911), the writer Balys Sruoga (1886–1947)

BELOW: a street café on a warm summer's day.

and author Jonas Basanavičius (1851–1927). The heart of Józef Piłsudski, the Lithuania-born Polish military general, who ensured eastern Lithuania was under Polish control from 1920 to 1939, is also buried here. The rest of his remains lie in a coffin in the crypts of Wawel Cathedral in Kraków, but as he always felt his heart was in Vilnius, his was buried along with his mother's body under a black granite slab.

Pushkin Museum

Just out of town to the southeast, on the far side of the Markučiai district, is the **Pushkin Memorial Museum** ❌ (Puškino memorialinis muziejus; Subačiaus 124; Wed–Sun 10am–5pm; charge) in the former home of Alexander Pushkin's son, built in 1867. One room contains the poet's possessions, and you can also see the 19-hectare (47-acre) grounds where the anti-tsarist uprising of 1863 was hatched.

West of the Old Town

To the west of the city, inside a crook in the meandering River Neris is **Vingis Park** ❶ (Vingio parkas), a popular place for cyclists and skaters. The park dates back to the 16th century, when it was part of the aristocratic Radvila (Radziwiłł) estate. Tsar Alexander I was at a ball in Radvila Palace, then in Vingis, when he received the news of Napoleon's invasion in 1812 – the episode is detailed in Tolstoy's book *War and Peace*.

The first **National Song Festival** took place here in 1947, and a special stage was built in 1960 to absorb the 20,000 singers, dancers and musicians who still flock here every five years to take part in one of the country's great celebrations.

The housing districts on the far side of the river are the work of Soviet-Lithuanian architects. In 1974 the designers of the new **Lazdynai District** received the Order of Lenin for their grey prefabricated ferro-concrete housing blocks. The **Karoliniškės district** to the west of the city on the right bank of the Neris is dominated by the **Television Tower** ❷ (Televizijos bokštas), which has become infamous for the massacre on the night of 12/13 January 1991 when Soviet tanks

TIP

Vilnius aspires to be Las Vegas. If you want to try your hand at gambling, visit Olympic Casino in the Radisson Blu Hotel Lietuva at Konstitucijos 20, on the north side of the River Neris (tel: 211 1110).

BELOW: Verkiai Palace.

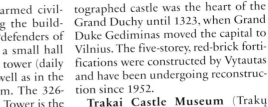

crushed and shot 14 unarmed civilians who were defending the building. The memory of the "defenders of freedom" is preserved in a small hall of fame at the foot of the tower (daily 10am–10pm; charge), as well as in the Lithuanian State Museum. The 326-metre (1,070ft) Television Tower is the tallest structure in Lithuania and has a restaurant halfway up, from where there is a breathtaking view of the suburbs with the centre just visible on a clear day.

The castle of Trakai

The former capital of the Grand Duchy of Lithuania, 27km (18 miles) to the west of Vilnius, is the most popular day trip from Vilnius. The resort village of **Trakai ❷** is surrounded by five lakes up to 48 metres (158ft) deep. In summer people swim and sail in Lake Galvė, which acts as a kind of moat around Trakai Castle's peninsula. *Galvė* is the Lithuanian for "head", and the story is that the lake would not unfreeze in spring unless it had been fed the heads of the Grand Duke's enemies. Lithuania's most pho-

tographed castle was the heart of the Grand Duchy until 1323, when Grand Duke Gediminas moved the capital to Vilnius. The five-storey, red-brick fortifications were constructed by Vytautas and have been undergoing reconstruction since 1952.

Trakai Castle Museum (Trakų pilies muziejus; daily 10am–7pm; charge) in the rooms around the internal courtyard offers an exhibition on prehistoric discoveries and the splendour of Lithuania's Grand Duchy, which extended from the Baltic to the Black Sea. In the outer buildings are antiques from the feudal houses of later centuries. The ruins of the town's earlier castle can be seen on the mainland nearby.

In the 14th century Grand Duke Vytautas "invited" his bodyguard of Crimean Karaite (or Karaim) to come to Trakai, where they settled around the castle. The Karaite are ethnically Turkish and practise a particular kind of Judaism, giving the royal town its distinctive touch and exotic flavour. Numbering somewhere in the region of 250, the Karaite are the smallest historically ethnic minority in Lithuania. Karaimų, the town's main street, is a good place to learn more about their culture.

At No. 22, the **Karaite Ethnographic Museum** (Karaimų Etnografijos muziejus; Wed–Sun 10am–6pm; charge) has traditional costumes, jewellery and photographs of the Karaite people alongside weaponry and cooking utensils. A *kenesa*, or prayer house, of this fascinating Judaic sect who also observe elements of the New Testament and Islam, is at Karaimų 30. Their cemetery, which dates back centuries, can be found by following Karaimų north past the castle and over a small bridge. Take the next left and it's a little further along on the left-hand side of the track.

There are a number of hotels in the area, and a music festival centring on the castle brings many visitors to Trakai in August.

KAUNAS

At the confluence of the Neris and Nemunas Rivers, Lithuania's second city is in many ways the centre of the country, with some of the best museums and a thriving commercial life

Lithuania's second city, **Kaunas ❸** represents the very heart of ethnic Lithuanian identity. Less than two hours from Vilnius, it can be enjoyed as a day trip, though visitors may want to stay longer. There is no shortage of places to stay. It was relatively unscathed by World War II, and large parts of the Old City remain untouched.

During its two decades as Lithuania's interim capital it developed from a hugely important Russian garrison town to a European city, and many of the Functionalist buildings from that period remain. It is the major commercial centre of the country, manufacturing textiles and food products, and if Vilnius now provides the country with intellectuals, Kaunas provides it with traders and businessmen.

Kaunas and Vilnius are connected by the River Neris. The point where it joins Lithuania's major river, the Nemunas, was chosen for the siting of the original castle from where the town grew. The Nemunas, once Lithuania's southern border, was on the German traders' route, and Kaunas became a Hansa town.

Town Hall Square

The city was first mentioned in 1361, and its historical heart is by the castle in **Town Hall Square ❹** (Rotušės aikštė), surrounded by numerous 16th-century German merchant houses. In the middle of this cobblestoned open area is the **Kaunas Town Hall** (Kauno Rotušė), known as The White Swan for its elegance and 53-metre (175ft) tower. Designed in late Baroque and early classical style, it was begun in 1542 as a one-storey building. The second floor and the tower were added at the end of the 16th century. The Gothic vaulted cellar of the tower served as a prison and a warehouse, the ground floor was reserved for traders and prison guards, and the first floor

Main attractions
PERKŪNAS HOUSE
CATHEDRAL-BASILICA OF STS PETER AND PAUL
LAISVĖS ALĖJA
MYKOLAS ŽILINSKAS ART MUSEUM
M.K. ČIURLIONIS STATE ART MUSEUM
CHURCH OF CHRIST'S RESURRECTION
NINTH FORT
OPEN-AIR MUSEUM, RUMŠIŠKĖS

LEFT: Kaunas Town Hall. **RIGHT:** café in Laisvės alėja.

Local blueberries, served with honey.

housed the magistrate's office, treasury and town archives.

Destroyed during fighting between the Russians and the Swedes, it was reconstructed in 1771 to house the local government. In 1824, under the tsarist regime, it was transformed into an Orthodox church and later it became the warehouse of the artillery. It served as the provisional residence of the tsar (1837) and as a theatre (1865–9). Under the Soviet regime it was used by the engineering department of Kaunas Polytechnic (1951–60). Renovated between 1969 and 1973, it now serves as a wedding palace, and happy couples and their entourages often line up for photographs in the square outside. The cellar of the Town Hall houses the small **Ceramics Museum** (Tue–Sun 11am–5pm; charge), and includes archaeological finds, 20th-century Lithuanian ceramics and temporary exhibitions.

St Francis' Church

The Jesuits started to buy land and buildings in Kaunas in the early 17th century. The construction of **St Francis' Church**

and Jesuit Monastery (Šv Pranciškaus bažnyčia ir Jėzuitų vienuolynas; Rotušės aikštė 7) was finished in the middle of the 18th century. After 1812 it served as a hospital and in 1824 it became the residence of the city's archbishop. In 1924 it was returned to the Jesuits, who used it for a boys' school. The church, which has a basilica layout, fine marble altars and woodcarvings, was built in 1666 and was frequently destroyed by fires. In 1825 it became the Alexander Nevski Orthodox Church and under the Soviets it was transformed into a vocational school. In 1990 it was returned to the Catholic Church.

Hunters' inn

The house at Rotušės aikštė 10, which has a Renaissance facade, was once a hunters' inn and now houses a hunters' restaurant decorated with the taxidermist's art. A statue for the Lithuanian poet and priest J. Mačiulis-Maironis has been erected in front of No. 13, where he lived from 1910 until his death in 1932. The Baroque building from the late 16th century served as a military hospital in 1812. During the 1861

Kaunas

0 — 500 m
0 — 500 yds

uprising against Russia its cellars were used as prisons. At Rotušės aikštė 19 there is a tribute to the country's communications through the ages, most interestingly in the form of antique telephones and stamps at the **History of Communications Museum** (Ryšių istorijos muziejus; Wed–Sun 10am–4pm; charge).

In the northwest corner of the square is the **Bernardine Monastery** (Bernardinų vienuolynas). With Renaissance and Gothic elements, it dates back to the late 16th century, when the first house was bought by nuns. The attached house of worship, the **Holy Trinity Church** (Šv Trejybės bažnyčia, 1668), was rebuilt in the Baroque style. In the 19th century it possessed nine wooden altars, but these were lost during World War I. In 1978 it was given back to the Catholic seminary. In 1933–4, the late-Renaissance belfry was incorporated into the seminary, which is located between the church and the belfry. This building was given back to the seminary in 1982.

The **Museum of Medicine and Pharmacy History** (Medicinos ir far-macijos istorijos muziejus; Rotušės aikštė 28; Tue–Sat 10am–5pm; charge) is a 17th-century building that used to house a pharmacy. On display are old instruments and a reconstructed interior of a pharmacy from the early 20th century.

Perkūnas House

From Town Hall Square walk down Aleksoto Street towards the Nemunas. At Aleksoto Street 6 is **Perkūnas House** (Perkūno namas). Historians cannot agree if the original purpose of this picturesque 15th-century Gothic brick building was a chapel or the Hansa office. The more romantically minded maintain it was the temple of Perkūnas, the god of thunder, since during renovation in 1818 workers found a 27cm (11in) tableau of a town and temples with three fishes which came to symbolise the rivers Nemunas, Neris and the god Perkūnas. The statue has since been lost but the name stuck.

Similar to St Anne's Church in Vil-

The Church of St Michael the Archangel.

BELOW: Town Hall Square.

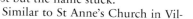

nius, Perkūnas House is one of the most original examples of late Gothic in Lithuania, and its rich architecture is a monument to the economic power of the Hansa and the German-speaking world of the time. After reconstruction in the early 19th century it served as a school, and in 1844 the first Kaunas Drama Theatre was established here. After 1863 the house fell into ruins. Renovated at the end of the 19th century it served as a religious school, and returned to the Jesuits.

On the banks of the River Nemunas stands **Vytautas Church** ❸ (Vytauto bažnyčia), built at the beginning of the 15th century for Franciscan monks. Here foreign merchants celebrated Mass. It was built in the Gothic style, and a tower was added at the end of the same century. Napoleon's troops used it to store ammunition in 1812, and in 1915, when the German Army occupied Kaunas, it was used as a potato warehouse. In 1990 the church, with its sober white interior, was re-opened for worship. The grave of priest and writer J. Tumas Vaižgantas (1869–1933), who organised the renovation

of the church in 1920, is in the outer walls on the left.

A pathway leads to the confluence of the Neris and the Nemunas Rivers. From the bank where they meet there is a good view of the Old Town spires, the Town Hall and the Jesuit and Vytautas churches. Midsummer's Eve (Joninės) on 23 June is celebrated every year on this piece of ground.

Castle and Cathedral

Situated on the banks of the Neris is **Kaunas Castle** ❹ (Kauno pilis). First mentioned in the 13th century, it was the earliest stone castle in Lithuania. The surrounding walls, 2 metres (7ft) wide and 13 metres (43ft) high, could not fend off the crusaders who destroyed the castle in 1362 after a three-week siege. Six years later a stronger castle was built with walls 3.5 metres (12ft) thick and four towers. Nevertheless, over the centuries it was washed away by the Neris and the northern walls with the towers collapsed. Today, only part of the castle remains.

Using Valančiaus Street, walk back to Town Hall Square and turn left

into Vilniaus Street at the **Cathedral-Basilica of Sts Peter and Paul**  (Šv Petro ir Povilo arkikatedra bazilika), which towers 42 metres (138ft) above the ground. The first church was built here in the early 15th century but its original shape is unknown. The naves were added in the 15th–16th century, and the construction was completed in 1655. Of particular interest are the Baroque high altar of 1775 and the neo-Gothic chapel to the right. It belonged to Augustine monks until 1895 when it became a cathedral. It was elevated to the rank of basilica in 1921. On the right, intersecting Vilniaus Street, Zamenhofo Street leads to **P. Stulga's Folk Music Museum** (Povilo Stulgos tautinės muzikos muziejus; Zamenhofo 12; Wed–Sun 9am–5pm; charge). Inside you will find a range of Lithuanian traditional instruments, including *kanklės*, usually a trapezoidal shaped piece of wood with strings attached *(see page 61)*.

Freedom Avenue

Continue along Vilniaus Street going towards the city centre. In a small yard is the **Prezidentūra** (Vilniaus 33; 10am–5pm, closed Mon; charge), the residence of the three Lithuanian presidents during the inter-war period. The one-storey building has been renovated and is now open to the public as a small museum.

Vilniaus Street leads into **Laisvės alėja** (Freedom Avenue), the main thoroughfare of the New Town often optimistically compared to the Champs-Elysées in Paris or Unter den Linden in Berlin. Kaunas residents love to stroll along the 1.6km (1-mile) pedestrian street, designed in the late 19th century.

In 1982 Laisvės alėja was closed to traffic and the central tree-lined pathway was dotted with numerous benches. Restful and green in the summer, it can be quite grey and depressing in winter. Between the wars a number of administrative buildings were put up along this classy avenue now lined with shops.

At the crossing of Sapiegos Street stands the **Monument to Vytautas the Great** . The bronze statue of "the creator of Lithuanian power" stands

Kaunas Cathedral.

BELOW: shopping for baskets in Laisvės alėja.

proudly over four defeated soldiers: a Russian, a Pole, a Tatar and a German crusader holding a broken sword, symbolising the defeat of the Teutonic Knights. A bronze plaque shows a map of medieval Lithuania extending from the Black Sea to the Baltic Sea.

In Miesto sodas, the city park facing the **Music Theatre ❻** (Muzikinis teatras) lies a granite monument where the name of Romas Kalanta is written into the pavement, marking the spot where the 19-year-old student protester immolated himself on 14 May 1972, sparking anti-Soviet riots.

Independence Square

The large pedestrian mall ends in **Independence Square** (Nepriklausomybės aikštė), which is dominated by the **Church of St Michael the Archangel** (Sv Mykolo arkangelo bažnyčia). The imposing blue neo-Byzantine building was built in 1893 by Russian architects as the Orthodox church for the army at Kaunas Castle. It was closed in 1960 and transformed into a permanent exhibition of stained glass and sculpture, but after independence it re-

opened as a Catholic house of worship. Inside are several interesting frescoes of the Evangelists and saints, and the stained glass represents the Assumption. In autumn, which is the favourite time for weddings in Lithuania, couples queue up outside the church to be married.

On the right-hand side of the square is the modern building of the **Mykolas Žilinskas Art Museum** (Mykolo Žilinsko dailės muziejus; Tue–Sun 11am–5pm; charge). The austere glass-and-granite building houses 1,670 works of art donated by Lithuanian-born Žilinskas (1904–92). It has Chinese, German and Dutch porcelain, Italian paintings of the 16th and 18th centuries and an interesting collection of 20th-century art. In front of the museum stands a statue of a naked man created by Petras Mazūras and put up in 1991 despite some objections.

Military Museum

Kaunas has some of the country's best museums. On Donelaičio Street, north of Laisvės alėja and running parallel, lies Unity Square (Vienybės aikštė), where the symbols of Lithuanian statehood have been re-erected. A hall of fame with the portraits of famous Lithuanian politicians and writers leads from the Liberty monument to the eternal flame, flanked by traditional wooden crosses remembering those who died for Lithuania's independence.

The entrance to the **Military Museum of Vytautas the Great ❻** (Vytauto Didžiojo karo muziejus; Tue–Sun 11am–5pm; charge) is on Unity Square. Lithuanian militaria is shown through the ages from prehistoric times to the present day. There is also the wreck of the *Lituanica*, the plane in which Steponas Darius and Stasys Girėnas attempted in 1933 to fly non-stop from New York (*see page 303*). Other exhibits show the history of the Vytautas Magnus University founded in 1922, closed in 1940 and reopened in 1990.

(*see page 303*).

BELOW: a corner on Laisvės alėja.

M.K. Čiurlionis Art Museum

The **M.K. Čiurlionis State Art Museum** (M. K. Čiurlionio valstybinis dailės muziejus; Tue–Sun 11am–5pm; charge) is situated in the building immediately behind the Military Museum and has its entrance at Putvinskio 55. Built in 1936, the gallery has some 360 works of the Lithuanian painter and composer, and it should not be missed.

The mystic and Modernist Čiurlionis (1875–1911) saw nature as an inexhaustible source of beauty. Of *Miške (In the Forest)*, Lithuania's first symphony, he wrote: "It begins with soft and wide chords, as soft and wide as the sighing of our Lithuanian pines." Čiurlionis wrote some 20 preludes, canons and fugues for the organ, and harmonised around 60 folk songs. In a special listening hall, visitors can hear some of his symphonies and orchestral works. (Concerts are also sometimes held in his former home, now a museum, in the spa town of Druskininkai, 124km/77 miles to the south, *see page 307*). The museum also has an exhibition featuring other Lithuanian artists.

A few houses away, at Putvinskio 64, is the **Devil Museum** (Velnių muziejus; Tue–Sun 11am–5pm; charge), an impressive collection of wooden devil statues amassed by the folk artist Antanas Žmuidzinavičius (1876–1966). It has grown over the years as new foreign devils have been added, and there are now more than 1,700, including Hitler and Stalin dancing over the bones of Lithuania.

Žaliakalnis district

From Putvinskio you can either take the Žaliakalnis funicular or climb 231 steps up to the Žaliakalnis district, which offers a splendid view of the city. One of the most interesting architectural monuments is the **Church of Christ's Resurrection** ⑪ (Kristaus Prisikėlimo Bažnyčia; charge for observation deck) at Žemaičių 31b, near the funicular terminal. It was started in 1932, although with the annexation by the USSR in 1940, the 63-metre (205ft) high church did not see completion until 2004. The massive white building is fairly plain inside but is worth a visit. An observation platform on the

TIP

Look out for concerts and choral works at the Kaunas Philharmonic (Kauno Filharmonija, Sapiegos 5, www.kaunofilharmonija.lt), which start at 5–6pm.

LEFT: exhibit at the Devil Museum.

Emma Goldman

Bob Dylan has supposed family roots in Kaunas and Sacha Baron Cohen, aka Borat, definitely has. Another infamous Kaunas Jew was a woman perhaps better known for something she's erroneously credited with saying than for who she ever was. Professional anarchist Emma Goldman (1869–1940) was born in Kaunas (or Kovno as it was then called), and despite being at one time America's Most Hated Woman after being implicated in the assassination of US President William McKinley in 1901, is credited with the immortal line, "If I can't dance, I don't want to be part of your revolution."

Despite a penchant for feminism, free love and human rights, there is not a lot of evidence to show Goldman's supposed love of the dance floor, rather she left in her wake a catalogue of trouble that saw her imprisoned for a year, deported to the Soviet Union and speaking out against the Spanish Civil War before she finally passed away in Toronto at the age of 70. Emigrating from tsarist Russia in her teens, Emma Goldman was a zealous defender of the proletariat, working as a seamstress on arrival in the United States before embarking on a remarkable political career that included the publication of several books that are still worth reading today. Not surprisingly, no statue of her stands in the city of her birth.

The Ninth Fort, where victims from the Kaunas ghetto died.

BELOW: Pažaislis Monastery.
RIGHT: Open-Air Museum at Rumšiškės.

roof can be reached via a lift for spectacular views.

The Ninth Fort

A visit to Kaunas is not complete without a tour of the **Ninth Fort ❶** (Devintasis Fortas; Žemaičių plentas 73; Wed–Mon 10am–6pm; charge), just off the A1 road towards Klaipėda. Built at the end of the 19th century as part of the outer town defences on the orders of Tsar Alexander II to strengthen the western border of the Russian Empire, it became infamous as a concentration camp during the Nazi occupation. In the fort you can visit the former prison cells where Jews from all over Europe were herded together awaiting execution. A silent reminder of the horrors are the inscriptions preserved on the walls of the cell. "*Nous sommes 500 Français*" ("We are 500 French"), wrote Abraham Wechsler from the French town of Limoges before being killed.

The **Way of Death** (Mirties kelias) leads to the place where some 30,000 Jews were shot. The museum housed in a concrete hall near the fort describes the deportations of Lithuanians by the NKVD (the predecessor of the KGB), the Nazi and the Stalinist terror, and the resistance fighters under the Soviet occupation who fought on until the early 1950s. An astonishing, 32-metre (105ft) reinforced-concrete monument dating from 1984 and commemorating the events at the fort is located nearby.

Pažaislis Monastery

Some 7km (4 miles) to the southeast of the town centre (take trolleybus No. 9 or 12) is Lithuania's Baroque gem, the **Pažaislis Monastery ❿** (Pažaislio vienuolynas). Isolated in the countryside above a dam on the River Nemunas, it was built in the 17th century with orchards and gardens that are still cultivated. Entrance is through the Holy Gate, and the church has a fine 45-metre (150ft) cupola, on the inside of which is a painting of the Virgin Mary. The marble and oak interior is enriched with frescoes restored under the aegis of the Čiurlionis Museum, which became responsible for it in 1966. Built for the obscure Camaldolese Order, it was briefly populated by Lithuanian-American nuns in the early 20th century, and again in 1992.

The huge reservoir beside the monastery is called the **Kaunas Sea** (Kauno marios) and is popular for recreation.

Open-Air Museum

Some 20km (12 miles) east of the city, on the A1, is the small village of Rumšiškės, the site of the **Open-Air Museum of Lithuania** (Lietuvos liaudies buities muziejus; Tue–Sun 10am–6pm, closed Oct–May; charge). The 176-hectare (435-acre) grounds make a good half-day out, and give time to appreciate the collections of old rural homes from all over the country. There are also re-creations of schools, pubs and a mill. It becomes quite crowded during holiday weekends, especially those related to pagan feast days. Inside the houses actors dressed as peasants work on traditional crafts.

AUKŠTAITIJA

This region follows the Castle Route beside the River Nemunas to the coast and heads north through agricultural land to Kernavė, one of the most important pagan sites in the country

Main attractions
PANEMUNĖ CASTLE
KĖDAINIAI
KERNAVĖ
AUKŠTAITIJA NATIONAL PARK
VISAGINAS

BELOW: lakes and hills, Aukštaitija.

The northern part of Lithuania between the Nemunas and Neris Rivers and the Latvian border is called Aukštaitija (literally, Highlands). The communities of Aukštaitija grew up around uniform, one-street villages, and small homesteads were created as land was divided among successive generations. The region was once known for growing flax. Primarily an agricultural area, Aukštaitija is moving towards more lucrative forms of income. In general, people from this part of the country have a reputation for being talkative, friendly and fond of songs.

Aukštaitija has two distinct regions: a rather flat western region, accessible from Kaunas, and a hilly eastern region, one of the nicest parts of the country.

The castle road

The willow-lined banks beside the 141, which follows the River Nemunas for 229km (143 miles) from Kaunas to the coast, are dotted with red-brick fortified manor houses looking out over the wide valley towards Lithuania's southern neighbours. Just beyond Jurbarkas the river forms the border with Kaliningrad. Castles were built all along here when the river marked the border between the Grand Duchy and the lands of the Teutonic Order. From the 17th century, merchants and aristocrats made their castle homes here.

The first stretch of the road, from Kaunas to Jurbarkas, is a pleasant 86km (53-mile) drive. The bizarre-looking castle at **Raudondvaris ❹** (Pilies takas 4; closed until 2011 for renovation) on the outskirts of Kaunas was built in the 17th century and remodelled in the 19th century by the Tiškevičius (Tyszkiewicz) family, who embellished it with a picture collection and a fine library. The 19th-century church was built by Lorenzo Anichini, who is buried here, and the interior statuary is by Lorenzo Pompaloni. There is also a 25-metre (82ft) tower overlooking the **Nevėžis Nature Reserve**.

At **Seredžius** there is a hill fort named after a legendary hero, Duke Palemonas, who is supposed to have been descended from Roman nobility. The actor and singer Al Jolson was born Asa Yoelson in this *shtetl* in 1886, five years before his family emigrated to the United States where he starred in the pioneering 1927 "talkie" *The Jazz Singer*.

Nearby is the old Belvedere Manor (Belvederio dvaras) on a high slope, but it has been rather neglected, as has the park in which it lies. Only the park is open to the public.

Veliuona is a small and fairly unremarkable town high on the river bank with a park and two hill forts: the Castle Mountain and the Gediminas Grave (Gedimino kapas) – it is thought that Lithuania's Grand Duke died here in 1341. The town has a 17th-century Renaissance church restored at the turn of the century, and this is the burial place of Juozas Radavičius (1857–1911), a famous organ master, and Antanas and Jonas Juška, two 19th-century Lithuanian folklorist brothers whose remains

Belvedere Manor, Seredžius.

were brought back here from Kazan in Russia, in 1990.

A few miles further on is **Raudonė**, a town in a similarly elevated position. Its park is full of ancient oaks. The 17th-century red-brick castle (Raudonės pilis; Mon–Sat 10am–4pm; charge), a mix of Renaissance and neo-Gothic, was built for a Prussian merchant, Krispin Kirschenstein. It was rebuilt in the 19th century and today it houses a school. There is a wonderful view from its tower, which is open to visitors.

The 17th-century **Panemunė Castle** (Panemunės pilis) in the village of **Vytėnai ❺** was built by a Hungarian merchant, Janush Eperjesh, on the site of a former Teutonic fort. Set on a hill with a park, the large and somewhat tumbledown building is surrounded by cascading ponds.

Jurbarkas

Beyond Skirsnemunė (called Christmemel by the Germans) is **Jurbarkas**. It has a population of 14,000, and the biggest employers are the gravel-extraction company, a logging concern

BELOW: Panemunė Castle.

and a flax mill. There is an interesting 19th-century part of the town, and the local park has a farmstead museum (Vinco Grybo memorialinis muziejus; Vydūno 31; closed until 2011 for renovation), devoted to the distinguished Lithuanian sculptor and Communist sympathiser Vincas Grybas, who lived here from 1926 until he was murdered by the Nazis in 1941.

Kaunas to Kėdainiai

The A8 (E67) leaves Kaunas past the Ninth Fort *(see page 294)*. After a few kilometres, the 144 turn-off leads up to **Kėdainiai** ❻, an administrative centre with chemical works and a sugar industry. The recommended Old Town is comparatively large and dates back to the 15th century, when it was owned by the dukes of Radvila.

Under their patronage industry expanded, schools and publishing houses grew up, and Lutheran, Roman Catholic and Reformed churches and a synagogue, all still standing, were built. The **Kėdainiai Regional Museum** (Kėdainių krašto muziejus; Didžioji 19; Tue–Sat 10am–5pm; charge) tells the story of the town from ancient times to the present, with particular attention paid to the Nazi and Soviet occupations.

Panevėžys

From Kėdainiai the A8 (E67) runs to **Panevėžys**, where it becomes the A10 (E67). Panevėžys is Lithuania's fifth-largest city, with a population of 113,000. It dates from the middle of the 16th century, when there was a community and a manor house on the River Nevėžis, where a park is laid out today. Its rapid expansion as an industrial centre has not improved its attractiveness. Since the 1960s its name has been linked with the Panevėžys Drama Theatre, which has built up an impressive reputation.

The **Ethnographic Museum** (Panevėžio kraštotyros muziejus; Vasario 16-osios 23; Tue–Sat 10am–5pm; charge) is in the oldest house in the area, dating from 1614. It also has a small collection of folk art a block away (Kranto 21; tel: 59 61 81 to arrange a visit; charge).

The karst region around **Pasvalys** ❼,

38km (24 miles) north of Panevėžys, has underground caverns, and in the town park there are signs where some of these have caved in. The less than stable terrain is also marked by sinkholes permanently filled with water; one of the best is the Green Spring (Žalsvasis šaltinis), which is located alongside the River Lévuo and Kalno Street.

Branching off the A10, Road 125 leads up to **Biržai** ❽. The old town of Biržai was built up around an artificial lake created in the 16th century at the confluence of the Apaščia and the Agluona. The castle that stood here was destroyed in the 18th century but restored in the 1980s, and there is a small museum inside. The newly reconstructed area around **Radvila Palace** is on the edge of a man-made lake. Inside is the beautiful Baroque Church of St John the Baptist (Šv Jono bažnyčia) and a monument on the town square to a local poet and revolutionary, Julius Janonis (1896–1917), who wrote under the pseudonym Vaidila Ainis. Also beside the lake is the 19th-century neoclassical Astravas Manor (Astravo dvaras), with a palace and park now used by a linen enterprise. Try some beer while you are here. There are a number of breweries in the town, giving Biržai the reputation as the beer capital of Lithuania.

Kaunas to Rokiškis

This route goes through the eastern edge of the Aukštaitija plains, following the River Šventoji. It leaves Kaunas on the A6 (E262), the former Warsaw to St Petersburg post-road which was paved in the early 19th century.

As the road enters **Ukmergė** ❾ there is a neoclassical post-house built in 1835 on the right. On the south side of the town at Vaitkuškis is the former country home of the Koskovskis family, arts patrons with a taste for literature who corresponded with Balzac.

After Ukmergė, Road 120 heads towards **Anykščiai** ❿, where wine is blended from imported grapes as well as local cherries, apples, rowan berries

and redcurrants in the **Anykščiai Wine** (Anykščių vynas) factory. Started in a small wooden house in the town centre in 1926 by Balys Karazija, it is now the largest winery in the Baltic States. The town is also known for its literary tradition. The most famous work from the town was a lyric poem written by Antanas Baranauskas (Antoni Baranowski, 1835–1902) in response to the felling by the tsar of Anykščių Šilelis, the 1,812-sq km (700-sq mile) pine forest 5km (3 miles) to the south. The poem became a milestone in the idea of conservation and the countryside. In the forest is the **Puntukas Stone** (Puntuko akmuo), one of the largest in the country, weighing 265 tonnes. These big rocks, brought by glacial drift, are scattered throughout the Baltics, and are sometimes called "presents from Scandinavia". The sculptor Bronius Pundzius turned one boulder into a monument to the transatlantic flyers Darius and Girėnas in 1943 (*see page 303*).

In the town's Exhibition Hall (Parodų salė; Vienuolio 4; daily 9am–6pm; charge) is the work of Stanislovas

A working windmill in Aukštaitija National Park.

BELOW: wild poppies in a barley field, a common sight in early summer.

The museum of wooden sculpture, Rokiškis.

BELOW: one of the many mass grave direction markers in Lithuania.

Petraska (1935–2009), a folk artist who ground stones into a paste before painting the remaining powder onto a canvas, with some interesting effects. The **Narrow Gauge Railway Museum** (Siauruko muziejus; Vilties 2; tel: 381 580 15; officially daily 10am–5pm) is interactive and fun, but is often closed. Calling the museum number usually leads to somebody rushing up the road with a set of keys. Organised excursions on an old narrow-gauge railway to a nearby lake, with food, wine and live musicians, are also on offer.

Niūronys Horse Museum

In the village of **Niūronys**, just 8km (5 miles) outside of the town, the **Horse Museum** (Arklio muziejus; daily 9am–6pm; charge) focuses on the role and importance of horses, which are highly regarded in Lithuania. Besides the animals, there are numerous carriages, horse-drawn buggies and agricultural machinery. There are also some areas dedicated to showing homes typical of the region. One weekend every June there is a lively horse gathering called Bėk, Bėk, Žirgeli (Run, Run, Horse),

and there are races all day, from donkeys to thoroughbreds.

From **Svėdasai** ⑪ beside a lake 24km (15 miles) further on, Road 118 goes northwest to **Kupiškis**, which is surrounded by manor houses, windmills and rural churches. Continuing 33km (20 miles) on Road 120 is **Rokiškis** ⑫, a regional centre with a hotel. Beside the main square is a country estate dating back to the 17th century and now housing a **museum of wooden sculpture** (Tyzenhauzų al. 5; Tue–Sun 10am–6pm; charge). The 19th-century neo-Gothic church dedicated to St Matthew (Šv Mato bažnyčia) on the opposite side of the square is richly decorated thanks to the Tyzenhauzas family.

Aukštaitija Uplands

The main A2 highway runs northwest from Vilnius towards Rīga and Tallinn until it reaches **Panevėžys**. On its western side, on the banks of the Neris 32km (20 miles) from Vilnius, is the town of **Kernavė**, which can be reached by following Road 108 to Road 116. Forming a triangle with Vilnius and

Holocaust Atlas

The genocide of the Jewish population in Lithuania began a few days before the German invasion of the Soviet Union on 22 June 1941. In a prelude to the systematic Nazi slaughter, many ethnic Lithuanians began killing Jewish men, women and children in the countryside, where their former neighbours for hundreds of years were tortured, raped, shot and buried in mass graves. An estimated 230 or so of these burial sites are believed to exist, some marked and others still not discovered or commemorated, many of them in Aukštaitija.

In 2010, the Vilna Gaon State Jewish Museum began an extensive project called the "Atlas of the Holocaust in Lithuania", which aims to remember the victims and help visitors find these important historical sites (www.holocaustatlas.jmuseum.lt).

Trakai, this was a major trading centre in the 13th and 14th centuries. A village of just 200 or so, the site includes five hill-fort earthworks built to repel the crusaders and probably used by Mindaugas. Settlement here has been found to go back 10,000 years, and it developed into an exceptionally large defence system. It was an important feudal town until the Teutonic Order destroyed it in the late 14th century. The area is considered such a significant pagan monument that in 2004 it was designated a Unesco World Heritage Site. Its prehistoric flavour and perfect setting, with a beautiful view over the Neris Valley, make it a popular gathering spot on Midsummer's Eve, when there are bonfires and all sorts of merry-making.

The **Green Lakes ⓭** (Žalieji ežerai) lie off the A14 just north from Vilnius. The area is a popular, hilly collection of summer homes, where the deep lake waters, tinted green, are a place for people from the city to cool off.

The Centre of Europe

After 26km (16 miles) north along the A14 there is a signpost directing you to the **Centre of Europe ⓮**. At longitude 25° 19', latitude 50° 54', members of the French National Geographic Institute "discovered" this fact in 1989, though few seem to have recognised it. More remarkable is the **Open-Air Museum at the Centre of Europe** (Europos parkas; daily 10am–sunset; charge) just south of Road 108. The area covers nearly 55 hectares (136 acres) of land, and has a growing number of sculptures by various artists from around the world who depict what Europe and its centre mean to them. The grounds also have a post office and restaurant. A speedier way to Europos parkas from Vilnius is to take Kalvarijų Street, veering right at the roundabout in Santariškės and following the Europos parkas signs; this road passes Verkių rūmai (Verkiai Palace) and the Green Lakes.

Aukštaitija National Park

Road 102 continues north into the **Aukštaitija National Park** (Aukštaitijos nacionalinis parkas), an area of 4,530 sq km (1,750 sq miles) of which 15 percent is lakes. Around three-quarters of the land is forested, and there is a great diversity of flora and fauna, with more than 700 species of plants, 100 species of mammals – including boar, elk, martens and beaver – and 78 species of fish. Canoeing and other water activities are popular, and there are many nature trails.

The best way to explore the park is to start in the tiny hamlet of **Palūšė ⓯**, where there is a handsome 19th-century wooden church and belfry. The park has an additional administrative centre at **Meironys**. Perhaps one of the quirkiest museums in the country is the folksy **Bee-keeper's Museum** in the village of **Stripeikiai** (Bitininkystės muziejus; 1 May–15 Oct Tue–Sun 10am–7pm; charge). There are various hives in the shapes of pagan gods, along with woodcarvings of bee-related deities. The area surrounding the cottage is where the

TIP

A detailed map is absolutely essential for navigating through the area, and can be obtained from the Aukštaitijos National Park Authority in Ignalina (tel: 386 474 78; www.anp.lt), or one of the bookshops listed on page 361.

BELOW: chair sculpture in Europos Park.

Aukštaitija is famous for its home-brewed beer, and for the songs of the flax and hay-harvesters, called valiavimai.

actual bee-keeping takes place. Honey, of course, can be procured and boats can be hired for a better view of the surrounding lakes. **Ginučiai**, **Šuminai**, **Strazdai** and **Salos** are all pleasant villages in the vicinity.

Ignalina ⑯, the main town close to Palūšė, is a centre for the area, and the **Švenčionys Uplands** on its eastern side are an attractive hilly area. It snows more in Ignalina than anywhere else in the country and the snow stays longer, which make it popular for winter sports.

To the north is Lithuania's youngest city, **Visaginas** ⑰. Most of the 30,000 or so who live here are Russian-speakers brought to the town in the 1970s and 1980s to work at the nearby nuclear power plant. Its main street, Taikos prospektas, looks more like a boulevard in Moscow than anything found in a small Baltic town, and is a prime example of Soviet social planning. The town is situated in a picturesque area of pine forests near a lake, in the shadow of the Ignalina Nuclear Power Plant (INPP) to the east, on the south bank of Lake Drūkšiai. Built in

1974, to the same design as the one used for disastrous Chernobyl, both INPP reactors have been decommissioned as part of the agreement for the country joining the EU.

On the Belarusian border

Vilnius is only 24km (15 miles) from the Belarusian border, and there are several places of interest in between. It is tempting to follow the roads into the neighbouring country, but the border has become closely guarded since Lithuania joined the EU, and most visitors will need a visa. The A3 has been the main highway to the east since the Middle Ages, and it goes to the Belarus capital of Minsk. **Nemėžis** is the first village on the road, settled by Tatars in Vytautas' time, and they have their own chapel and cemetery here. On the opposite side of the valley are the remains of a 19th-century country estate and park.

The road is now in the **Medininkai Uplands**, an area of wide valleys, fewer depressions and fewer forests, formed in an earlier glacial age than other uplands in the country. At the frontier customs post are seven crosses in memory of the young Lithuanian border guards killed in July 1991. Just before the border an old track goes down to the right to **Medininkai** and the remains of Medininkai Castle, a stone defence work from the 14th century, where Lithuania's patron saint St Casimir spent part of his childhood. The castle is in ruins, and the surroundings offer some spectacular walks.

Just over 3km (2 miles) to the south there is a signpost to **Juozapinė Hill** (Juozapinės kalnas), formerly the highest point in Lithuania at a meagre 292.7 metres (963ft) and recently knocked into third place by more accurate measurements. Just over the border there are castles of ancient Lithuania at **Lyda** and at **Navagrudak** (Naugardukas in Lithuanian), where there is an exhibition about the history of the two countries. The poet Adam Mickiewicz was born here in 1798.

BELOW: carved figure at the Beekeeper's Museum in Stripeikiai.

Basketball Flyer

Basketball is Lithuania's favourite game, and one of its heroes is also remembered, with his co-pilot, for a fatal pioneering flight

The sport at which Lithuania excels is basketball. Seven Lithuanians have Olympic gold medals. A few were even drafted into the North American National Basketball Association, including, most notably, Šarūnas Marčiulionis, who has put his money into a hotel and other businesses in Vilnius. Arvydas Sabonis, another legend, has followed suit; he owns a hotel in Palanga and has a stake in the Kaunas-based Žalgiris team.

The history of the game in Lithuania begins with one of the country's great heroes, Steponas Darius. The village of Rubiškė on the coast where he was born in 1896 has since changed its name to Darius. In 1907, his family emigrated to the US and as a student he excelled at baseball and football as well as basketball. He signed up for the army in 1917 and fought in France where he was wounded and decorated. In 1920 he was a US volunteer for the Lithuanian Army and as a pilot he took part in the Klaipėda Revolt in 1923. He introduced basketball into his home country and laid down a sporting tradition that has continued to this day.

Epic flight

Darius returned to the US in 1927 and founded a Lithuanian flying club, called Vytis. Five years later he and a colleague, Stasys Girėnas, set out to bring fame and glory to their newly independent nation by embarking on an epic flight from New York to Lithuania. They found enough money to buy an old plane they called *Lituanica*, but there was not enough for radio equipment.

The plane left New York on 15 July 1933 and flew across the Atlantic, covering 6,411km (3,984 miles) in 37 hours 11 minutes. Nobody knows why, but it never reached Lithuania and crashed at Soldin in Germany (now the town of Myślibórz in north-western Poland). Their bodies were brought to Kaunas, where 60,000 people turned out for their funeral. The duo's portraits appeared on postage stamps, and 300 streets, 18 bridges and 8 schools were named after them. Their faces currently appear on the Lithuanian 10 Lt banknote.

Monument to the pilots

The most popular monument to the heroes is near Anykščiai (between Panevėžys and Ignalina) on a huge boulder called Puntukas. In 1943 a Lithuanian sculptor, Bronius Pundzius, was in hiding from the Germans and he made himself a shelter beside the boulder. To while away his vigil, he sculpted a relief of the faces of the pilots in the stone, adding the text of their will, written before they set off.

Remnants of the aeroplane are on display in the Military Museum of Vytautas the Great in Kaunas. On the main road from Klaipėda, there is a signpost marked "S. Darius tėviškė" leading 9km (5½ miles) to the village of Darius and a memorial museum. ❑

ABOVE: the national sport. **RIGHT:** Darius memorial in the village named after its most celebrated son.

THE SOUTH

In the attractive south lies the spa town of Druskininkai, forever more associated with the composer and artist M.K. Čiurlionis, as well as the outrageous Grūtas Park, the world's first Soviet theme park

The southernmost part of the country is split in two by the River Nemunas, which flows up from the Belarusian border just beyond Druskininkai to Kaunas. To the west is the region of **Suvalkija**. To the east is **Dzūkija**. Suvalkija was the land of the Sūduva and Jotvingiai tribes until it was joined to the Grand Duchy of Lithuania after the Teutonic Knights were crushed in 1410. In the following years of peace, people from Žemaitija and other neighbouring regions came to settle here, but the main villages and townships were not founded until the 17th and 18th centuries.

From 1867 to 1915 the area was part of the Russian province of Suvalkai, and although the region still bears the name, the town of Suvalkai (Suwałki) is in Poland today. After serfdom was abolished in the 19th century, peasants settled in farmsteads and a great number were able to afford to educate their own children. Since the bulk of the first group of educated people in the country came from here, their local dialect became the basis of the modern Lithuanian literary language.

People of Suvalkija have a reputation of being stingy and thrifty. They also have a reputation for hard work, summed up in the expression, "It would be better if father fell off the roof than a grain or a drop is lost."

The Suvalkija plain

Marijampolė ⓲ (pop. 48,600), the principal city of the region, is 150km (94 miles) west of Vilnius and 60km (38 miles) south of Kaunas across one of the most fertile plains in the country. It lies in a rather dull plain relieved only by the Šešupė, the region's main river. The town manufactures car parts and has one of the largest car markets in the country. The related transport and freighting businesses also generate a great deal of the city's wealth. The town takes its name from an 18th-century

Main attractions
DRUSKININKAI
ČIURLIONIS MEMORIAL MUSEUM
GRŪTAS PARK
DZŪKIJA NATIONAL PARK

LEFT: wooden church at Marcinkonys.
RIGHT: tranquil countryside near Lazdijai.

Composer M.K. Čiurlionis. Recitals are given at his Druskininkai house every Sunday in summer.

BELOW: Liškiava church. **BELOW RIGHT:** musician accompanists on Čiurlionis Way.

Marian monastery and in the 19th century it was a centre of enlightenment. The only town in Lithuania to change its name during the Soviet occupation, when it was known as Kapsukas in honour of one of the founders of the Lithuanian Communist Party, Marijampolė is on the main north–south Via Baltica, a fact that blesses it with the best hotels in the region.

Among half a dozen local museums is the local **Marijampolė Ethnographic Museum** (Marijampolės etnografijos muziejus; Vytauto 29; Mon–Fri 8am–noon and 1–5pm; charge), which has a collection of local history.

Further up the River Šešupė on the A5 (E67) is **Kalvarija** ⓳. The old part is attractive with a post-house (1820) and the remains of a large jail built in 1810 to contain 1,000 prisoners. The classical-style church was built in 1840 and rebuilt in 1908, and it has some good paintings inside. A large Jewish community that settled here in the 17th century was exterminated by the Nazis and their ethnic Lithuanian helpers.

To the west of Marijampolė, the A7 (E28) leads to the Polish border, passing through **Vilkaviškis** ⓴, a local centre that was burnt to the ground in World War II. Nearer the frontier is the **Paežeriai Manor** (Paežerių dvaras), an 18th–19th-century palace set in a park with a lake. It contains a regional museum and a cultural centre. Beyond it is **Kiršai** ㉑, birthplace of the controversial poet Salomėja Nėris (1904–45).

To the south is a hilly, attractive corner of the country. In the southwest corner on Road 186 is **Vištytis**, a border town by a 180-sq km (70-sq mile) lake of the same name. Vincas Kudirka (1858–99), author of both the words and the music to the Lithuanian national anthem, was born and buried in **Kudirkos Naumiestis**, further north on Road 186.

Sūduva land

The southern part of Suvalkija, often called Sūduva, is a picturesque region of lakes and hills, centred on **Lazdijai** ㉒. Road 134 continues for 18km (11 miles) towards hills, forests, valleys and a lovely labyrinth of lakes around

Veisiejai, which has a number of pleasant corners to stop for a rest. The old part of the town has a beautiful park and an early 19th-century church. Lazar Zamenhof (1859–1917), the Białystok-born physician who devised Esperanto, lived here briefly in 1886–7.

To the east of Lazdijai is **Seirijai ㉓**, from where Road 181 goes through forests and around the largest lakes in the region. The biggest of these is the 139-sq km (50-sq mile) **Lake Metelys** (Metelio ežeras), which has clear water up to 15 metres (50ft) deep and is teeming with fish. **Meteliai**, near the lake, has a 19th-century church with good interior decoration, as does the 16th-century church in nearby **Simnas**. To the north is the 100-sq km (40-sq mile) **Lake Žuvintas** (Žuvinto ežeras), surrounded by a large nature reserve, a boggy area which supports more than 600 species of plants and more than 250 species of birds.

Alytus ㉔, 24km (15 miles) east of Simnas on Road 131, lies in a deep valley of the Nemunas, surrounded by dry forests and deciduous woods on the heights above. Because the ancient town straddled the river, it developed slowly. Today it has a population of around 70,000 and up-to-date industries in building materials, machinery, textiles, food processing, and Alita, makers of the country's best champagne. It is also the cultural centre of Dzūkija. There is a local museum and two 18th- and 19th-century churches. In Vidugiris, a forest in the southern part of the city, a monument has been erected to 35,000 victims of the Nazis. The bridge over the Nemunas is named after Antanas Juozapavičius, an officer killed here during the battle for independence in 1919.

Druskininkai

Lithuania's best-known artist and composer, Mikalojus Konstantinas Čiurlionis (1875–1911), grew up in **Druskininkai ㉕**, the first main town on this road, 150km (96 miles) southwest of Vilnius. It is a spa town and resort of wide boulevards and old and new villas. Around 100,000 people visit each year, many of them Poles and Belarusians. The spa opened in 1832 when salty mineral water was first used for treatment: the name Druskininkai comes from *druska*, meaning salt. Every litre of water contains 3g (0.1oz) of minerals, and it arrives at the surface, both tepid and hot, from a depth of 72 metres (235ft).

There are several parks, and treatments offered in the Remedial Gymnastics and Climatotherapy Park, where visitors queue up with their special cups to sample the waters in doses often prescribed by their doctors. Near the health park is a wonderful riverside walk, which traces the River Ratnyčia for 7km (4 miles) past carved seats and follies inscribed with poems and sayings. At one point the river is wide and deep enough to swim.

Čiurlionis Museum

The middle of Druskininkai has a 20th-century neo-Gothic church and nearby is a memorial to Čiurlionis. His family came here when he was three, and until

Raižiai is a small village of 100 Tatars just northeast of Alytus. These Turkic-speaking Asian people began to settle in Lithuania in the 14th century after serving Grand Duke Vytautus, who gave them privileges.

BELOW:
Druskininkai spa.

Folk totem, Dzūkija National Park.

the age of 14 he lived in the family home in the street named after him in the south of the town. This timbered, single-storey building is now preserved as the **Čiurlionis memorial museum** (Čiurlionio Memorialinis Muziejus; Čiurlionio 35; Tue–Sun 11am–5pm; charge). Famously, piano concerts are held inside during the summer, while the audience sits outside in the shade of the pretty garden. At the other end of town, at Čiurlionio 102, is **Echo of the Forest** (Miško aidas; Wed–Sun 10am–6pm; charge), run by the Lithuanian Foresters' Union in a building that has "the forest inside of it", which basically means an oak tree coming up through the building. This is Frank Lloyd Wright's idea of architecture taken to an extreme.

Grūtas Park

Tucked in the woodlands around Druskininkai, which are abundant with mushrooms in autumn, there are some ancient farmsteads: at **Latežeris**, for example, just to the east. Nearby is the small village of **Grūtas** and its famous **Grūtas Park** (Grūto Parkas,

see box opposite; tel: 313 55 511; daily 9am–8pm; charge). A controversial and rather startling place, it has collections of former Soviet leaders and various Communist bigwigs acquired from the scrap heaps of the early independence years.

Dzūkija National Park

Merkinė ㉖, 27km (17 miles) to the northeast, is at the confluence of the Rivers Nemunas and Merkys. Russia's Peter I stayed here and Władysław IV Waza, the King of Poland, fell ill and died here in 1648. North of Merkinė, forests cover the light plains on both sides of the road from Druskininkai. The route, lined with more than 20 traditional wooden sculptures, is called the **Čiurlionis Way**, since it leads 50km (31 miles) from the family home to Varėna (see opposite), the artist's birthplace. The sculptures, based on ideas from his music and paintings, were erected in 1975 on the centenary of his birth.

Merkinė also has a small museum of local lore opposite the visitor centre for the 560-sq km (215-sq mile) **Dzūkija**

BELOW: Grūtas Soviet Sculpture Park.

National Park (Mon–Fri 8am–noon and 1–5pm), where you can walk, ride and canoe on the tributaries of the Nemunas. There is another visitor centre in the woodlands at **Marcinkonys** to the southeast, near the Cepkeliai Marshes. The woodland of Dzūkija is often called Dainava (from *dainuoti*, meaning to sing). The Dzūkai who live here are known for their cheerfulness and their great singing voices, as well as for an ability to scratch a living out of poor soil. They used to be said to have no saws, only axes; no bricks, only clay. One saying that still persists is, "If it weren't for the mushrooms and berries, Dzūkai girls would walk around naked." These berries and mushrooms that keep clothes on the women's backs are sold along the highways in season.

Independent Perloja

Continuing east on the A4, just outside the national park in woodland beside the River Merkys, is the small town of **Perloja** 27 (pop. 100), a place of independent-minded people. It declared itself the Perloja Republic (Perlojos Respublika) in 1918, a status it stubbornly maintained for five years, with a government and an armed guard of 50 men, defiant against Russians, Poles, Germans and both red and white Lithuanian factions. In the centre of the town square is a hugely patriotic statue to Vytautas, Grand Duke of Lithuania, sculpted by Petras Tarabilda (1905–1977) in 1930.

Senoji Varėna (Old Varėna) was burnt down during World War II and replaced with the new town of **Varėna** 28 on the River Merkys, 5km (3 miles) to the south. The town is perhaps best known locally for its annual Mushroom Festival (Grybų šventė) held each September.

Heading towards Vilnius, the road passes more hilly, sandy woodland and the resurrected village of **Pirčiupiai** 29, where there is a monument called *Pirčiupiai Mother (Pirčiupių motina)*, by Gediminas Jokūbonis (1927–2006). It was commissioned in remembrance of the village that was burnt to the ground, along with all 119 inhabitants, on 3 June 1944 by the Nazis. The memorial is inscribed with each of the victims' names. ❏

BELOW: Lenin and Stalin at Grūtas Park.

"Stalin World"

Grūto Parkas (Grūtas Park) is the planet's first Soviet theme park. It is the audacious idea of Viliumas Malinauskas, one of Lithuania's wealthiest businessmen who made his fortune in canned mushrooms off the back of the very same Soviet system he now mocks with his park. This is a $1-million mock-up of a Soviet prison camp, surrounded by barbed wire and watchtowers and populated by bronze and granite statues of former Soviet leaders and communist bigwigs that Malinauskas has collected.

Visitors can drink shots of vodka and eat cold borscht while loudspeakers broadcast old communist hymns. There are said to be controversial plans to build a railway for cattle wagons from Vilnius to give younger Lithuanians an idea of what it would feel like to be deported.

THE BALTIC SEA

Partially enclosed and surrounded by nine countries, including Estonia, Latvia and Lithuania, the Baltic Sea is beset by a number of challenging ecological problems

The Baltic Sea is not deep, at an average of 55 metres (180ft), but it is tideless, and nearly half of it, including the waters around Estonia, Rīga Bay and the Courland Lagoon, freeze over each winter, and ice can remain until early spring. However, as the planet warms up, algal blooms are developing – in 2010, when the water temperature at Narva Joesuu in northeast Estonia reached 26°C (79°F), a bloom the size of Germany was detected by satellite in the middle of the sea.

With only a narrow channel between Sweden and Denmark for its exit into the North Sea, the same water remains for about 30 years. It is one of the largest bodies of brackish water in the world, which means that its saltiness is somewhere between fresh water and sea water. This presents the worst possible living conditions for aquatic organisms, and the few species that survive in the waters are vulnerable to ecological change. The Baltic Sea herring has evolved as a smaller species than its Atlantic relative, while sprats seem to have benefited from the warming water. There are also cod, eel, flounder, hake, plaice, salmon, sea trout and turbot. Grey and ringed seals, once found in large numbers, are diminishing, in part because warmer winters mean seal pups are leaving their ice bases too early, and because seals are often found covered with films of oil. Harbour porpoises are all but extinct.

This does not mean that the sea around Estonia, Latvia and Lithuania is unfit for bathing: all three countries have beaches with Blue Flag status, and the waters are generally shallow and safe. The dunes that line much of the shore are susceptible to storm damage and human depredation, so grasses and trees are important in preventing erosion.

ABOVE: leisure sailing off Pirita, reconstructed for the 1980 Olympic Games. Estonia's popular harbour has berths for around 300 yach[

BELOW: an Estonian-registered tanker trapped in thick ice is pulle[clear by a tug in March 2010.

LEFT: an avocet is one of many waders to be seen on the coast, which lies on one of the world's main migration routes.

ABOVE: local fishermen set out their nets and pots all around the coast, hauling in smelt and flounder from the shallow water.

LEFT: rising sea temperatures have had beneficial effects on stocks of sprats, which have been increasing in numbers.

CAUSE FOR CONCERN

Rivers and streams all around the Baltic have been dumping toxic matter into the sea for years, so that today it is one of the world's most threatened marine ecosystems. It has seven of the world's biggest marine dead zones, where oxygen depletion has been caused by an overdose of nutrients from fertilisers and sewage.

Some 90 million people live in countries around the sea, and about 2,000 vessels are out on the water every day. There are many wrecks – three British warships sunk by mines in 1919 were discovered off the Estonian island of Saaremaa only in 2010. The Baltic Sea was also the scene of fierce fighting, and there are an estimated 80,000 unexploded mines left over from World War II. Munitions had to be removed to allow for the 1,223km (750-mile) long Russian gas pipeline, operated by Nord Stream and opening in 2011 with a second one in 2012, to run from the Gulf of Finland to Germany. Oil leakage and spillage are a constant threat.

A number of initiatives have been taken by the Baltic countries since the 1990s, but pledges have proved hard to implement. All the countries around the sea are signed up to HELCOM, the Baltic Marine Environment Protection Commission, with a rotating presidency. In has an Action Plan to "restore the good ecological status of the Baltic marine environment" by 2021.

ABOVE: a World War II mine is detonated off Lithuania in Operation Open Spirit, an ongoing multinational effort to clear the sea of munitions.

LEFT: dunes such as these in Latvia are delicate ecologies and have to be planted to prevent erosion.

RIGHT: windsurfing on the Baltic.

ŽEMAITIJA AND THE COAST

The Amber Coast includes the Curonian Spit,
one of the world's great sand-dune nature areas,
while inland is the man-made Hill of Crosses,
a place of extraordinary devotion

Vilnius

The province of Žemaitija covers about a quarter of Lithuania, and roughly corresponds with the Žemaitija Upland. The adjacent coastal area, known as Mažoji Lietuva or Lithuania Minor, stretches south into the Russian exclave of Kaliningrad. Although the ancient tribes probably took their names from the places they came from, the Žemaitijans (Žemaičiai) lived not in the Upland but around the mouth of the Nemunas, trading with the Aukštaitijans towards the river's source. On this coast there is also archaeological evidence of Romans and Vikings, and of Bronze Age trade with Britain and the Mediterranean.

A mysterious land

For 200 years the Žemaitijans had a running battle with the Germanic crusaders of the Livonian Order who had established their Baltic base in Rīga, and with the Teutonic Knights who harried them from the west. Between 1382 and 1404 the Grand Dukes of Lithuania ceded Žemaitija to the knights, but in the 15th century it became a self-governing district and duchy.

To outsiders Žemaitija long seemed a rather mysterious, wild and pagan land, an image enforced by the French dramatist Prosper Mérimée's 1869

novel *Lokis*. The Žemaitijans maintain a strong regional dialect that's a mystery even to many Lithuanian-speakers, and they keep their links with the past.

Inhabited by men of few words, this is not a land of songs. Most of the countryside is rather severe, and the western slope of the Upland is windier, foggier and wetter than elsewhere. The trees are mostly firs and once-sacred oaks, and the landscape is dotted with old wooden crucifixes in roadside shrines and cemeteries. The main motorway from Vilnius to Klaipėda via Kaunas

Main attractions
OGINSKIS MANOR AND ESTATE
LITHUANIA MINOR MUSEUM
AMBER MUSEUM
CURONIAN SPIT
NIDA
NEMUNAS DELTA REGIONAL PARK
KRETINGA MUSEUM
HILL OF CROSSES

LEFT: Neringa looks out for sailors at Witches' Hill sculpture park. **RIGHT:** sand dunes at Nida.

A typical rural dwelling, Neringa.

BELOW: the coast near Nida.

is the well-maintained A1 (E85) dual carriageway. To the north and somewhat parallel to the A1 runs the A9 (E272) from Panevėžys, which becomes the A11 (E272) west of Šiauliai. The A12 (E77) runs horizontally to these roads and connects Šiauliai with Tauragė. Connecting the northerly town of Mažeikiai to southerly Tauragė (via Plungė) is the 164.

Kaunas–Klaipėda Highway

The A1(E85) motorway from Vilnius via Kaunas to the coast is a lovely 311km (193-mile) stretch. There are a number of diversions not far from the main road should you want to explore lesser-known parts of the country. The first of these that falls within the Žemaitija region is **Raseiniai** ㉚, 86km (53 miles) west of Kaunas and about 5km (3 miles) off the A1 on Route 146. This town is typical of the region and worth visiting for this reason alone. Historically significant, it was one of the focal points of the 1831 rebellion against the tsar. The 18th-century church and abbey is dedicated to the Assumption of the Holy Virgin (Švč

Mergelės Marijos Ėmimo į Dangų bažnyčia; Bažnyčios 2). Also of interest further into town and past the city's park is the **Raseiniai Regional History Museum** (Raseinių krašto istorijos muziejus; Muziejaus 3; Tue–Fri 8am–noon and 1pm–6pm, Sat 11am–4pm; charge) in a former prison building, which includes photographs of prisoners from 1940–52 and exhibits about the area and the diaspora from this region. There is also an area dedicated to flax, national patterns, ceramics, early 20th-century household utensils and folk art.

Šiluva

About 17km (10 miles) north of Raseiniai on Route 148 is **Šiluva** ㉛, which has the beautiful twin-towered **Basilica of the Birth of the Blessed Virgin** (Švč Mergelės Marijos gimimo bazilika; Jurgaičio 2), a Baroque building dedicated to the "Lourdes of Lithuania". It is believed that in the mid-17th century the Virgin Mary appeared on a rock near the site of a former church which had been seized by Calvinists, and she wept for its destruction. Moved

by these tears, a passing blind man was able to remember that a former church had stood on the grounds and he was able to locate both an icon of the Virgin and the original deed to the land, and through this apparent miracle he regained his sight. The existing church was returned to the Catholics. Although this miracle was historically advantageous, many still come here to worship. Large congregations attend services on major holidays to see both the icon, which is now partially covered in gold, and the holy rock.

Tytuvėnai ㉜ is about 10km (6 miles) north on Route 148. The area surrounding the town is popular due to its lakes and forested areas. The 17th–18th-century **Church of the Holy Virgin Mary** (Švč Mergelės Marijos bažnyčia) is one of the largest and most important religious houses in Lithuania, with a two-storey monastery, where concerts take place in summer.

Village detours

Heading out of Raseiniai, Route 196 runs parallel to the significantly faster A1, or you can return to the A1 via Route 146. About 5km (3 miles) outside the tiny settlement of **Kryžkalnis** there is a small sign for **Bijotai** village. Follow the signs towards D. Poška Baubliai (closed for renovation until 2011) in order to find Dionizas Poška's hollowed-out oak-tree trunks with pagan carvings in them.

Along the same road, heading away from the A1, is the town of **Girdiškė**. Its church, dedicated to the Virgin, has an oak altar with six main branches shooting upwards and intertwined. Continue along the road and circle around the church in the village of **Upyna** to return to the A1 at the town of Prienai via Gudirvės. Stasys Girėnas, the doomed transatlantic aviator, was born into a peasant family in 1893 in **Vytogala**, a little further west (see page 303). He was the youngest in a family of 16 children.

Another detour from the A1 is along Route 164 towards the town

of **Rietavas**, an ancient settlement (pop. approx. 4,000) centred around an old square. The main attraction is the **Manor House and Estate of the Oginskis (Ogiński) Family** (Rietavo Dvaras sodyba; Parko 10; tel: 69 82 14 26; Mon–Fri 8am–5pm, Sat–Sun by appointment; charge). From 1812 to 1909 they ruled over their own autonomous domain, with their own laws and even their own currency. In 1835 they granted civil rights to their peasants, organised agricultural exhibitions, promoted Lithuanian culture and written language, and started publishing the Lithuanian calendar. They established a music school in the town, and in 1872 mustered a famous brass band. The manor house is famous for being the first residential property in Lithuania to have electric lighting, courtesy of its own power station, in 1892, and the building is an intriguing place to spend an hour or so. In 1874 a beautiful church in the Venetian style was built on their orders by the Prussian architect Friedrich August Stüler.

The road continues through 50km (30 miles) of uninhabited forest. At

Summer in Klaipėda.

BELOW: amber at Klaipėda.

One of the few surviving half-timbered buildings in old Klaipėda.

BELOW: by the river in Klaipėda.

Endriejavas there is a small lake and 8km (5 miles) to the north is the former village of Ablinga. On 23 July 1941 it was burnt down by the Nazis and its 42 inhabitants perished. A wooden sculpture has been erected to each of the dead.

Baltic coast

The coastal plain, Pajūris, is 15–20km (10–13 miles) wide and rises to around 40 metres (132ft). The landscape is diverse, consisting of fertile clay soils, dunes, sandy forests and wet bogs. In the south is the swampy Nemunas Delta and the 1,600-sq km (618-sq mile) and 4-metre (13ft) deep **Curonian Lagoon** (Kuršių marios). The coastline has urbanised resorts, around Palanga in the north, and in Neringa along the Curonian Spit (Kuršių Nerija), which like much of the area was part of Prussia's Memelland. Neringa is not actually a town, but an administrative area with its capital at Nida, near the border with Kaliningrad at the southern end of the spit. The area has many miles of empty beaches and some nature reserves.

Klaipėda

Klaipėda ㉝ is the main city on the coast, situated at the mouth of the River Danė at the far northern end of the Curonian Spit and Lagoon. It suffered colossal damage during World War II, when it was used by the Germans as a submarine base. Since the 1970s, when investment was ploughed into local industry, its population has dramatically risen and then fallen. It is currently around 185,000, making it the third-largest city in Lithuania. In 1252 the Livonian Order built a castle here, called Memelburg, and the city became known as Memel in German. Today the port city has a flourishing shipbuilding industry, a thriving expat community and ferry services to Germany and Sweden.

What is left of the Old Town is strung out along a small network of cobbled streets on the left bank of the Danė, where there are some decent bars and restaurants plus a few remaining half-timbered (*Fachwerk*) buildings. The city also has two theatres, from one of which Hitler spoke from the balcony in March 1939 in the old town square

where the resurrected Annchen von Tarau statue now stands. The original, erected in 1912, was dedicated to the native Prussian German poet Simon Dach, and it is still a matter of debate whether it fell into the hands of the Nazis or Soviets.

Also of interest in the Old Town is the **History of Lithuania Minor Museum** (Mažosios Lietuvos istorijos muziejus; Didžioji Vandens 6; Tue–Sat 10am–6pm; charge), which houses all sorts of ethnic, archaeological and historical pieces related to the area and its former inhabitants. Most attention-grabbing are the eerie photographs of the city during World War II.

South of the Old Town is the **Blacksmiths' Museum** (Kalvystės muziejus; Saltkalvių 2a; Tue–Sat 10am–6pm; charge), which is both a museum and a working smithy, where perspiring blacksmiths forge all types of ironwork.

On the other side of the Danė, the **Klaipėda Timepiece Museum** (Klaipėdos laikrodžių muziejus; Liepų 12; Tue–Sat noon–5.30pm, Sun noon–4.30pm; charge) is another strangely satisfying museum. Centred around clocks and how they are made, it displays mechanisms from sundials to atomic clocks. In the rear courtyard is a splendid sundial.

Almost next door at Liepų 12 is the magnificent, 19th-century neo-Gothic **Post Office**. A 48-bell carillon in its tower is played to startling effect by local enthusiasts every Saturday and Sunday at noon.

Sculpture park

Continuing along Liepų leads to the **M. Mažvydas Sculpture Park** (M. Mažvydo skulptūrų parkas), which is bordered by Daukanto, Liepų and Trilapio Streets. The park was the city's main cemetery until the 1970s, when it was closed. Some of the crosses were salvaged and are now housed in the Blacksmiths' Museum *(see above)*. The 10-hectare (25-acre) park, which contains around 180 sculptures by more than 50 artists, is a nice way to come across many and disparate styles of sculpture, most with more than a touch of whimsy. In the far northern section of the park is the wonderfully

BELOW LEFT: Klaipėda Timepiece Museum. **BELOW:** engraved padlocks on a Klaipėda bridge ensure the couples who put them there stay together.

Amber

Amber is interwoven in Lithuanian folklore, and leaving the country without a piece or two of amber is bordering on sin

There is amber everywhere in the southern half of the Baltics. At any opportunity, stalls are set up to sell bracelets, necklaces, earrings, key rings and brooches. In its raw state, buffeted by tides and exposed to the elements, these are dull stones, scattered like pebbles the length of the beaches. People are always on the lookout for them, particularly after storms, though most of the

amber bought today will have been dug out of the ground by excavators in Kaliningrad.

Amber is not in fact a stone, but fossilised resin of primeval pine trees. The amber deposit, dating back 40 million years, forms a seam 60–90cm (2–3ft) thick beneath the surface of the seabed. In spring, fishermen used to comb the beaches with large nets to pull in flotsam that might contain amber. The Curonian Lagoon was also a source of it. In the 19th century Juodkrantė was known as Amber Cove: the Stantien and Becker company used to dredge up to 85 tonnes of it here every year.

Unusual attraction

The stone's peculiarity is that, while it was sticky resin, insects were attracted to it, and it often solidified while they were trapped by its surface. If you hold a polished stone to the light you will see flies and mosquitoes perfectly preserved inside. The 18th-century English poet Alexander Pope wrote:

Pretty! in amber, to observe the forms
Of hairs, or straws, or dirt, or grubs or worms;
The things, we know, are neither rich nor rare,
But wonder how the devil they got there.

Amber was a commodity that the earliest tribes could easily trade: according to Tacitus, the price it fetched astonished them. It has been found in the tombs of Mycenae, and Tutankhamun's treasure included an amber necklace. The Baltic shoreline was first called the Amber Coast by the ancient Greek poet Homer, who described the brilliant "electron" on his warriors' shields. The best place to see amber is at the Amber Museum in Palanga.

A palace of amber

A local legend tells how "Lithuanian gold" was created. There was once a Baltic queen named Jūratė who lived in a submarine palace made of amber. She was to be the bride of Patrimpas, god of water, but she fell for a mortal fisherman called Kastytis whom she visited in his hut on the banks of the Nemunas near Klaipėda at sunset every night for a year. The liaison came to the attention of Perkūnas, god of thunder, and in a rage he threw down bolts of lightning, killing Jūratė and shattering her amber palace into 10,000 pieces. Perkūnas then punished Kastytis by binding him to a rock on the seabed. It is said that when the west wind blows Kastytis can be heard moaning for his love, and when the wind dies the shore is strewn with fragments of Jūratė's palace. ❑

ABOVE LEFT: insects preserved in amber are millions of years old. **LEFT:** a hoard of "Lithuanian gold".

bombastic **Monument to the Port Liberators** (Paminklas uostamiesčio išvaduotojams), depicting the Soviet military in all its glory and unveiled in 1980 to commemorate the liberation of the city from the Nazis on their final push to Berlin.

Palanga

At 33km (20 miles) and 46km (29 miles) north of Klaipėda on the A13 respectively are the two resorts of Palanga and Šventoji. An old settlement of fishermen and amber-gatherers, **Palanga** ㉞ became popular in the late 19th century when it developed as a spa and health resort. Considered the wildest of the resorts on the Lithuanian coast, Palanga still manages to maintain its charm even with the heavy influx of hotels, restaurants and bars that open their doors the moment the weather turns warm.

Meilės alėja (Lover's Lane), which runs parallel to the Baltic Sea, and Basanavičiaus, which leads into the pier, are the two most popular places to take a stroll, especially as the sun is setting. A trip to Palanga without watching the sun set over the sea is a wasted trip indeed.

Despite the bars and cafés touting karaoke, drinking contests or just playing loud thumping music that leaves the sound of the ocean unheard, peace reigns in some parts of the resort. One of the best places to visit besides the beaches is the 110-hectare (272-acre) **Botanical Park**, which lies alongside the Baltic Sea. In summer, concerts take place regularly throughout the park, where there are more than 500 plant species, dominated by pine trees.

Amber Museum

In the centre of the park is Count Tiškevičius's mansion, which is now home to the **Amber Museum** (Gintaro muziejus; Vytauto 17; Tue–Sat 10am–8pm; charge). After touring the museum there will be no question left unanswered about Baltic gold (*see opposite*). Numerous pieces of amber contain particles of animal or vegetable life, which adds to their fascination. Behind the mansion is a garden full of fragrant roses.

Also in the park is **Birutė's Hill** (Birutės kalnas), the tallest point in town and on which a small chapel now stands. The hill is considered to be a former pagan shrine, and the presence of a large oak – sacred in local pagan tradition – at the foot of the hill supports this theory. In the middle of the park sits one of the most famous statues in the town, of the mythical Eglė. According to the legend, Eglė met an enchanted lake-living prince during a swim. The two married, had children and tried to live happily ever after in their lake. However, when Eglė brought her children to meet their grandparents, her brothers killed her husband. In despair Eglė turned herself and her children into trees.

Another worthwhile stop is the **Antanas Mončys House Museum** (Antano Mončio namai muziejus; Daukanto 16; Wed–Sun 1pm–7pm; charge). All the wooden pieces by the sculptor (1921–93) can be handled by

The beach at Palanga.

BELOW: Palanga waterfront.

visitors; in fact, the artist requested this in his will.

Šventoji ㉟, a little further up the coast, is a quieter resort. On the mouth of the small River Šventoji, it is famous for its sand dunes, beach and bogs. Shown on Hansa maps, it became a resort at the beginning of the 20th century. A community of small cottages and simple houses, this is the place to go if you want peace and quiet.

The Curonian Spit

The Curonian Spit (Kuršių Nerija) is named after the Curonians (Kuršiai), an ethnic group who lived in the region from the 5th to the 16th century. It was formed about 5,000 years ago and geologically it is the youngest part of the country. It has no rivers, a few lagoons and along its shore lies a chain of man-made beaches and dunes. A bird's-eye view is a wonderful picture of white, sandy hills against a dark blue background, and it was the sight of these extraordinary dunes that inspired the German naturalist Alexander von Humboldt to write in 1809: "[the] Curonian Spit is such a peculiar

place as Italy or Spain. One must see it to give pleasure to one's soul." It was awarded Unesco World Heritage Site status in 2000.

Winds formed the long, narrow coastal spit no more than a mile wide and 60 metres (200ft) high. It runs 98km (60 miles) from Klaipėda south to Kaliningrad; 51km (32 miles) of the spit are in Lithuania. The lagoon on the inland side is formed by the mouth of the Nemunas. On the tip of the spit opposite Klaipėda is **Smiltynė**, reached by regular ferries from the port.

The Lithuanian Sea Museum (Lietuvos jūrų muziejus; Smiltynės 3; Tue–Sun 10.30am–6.30pm; charge) is home to a number of seals, penguins and dolphins. The dolphin show is especially enjoyable for younger visitors. Nearby is Klaipėda Yacht Club, one of the venues of Klaipėda's annual Sea Festival.

Lagoon-side villages

Most of the peninsula, however, lies to the south, where all tourist traffic needs to pay a toll. All the little villages along here face the lagoon. Until 1992,

BELOW: the Curonian Spit close to Nida.

the white sandy coast was occupied by the Soviet Army. Shifting sands have meant many of the villages have constantly been on the move. During the 18th and 19th centuries more than a dozen were affected, some of them covered over by sand. **Pervalka** and **Preila** are typical small seaside communities with signs for *žuvis* (fish) and locals quietly going about their business. **Juodkrantė** is larger and has a harbour once known as Amber Cove because of the amount of the material that was dredged up for the local industry.

Witches' Hill

Also of note when driving through town is **Witches' Hill** (Raganų kalnas), which was established in the 1980s by a group of local sculptors. This large wooden sculpture park filled with fabled figures – such as the main pagan god, Perkūnas, and Neringa, a local girl who became a giant and helped sailors in trouble – makes a pleasant excursion through the pine trees. This spot is especially appreciated by children, as some of the sculptures double as slides and see-saws. Look for the sign on your right as you are heading south through town. A walk beside the lagoon path with its stone sculptures provides a pleasant contrast.

Nida

At the southern end of the spit, just before the border with Russian Kaliningrad, is **Nida** ㊱, which has moved several times to escape the mobile sand. This is the largest of the resorts (pop. 1,650, rising to more than 10,000 in summer), with the best facilities. It is the sunniest and most famous place on the Lithuanian part of the peninsula.

Nida has a distinctive landscape, created by the wind and the sea. White sand dunes stretch away like a desert to the south, and trunks of trees show where ancient forests once flourished. It is known among Lithuanians as a place where the landscape forces you to take stock of your life. The area is fantastic, and exploring the dunes is an integral part of any visit. Because of the fragile ecosystem, however, it is forbidden just to traipse through them. Instead, visitors are asked to walk through the forest at the end of Naglių

Nida's coat of arms and flag. Every village along the Curonian Spit has its own.

BELOW LEFT:
Nida lighthouse.
BELOW:
a typical late
19th-century
house.

to view them or to walk alongside the beach and then climb the steps.

Those who plan on visiting the area's beaches should pay particular attention to the signposting as some are women-only, others are men-only. According to local custom, however, men are allowed to cross women-only beaches if they are close to the water and not disruptive.

To find out more about local life, there is a small recreated fisherman's house, the **Ethnographic Fisherman's Museum** (Žvejo etnografinė sodyba; daily 10am–6pm; charge) from the 19th century at Naglių 4. For some local shopping and further information, head for the **Amber Gallery** (Gintaros galerija; Pamario 20; 10am–7pm). Further along is the **Neringa History Museum** (Neringos istorijos muziejus; Pamario 53; daily 10am–6pm; charge), which houses amber figures from the Stone Age as well as numerous exhibitions chronicling life on the spit as it used to be. The writer Thomas Mann lived in Nida for three consecutive summers between 1930 and 1933. There is a museum in the house he

had specially built, the **Thomas Mann Memorial Museum** (Thomo Manno memorialinis muziejus; Skruzdynės 17; June–Sept daily 10am–6pm; charge). Information is in Lithuanian and German.

Nemunas Delta

From Klaipėda, Road 141 runs southeast through Šilutė and Pagėgiai, following the north bank of the Nemunas to Kaunas. From the small town of **Priekulė**, Road 221 goes south, past the fishing village of **Kintai**, as it enters the **Nemunas Delta Regional Park** (Nemuno deltos regioninis parkas), an area of islands and waterways teaming with fish, and a main port of call for migrating birds.

Among the typical fishing villages here are **Mingė**, the "Venice of Lithuania", where the River Minija serves as its main street, and **Skirvytėlė**, whose traditional houses are made of timber and reeds and include an ethnological farm museum. At the western edge of the park is **Ventės Ragas ③**, marked by a lighthouse built in 1863. The main reason

for coming to this backwater is the wildlife. An important bird-ringing centre, which keeps track of the many coastal migrants, has been operating here since 1929. It has vast bird-catching nets. A small museum with erratic opening times has display cases of stuffed birds.

From Saugos the 141 falls down into the Nemunas Delta plain, passing through **Šilutė** ㊳ on the River Šyša. The town of Šilutė spent most of its time under German rule and was only integrated into Lithuania in 1923. Most of its economy centres on textiles, livestock and machinery plants. The city has its own museum (Šilutės muziejus; Lietuvininkų 36; Mon–Thu 8am–5pm, Fri 8am–4pm; charge), which displays a vast amount of ethnic costumes, weaponry, folk art and photographs.

In the village of **Macikai**, just off the 141 to the east of Šilutė, the former Stalag Luft VI prisoner-of-war camp for Allied airmen, and later a KGB prison for Lithuanian dissidents, opened to the public in 1995. There are photographs and lists of prisoners along with their journals and drawings. The eerie and harrowing museum (15 May–1 Oct Tue–Sat 10am–4pm) is not suitable for youngsters.

Island town of Rusnė

Just west of Šilutė in the Nemunas Delta is 45-sq km (17-sq mile) **Rusnė** ㊴, Lithuania's only island town, which rises just 1.5 metres (5ft) above sea level. It has a community of around 3,000, who earn a living by fishing and breeding cattle. The main town for the Nemunas Delta Regional Park, it has information on hiring boats and bikes. There is also an ethnographic fisherman's farmstead (Skirvytėlės 8; 15 May–15 Sept daily 10am–6pm; admis-charge), which shows an authentic farmhouse of Lithuania Minor.

The next town of any size on the 141 is **Pagėgiai**, 38km (22 miles) south of Šilutė. During World War II, in the forest to the west behind a tangle of barbed wire, the Germans kept prisoners of war under the open sky: 10,000 of them died. The ground is very hilly, and prisoners tried to bury themselves to escape the cold. From Pagėgiai the A12 (E77) goes 32km (20 miles) north-

Lithuania's national bird is the stork, seen in large numbers from April to September. Every spring and autumn around a million birds of many species pass over the Nemunas Delta.

BELOW: still life in the lagoon.

BELOW AND BELOW RIGHT: artwork at Gargždelė.

east to **Tauragė**, which gave its name to the Tauragė (Tauroggen) Convention, signed in 1812 between General Yorch for Prussia and General Diebitsch for Russia in Požeronys Mill: a monument records the event. The A12 joins with the Kaunas–Klaipėda (A1) highway.

North Žemaitija

One of the most interesting diversions in northern Žemaitija is the regional capital of **Kretinga** ❹ (pop. 22,000). Although parts of the city are not particularly eye-catching, all is made up for by the **Kretinga Museum** (Kretingos muziejus; Vilnaus 20; Wed–Sun 10am– 6pm; charge). It is housed in a former mansion of Count Tiškevičius (Tyszkiewicz, 1814–73) and has collections of numerous Žemaitijan craftwork and articles belonging to the count and his family. There are also objects found from archaeological digs displayed in the cellar. The winter garden (Kretingos Žiemos Sodas) is one of the most spectacular displays in the area; it is covered by plants, their leaves regularly dusted by women attendants. The indoor café adds to the experience. The town has

an important Franciscan monastery, founded in 1602, and concerts are sometimes given in its courtyard.

On the A11 (E272) between Kretinga and the next main town of Plungė is **Kartena** ❹, situated in the beautiful valley of the Minija. It has a 19th-century wooden church, which is dedicated to the Assumption of the Virgin (Kretingos 4).

Before reaching Plungė, an interesting diversion can be found by turning north on Route 169 towards Salantai. Here in the village of **Gargždelė** ❹ is the **Orvydas Farmstead Museum** (open Tue–Sun 10am–6pm; donation), a tribute to all things wacky, serious and religious. The owner's eccentric son, Vilius Orvydas (1952–92), is now considered part of the Naïve artist movement, and the area around the farmhouse features an arresting amount of carved stones, boulders, rescued crosses and other pieces of art he created during his short life.

Mosėdis

An even more bizarre diversion is to be found further north in the town of

Mosėdis ㊽ at the **Museum of Stones** (Akmenų muziejus; Salantų 2; daily 8am–8pm; charge), which is a collection of more than 20,000 stones and rocks from around the world. The point of this rock gathering may have most people scratching their heads, but the sheer willpower inherent in this museum's existence does have a certain appeal. Interestingly, many of the rocks have not enjoyed their captivity and spilled out over the town.

Plungė ㊹ (pop. 23,000) is a little larger than Kretinga and a centre of light industry and administration, with a long tradition of folk art. It became rich after the Oginskis family arrived to buy up the local manor. They enlarged and cultivated the 18th-century park that surrounds the manor, and in 1879 entrusted the architect Karl Lorens with the building of a neo-Renaissance palace imitating the 15th-century Palazzo Vecchio in Florence. In 1889 they also sponsored the education of the painter and musician M.K. Čiurlionis. Today the building is the **Žemaitija Art Museum** (Žemaičių dailės muziejus; Parko 1; 15 Wed–Sun 10am–5pm; Nov–15 May Wed–Sun 10am–5pm, closed the last Friday of every month; charge), which houses mostly paintings executed by Žemaitijan artists either living in Lithuania or abroad. There is also a small area dedicated to the folk art of the region.

Žemaitija National Park

Due east of Salantai is **Plateliai**, the heart of the **Žemaitija National Park** (Žemaitijos nacionalinis parkas) and its main tourist information centre (Didžioji 8; www.zemaitijosnp.lt). Though lying 146 metres (480ft) above sea level, there is a large lake beside it: **Lake Plateliai** (Platelių ežeras) is nearly 12 sq km (5 sq miles) in size and 46 metres (150ft) deep, and it has seven islands. There are boating facilities on its western side near the town, where there is an 18th-century wooden church and a ruined manor.

Other attractive small towns in this region, which is rich with festivals and calendar customs, include

18th-century wooden church on the shores of Lake Plateliai.

BELOW: Lake Plateliai.

Alsėdžiai and Seda and Žemaičių Kalvarija, a pretty village that has 10 days of pilgrimage celebration every July.

Telšiai, on the A11, is an industrial town with a population of 30,000, but before World War II it was an important religious and cultural centre for both Catholics and Jews, with a bishop's see and seminaries for priests and rabbis. It still has a school of applied art and the **Alka Museum** (Žemaičių muziejus Alka; Muziejaus 31; Wed–Sat 9am–5pm; charge), featuring the usual collections of local interest as well as the extraordinary, recently rediscovered photographs of the local Jewish salon photographer Chaimas Kaplanskis (Chaim Kaplan, c. 1860–1935).

On the southeast of the town is **Rainiai Forest** (Rainių miškelis), where 73 Lithuanian nationalists and Nazi collaborators were executed by the KGB in 1941; 50 years later a chapel was built in their remembrance. East from here is **Luokė**, famous for its folklore festivals, and **Lake German-tas** (Germanto ežeras), where there are holiday facilities and an airfield for pleasure flights.

Šiauliai

Heading east, at the junction of the A11 and A12, **Šiauliai** **45** (pop. 134,000), Lithuania's fourth-largest town, is an industrial centre, of shoes, textiles and, notably, bicycles, and there is a **Bicycle Museum** (Dviračių muziejus; Vilniaus 139; Tue–Fri 10am–6pm, Sat 11am–4pm; charge). There is also a **Museum of Radio and Television** (Radio ir Televizijos muziejus; Vilnaus 174; Wed–Sun 11am–5pm; charge). Šiauliai's vast 17th-century cathedral was rebuilt in 1954, as, like most other buildings in the town, it was flattened in World War II. Its spire is one of the tallest in the country. To the south are picturesque hills and lakes around **Bubiai** and **Kurtuvėnai**.

Hill of Crosses

Šiauliai is most famous for the **Hill of Crosses** **46** (Kryžių kalnas), which lies in the countryside about 14km (9 miles) to the northeast on the A12 (E77). Nobody is sure of its origins, but it has been a religious site since at least the end of the 19th century. People come from all over the world to add their crosses to the thousands already here. The sight is nothing short of awe-inspiring. The hill itself is only a small hump. The Soviets bulldozed it three times, the first time in 1960, destroying an estimated 5,000 crosses. Each time they reappeared and today there are thousands of crosses, rosaries, pebbles, branches and other offerings.

The large statue of Jesus at the entrance was a present from the late Pope John Paul II during his visit in 1993. The Pope subsequently encouraged Italian Franciscans to build a monastery for Lithuanian novitiates, and this opened in 2001 on the north side of the hill. The monastery is also open to pilgrims. The annual pilgrimage to the hill takes place on the third Sunday in July. ❑

Rural traffic in Plateliai.

BELOW: marshland in Žemaitija National Park.
RIGHT: the Hill of Crosses.

INSIGHT GUIDES **TRAVEL TIPS**

ESTONIA, LATVIA & LITHUANIA

Transport

Accommodation

Eating Out

Activities

A – Z

Language

Further Reading

TRANSPORT

GETTING THERE AND GETTING AROUND

GETTING THERE

By Air

Estonia

The discount airline easyJet.com offers a direct, daily London–Tallinn service, while the national carrier Estonian Air flies the route twice weekly. Other airlines such as SAS and Finnair offer flights that connect through Stockholm, Copenhagen and Helsinki, though these routes are usually more expensive. Rīga's airport is far better connected than Tallinn's, and travellers often use it as a gateway to Estonia, making the final leg either by air or by coach. Another option is to find a cheap flight to Helsinki and take a ferry to Tallinn.

Lennart Meri Tallinn Airport (TLL) is one of Europe's most modern as well as one of its smallest.

Taxis and buses wait just outside the arrivals area's main door. The airport is remarkably close to the centre of the capital, and a taxi ride can take as little as 10 minutes. The fare should be €7–8. City bus No. 2, which will take you to the A. Laikmaa stop next to the Viru shopping mall in the centre, departs from the airport roughly every 20–30 minutes. Its timetable is posted under the blue-and-white bus sign outside. The journey takes about 15 minutes and costs €1.60. Pay the conductor as you board or buy tickets at the kiosk in the arrivals hall for €0.95, or €6.40 for a book of 10.

Landing at one of Estonia's other airports may be more convenient, depending on your plans. The Latvian carrier AirBaltic flies twice daily from Rīga to Tartu, and Estonian Air offers direct, though infrequent, flights from Stockholm to Tartu, Pärnu and Kuressaare.

Latvia

The national carrier AirBaltic is partially owned by the Latvian government and has successfully adopted a budget-airline business model. The airline offers affordable direct flights to Rīga from London, Manchester, Dublin, Brussels, Berlin, Stockholm and several other cities in Europe, Central Asia and the Middle East.

Ryanair www.ryanair.com also flies direct from the UK to Rīga, and booking is by internet only. Uzbekistan Airways operates the only direct flight to Rīga from New York twice weekly.

Rīga International Airport (RIX) is a shiny modern complex 13km (8 miles) outside the city centre and is easily accessed by taxi or bus. Flights arrive and depart from only three small terminals, so getting lost is impossible. In addition to AirBaltic and Ryanair, Rīga is served by several other major European airlines, including Lufthansa, Finnair and Wizz Air. For more information visit www.riga-airport.com.

A queue of reputable taxis is always available outside, and the trip to the city centre takes roughly 20 minutes and should cost no more than 10Ls. City bus 22 picks up passengers on the far side of the car park when leaving the arrivals hall. Tickets are 0.70Ls, and another may be required for luggage. The Airport Express shuttle departs every 30 minutes between 05.30–00.45 to five different hotels throughout the city for 3Ls.

Lithuania

After a rather ridiculous episode in which the Lithuania national airline FlyLAL tried to sell itself back to the state, the company took a spectacular nosedive in January 2009. Filling the void is Star 1, a private, low-cost enterprise currently operating flights between Vilnius and several European destinations including Barcelona, Dublin, Edinburgh, London Stansted and Milan.

The country's second airport at Kaunas has become a major hub for Ryanair, which currently flies between the city and 21 European destinations.

Vilnius International Airport (VNO, Tarptautinio Vilniaus oro uostas) is 5km (3 miles) south of the capital. The cheapest way into town is bus No. 1 to the train station or No. 2, which stops at both Gedimino and Konstitucijos avenues. Both can be picked up right outside the arrivals hall. For one litas more you can also take minibus Nos 15, 21, 23 or 47, all of which stop in the city centre on Gedimino. Bus drivers do not speak English.

The taxis parked outside will happily deliver fresh arrivals to the city centre for a sky-high price of around 50lt. Alternatively, call one in advance and save up to 70 percent. Two taxi companies are listed on *page 333*.

Kaunas Airport (KUN, Kauno Aerouostas) is located in the small settlement of Karmėlava, 15km (9 miles) north of the city. Microbus No. 120 runs from outside the terminal building and goes to the castle for 2lt. A regular minibus service operates from the airport to Vilnius and Klaipėda. More information can be found at www.airport-express.lt.

Flight Contacts

Estonia

Tallinn Airport
Tel: (+372) 6058 888
www.tallinn-airport.ee
Estonian Air
Tel: (+372) 6401 233
www.estonian-air.ee
UK Ticket Office, London
Tel: 01293 596 661
Email: sales.estonian-air@aviareps-group.com
Gatwick Airport: Skybreak
(Departure Hall, Zone H)
Tel: 01293 555 700
Email: reps@skybreak.co.uk

Flights from the UK

easyJet www.easyjet.com

Latvia

Riga Airport
Tel: (+371) 1187 or (+371) 2931
1187 if calling from abroad
www.riga-airport.com
AirBaltic
www.airbaltic.com
Tērbatas iela 14, Rīga
Tel: (+371) 9000 1100 or (+371)
6700 6006 from abroad

Flights from the UK

Ryanair www.ryanair.com
Wizz Air www.wizzair.com

Lithuania

Vilnius Airport
Tel: (+370) 5273 9305
www.vilnius-airport.lt
Star 1 Airlines
Tel: (+370) 5247 7744
www.star1.lt
In UK: Gatwick Airport
Tel: 01293 579 900
Email: info-greatbritain@lal.lt
Heathrow Airport:
Tel: 020 8759 7323

UK Airlines

easyJet www.easyjet.com
Ryanair www.ryanair.com
British Airways, tel: 0844 493 0787
www.britishairways.com

From outside Europe

One of the only direct flights to the Baltic States from outside Europe is from New York to Rīga, so in most cases you must link with one of the carriers from the Baltic States (see panel) or from neighbouring countries: Aeroflot, British Airways, Czech Airlines, Finnair, KLM, Lufthansa, LOT Polish Airlines or Scandinavian Airlines (SAS). Connections from the US are possible with SAS, Finnair, Uzbekistan Air,

American Airlines, Continental Airlines, Delta Airlines, Northwest Airlines and United Airlines, although many will require at least two stopovers.

From Australia and New Zealand it is cheapest to fly to London and connect to a budget flight.

By Rail

There are some local first-class trains, such as the twice-daily train from Tallinn to Tartu (free tea/coffee, WiFi access), but services through the region tend to be cumbersome, with a change of trains in the border towns. For long-distance travel, however, trains can provide a far better level of comfort and a greater chance of getting some sleep. A luxury express train from Berlin to St Petersburg has been talked about for years but has yet to come to fruition.

Estonia There is an overnight train from Tallinn to Moscow. Contact: GoRail, Tallinn Train Station, Toompuiestee 37; tel: 6310 044; email: reisid@gorail.ee; www.gorail.ee.
Latvia There are daily convenient and comfortable overnight trains from Moscow and St Petersburg to Rīga. For more information contact: Latvian Railways; tel: 6723 1181; www.ldz.lv.
Lithuania Lietuvos Gelez+inkeliai, the Lithuanian rail network, connects with Poland and Germany. Train timetables and other useful information in English can be viewed on the Lithuanian rail website, www.litrail.lt.

By Car

When driving in the Baltics, be sure you carry a valid driver's licence, vehicle registration and/or ownership documents and a Green Card extending your regular car insurance. Vehicles are required to carry a fluorescent warning triangle, fire extinguisher and first-aid kit. You must also have a national identity sticker on the rear of your vehicle. Breakdown insurance is advisable; consult your insurer before travelling.

The three countries are linked by the Via Baltica (E-67), the main highway that runs 670km (416 miles) from the Lithuanian border with Poland to Tallinn.

Because all three Baltic countries are in the Schengen visa area, there are usually no border checks between them, or on routes in from Western countries. However, border guards regularly stop vehicles along the highway to check passports.

High-grade petrol is available, and garages also sell maps (Regio produces good maps for Estonia, Jana Seta for Latvia and Lithuania), which are essential for getting around.

There are a number of hotels and rest stops en route.

The speed limit on motorways is 90kph (55mph) and 60kph (37mph) in residential areas.

Headlights must be turned on at all times.

See Rules of the Road, page 334.

By Bus

Travelling by bus can be significantly cheaper and faster than travelling by train. From London, Eurolines (www.eurolines.com) offers a service from numerous destinations in Europe to the major Baltic cities and is the main means of transport between the countries.

By Sea

Estonia

In summer, dozens of ships make the quick, 85km (53-mile) crossing from Helsinki to Tallinn throughout the day, and larger ferries bring in passengers from other cities across the Baltic. There are several hydrofoils making regular crossings from Helsinki to Tallinn with a journey time of between one and two hours depending on the particular craft and the weather. In winter, the route is restricted to ferries, which take between two and four hours. Overnight ferries make slow but inexpensive connections from Stockholm.

Tallinn harbour (sadam) is a 15-minute walk from the Old Town. On trams 1 or 2 coming from the Old Town or the centre, the harbour is the next stop after Mere Puiestee, or from the opposite direction, two stops after the railway station. Note that all ships operated by Tallink leave from the harbour's D-Terminal, about 500 metres/yds northwest.
Main operators:
Ekerö Line, Mannerheimintie 10, Helsinki; tel: (+358) 9 228 8544; and Passenger Port, A-Terminal, Tallinn; tel: 6646 000; www.ekeroline.ee. Inexpensive, slow ferries from Helsinki to Tallinn.
Linda Line Express, Makasiiniterminaali, Eteläsatama, Helsinki; tel: (+358) 600 0668; and Linnahall Port, Mere pst. 20, Tallinn; tel: 6999 333; www.lindaline.fi. Helsinki–Tallinn hydrofoil service offering several 90-minute crossings

a day. Subject to weather; does not operate Jan–March.

Tallink, Olympiaterminal, Eteläsatama, Helsinki; tel: (+358) 9 646 635; and A. Laikmaa 5, Tallinn; tel: 6409 808; fax: 6118 895; www.tallink.ee. Numerous daily express services and larger ferries from Helsinki to Tallinn; overnight services from Stockholm to Tallinn.

Viking Line, Lönnrotinkatu 2, Helsinki; tel: (+358) 9 12351; and Hobujaama 4, Tallinn; tel: 6663 966; www.vikingline.fi. Viking Line operates ferries from Stockholm to Helsinki, and Helsinki to Tallinn.

Latvia

Tallink offers a luxurious ferry service to Rīga from Stockholm every day. For more information visit www.tallink.lv. Ferries from Rīga to Lübeck (Travemunde) in Germany depart twice weekly. The cities of Nynashamn (near Stockholm), Sweden, as well as Lübeck (Travemunde) in Germany are serviced by regular ferries from the western Latvian cities of Liepāja and Ventspils. Tallinn and Rīga are major ports of call on Baltic cruises. The main operators are:

Aveline, Rīga, Zivju 1; tel: 2944 4999; www.aveline.lv.

Scandlines, Ventspils, Dārzu 6; tel: 6362 0783; www.scandlines.lv. Passenger and cargo links from Ventspils and Liepāja to Lübeck, Germany, and Nynashamn, Sweden (60km/37 miles from Stockholm).

Tallink, Eksporta 3a; tel: 6709 9700; www.tallink.lv. Regular ferry service between Rīga and Stockholm.

Lithuania

A handful of car ferries link the Lithuanian port of Klaipėda to Kiel and Sassnitz in Germany and Karlshamn in Sweden. Journeys tend to be overnight.

The international ferry terminal is located several kilometres south of the city centre and can be reached by taxi for about 50lt.

DFDS Seaways; tel: (+370) 46 393 600; www.dfdslisco.com. Klaipėda's sole remaining ferry operator was at the time of writing merging with Norfolkline, although it was unclear whether services would be reduced or improved as a result.

Tour Operators

Because of the special rates they enjoy from airlines and hotels, prices for holidays booked through tour operators should cost little or no more than those booked direct.

Baltic Holidays
Individual and group arrangements.
5 Wood Road, Manchester M16 9RB; tel: 0845 070 5711, www.balticholidays.com.

Martin Randall Travel
A regular programme of group tours specialising in art, architecture and music festivals.
Voysey House, Barley Mow Passage, London W4 4GF; tel: 020 8742 3355; www.martinrandall.com.

Naturetrek
Specialists for bird-watching tours in the Baltics.
Cheriton Mill, Cheriton, Alresford, Hants SO24 0NG; tel: 01962 733 051; www.naturetrek.co.uk.

Operas Abroad
Individual arrangements to opera and musical concerts; part of Regent Holidays; www.operasabroad.com.

Regent Holidays
Specialists in the Baltic States since 1992, both with group tours and individuals. It also organises city breaks throughout the year.
Mezzanine Suite, Froomsgate House, Rupert Street, Bristol BS1 2QJ; tel: 0117 921 1711; www.regent-holidays.co.uk.

Entry Requirements

Citizens of the EU, US, Canada, Australia and New Zealand need only a valid passport. Citizens of South Africa need a visa to visit the Baltic States, but can enter Estonia if they have a valid visa for Latvia or Lithuania.

Customs and Export

Individuals entering and leaving the Baltic States may carry with them most articles, personal property and other valuables in unlimited quantities. However, weapons and ammunition of any kind, drugs and psychotropic substances are not allowed. Lithuania also forbids the import of meat, dairy products, eggs and sausages and the export of more than 10kg of fresh and 5kg of dried mushrooms or berries.

Getting Around

Public Transport

Estonia

A system of **buses, trams** and **electric trolleybuses** makes up Tallinn's public transit system. The trams mainly service the centre of town, whereas the buses are for

reaching outlying areas. Detailed maps posted on most bus stops will show you how to make your journey. (You can also buy good transport maps published by Regio.) All three modes of transit use the same ticket, available from a kiosk for €0.95 (a book of 10 is €6.40), which you must punch after you board. Each ticket is good for one ride.

Taxis Most of the city is walkable, but if you do need a taxi, it is best to order one by phone. Dispatchers at Linnatakso, tel: 1242, and Tulika Takso, tel: 1200, usually speak some English. The biggest complaint among tourists in Tallinn is taxi drivers who overcharge. Before starting out, check the rates listed on the taxi's window. Typical rates are €2–3 starting fee, then about €0.50/km. If in doubt, ask a driver for an estimate before getting in.

Buses Long-distance buses are the most convenient and widely used method of getting from city to city in Estonia. In Tallinn, the bus station is located at Lastekodu 46; tel: 12550. Bussireisid has complete bus timetables in English on its website, www.bussireisid.ee. It also offers online booking.

Internal flights Estonian Air offers regular services to Kuressaare on Saaremaa six days a week. The private company Avies flies to Kärdla on Hiiumaa daily.
Avies: Tallinn Airport; tel: 6058 022; www.avies.ee.

Latvia

All public transport in Rīga, including **trams**, **buses**, and **trolleybuses**, costs a flat fee of 0.70Ls for the duration of your trip, if you buy a ticket from the driver. If you get off a tram and hop on the next available one you will have to pay

BELOW: a Tallinn tram.

for another ticket. Cheaper tickets called e-talons can be purchased at newsstands and supermarkets and cost 0.50Ls (one trip), 2.50Ls (5 trips), 4.75Ls (10 trips) and 9Ls (20 trips). Tickets for one, three and five days of travel are also available. You must touch the electronic ticket readers with your e-talons upon entering the vehicle. For more information in English visit the Tram and Trolleybus Authority's excellent site, www.rigassatiksme.lv.

Minibuses called mikroautobusi, or mikriņi for short, can also be a convenient way of travelling as they will stop at any point along a given route, and are a fast way of getting around, though they are often packed.

Trams Electric trams have been in use in Rīga since 1901. Today, there are nine different tram lines , which operate from 5.30am to midnight, and night trams are in service roughly every hour on weekend nights. There are also 21 trolleybus routes for which the same rules for trams apply.

Taxis Taxis in Rīga are notoriously dodgy and will often overcharge any person who doesn't speak Latvian or Russian. To avoid exorbitant prices always call a cab or ask the receptionist at your hotel to order a reputable taxi for you. Despite their dubious reputation in general, there are a few taxi companies that can be trusted. Try Baltic Taxi, tel: 2000 8500, run by AirBaltic, or Lady Taxi, tel: 2780 0900, which employs only female drivers. Most taxis accept credit cards.

Lithuania

Public transport has never been the most pleasant part of a stay in Vilnius. Most systems operate from 5.30am– 11pm, so late-night travel is by foot or taxi. Public transport is, however, inexpensive and covers most of the city, excluding the Old Town.

City buses The newer-looking buses are city-owned. Tickets can be purchased at a Lietuva spauda kiosk (2lt) or on board the bus (2.50lt). Once on the bus you must validate your ticket in one of the boxes provided. Failure to do so will result in a fine by the ticket inspectors, who constantly patrol the buses. Private bus company tickets can only be bought on board buses and currently cost 2lt.

Trolleybuses Riding a trolleybus in Vilnius is the easiest way to travel back in time to the Soviet era. As on the city's buses, tickets can be purchased on board for 2.50lt or from Lietuva spauda kiosks for 2lt, but must be validated on board.

Car Hire Firms

Tallinn

Avis: at the airport; tel: 6058 222; in the city at Pärnu mnt. 141; tel: 6671 500; www.avis.ee.
Budget: at the airport; tel: 6058 600; www.budget.ee.
Hertz: at the airport; tel: 6058 923; in the city at Ahtri 12; tel: 6116 333; www.hertz.ee.
R-Rent: at the airport, tel: 6058 929; in the city at Rävala pst. 4; tel: 6612 400; www.rrent.ee.
Sir Rent: Juhkentali 11; tel: 6614 353; www.sirrent.ee.
Sixt: at the airport; tel: 6058 148; in the city at Rävala 5; tel: 6133 660; www.sixt.ee.

Riga

AddCar Rental: at the airport; tel: 2658 9674; www.addcarrental. com.
Auto Cars Rent: tel: 2958 0448; www.carsrent.lv. Delivers cars to any

location in Rīga and also offers drivers.
Avis: at the airport; tel: 6720 7353; in the city at 11. novembra krastmala 29; tel: 6722 5876; fax: 6783 0991; www.avis.lv.
EgiCarRent: tel: 2953 1044; www. egi.lv. Delivers cars to any location in Rīga.
Europcar: at the airport; tel: 6720 7825; in the city at Torņa 4, 3C-102; tel: 6722 2637; fax: 6782 0360; www.europcar.lv.
Sixt-Baltic Car Lease: at the airport; tel: 6720 71 21; fax: 6720 71 31; www.sixt.lv.

Lithuania

Avis: at the airport; tel: 8-5 232 9316; www.avis.lt.
Budget: at the airport; tel: 8-5 230 6708; www.budget.lt.
Sixt: at the airport; tel: 8-5 239 5636; www.sixt.lt.

Microbuses This is the fastest and cleanest form of transport through the city. Microbus routes are subject to change as they are privately owned and operated. Most have signs in their front windows giving a general idea of their trajectory. To get on one, just flag it down, get in, sit down and tell the driver where you would like to be dropped off. As no one usually speaks English, it is best to have decent Lithuanian pronunciation skills or have your destination written down (see Language, page 373). Tickets cost 3lt.

Taxis Generally, taxi drivers like to take advantage of foreigners. Most horror stories of inflated taxi prices occur when foreigners are inebriated or when the meter clicks away at a super-fast rate and goes unnoticed until the arrival at the destination. Your best bet for not getting ripped off is merely to pay attention to your surroundings. If possible, always try to call for a taxi instead of hailing one off the street as the price will be significantly cheaper.

Two reputable firms that occasionally have English-speakers on their staff are Martono taksi (tel: 240 00 04, 1.50lt/km) and Vilniaus taxi plius (tel: 261 61 61, 1.25lt/km).

Long-distance buses Buses are more popular and expensive than trains for most domestic destinations. The bus station (autobusų stotis) is at Sodų 22, www.toks.lt, across from the train station.

Trains Tickets can be purchased at the train station (geležinkelio stotis), www.litrail.lt, located at Geležinkelio 16. On overnight trains to Russia there are three different classes of tickets. The cheapest is obschii, which is a sitting place only. Platzkart is an open compartment with dormitory-style beds and coupe is a softer bed in a four-person compartment with a door that locks.

Women travelling alone should be aware that it is not uncommon for them to end up in a coupe with three men overnight, although a word in the ear of the train compartment manager once on board can sometimes result in the sleeping arrangements being changed.

There is no first class in Lithuania, and only a handful of second-class services.

Car Hire

Hiring a car is generally the best way to explore the three countries, and is simple and relatively inexpensive. You must be at least 21 years of age and must possess a valid driving licence, passport and major credit card, and must have had a licence for at least two years. Most of the major international car hire agencies operate in the cities and have desks at the airports. In most cases cars can be delivered to your hotel.

Mileage is unlimited, but hirers are expected to fill the tank just before returning the car. Otherwise a top-up fee will be added to the bill, along with the price of the fuel. Prices in comparison tend to be lower than in Western Europe and the US. Pricing structures are the same as in most countries, with added fees for an additional driver, insurance, mileage and the like.

If you plan to take your hire car outside the country, you may need special documents for the border. However, many hire companies have special deals even for one-way travel within all three Baltic States.

Driving

Road conditions vary from good to poor. Estonian drivers range from the careless to the aggressive, while Latvians are not above passing on blind turns or suddenly driving in the opposite lane of oncoming traffic to avoid a pothole. Your only recourse is to drive defensively.

Weather is an issue, particularly in winter when patches of ice appear on roads. If you are not experienced at driving in winter conditions, this is not the place to learn.

Also, because markings on rural routes can often be confusing, it is essential to have a good road atlas to refer to.

Take it Easy

Latvia once had the highest proportion of road-accident casualties in Europe, with around 44,000 traffic accidents each year in which nearly 7,000 were injured and around 500 killed. More stringent drink-driving laws have lowered these statistics to just over 35,000 accidents, 3,160 injuries and 254 deaths in 2009.

Parking

Parking in the centre of the three capitals can be a battle. Most street parking is paid parking, and tickets are sold in vending machines.

In **Tallinn** car parks can be found under Freedom Square (Vabaduse väljak), on Rävala 5, and at the Viru Hotel, Viru väljak 4. See www.europark.ee for a map of more options. The cost is typically €1.60–3.20/h.

Rīga has plenty of guarded and multi-storey car parks around town. To find the most convenient location, visit www.europark.lv.

Although you can now enter Old Rīga free of charge, you have to pay high fees for hourly parking. To make things worse, you can only pay for parking using a complicated mobile phone SMS system, which isn't very advantageous for visitors. If you would like to learn more about how to pay for parking in Old Rīga, visit www.mobilly.lv.

Parking in **Vilnius** is paid by the hour, Mon–Sat 8am–8pm. In Vilnius there are human ticket takers; tickets should be displayed on the dashboard along with a marking clock (usually provided by car-hire companies) or a note indicating the time you parked.

Some **national parks** and the Latvian seaside of Jūrmala charge drivers a small entrance fee.

Rules of the Road

Traffic signs and symbols follow the European standard.
• Drive on the right and overtake on the left.
• Headlights must be kept on at all times, day and night, even in the city.
• Passengers in both front seats must wear seatbelts at all times; on the highway, the same rule applies to back-seat passengers.
• Children under 12 are not allowed

In Case of a Breakdown

Estonia: call the Estonian Automobile Club, tel: 1888, for 24-hour towing services.
Latvia: LAMB; tel: 1888; www.lamb.lv; offers a 24-hour service.
Lithuania: Atlas Assistance (tel: 8-5 240 23 80) provides all types of help for a modest fee. All accidents, no matter how small, must be reported to the police or it will be impossible to make an insurance claim.

to travel in the front seat.
• Winter tyres must be used from October to April.
• The use of mobile phones by drivers is prohibited without hands-free equipment.
• Drivers are considered under the influence and therefore subject to arrest if they have a 0.4 percent alcohol level in their blood – about a half-litre of beer. It is best not to drink at all if you are driving. If caught in Latvia, you can also expect a mandatory 10-day jail sentence in addition to a large fine and the loss of your driving licence.
• The basic speed limit outside built-up areas is 90km/h (55mph), in built-up areas 50–60 km/h (31–37mph), and in residential areas 20km/h (13 mph). Some roads are marked with their own limits, particularly large motorways, where cars are permitted to go 110km/h (69mph) in summer. On the Vilnius–Kaunas motorway speed limits are 100km/h (62mph). On all other Lithuanian motorways the limits range from 90km/h (55mph) to 130km/h (80mph).
• Drivers must have a valid driving licence and car documents with them at all times.

Police are stationed at most major thoroughfares, and most drivers opt to pay their fines in cash on the spot in order to avoid having to go to a particular police station to pay the fine.

Even if you are driving by lakes and forests, remember that the town's limits extend up to the point where the sign of the town with a cross through it stands. Often police will have speed traps in these non-populated areas that are still within the town or city limits. Fines may also be imposed on drivers who fail to stop at pedestrian crossings.

If you have an accident, you are not supposed to move your vehicle until the police have arrived.

BELOW: there are regular ferries from Rīga and Ventspils to Germany and Sweden.

A CCOMMODATION

HOTELS, SPAS, HOSTELS, BED & BREAKFAST

There have been a large number of three- and four-star hotels built throughout the region since around the turn of the millennium, and all three capitals offer a choice of world-class hotels, with stylish rooms, in-room internet connections, free WiFi, business centres, top-notch restaurants and other luxury amenities, including health spas and saunas, both of which are specialities of the Baltics. Most larger hotels also have rooms or entire floors designated for non-smokers, as well as rooms equipped for disabled guests. A growing number of cosy boutique hotels, often built into refurbished Old Town buildings and rural manor houses, offer the same level of luxury in a more intimate environment. Hotels in smaller cities and in the countryside tend to be more basic, but even here, standards of quality are usually similar to Western European levels. Travellers on a tight budget should consider bed & breakfast, hostel, home stay, or tourist farm accommodation. All hotels take credit cards unless otherwise noted.

ACCOMMODATION LISTINGS

ESTONIA

Thanks to a tourism boom, the choice of hotels and spas in Estonia has mushroomed over the last decade. Even so, book early during the high season (May to August) to get the best deals. Tallinn offers the widest range of choice, from medieval-style boutique hotels to ultra-modern high-rises, many with spa treatment facilities. If you're travelling in a small group and spending any length of time in the capital, renting a flat is worth considering; an increasing number of firms specialise in rentals. Anyone visiting Tallinn on a tight budget should first try to find space in one of the few Old Town guesthouses and hostels, then look to the outskirts for super-cheap accommodation.

Prices for rooms elsewhere in Estonia are usually drastically lower, but even here there are ways to economise.

Tourist farms (rural B&Bs) offer simple double rooms at hostel prices, though your hosts may not speak English. Many tourist farms, and even a few guesthouses in the city suburbs, will also let you pitch a tent in their garden – and use their facilities – for a small fee.

A database listing every registered accommodation facility in Estonia, with prices and links to web pages, can be found at the Tourism Board's website: www.visitestonia.com. Rooms in private homes in Tallinn, Pärnu and Kuressaare can be booked through Rasastra (tel: 6616 291; www.bed breakfast.ee).

Campers should note that at Estonia's official "Kämping" sites you won't even need a tent. These are typically patches of forest filled with simple little camp huts. All you need to bring with you is a sleeping bag and lots of mosquito repellent.

HOTELS

Tallinn

Barons
Suur-Karja 7/Väike-Karja 2
Tel: 6999 700
Fax: 6999 718
barons@baronshotel.ee
www.baronshotel.ee
Steeped with elegance, this small luxury hotel is housed in a 1912-era bank building and still has the original vaults to prove it. Amenities include mini-bar, hairdryer, bathrobe and slippers. €€

Braavo
Aia 20
Tel: 6999 777
Fax: 6412 317
braavo@braavo.ee
www.braavo.ee
The 36-room Braavo is a decent budget choice thanks to its Old Town location and ultra-modern rooms, though don't expect

PRICE CATEGORIES

Ranges given are for a hotel double room, per night:
€ under €50
€€ €50–100
€€€ €100–150
€€€€ over €150

ABOVE: The Three Sisters Hotel.

much from the view. It's attached to a busy sports club to which guests have free entrance. €€

City Hotel Portus
Uus-Sadama 23
Tel: 6806 600
Fax: 6806 601
portus@tallinnhotels.ee
www.portus.ee
Located in the passenger port area, this modern, 107-room hotel offers colourful rooms and an overall cheerful ambience. Plusses include free parking, a kids' playroom and a retro-style café. €€

Meriton Grand Conference & Spa Hotel
Toompuiestee 27
Tel: 6677 111
Fax: 6288 101
reservation@meritonhotels.com
www.meritonhotels.com
Considered one of Tallinn's finest hotels, the Grand doubled its size in 2009, adding an extensive aqua and wellness centre as well as hundreds more rooms. Located near Toompea Castle, within easy walking distance of the main sights. €€

Meriton Old Town Garden Hotel
Pikk 29/Lai 24
Tel: 6677 111
Fax: 6288 101
reservation@meritonhotels.com
www.meritonhotels.com
The Garden stretches between two of the Old Town's most picturesque streets, with a separate entrance on each one. It approximates the feel of

Tallinn's exclusive boutique hotels, but at a much lower cost. €€

Nordic Hotel Forum
Viru väljak 3
Tel: 6222 900
Fax: 6222 901
info@nordichotels.eu
www.nordichotels.eu
This full-service, ultra-modern hotel is prized for its comfortable interior, professional service and highly central location. €€

Radisson Blu Hotel Olümpia
Liivalaia 33
Tel: 6315 333
Fax: 6315 325
info.olumpia.tallinn@radissonblu.com
www.radissonblu.com
Contemporary four-star monolith offering business facilities, a comfortable restaurant, lunch café, English-style pub, and nightclub. €€€

Radisson Blu Hotel Tallinn
Rävala pst. 3
Tel: 6823 000
Fax: 6823 001
info.tallinn@radissonblu.com
www.radissonblu.com
Everything one would expect from a world-class chain hotel. A five-minute walk from the Old Town, the building is one of the city's tallest; request a room on the town side for the best views. €€€

Schlössle
Pühavaimu 13/15
Tel: 6997 700
Fax: 6997 777
sch@schlossle-hotels.com
www.schloesslehotel.com
Impressive ambience and

impeccable service. Ancient stone and heavy wooden beams give the lobby its medieval look, while rooms are furnished in a lavish, antique style. €€€€

Sokos Viru Hotel
Viru väljak 4
Tel: 6809 300
Fax: 6809 236
viru.reservation@sok.fi
www.sokoshotels.fi
Tallinn's most famous Soviet-era high-rise hotel has evolved into a quality, international-style establishment popular with Finns. Adjacent to the Old Town and attached to the city centre's largest shopping complex. €€

Swissôtel
Tornimäe 3
Tel: 6240 000
Fax: 6240 001
tallinn@swissotel.com
www.swissotel.com/tallinn
Tallinn's branch of this well-known, international hotel chain is an immense glass tower in the city centre. In addition to sweeping views, it offers luxuries from spa facilities to iPod docking stations. €€

Tallink Spa & Conference Hotel
Sadama 11a
Tel: 6301 000
Fax: 6301 010
spahotel@tallink.ee
www.hotels.tallink.com
One of several hotels owned by Estonia's major ferry operator, this cutting-edge establishment next to the passenger port caters to guests who come with relaxation in mind. It's centred around a decadent, indoor pool area, with waterfall. €€€

Telegraaf
Vene 9
Tel: 6000 600
Fax: 6061 601
info@telegraafhotel.com
www.telegraafhotel.com
Telegraaf, the newest of the Old Town's five-star luxury hotels, has a palpable air of exclusivity and class. Among its amenities are a day spa and a top-notch Russian-French fusion restaurant. €€€€

The Three Sisters
Pikk 71/Tolli 2
Tel: 6306 300
Fax: 6306 301
info@threesistershotel.com
Built inside Tallinn's famous Three Sisters, a trio of 14th–15th-century houses, this five-star hotel offers unmatched lavishness from the candles in the lobby chandelier to the amazing room decor. €€€€

Unique Hotel Mihkli
Endla 23
Tel: 6664 802
Fax: 6664 888
reservationsmikhli@uniquestay.com
www.uniquestay.com
This trendy hotel, five minutes' walk from the Old Town, offers good value and frequent specials on its website. Rooms are all freshly renovated, fashionably decorated and come with their own computers. €€

Haapsalu

Baltic Hotel Promenaadi
Sadama 22
Tel: 4737 250
Fax: 4737 254
promenaadi@baltichotelgroup.com
www.promenaadi.ee
Part new and part built into a 19th-century villa, Promenaadi offers decent rooms and a restaurant-café overlooking the waterfront. €€

Fra Mare Thalasso SPA
Ranna tee 2
Tel: 4724 600
Fax: 4724 601
framare@framare.ee
www.framare.ee
Haapsalu's best-equipped hotel is beside the town's swimming beach. The 115-room facility offers modern accommodation, spa-treatment packages, beauty parlour, restaurant and a seawater pool. €€

Kongo
Kalda 19

PRICE CATEGORIES

Ranges given are for a hotel double room, per night:
€ under €50
€€ €50–100
€€€ €100–150
€€€€ over €150

Tel: 4724 800
Fax: 4724 809
kongohotel@hot.ee
www.kongohotel.ee
A cosy, 21-room hotel in the quaint wooden-house district of Haapsalu. The location, near the castle and city attractions, is a plus, as are the restaurant and sauna. €€€

Kuressaare

Arensburg Boutique Hotel & Spa
Lossi 15
Tel: 4524 700
Fax: 4524 702
arensburg@arensburg.ee
www.arensburg.ee
This 46-room, luxury hotel makes its home in a 300-year-old building on historic Kuressaare's main street. Smartly decorated rooms, spa facilities, two restaurants and a wine cellar are on offer. €€

Georg Ots Spa Hotel
Tori 2
Tel: 4550 000
Fax: 4550 001
info@gospa.ee
www.gospa.ee
A large, state-of-the-art spa hotel right on the water. Facials to foot massage, swimming pools, in-room stereo systems. €€

Grand Rose Spa Hotel
Tallinna 15
Tel: 6667 000
info@grandrose.ee
www.grandrose.ee
Estonians who want to pamper themselves prefer this exclusive, rose-themed spa to Kuressaare's larger, group-orientated establishments. Reasonably priced for this level of luxury. €€

Narva

Narva Hotell
Puškini 6
Tel: 3599 600
Fax: 3599 603
hotell@narvahotell.ee
www.narvahotell.ee
Large, central and completely up to date, this four-storey edifice is Narva's nicest hotel. Rooms are decorated with natural

materials, and many have excellent views of Ivangorod Castle. €€

Otepää

Bernhard Spa Hotell
Kolga tee 22a
Tel: 7669 600
Fax: 7669 601
hotell@bernhard.ee
www.bernhard.ee
A 32-room spa hotel in a peaceful, lakeside setting. Bernhard is a good choice both in summer and during ski season, with a number of packages available to let guests make the most of its pools, hot tubs and spa treatments. €€

Pühajärve Spa & Holiday Resort
Pühajärve village
Tel: 7665 500
Fax: 7665 501
pjpk@pjpk.ee
www.pyhajarve.com
Built around a historic manor house on the shore of Lake Pühajärve, this busy hotel offers by far the widest range of services and amenities available in the area, including a full spa, bowling alley, and an elegant tower café with a view. €€

Pärnu

Ammende Villa
Mere pst. 7
Tel: 4473 888
Fax: 4473 887
sale@ammende.ee
www.ammende.ee

Pärnu's most luxurious hotel makes its home in a stunning, 1905-era Art Nouveau villa that's entirely decorated in the style of that period. Guests can enjoy the villa's surrounding garden and fountains, as well as its gourmet restaurant. €€€–€€€€

Konse Holiday Village
Suur-Jõe 44a
Tel: 53 435 092
Fax: 4475 561
info@konse.ee
www.konse.ee
A riverside guesthouse/campsite offering basic double rooms and a café, as well as places for caravans and tents. About 10 minutes' walk from the centre. €–€€

Hotell Pärnu
Rüütli 44
Tel: 4478 911
Fax: 4478 905
hotparnu@pergohotels.ee
www.pergohotels.ee
Despite the outdated, blocky exterior, this 80-room hotel is entirely modern and cheerful once you get past the front doors. Its main draws are its heart-of-city-centre location, balcony views and full array of services. €€

Scandic Rannahotell
Ranna pst. 5
Tel: 4432 950
Fax: 4432 918
rannahotell@scandichotels.com
www.scandichotels.com
An amazing example of Functionalism from 1937, the beautiful and stylish

Rannahotell sits right on the beach. Ask for a sea-facing room with a balcony. May be closed during low season. €€€

St Peterburg
Hospidali 6
Tel: 4430 555
Fax: 4430 556
info@stpeterburg.ee
www.seegimaja.ee
A history-themed hotel in Pärnu's Old Town. Some rooms are decorated in tsarist-era style, others reflect the 17th-century Swedish period. €€€

Tervise Paradiis
Side 14
Tel: 4479 219
Fax: 4451 601
sales@spa.ee
www.terviseparadiis.ee
A full-service spa, the "Health Paradise" is a very family-oriented hotel near the beach, with several restaurants, a casino, bowling alley and a huge indoor water park. €€–€€€

Tartu

Barclay
Ülikooli 8
Tel: 7447 100
Fax: 7447 101
barclay@barclay.ee
www.barclay.ee
Set in what was once the local headquarters of the Soviet Army, the reconstructed Barclay Hotel exudes early 19th-century elegance. Ask for the Dzhokhar Dudayev room, named after the first

BELOW: Ammende Villa.

ABOVE: a hotel internet café.

president of Chechnya, who was stationed here from 1987–91 while an officer in the Soviet Army. €€

Dorpat
Soola 6
Tel: 7337 180
Fax: 7337 181
info@dorpat.ee
www.dorpat.ee
With 205 rooms, this newly built hotel on the banks of the River Emajõgi is by far Tartu's largest. Special packages are available, including luxury meals, theatre tickets and treatments in the Dorpat's spa centre. €€

London
Rüütli 9
Tel: 7305 555
Fax: 7305 565
london@londonhotel.ee
www.londonhotel.ee
A modern, luxury hotel in the heart of Tartu's Old Town. Count on stylish

rooms, many with rooftop views. €€

Pallas
Riia 4
Tel: 7301 200
Fax: 7301 201
pallas@pallas.ee
www.pallas.ee
On top of a business centre overlooking the city, the hotel has 61 rooms, and the luxurious suites are wonderfully decorated according to the designs of 20th-century Estonian painters, all of whom were students of the Pallas Art School, located here before World War II. €€

Tartu Hostel
Pepleri 14 and Narva mnt. 27
Tel: 7409 955
Fax: 7409 958
hostel@kyla.ee
www.tartuhostel.eu
Surprisingly modern single and twin rooms in two of the university's dormitory buildings. Kitchenette, WC and shower are either in-room or shared with two others. €

Tartu Hotel
Soola 3
Tel: 7314 300
Fax: 7314 301
info@tartuhotell.ee
www.tartuhotell.ee
Situated next to the bus station, this friendly, newly renovated hotel has cheaper rooms than elsewhere in town, particularly its bargain-priced hostel rooms. Some spa facilities are available. €€

Viljandi

Grand Hotel Viljandi
Tartu 11/Lossi 29
Tel: 4355 800
Fax: 4355 805
info@ghv.ee
www.ghv.ee
Opened in 2002 in a late-1930s building, the stylish, 49-room hotel offers Art Deco furnishings, a restaurant, gym, sauna and beauty salon. €€

HOSTELS

Budget travellers should bear in mind that the term "hostel" has a much wider definition in Estonia than the familiar, friendly, backpackers' stopover, encompassing also cheap hotels and guesthouses. The latter typically offer only private rooms and lack kitchen and laundry facilities. The larger, traditional hostels offer private, bare-bones singles, doubles and triples (€20–50), as well as dorm beds (€10–16).

The Estonian Youth Hostel Association, part of Hostelling International, has given its stamp of membership to 18 hostels and guesthouses in Tallinn, as well as other establishments around the country, but does not cover the most popular, recommended venues.

Booking and information can be found at www.hotels.ee. You do not have to be a member of a hostelling association to stay at any of them.

Tallinn

Tallinn Backpackers
Olevimägi 11
Tel: 6440 298
Fax: 6166 754
info@tallinnbackpackers.com
www.tallinnbackpackers.com
Staffed mainly by backpackers, this Old Town hostel is a full-service affair, complete with bar, sauna, internet, movie nights and even day trips to Paldiski and Lahemaa. €

Vana Tom Hostel
Väike-Karja 1
Tel/fax: 6313 252
hostel@hostel.ee
www.hostel.ee
Vana Tom is a long-time favourite due to its central location, fun-loving decor and wide range of facilities. It's located amid the Old Town's most popular bars, so request a quieter room at the back. €

Pärnu

Lõuna Hostel
Lõuna 2
Tel: 4430 943
hostel@eliisabet.ee
www.hostellouna.eu
Bare-bones hostel accommodation in the centre. More expensive double rooms are newer and have their own shower/WC. €

Tartu

Terviseks Backpackers
Raekoja plats 10
Tel: 5841 7728
hostelterviseks@gmail.com
http://hostelterviseks.blogspot.com
An unbeatable location right on Town Hall Square and a relaxed, social atmosphere make this 24-bed hostel a great choice for travellers who like to mingle. Services range from free internet to city tours. Light breakfast is included. €

BELOW: inside the London Hotel, Tartu.

LATVIA

Rīga has many expensive luxury hotels as well as many medium-range hotels, but only Old Town hotels need to be booked well in advance. When travelling throughout the country, you will find the majority of towns have at least one good hotel where facilities are usually basic but acceptable. Large towns have at least one three- or four-star hotel, and several have more.

Private bed & breakfast accommodation has flourished in Rīga and usually costs much less than a hotel room. Farmhouse and cottage accommodation can be arranged through Lauku ceļotājs (Country Traveller), Kalnciema 40, Rīga; tel: 6761 7600; www.celotajs.lv.

HOTELS

Rīga

HOTELS

Rīga

Dodo Hotel
Jersikas 1
Tel: 6724 0220
Fax: 6724 0218
www.dodohotel.com
This modern budget hotel offers small yet affordable rooms with satellite TV, and private bathrooms in a recently built building a few tram stops beyond the Central Market. **€**

Hotel Bergs
Berga Bazārs
Tel: 6777 0900
Fax: 6777 0940
www.hotelbergs.lv
Five minutes' walk to the Old Town, this fantastic work of design by architect Zaiga Gaile was among *Condé Nast Traveller*'s Best Hotels of the World, 2004. Rooms are spacious and light. Family apartments with small kitchens also available. **€€€€**

Hotel Centra
Audēju 1
Tel: 6722 6441
Fax: 6722 3733
www.hotelcentra.lv

Located in the Old Town, but the interior is modern and minimalist. Rooms are spacious with high ceilings and offer great views over the Old Town from the top floors. **€€**

Hotel de Rome
Kaļķu 28
Tel: 6708 7600
Fax: 6708 7606
reservation@derome.lv
www.derome.lv
One of the smartest places to stay in Latvia, this hotel is centrally located on the edge of the Old Town facing the Freedom monument. Treat yourself to a nibble in the Otto Schwarz restaurant if your budget stretches to it. **€€€€**

Hotel Neiburgs
Jauniela 25/27
Tel: 6711 5522
Fax: 6755 9562
www.neiburgs.com
One of Old Rīga's most beautiful Art Nouveau buildings has been completely renovated and converted into a stylish design hotel. All rooms are essentially apartments with modern amenities and fantastic views. It also boasts a top-notch restaurant. **€€€€**

Islande
Ķīpsalas 20
Tel: 6760 8000
Fax: 6760 8001
www.islandehotel.lv
Scandinavian minimalist design, excellent service and a top-floor restaurant with fantastic views of Old Rīga are just a few reasons to stay here. Bowling alley also available. **€€€**

Kolonna Hotel Rīga
Tirgoņu 9
Tel: 6735 8254
Fax: 6735 8255
www.hotelkolonna.com
Located on a bustling Old Rīga street among cafés, bars and souvenir shops, this affordable hotel provides over 40 rooms with standard amenities next to the Old Town's central square, Doma laukums. Great value for money. **€€**

Konventa Sēta
Kalēju 9/11
Tel: 6708 7507
Fax: 6708 7515
reservation@konventa.lv
www.konventa.lv
Housed in a medieval convent in the heart of the Old Town, the "Convent Courtyard" (Konventhof) is run by the same team as the Hotel de Rome. **€€**

Metropole
Aspazijas bulv. 36
Tel: 6722 5411
Fax: 6721 6140
metropole@metropole.lv
www.metropole.lv
A Swedish-run top-quality hotel on the edge of the Old Town. **€€€**

Radisson Blu Hotel Elizabete
Elizabetes 73
Tel: 6778 5555
Fax: 6778 5554
www.radissonblu.com/elizabetehotel-riga
Completed in 2008, this stylish glass-and-metal building provides comfortable rooms decorated by a top-rated London design firm, a central open-air courtyard, a trendy restaurant and excellent views of the adjacent park. **€€€**

Radi un Draugi
Mārstaļu 1/3
Tel: 6782 0200
www.draugi.lv
This British-Latvian joint venture has been booked up ever since it opened, and with good reason: it offers moderately priced accommodation in the heart of the Old Town. Reservations are essential. **€€**

Tallink Hotel Riga
Elizabetes 24
Tel: 6709 9760
Fax: 6709 9762
www.hotels.tallink.com
Owned by a huge Baltic ferry company, this modern four-star hotel across the street from the train station is always full of Scandinavian guests. Two restaurants, a bar and a fitness and sauna complex are also available. **€€€**

Bed & Breakfast

Jacob Lenz
Lenču 2
Tel: 6733 3343
Fax: 6733 1378
www.guesthouselenz.lv
Only a stone's throw from Rīga's Art Nouveau and embassy district, this quiet bed & breakfast provides a variety of comfortable rooms for individual travellers, couples and families. **€**

Hostels

Central Hostel
E. Birznieka-Upīša 20
Tel: 2232 2662
www.centralhostel.lv
Although not in the Old Town, Central offers much more privacy than most Rīga hostels, and it's a short walk from the train station. A common room with video games, TV, a library and internet access is also available. **€**

Riga Old Town Hostel
Vaļņu 43
Tel: 6722 3406
www.rigaoldtownhostel.lv
The first "real" hostel to open in Rīga, it's a haven for students and budget-minded backpackers who can often be seen enjoying a beer at the bar, that also serves as a reception area. **€**

The House Hostel
Barona 44 (entrance from Lāčplēša)
Tel: 2938 9450
www.riga-hostel.com
Run by an Australian expatriate who also

PRICE CATEGORIES

Ranges given are for a hotel double room, per night:
€ under €40 (under 28Ls)
€€ €40–80 (28–56Ls)
€€€ €80–120 (56–84Ls)
€€€€ over €120 (56–84Ls)

(right margin, vertical text: TRANSPORT · ACCOMMODATION · EATING OUT · ACTIVITIES · A–Z · LANGUAGE)

RURAL LIVING

Countryside Holidays, www. celotajs.lv, has a catalogue and online reservation system for a variety of countryside accommodation in all three Baltic States. It has more than 300 guesthouses, castle hotels, self-catering apartments, cottages, farmhouses and campsites to choose from.

organises tours and excursions, this laid-back hostel offers comfortable rooms, a full kitchen and a relaxation area to watch TV or hang out with other guests. €

The Naughty Squirrel Backpackers
Kalēju 50
Tel: 2646 1248
www.thenaughtysquirrel.com
This popular hostel offers a big bar for its guests, corridors painted by local graffiti artists and speakers in each room that can be attached to your iPod. Three free computers with internet access are also available. €

Apartments

Agency Lilija Plus
Ridzenes 25
Tel: 6721 6040
www.lilarealty.lv
Furnished apartments in Old Rīga and the city centre for long- or short-term rental. €€
Agency STES Latvia
Dzirnavu 55
Tel: 2644 8510
www.stes.lv

BELOW: Liepāja waterfront.

Modern, renovated apartments in Old Rīga, the city centre and Jūrmala, as well as luxury cottages by the sea. €€€

Bauska

Brencis Motel
On the A7 just north of Bauska, 38km (22 miles) from Rīga.
Tel: 6392 8033
motelisbrencis@inbox.lv
www.brencis.viss.lv
Unusual and welcome motel accommodation in a rural setting. €
Kungu Ligdza
Rīgas 41
Tel: 6392 4000
Fax: 6392 4000
kungu@inbox.lv
A renovated 18th-century building on a bank of the River Mēmele is the perfect place to rest your head in Bauska. Don't leave without trying a local brew in its beer cellar. €€
Mežotne Manor House
Mežotne
Tel: 6396 0711
pils@mezotnespils.lv
www.mezotnespils.lv
Splendidly renovated historic building, comfortable rooms with modern facilities, beautiful countryside around. Near Rundāle Palace. €€

Cēsis

Kolonna Hotel Cēsis
Vienības laukums 1
Tel: 6412 0122
Fax: 6412 0121
www.hotelkolonna.com
Comfortable three-star hotel in the centre of this popular medieval town. €€

Gulbene

Hotel Vecgulbenes Muiža
Brīvības 12
Tel: 6447 4800
www.baltapils.lv
Have a regal yet affordable stay in a renovated manor house that includes a spa. €€

Daugavpils

Park Hotel Latgola
Ģimnāzijas 46

Tel: 6540 4900
www.hotellatgola.lv
Renovated three-star hotel. Comfortable rooms, sauna, beauty treatments, guarded parking. €€

Jūrmala

Baltic Beach Hotel
23/25 Jūras iela, Majori
Tel: 6777 1400
Fax: 6777 1402
www.balticbeach.lv,
This four-star spa hotel in Jūrmala has 165 spacious rooms with balconies, spa facilities, swimming pool with sea water, terrace restaurant and guarded parking. Practically on the beach. €€€
Guest House Vēju Roze
41 Bulduru prosp. Bulduri
Tel: 6775 1752
info@vejuroze.lvwww.vejuroze.lv
Small, renovated cottage only 100 metres/yds from beach, among centuries-old pine trees. All rooms en suite. Prices depend on season and room size.
Hotel Eiropa
56 Jūras iela, Majori
Tel: 6776 2211
Fax: 6776 2299
www.eiropahotel.lv
Elegant four-star hotel in a traditional wooden cottage-style building 100 metres/yds from the beach and five minutes' walk from the main Jūrmala restaurant and shopping street. Cosy rooms, spa facilities, facilities for children. Room price includes breakfast, saunas and fitness hall. Parking. €€€€
Hotel Jūrmala Spa
Jomas 47/49, Majori
Tel: 6778 4400
booking@hoteljurmala.com
www.hoteljurmala.com
Located on Jūrmala's bustling pedestrian street, this is without a doubt the resort's best and most stylish hotel. €€€
Hotel MaMa
22 Tirgoņu iela, Majori
Tel: 6776 1271
www.hotelmama.lv
This charming boutique hotel, a 10-minute walk from the beach, looks like a gingerbread house from a

Brothers Grimm fairy tale. Apartments and an upmarket restaurant are also available. €€€€
Hotel Pegasa Pils
60 Jūras iela, Majori
Tel: 6776 1149
Fax: 6776 1169
www.hotelpegasapils.com
Quirky hotel in 19th-century wooden building. All rooms with French balconies, 100 metres/yds to the beach. Bridal suites available. Tennis courts, children's facilities, parking and a spa. €€€
Villa Joma
90 Jomas iela, Majori
Tel: 6777 1999
Fax: 6777 1990
www.villajoma.lv
Family-run small hotel in historical wooden building on the main Jūrmala promenade. A lot of character. Two minutes to beach. Parking. €€

Kuldīga

Hotel Metropole
Baznīcas 11
Tel: 6335 0588
www.hotel-metropole.lv
Completely renovated hotel with a restaurant and rooms with views of the Alekšupīte river. €€
Jāņa Nams
Liepājas 36
Tel: 6332 3456
Fax: 6332 3785
www.jananams.lv
Quaint two-storey hotel with a sauna, situated in the centre of town. €

Liepāja

Fontaine Hotel
Jūras 24
Tel: 6342 0956
Fax: 6342 0966
www.fontaine.lv
Located in a renovated 100-year-old wooden house, this is most likely the

PRICE CATEGORIES

Ranges given are for a hotel double room, per night:
€ under €40 (under 28Ls)
€€ €40–80 (28–56Ls)
€€€ €80–120 (56–84Ls)
€€€€ over €120 (56–84Ls)

hippest boutique hotel in the Baltics. €

Fontaine Royal Hotel
Stūrmaņu 1
Tel: 6348 9777
www.fontaineroyal.lv
Located on the Liepāja promenade, this former warehouse offers affordable rooms, a steakhouse and a day spa. €

Hotel Kolumbs
Kuršu 32
Tel: 2201 9385
www.hotelkolumbs.lv
This modern hotel includes stylish rooms, free parking, a small spa, a billiard bar and offers a great breakfast. €€

Madona

Jumurda Country Hotel
Jumurda, Madona distr.
Tel: 6487 1791
www.hoteljumurda.lv
Beautiful and quiet location by the lake. All rooms have lake view. Boats, bicycles available for hire. €€

Marciena Manor
Marcienas pagasts
Madona distr.
Tel: 6480 7300
www.marciena.com
Spa resort situated on a large estate with delightful farm buildings, outdoor bathtubs and a lake for swimming. €€

Sigulda

Aparjods
Ventas 1a
Tel: 6797 2230
Fax: 6797 6737
www.aparjods.lv
A fantastic Latvian timber building with a thatched roof and modern amenities, not far from the city centre. €€

Guest House Līvkalns
Peteralas iela
Tel: 6797 0916
Fax: 6797 0919
www.livkalns.lv
Lots of character, with swimming pool, sauna, horse riding, bicycle hire and walking trails. €€

Hotel Santa
Kalnjāņi
Tel: 6770 5271
Fax: 6770 5278
www.hotelsanta.lv

ABOVE: the ornate interior of Kukšu muiža.

Beautiful and peaceful location by the lake. A bit away from the centre. €€

Sigulda
Pils 6
Tel: 6797 2263
www.hotelsigulda.lv
Comfortable accommodation in the city centre in either a historic stone building or its new addition. €€

Talsi

Martinelli
Lielā 7
Tel: 6329 1340
www.martinelli.lv
Stylish, family-run design hotel with an excellent café and rooms decorated with antiques. €€

Saule Hotel
Saules 19
Tel: 6323 2232
www.saulehotel.lv
Located in what used to be the servants' quarters of a 19th-century manor, this hotel offers affordable rooms next to the lake. €

Tukums

Kukšu muiža
Tukuma novads
Jaunsatu pag., Kuksas
Tel: 6318 1545
www.kuksumuiza.lv/eng/eng
A short distance west of Tukums, this superbly restored manor house is a wonderful place to stay.

Sumptuous, ornate interiors and 13 very individual guest rooms. €€€€

Ventspils

Guest House Sārnate
Užava, Ventspils distr.
Tel: 6591 5519
www.sarnate.lv
On the Baltic coast, offering a variety of activities, including boating and cycle hire. A beautiful and quiet place. €€

Kupfernams
Kārļa 5
Tel: 6362 6999
kupfernams@inbox.lv
Pleasant guesthouse in a historic wooden building in the city centre with a restaurant-café. €€

Spicīte
Saules 145
Tel: 2950 8200
www.spicite.lv
Just outside the city centre, this family-run hotel offers affordable, renovated rooms and a café. €

CAMPING

Rīga

Rīga City Camping
Ķīpsalas 8
Tel: 6706 5000
www.bt1.lv/camping
Located on an island overlooking the Old Town.

Offers modern facilities as well as hire of equipment, including tents, bicycles, barbecues. Laundry service.

Cēsis

Apaļkalns
Raiskums (9km/5½ miles from Cēsis)
Tel: 2944 8188
Located on the shore of Lake Raiskums, it offers cottages, camping places for tents with picnic tables and barbecues, as well as sites for caravans.

Ludza

Dzerkaļi
Dzerkaļi (8km/5 miles from Ludza)
Tel: 2632 4735
Huge recreation complex on the shore of Lake Cirma provides small cottages, tent and caravan sites as well as a sauna, volleyball courts, fishing, boat and jet-ski hire and even paintball.

Guest House & Camping Meldri
Nirza, Ludza distr.
Tel: 2948 5444
Recreation centre by Lake Nirza. Cottages, tent sites, country sauna, picnic spots, a garden fireplace, sports grounds and boat hire. Traditional Latgale meals available.

Ventspils

Camping PieJuras
Vasarnīcu 56
Tel: 6362 7925
www.camping.ventspils.lv
Surrounded by pine forest, next door to the Open-Air Ethnographic Museum and 500 metres/yds to beach. Excellent facilities, cosy cabins, places for tents and caravans. Book ahead.

Usmas Camping
Usma distr.
Tel: 2633 4500
www.usma.lv
On the shores of Lake Usma. Camping with comfortable cabins. Hotel and spa next door. Boats, paddle boats, windsurfing boards and bicycles for hire.

LITHUANIA

ABOVE: hotel standards have risen in the past few years.

A great deal of time, effort and money has been spent to produce some swish establishments in which the visitor can rest his or her weary head. Most hotels are child-friendly, but not always pet-friendly. Rates in Vilnius, as opposed to the coastal regions, tend not to fluctuate seasonally. However, hotel prices can sometimes be lower in winter as hotels scramble to fill up their empty rooms. Breakfast is usually included in most hotels, although guests are under no obligation to eat the Soviet timewarp, squeaky omelette-style breakfasts still served in many of the cheaper places to stay.

It is always best, although not vital, to have a reservation before entering the country. Many of the newer hotels have online booking systems, making the experience hassle-free. Large hotels are hardly ever booked to capacity, but the cosier bed & breakfast or cheaper options fill up quickly in the summer. If you arrive without a reservation, there is a Vilnius Tourist Information Centre in the train station that can give you listings of accommodation in the city.

All hotels are graded by the Lithuanian Tourism Board, but the star system is based on the amount of amenities on offer, not by the level of service.

Most hotels do not have facilities for wheelchair-bound customers. It is best to ask pointed and numerous questions about the facilities if you are disabled. Those travelling with these sorts of concerns should check out newer hotels, as zoning laws tend to make them more wheelchair-friendly.

HOTELS

Vilnius

Amberton Hotel
L. Stuokos-Gucevičiaus 1
Tel: 8-5 210 7461
Fax: 8-5 210 7460

www.ambertonhotels.com
Occupying one of the best locations in the city opposite the cathedral, the Amberton is a relatively modern hotel featuring every possible comfort. The in-house Italian restaurant is also exceptionally good. €€€

Atrium
Pilies 10
Tel: 8-5 210 7777
Fax: 8-5 210 7770
www.atrium.lt
The rooms are more than ample and the leather sofas and cordless phones are noteworthy touches. Restaurant and sauna. €€€

Centro Kubas – Angel
Stiklių 3
Tel: 8-5 266 0860
Fax: 8-5 266 0863
www.hotel.centrokubas.lt
Small but charmingly decorated with antiques and all conveniences. One room is specifically designed for wheelchair-bound guests. €€€

Crowne Plaza Vilnius
M.K. Čiurlionio 84
Tel: 8-5 274 3400
Fax: 8-5 274 3420
www.cpvilnius.com
This renovated Intourist classic near Vingis Park is exceptionally soothing. Lovely touches are to be found throughout its 108 five-star rooms; 24-hour room service; 16th-floor bar with views. €€€

Domus Maria
Aušros Vartų 12
Tel: 8-5 264 4880
Fax: 8-5 264 4878
www.domusmaria.lt
Rooms in this renovated monastery are basic and a bit small, but the location alongside the Gates of Dawn and the windows looking out onto the city make this a sound option for inexpensive accommodation. Breakfast included. Parking. €€

Europa Royale Vilnius
Aušros Vartų 6
Tel: 8-5 266 0770
Fax: 8-5 261 2000
www.groupeuropa.com
The ground-zero locale and

the abundance of windows add distinctiveness to this mid-sized hotel. Some rooms have balconies with views of the Gates of Dawn, others have views onto the Old Town. Breakfast included. Restaurant and parking. €€€

Grotthuss
Ligoninės 7
Tel: 8-5 266 0322
Fax: 8-5 266 0223
www.grotthushotel.com
Absolutely charming, with attentive staff. Try to book a room overlooking the garden. Breakfast included. Restaurant, parking and conference facilities. €€€

Mabre Residence
Maironio 13
Tel: 8-5 212 2087
Fax: 8-5 212 2240
www.mabre.lt
Situated around a courtyard at the edge of the Old Town, this former Orthodox monastery has pleasant, insular surroundings. Breakfast is not included. Restaurant, sauna, parking. €€€

Novotel Vilnius
Gedimino 16
Tel: 8-5 266 6200
Fax: 8-5 266 6201
www.novotel.com
Clean and crisp, the Novotel has jazzed up the otherwise drab Gedimino hotel options. Works of art in the rooms add a delightful quirkiness. All the amenities – mini-bars, satellite TV, fitness and business centres – plus wheelchair access. €€€

LITHUANIA

Vilnius

Radisson Blu Astorija
Didžioji 35/2
Tel: 8-5 212 0110
Fax: 8-5 212 1762
www.radissonblu.com
Geared to an international business clientele, so expect all comforts, including in-room safes, modem points and mini-bars. Restaurant. €€€€

Radisson Blu Hotel Lietuva
Konstitucijos 20
Tel: 8-5 272 6272
Fax: 8-5 272 6270
www.radissonblu.com
Just across the pedestrian White Bridge (Baltasis tiltas), this beautiful 300-room hotel has a restaurant, 22nd-floor bar and casino. Executive-class rooms have balconies. €€€

Relais & Châteaux Stikliai
Gaono 7
Tel: 8-5 264 9595
Fax: 8-5 212 3870
www.stikliaihotel.lt
This lovely upscale hotel has been setting the standards for class in this town for decades. A truly exceptional experience. Staff wait on you hand and foot. Apartment rentals are also available. Restaurant, sauna and pool. €€€€

Shakespeare Boutique Hotel
Bernardinų 8/8
Tel: 8-5 266 5885
Fax: 8-5 266 5886
www.shakespeare.lt
The city's original boutique hotel, with each room devoted to a literary genius. All rooms have an touch of decadence. Both the in-house restaurant and bar are knockout. €€€€

Guesthouses

Bernadinų B&B House
Bernardinų 5
Tel: 8-5 261 5134
Fax: 8-5 260 8410
www.avevita.lt
A good option for the budget traveller, this recommended guesthouse that likes to think it's a B&B when it's not, is located in the Old Town, and rooms, though small, are clean and comfortable. Parking. €

Litinterp Guest House
Bernardinų 7–2
Tel: 8-5 212 3850
Fax: 8-5 212 3559
www.litinterp.lt
In the Old Town. Litinterp is known throughout Lithuania, offering the best range of accommodation with extremely reasonable pricing. Rooms with or without hosts are available also in Kaunas, Klaipėda, Nida and Palanga. €

Outside Vilnius

Le Méridien Vilnius
A-2 motorway 19km (12 miles) north of Vilnius
Tel: 8-5 273 9700
Fax: 8-5 265 9730
www.lemeridien.com
If you can afford to stay here you can afford the regular 20-minute taxi rides required to get in and out of the city. Featuring luxurious rooms overlooking lakes and forests; it even has its own 18-hole gold course. Amenities are plentiful. €€€

Trakai

Trakai
Apvalaus Stalo Klubas
Karaimų 53a
Tel: 8-6 6991 3769
Fax: 8-5 285 1760
www.apvalaus-stalo-klubas.com
The best address in town, the curiously named Round Table Club is both a chintzy hotel and two restaurants in one (international and pizza). €€€

Druskininkai

Druskininkai
Kudirkos 43
Tel: 8-313 525 66
Fax: 8-313 513 45
www.hotel-druskininkai.lt
A classy hotel in the town centre with all amenities imaginable, the Druskininkai now has its own modern pool and spa complex out the back. Breakfast included. €€€

Regina
Kosciuškos 3
Tel: 8-313 590 60
Fax: 8-313 590 61

www.regina.lt
The Regina is a very classy full-service hotel. Numerous weekend packages are available to entice reticent visitors. €€

Kaunas

Amberton Cozy
Kuzmos 8
Tel: 8-37 229 981
Fax: 8-37 220 355
www.ambertonhotels.com
Right off Vilniaus, this recommended, 28-room hotel offers clean and comfortable surroundings and a decent in-house international restaurant. €€

Apple Economy Hotel
Valančiaus 19
Tel: 8-37 321 404
Fax: 8-37 321 404
www.applehotel.lt
An absolute delight. Rooms are bright, non-smoking, and previous guests send along toys and trinkets which make up the lobby decor. Parking available. €

Best Western Santaka
J. Gruodžio 21
Tel: 8-37 302 702
Fax: 8-37 302 700
www.hotelsinlithuania.eu
Lithuania's first Best Western hotel is set in an old red-brick warehouse in a side street. The 40 rooms are refurbished and comfortable. €€€

Kaunas
Laisvės 79
Tel: 8-37 750 850
Fax: 8-37 750 851
www.kaunashotel.lt
This is one of the most luxurious hotels in the city centre. The less modern rooms overlook the bustle of Laisvės, but the more modern rooms are further into the building. €€€

Litinterp
Gedimino 28–7
Tel: 8-37 228 718
Fax: 8-37 425 120
www.litinterp.lt
Offers excellent value bed & breakfasts in the city centre. Also rents cars. €

Park Inn Kaunas
Donelaičio 27
Tel: 8-37 306 100
Fax: 8-37 306 221

www.parkinn.com
Essentially a budget version of the Radisson brand, the Kaunas Park Inn can be found in a central location and offering a good standard of rooms and amenities. €€

Perkūno Namai
Perkūno 61
Tel: 8-37 320 230
Fax: 8-37 323 678
www.perkuno-namai.lt
What this hotel lacks in centrality it makes up for in gorgeous furnishings and exquisite attention to detail. Rooms with a balcony in this hilltop hotel situated near a park are spectacular. €€€

Klaipėda and the coast

Amberton Klaipėda
Naujoji Sodo 1
Tel: 8-46 404 372
Fax: 8-46 404 373
www.ambertonhotel.lt
This vast monster in three buildings is more of a village than a hotel. Expect comfort and a wealth of extras, including bars, restaurants, clubs and gym. €€

Europa Royale Klaipėda
Žvejų 21/1
Tel: 8-46 404 444
Fax: 8-46 404 445
www.groupeuropa.com
Excellent Old Town location, refreshingly friendly and helpful staff, amenities by the bucketload and an in-house bar popular with the local expat community. One of the best if you can afford the price tag. €€€

Litinterp
Puodžių 17
Tel: 8-46 410 644
Fax: 8-46 420 176
www.litinterp.lt
Great budget accommodation inside its own building as well as a number of hosted options around the city and on the coast. €

Lūgnė
Galinio Pylimo 16
Tel/Fax: 8-46 411 884
www.lugne.lt
Right outside the Old Town, this 47-room hotel provides a choice of rooms for most

TRANSPORT
ACCOMMODATION
EATING OUT
ACTIVITIES
A – Z
LANGUAGE

CAMPING

Nature-lovers that they are, the population of Lithuania likes nothing better during the summer than to head for the countryside and pitch a tent. This is always an option, although if it's facilities you're after, try one of the following. Note that the country's official campsites operate from around May until September.

Vilnius
Vilnius City Camping
Parodų 7
Tel: 8-5 6803 2452
www.camping.lt
Not far from the centre; amenities include spaces for tents and camper vans. Extras include electricity, washing facilities and even internet.

Klaipėda
Pajūrio Kempingas

Šlaito 3 (Giriuliai)
Tel: 8-46 6777 3227
www.klaipedainfo.lt
Giruliai is a tiny village 15 minutes north of the centre on the main railway route. Facilities at this municipality-owned campsite include spaces for tents and camper vans, plus there are several basic chalets. The location very close to the sea is superb.

Nida
Nidos Kempingas
Taikos 45a
Tel: 8-469 52 045
www.kempingas.lt
Places to pitch tents and camper vans, plus basic wooden chalets dating from Soviet times, all in a forest clearing within easy walking distance of the lagoon.

Fax: 8-460 41 415
www.palangahotel.lt
A better location and better view onto the pine-tree forests is hard to find. The rooms are extremely stylish.
€€€

Pušų Paunksnėje
Darius ir Girėno 25
Tel: 8-460 49 080
Fax: 8-460 49 081
www.pusupaunksneje.lt
Owned by the former world-class basketball player Arvydas Sabonis, this chalet-style hotel is pure luxury. Fireplaces and wooden decor ensure a romantic feel in every room.
€€€€

Šachmatinė
Basanavičiaus 45
Tel: 8-460 51 655
Fax: 8-460 51 655
www.sachmatine.lt
Flashy 11-room hotel set behind the dunes, next to the beach, at the end of the town's most lively street.
€€

Villa Ramybė
Vytauto 54
Tel: 8-460 54 124
www.vilaramybe.lt
Few people can run an adorable 12-room hotel so perfectly. Reservations are an absolute must. **€**

tastes and budgets, although the cheaper rooms offer the best value. Lovely staff. Parking. **€**

Park Inn Klaipėda
Minijos 119
Tel: 8-46 380 803
Fax: 8-46 482 030
www.parkinn.com
Basic, business-class accommodation in a tall building way out of the centre. It's a great hotel, but think twice if you want easy access to the sights. **€€**

Radisson Blu Hotel Klaipėda
Šaulių 28
Tel: 8-46 490 800
Fax: 8-46 490 815
www.radissonblu.com
Leave it to the Radisson people to class up a drab hotel scene. The lovely nautical-themed hotel, in a central location, has beautiful rooms. Expect all the pleasant trappings of a large hotel. **€€€**

Neringa

Ažuolynas
Rézos 54 (Juodkrantė)
Tel: 8-469 533 10
Fax: 8-469 533 16
www.hotelazuolynas.lt
The large water slide is the first clue that this place is geared toward the happy-go-lucky. The 52 rooms, doubles or apartment, are comfy and spacious. **€€**

Inkaro Kaimas
Naglių 26-1 (Nida)

Tel: 8-469 52 123
www.inkarokaimas.lt
Three apartments make up this lodging. Its location right on the main street and in spitting distance of the water make it a fabulous option for those not fussed by less than noble surroundings. **€€**

Jūratė
Pamario 3 (Nida)
Tel: 8-469 523 00
www.hotel-jurate.lt
A grand-looking German-style hotel close to the bus station and the main places to eat and drink. The rooms and apartments are nothing to write home about but they do at least do the job.
€€–€€€

Nerija
Pamario 13 (Nida)
Tel: 8-469 527 77
www.nerijahotels.lt
Everything from singles to apartments, plus a basketball court and a reasonable restaurant. A fairly safe bet for the price. **€€**

Nidos Smiltė
Skruzdynės 2 (Nida)
Tel: 8-469 52 221
www.smilte.lt
Three villas in one location close to the centre and the lagoon. Choose from basic rooms through to apartments for a little more money. One villa houses a collection of Expressionist paintings by former minor celebrity guests. **€€**

Santauta
Kalno 36 (Juodkrantė)
Tel: 8-469 3 346
By far the cheapest option in town, this hotel has both shared dorm rooms and some private rooms. **€**

Villa Banga
Pamario 2 (Nida)
Tel: 8-469 51 139
Fax: 8-469 52 762
smilte@is.lt
A seven-room house that looks like something out of a fairy tale. Privacy is in lieu of amenities. **€€**

Vila Simona
Pamario 21a (Nida)
Tel: 8-469 527 20
www.vilasimona.ot.lt
In a good central location, Vila Simona is a fairly new guesthouse designed to look like a traditional fisherman's cottage. Fridges in all the rooms help keep the cost down.
€€–€€€

Palanga

Mama Rosa Villa
Jūratés 28a
Tel: 8-460 48 581
Fax: 8-460 48 189
www.mamarosa.lt
Palanga's prime villa has eight rooms in the centre of town. It's popular, so book ahead. Beware of the temperamental chef on a Sunday morning. **€€€**

Palanga
Birutés 60
Tel: 8-460 41 414

Siauliai

Šaulys
Vasario 16-osios 40
Tel: 8-41 520 812
Fax: 8-41 520 911
www.saulys.lt
This mid-sized hotel in the city centre is among the best in town. Breakfast included. **€€**

Turnė
Rūdės 9
Tel: 8-41 500 150
Fax: 8-41 429 238
www.turne.lt
A bit on the drab side, but the attentive staff makes up for any decor faux pas. Breakfast included. **€**

PRICE CATEGORIES

Ranges given are for a hotel double room, per night:
€ under €40 (under 28Ls)
€€ €40–80 (28–56Ls)
€€€ €80–120 (56–84Ls)
€€€€ over €120 (56–84Ls)

TRANSPORT

E ATING OUT

ACCOMMODATION

RECOMMENDED RESTAURANTS, CAFÉS & BARS

One new establishment opens every month in each of the capital cities and you can feast on French haute cuisine, sample Japanese sushi or Armenian shashlik and wolf down vegetarian dishes. In the main cities, some of the bars and clubs here are so funky that they would stand out in Paris, London or New York. Most waiting staff speak English – if they don't speak English, the menu will certainly be in either English, German, French or Russian. The best hotels and restaurants have imported top international chefs, serving first-class international food.

Most restaurants accept Visa and MasterCard unless otherwise noted. As there is not enough room here to give a full list of restaurants, we have tried to recommend the most notable establishments, with the stress on local cuisine.

Tipping: Service is not included in most bills. Round up the sum of the bill and add a little if service was appreciated. No more than 5 percent is expected.

For an informed, general read about what to eat, see pages 77–82.

EATING OUT

RESTAURANT LISTINGS

ESTONIA

ACTIVITIES

Despite Estonia's small size, its restaurant scene is marked by sophistication and variety. Diners can find anything from medieval fare to cutting-edge fusion. Tallinn's Old Town in particular is awash with theme restaurants, and it is not uncommon to see waiters in elaborate costumes roaming the streets, handing out coupons and flyers.

One thing that is surprisingly hard to find in the city, however, is a restaurant that serves Estonian food. Even at the casual lunch cafés and pubs favoured by locals, the choices are typically *seljanka* (a thick, Russian soup) or *schnitzel*, which are not originally Estonian. The reason for this conspicuous absence of traditional fare is that Estonian cuisine is

for the most part a simple – some would say bland – affair with country roots. Favourites are *sült* (jellied meat), *mulgikapsas* (fatty sauerkraut), *rollmops* (soused herrings) and *kama* (a mixture of ground cereals taken as dessert). Estonians think of this cuisine as something they make at home, but wouldn't look for when they go out, hence its scarcity in the restaurant world. That said, visitors who know where to look can find one or two decent places to sample the local food. Not surprisingly, however, these are mainly aimed at tourists.

Out in the country it is different, and this is the place to head for if you really want to find more of the local flavour, especially locally smoked fish and meat, which you should try.

RESTAURANTS

Tallinn

Chakra
Bremeni käik 1
Tel: 6412 615
info@chakra.ee
www.chakra.ee
Sun–Thur noon–midnight, Fri–Sat noon–1am
Owners of this serene little Indian restaurant have put together a crew of Estonia's best South Asian cooks to create a first-rate dining experience. When ordering, tell them how spicy or mild you prefer your meal. **€€**

Controvento
Vene 12
Tel: 6440 470
info@controvento.ee
www.controvento.ee
Daily noon–11.45pm
Set in a cosy medieval

building in the Katariina passageway, this Italian restaurant is a long-time favourite of Tallinn's expatriate elite. Consistently high-quality cuisine and professional service. Reservations essential.
€€€

Gloria
Müürivahe 2
Tel: 6406 800
Fax: 6406 810
gloria@gloria.ee
www.gloria.ee
Open daily noon–midnight
This luxuriously decadent restaurant has hosted a number of statesmen, dignitaries and even Pope

PRICE CATEGORIES

For a three-course meal per person without drinks:
€ = under €15
€€ = €15–25
€€€ = €25–35
€€€€ = over €35

A – Z

LANGUAGE

John Paul II. An interesting mix of French, Italian, Baltic and Russian creations makes up the menu. €€€€

Kaerajaan
Raekoja plats 17
Tel: 6155 400
Fax: 6155 402
kaerajaan@kaerajaan.ee
www.kaerajaan.ee
Sun–Thur 11am–11pm, Fri & Sat 11am–midnight
A modern take on traditional Estonian cuisine, not to mention interior design, is the speciality at Kaerajaan, an airy restaurant overlooking Town Hall Square. Its ground-floor "lounge" has a more casual feel. €€€

Kohvik Moon
Võrgu 3
Tel: 6314 575
Fax: 6314 575
kohvik@kohvikmoon.ee
www.kohvikmoon.ee
Tue–Sat noon–11pm
Run by some of Tallinn's top chefs, this high-quality restaurant is worth seeking out despite its out-of-the-way location. The menu is general European with some Russian leanings. €€

Olde Hansa
Vana turg 1
Tel: 6279 020
Fax: 6279 021
reserve@oldehansa.ee
www.oldehansa.ee
Daily 10am–midnight
A visit to Tallinn wouldn't be complete without experiencing this medieval-style restaurant. Far more intricate and authentic than a typical theme restaurant, it offers an intriguing menu, costumed waitresses, candlelight and minstrels. Reserve on weekends. €€€€

Ribe
Vene 7
Tel: 6313 084
info@ribe.ee
www.ribe.ee
Daily noon–11pm
Founded by three veteran waiters, this Old Town restaurant has become a favourite for its elegant, modern interior, cutting-edge, European menu and superior food. Fillets comprise most of the mains. €€

Troika
Raekoja plats 15
Tel: 6276 245
restoran@troika.ee
www.troika.ee
Daily 10am–11pm
A lavishly decorated Russian restaurant resembling something out of a tsarist-era fairy tale. The menu ranges from blinis to Kuban mutton and even includes bear Stroganoff. Reserve in advance. €€€

Vanaema Juures
Rataskaevu 10/12
Tel: 6269 080
vanaema.juures@mail.ee
www.vonkrahl.ee/en/toit/vanaemajuures
Mon–Sat noon–10pm, Sun noon–6pm
Just as you might expect from a restaurant called Grandmother's Place, this cosy cellar venue is bursting with antiques, old photographs and friendly attitudes. An excellent place to try Estonian national dishes. €€

Zebra Cafe
Narva mnt. 7
Tel: 6109 230
info@zebracafe.ee
www.zebracafe.ee
Daily 11am–midnight
Set in a futuristic-looking structure, this casual-chic restaurant sits at the trendier edge of Tallinn's dining spectrum. Order salads and fillets from the menu, or just pick out sushi, pastries and desserts from the counter. €€

Islands

Alexander
Pädaste Manor
Muhu Island
Tel: 4548 800
Fax: 4548 811
info@padaste.ee
www.padaste.ee
Daily 1–2.30pm & 7–9pm
A highly respected gourmet restaurant built into a restored manor house on the road to Kuressaare. Guests can sit inside by the fireplace or, in summer, take lunch on the Sea House Terrace. Reservations are required. €€€€

Pärnu

Ammende Villa
Mere pst. 7
Tel: 4473 888
Fax: 4473 887
sale@ammende.ee
www.ammende.ee
Tue–Sat noon–11pm, Sun–Mon noon–10pm
Pärnu's finest hotel is also home to its most upscale restaurant. Fine Estonian and European cuisine is served in the Art Nouveau mansion's elegant, old-fashioned dining rooms. €€€

Si-Si
Supeluse 21
Tel: 4475 612
info@si-si.ee
www.si-si.ee
Daily noon–2am
This combination restaurant and lounge is a relaxing

choice for diners in search of a well-prepared Italian meal. €€

Steffani Pizzarestoran
Nikolai 24
Tel: 4431 170
info@steffani.ee
www.steffani.ee
Sun–Thur 11am–midnight, Fri & Sat 11am–2am
A long-time favourite, Steffani is wildly popular not just for its pizza and pasta, but for its cosy, fun-loving ambience. In summer it operates a second location at the beach. €€

Tartu

Eduard Vilde Lokaal
Vallikraavi 4
Tel: 7343 400
vilde@vilde.ee
www.vilde.ee
Mon–Thur noon–midnight, Fri & Sat noon–2am, Sun noon–11pm
Built in a historic printing house, Vilde has become a Tartu landmark, and is worth seeing for its elaborate decor alone. The art-filled café serves excellent cakes. €€

Gruusia Saatkond
Rüütli 8
Tel: 7441 386
gruusiasaatkond@gruusiasaatkond.ee
www.gruusiasaatkond.ee
Mon–Sat noon–midnight, Sun noon–10pm
The comfortable Georgian Embassy, right next to Tartu's Town Hall Square, is an excellent place to get acquainted with Georgian cuisine. Try *shashlyk* (kebab) and *hatchapuri* (cheese-filled bread). €€

Kung Fu
Ülikooli 5
Tel: 7400 787
www.kungfu24.ee
Sun–Thur noon–11pm, Fri noon–midnight
Supporting its claim to be "100 percent Chinese", Kung Fu delivers a level of quality and authenticity that's rare among its rivals in the Baltics. €–€€

La Dolce Vita
Kompanii 10
Tel: 7407 545
ladolcevita@ladolcevita.ee
www.ladolcevita.ee
Mon–Thur 11.30am–10pm, Fri &

BELOW: Olde Hansa restaurant in Tallinn.

DRINKING NOTES

Although vodka (viin) has a strong presence in Estonian drinking culture, its proliferation is actually due to last century's Russian influence. Without question, Estonia's national drink is beer (õlu), brewed at home by farmers since time immemorial. The most popular brands are Saku and A. Le Coq, which are served on tap throughout the country.

In the past few years, cider (siider) has become popular. For urbanites,

wine (vein) has also held a growing sway, giving rise to several swanky wine bars in the capital. Mostly, however, drinking establishments come in three varieties: old-fashioned cellar bars or trahters (taverns), English- or Irish-style pubs and, more recently, trendy, cosmopolitan lounges.

During the all-too-brief summer season Estonians will drink at any establishment, just so long as it has an outdoor table.

Sat 11.30am–midnight, Sun noon–10pm
Run by Italians, this cosy Old Town cellar restaurant serves up a huge variety of tasty pizzas and pastas. A local favourite. €€

Ülikooli Kohvik
Ülikooli 20
Tel: 7375 405
Fax: 7375 401
kohvik@kohvik.ut.ee
www.kohvik.ut.ee
Mon–Thur noon–11pm, Fri & Sat noon–1am, Sun noon–8pm
The University Café's sprawling, old-fashioned rooms lend it an air of history and style that put it a cut above most Tartu venues. An equally worthy ground-floor buffet/café opens early for breakfast. €€

FAST FOOD

International burger barons McDonald's (Viru 24) and the Finnish chain Hesburger (Viru 27) have both staked out territory in and around Tallinn.

For pizza on the run, try the thin-crust Peetri Pizza (Mere pst. 6) or the thick, deep-dish variety at Pizza Americana (Müürivahe 2).

For a more authentic Estonian option, order filled pancakes, which are available in both meat and dessert varieties at most cafés and pubs.

CAFÉS

Estonian urban café culture is very much alive with a new breed of entrepreneurs competing to supply caffeine – and ambience – to discerning city dwellers.

Tallinn

Kehrwieder
Saiakang 1
www.kohvik.ee
Sun–Thur 8am–midnight, Fri & Sat 8am–1am
Three artfully decorated, cave-like rooms make up this popular café on Town Hall Square. Its main features are excellent gourmet coffee, eclectic furniture and a hip, young clientele.

NOP
Köleri 1
Tel: 6032 270
info@nop.ee
www.nop.ee
Daily 8am–8pm
This earthy little café in the Kadriorg district is worth seeking out for its selection of healthy soups, salads and sandwiches, not to mention tasty pastries.

Reval Café
Müürivahe 14
Tel: 6418 100
reval@revalcafe.ee
www.revalcafe.ee
Daily noon–midnight
Comfy sofas, soft jazz and candlelight make the

flagship of this café chain a fine place for a cappuccino or a cognac. Full meals are served at the back.

Spirit
Mere pst. 6e
Tel: 6616 151
info@kohvikspirit.ee
www.kohvikspirit.ee
Mon–Thur noon–11pm, Fri & Sat noon–1am, Sun 1–10pm
A smart, upscale venue that's popular with Tallinn's chic set. The menu includes soups, pastas, fillets and sushi.

Pärnu

Supelsaksad
Nikolai 32
Tel: 4422 448
kohvik@supelsaksad.ee
www.supelsaksad.ee
Sun–Thur 8am–9pm, Fri & Sat 8am–11pm
This apartment-like café, filled with a hotchpotch of old furniture, is a cosy spot for a light meal or an evening glass of wine.

Teatrikohvik
Keskväljak 1
Tel: 4420 664
kohvik@endla.ee
www.endla.ee
Mon–Thur 8.30am–10pm, Fri 8.30am–midnight, Sat 11am–midnight, Sun 11am–10pm
A favourite of the local cultural elite, the upstairs section of the Endla Theatre's modern café is also known for its summer terrace.

Tartu

Crepp
Rüütli 16
Tel: 5528 710
crepp@crepp.ee
www.crepp.ee
Daily noon–11pm
Quiches, galettes, soups and, of course, crêpes are the speciality at this stylish, little café that brings a touch of old Paris to the heart of Tartu.

Werner
Ülikooli 11
Tel: 7426 377
cafe@werner.ee
www.werner.ee
Mon–Thur 7.30am–11pm, Fri & Sat 8am–1pm, Sun 9am–9pm

Its interior may be ultra-modern, but this historic bakery-café has been providing caffeine and cheap meals to students since the early 20th century. Gourmet restaurant upstairs.

BARS

Tallinn

Clayhills Gastropub
Pikk 13
Tel: 6419 312
clayhills@clayhills.ee
www.clayhills.ee
Sun–Thur 10am–midnight, Fri & Sat 10am–2am
Estonia's first gastropub is a big step up in sophistication from the average Old Town bar, offering an inventive menu and tasteful surroundings.

Hell Hunt
Pikk 39
Tel: 6818 333
hellhunt@hellhunt.ee
www.hellhunt.ee
Daily noon–2am
Expats and locals gather for drinks in a comfortable, relaxed milieu. The tasty Hell Hunt beer served here is brewed exclusively for this pub.

Karja Kelder
Väike-Karja 1
Tel: 6441 008
karjakelder@hot.ee
www.karjakelder.ee
Sun & Mon 11am–midnight, Tue–Thur 11am–1am, Fri & Sat 11am–3am
This lively cellar pub is one of the few truly Estonian places to drink in Tallinn's Old Town. Karja Kelder gets crowded in the evenings, so arrive early and be prepared to pay for the cloakroom.

Molly Malone's
Müündi 2
Tel: 6313 016

PRICE CATEGORIES

For a three-course meal per person without drinks:
€ = under €15
€€ = €15–25
€€€ = €25–35
€€€€ = over €35

www.mollymalones.ee
Sun–Thur 9am–2am, Fri & Sat
9am–4am
Situated in a prime location
overlooking Town Hall
Square, this spacious Irish
pub is a great favourite
with expats and tourists.
Football matches
are shown on multiple
screens here.

Pärnu

Pärnu Kuursaal
Mere pst. 22
Tel: 4420 367
Fax: 4420 366
info@kuur.ee
www.kuur.ee
Sun–Thur noon–2am, Fri & Sat
noon–4am (shorter hours in winter)

WEIGHT WATCHER

The Baltics use the metric
system and vodka is
often ordered in grams –
50g equates to a single
measure, 100g is a
double.

Dubbed "Estonia's biggest
tavern", this is a vast beer
hall built inside Pärnu's
century-old resort hall
adjacent to the beach.
In summer, live bands
keep it buzzing late into
the night.
Postipoiss
Vee 12
Tel: 4464 864
Fax: 4464 861
postipoiss@ag.ee

www.trahterpostipoiss.ee
Sun–Thur noon–11pm, Fri & Sat
noon–2am
What was an old post
station is now a casual
Russian (actually "Slavic")
theme restaurant. In the
evenings, it turns into a
hotspot for drinking and
dancing. Give its Emperor
beer a try.

Tartu

Maailm
Rüütli 12
Tel: 7429 099
restoran@klubimaailm.ee
www.klubimaailm.ee
Daily 11.30am–1.30am (kitchen
closes 11pm)
This funky pub-restaurant is

a wonderful example of
Tartu's brand of eccentricity.
The menu ranges from
African salad to
cheeseburgers, and the
artsy interior borders
on the odd.
Ristiisa
Küüni 7
Tel: 7303 970
Fax: 7303 974
ristiisapubi@hot.ee
www.ristiisapubi.ee
Sun & Mon 11am–midnight, Tue–
Thur 11am–1am, Fri & Sat 11am–
3am
A truly unexpected find in
downtown Tartu, the popular
Godfather Pub is decorated
in an Al Capone theme and
filled with mobster
memorabilia.

LATVIA

Being a nation of farmers
for so many years, Latvia's
national foods are, to put it
mildly, rustic in nature.
Pīrāgi are small pastry buns
traditionally, although not
exclusively, filled with
chopped ham and onions. A
bowl of boiled grey peas
fried with bacon and onions
is also a favourite treat,
often topped with *kefīrs*, a
dairy drink similar to
yoghurt.

Latvians also pride
themselves on a wide
variety of sausages, which,
when compared to German
bratwurst or *knockwurst*,
sadly, just don't cut the
mustard. However, the thin
mednieku desiņas, or
hunters' sausages, are
definitely worth a try.

Although difficult to find
in Rīga, *grūdenis* is a thick
country stew that uses half
a pig's head as a base.
The pork chop or
karbonāde is the most
prevalent national dish,
usually complemented by
potatoes, *sauerkraut* and a
slice of delicious rye or
black bread baked only with
natural ingredients. Due to
so many years of culinary
isolation, dill and caraway
seeds are often the only
seasonings used by chefs
at Latvian restaurants.

Rīga is a food haven with
ethnic cuisines from Tex-
Mex to Korean. There are
excellent (and expensive)
upmarket restaurants in
dozens of luxurious hotels
throughout the city. Hotel
Bergs and Hotel Neiburgs
are among the best.

Good Latvian home
cooking is served in a
number of Lido
establishments, notably at
Alus Sēta, Dzirnavas, Lido
Atpūtas Centrs or
Vērmanītis *(further details
are given below)*. These
places have made country
cooking their trademark,
but do not accept credit
cards.

RESTAURANTS

Rīga

Alus Sēta
Tirgoņu 6
Tel: 6722 2431
Daily 11am–11pm
Latvian home cooking in a
self-service cafeteria-style
establishment. Help yourself
to the grey peas and ribs that
are grilled in front of you or
choose its speciality – baked
pork knuckle. **€**
Aragats
Miera 15

Tel: 6737 3445
Tue–Sun 1pm–11pm
Owned and operated by an
Armenian family from
Yerevan, this is the place to
go for delicious food and
drink from the Caucasus
Mountains served by
friendly staff. **€€**
Bergs
Elizabetes 83/85
Tel: 6777 0957
www.hotelbergs.lv
Noon–11pm, closed Sun
Without doubt the best
restaurant in Rīga. A
unique interior and plenty
of open space mask its
location in the hotel of the
same name, listed in the
top 100 hotels of the world
by *Condé Nast Traveller*.
€€€
Charlestons
Blaumaņa 38/40
Tel: 6777 0572
www.charlestons.lv
Daily noon–midnight
Charlestons is a classy and
trendy restaurant with a
beautiful outside terrace.
It's popular, especially in
the summer, so
reservations are
recommended. **€€**
Fabrikas restorāns
Balasta dambis 70
Tel: 6787 3804
www.melniemuki.lv
Daily 11am–midnight
Trendy restaurant on

Ķīpsala island in restored
factory building with views
of the Old Town. **€€€**
Lido Atpūtas Centrs
Krasta 76
Tel: 6750 4420
Daily 11am–midnight
This vast food court on
three levels serves only
Latvian fare. The Lido
Leisure Centre, slightly out
of town, is packed to the
rafters on weekends with
Latvian families out for a
cheap and hearty meal.
Beer is brewed on the
premises. **€**
Melnie mūki
Jāņa sēta 1
Tel: 6721 5006
Daily noon–midnight
The Black Monks, which is
situated in the heart of the
Old Town, has quickly
become one of Rīga's most
popular modestly priced
restaurants, which means
that reservations for dinner
are essential. **€€**
Neiburgs
Jauniela 25/27
Tel: 6711 5544
www.neiburgshotel.com
Daily noon–11pm

PRICE CATEGORIES

For a three-course meal per
person without drinks:
€ = under €7 (5Ls)
€€ = €7–14 (5–10Ls)
€€€ = over €14 (10Ls)

FAST FOOD

McDonald's followed swiftly after independence, opening in the heart of Rīga. Scandinavia's most beloved burger joint **Hesburger** also opened its doors in Old Rīga and at the train station.

Turkish kebabs have taken the city by storm, and the most authentic can be had at Food Box (Antonijas 6a; Mon–Fri 11.30am–8pm, Sat 1–6pm). Russian-style meat dumplings can be had at **Pelmeņi XL** (Kaļķu 7; daily 9am–4am). For cheap pancakes of all sorts look no further than **Šefpavārs Vilhelms** (Šķūņu 6; daily 9am–10pm). For an inexpensive buffet of delicious food try **Olé** (Audēju 1; Mon–Fri 11.30am–5pm).

Pizzerias can be found all over town, most with their own delivery services. For American-style pizza try **Pizza Lulū** (Blaumaņa 5a; tel: 8000 5858; www.lulu.lv; 24hrs).

Čili Pica (Brīvības 26; tel: 8000 3355; Sun–Wed 8am–3am, Thur–Sat 8am–6am) and **Vairāk saules** (Dzirnavu 60; tel: 6728 2878; daily 9am–11pm) serve dozens of delicious thin-crust pizzas.

The ground floor of one of Rīga's best design hotels is also home to a stylish restaurant that serves anything from breakfast food and gourmet burgers to duck breasts and seafood. €€
Vincents
Elizabetes 19
Tel: 6733 2634
Mon–Sat 6pm–11pm
This culinary institution, made popular by the renowned local chef Martins Ritins, is a firm favourite with the rich and famous, among them Elton John and Prince Charles. €€€

Cēsis

Café Popular
Vienības laukums 1
Tel: 6412 0122
Daily 11am–10pm
This cosy cellar restaurant specialising in pizzas has long been a favourite with locals and tourists. In the summer an outdoor terrace is also at your disposal. €
Sarunas
Rīgas 4
Tel: 6410 7173
www.bars-sarunas.lv
Sun–Thur 10am–11pm, Fri & Sat 10am–4am
Stylish bar with a variety of dishes, including a full breakfast. €

Daugavpils

Gubernators
Lāčplēša 10
Tel: 6542 2455
Sun–Thur 11am–midnight, Fri & Sat 11am–1am
Part beer hall, part restaurant, Gubernators offers a good selection of brews, good atmosphere and sports via satellite TV. €

Ikšķile

Meidrops
Rīgas 18
Tel: 6503 0466
www.meidrops.lv
Daily noon–11pm
Sandwiched between the highway and the River Daugava, this huge log cabin offers great food and good service, not to mention a beach volleyball court, sauna and great views. €€

Jelgava

Tami-Tami
Lielā 19a
Tel: 6302 2259
Sun–Tue 12am–midnight, Wed–Sat 11am–5am
Jelgava's most popular pizzeria, decorated with black-and-white photographs and funky modern paintings, is also a cocktail bar and music club with a wide selection of drinks. €–€€

Jūrmala

Café 53
Jomas 53, Majori
Tel: 6781 1771
www.cafe53.lv
Daily 10am–10pm
This café/bar has been around for ages and has remained popular due to its inexpensive international food, excellent location and good beer and cider selection. €
Orients Jūra
Dzintaru prosp. 2, Dzintari
Tel: 6776 1424
www.restoran-orient.lv
Daily noon–midnight
A huge seafood restaurant on two floors that has taken its kitschy nautical theme seriously, with plenty of life preservers, seashells and fishing nets hanging from the walls and ceiling. €€
Slāvu restorāns
Jomas 57, Majori
Tel: 6776 1401
Daily noon–11pm
Sample Slavic cuisine here as diverse as meat dumplings, grilled sturgeon and bortsch. Don't leave without trying one of its vodkas flavoured with garlic or horseradish. €€
Sue's Asia
Jomas 74, Majori
Tel: 6775 5900
Daily noon–11pm
One of the country's few Indian restaurants also serves delicious Thai food on Jūrmala's most popular pedestrian street. €€–€€€

Kuldīga

Stenders
Liepājas 3
Tel: 6332 2703
Sun–Thur 11am–11pm, Fri & Sat 11am–4am
Take the stairs to the second floor of this wooden building to find the city's best bar/café. It's also a favourite evening hangout, attracting crowds of locals at the weekends. €–€€

Lielvārde

Kante
Laimdotas 1 (A6)

BELOW: Vincents restaurants, Rīga.

TRANSPORT

ACCOMMODATION

EATING OUT

ACTIVITIES

A – Z

LANGUAGE

Tel: 6507 1829
Daily 11am–midnight
Friendly service, inexpensive
Latvian food and local
Lāčplēša beer on draught
make this a popular stop on
the way to Daugavpils. €

Liepāja

Latvia's 1st Rock Café
Stendera 18/20
Tel: 6348 1555
www.pablo.lv
Sun–Thur 9am–midnight, Fri & Sat
9am–6am
Covering three floors and a
cellar, this huge bar, club
and restaurant is one of the
largest entertainment
complexes in Latvia. It also
boasts live music nearly
every night. €-€€
Pastnieka māja
Brīvzemnieka 53
Tel: 6340 7521
www.pastniekamaja.lv
Daily 11am–11pm
This historic building is now
the setting for the
Postman's House, one of
the city's best restaurants.
It serves its menu inside an
envelope. €€€€

Ragana

Raganas Ķēķis
Ragana A3, Rīga–Valmiera highway
Tel: 6797 22 66
www.raganaskekis.lv
Sun–Thur 9am–11pm, Fri & Sat
9am–midnight
Undoubtedly the best place
to eat in the area, this
charming roadside tavern
offers typical Latvian dishes
like pork chops and
potatoes at cheap prices. €

Rēzekne

Mols
Latgales 22/24
Tel: 6462 5353
Daily 10am–10pm
Part art gallery, part café,
Mols offers unique Latgalian
cuisine and has an
interesting interior decorated
with ceramics and paintings
that are all for sale. €

Rubene

Mazais Ansis
A3 Rubene, Rīga–Valmiera highway

DRINKING NOTES

Like its neighbours, Latvia
has delicious beers (alus),
most notably Užavas,
Tērvetes and Bauskas.
Local vodka is also good.
However, the most
distinctive Latvian drink is
Riga Black Balsam,
(Melnais balzams), a bitter
liqueur made of dozens of
herbs whose recipe hasn't
changed since it was first
concocted by a
pharmacist in the late
18th century.

Tel: 6423 4066
www.mazais-ansis.lv
Only 6km (4 miles)
southwest of Valmiera, this
beautiful log cabin-style
building offers excellent
food and atmosphere as
well as having a playground,
outdoor barbecue, boat
hire on the lake and
accommodation above
the bar. €

Sigulda

Aparjods
Ventas 1a
Tel: 6797 4414
www.aparjods.lv
Daily noon–midnight
Housed in a rustic building
with a wood-shingled
roof, this charming
restaurant is decorated
with antiques and is the
best place to eat in
Sigulda. €€

Kropotkins
Pils 6
Tel: 6797 2263
www.hotelsigulda.lv
Tue–Sun noon–11pm
Named after the family that
once ruled this ancient
town, this upmarket
restaurant serves
international cuisine in an
ivy-draped fieldstone
building. €€

Ventspils

Bugiņš
Lielā 1/3
Tel: 6368 0151
Daily 11am–11pm
This Latvian pub and
restaurant has a traditional
interior of wood and linen,
and offers plenty of local
cuisine and beer for
reasonable prices. €
Melnais sivēns
Jāņa 17
Tel: 6362 2396
www.pilskrogs.lv
Daily 11am–11pm
Located in the restored
Livonian Order castle, this
medieval-style restaurant
specialises in its namesake
– roast suckling pig. €€

CAFÉS

Rīga

Boulangerie Bonjour
Jēkaba 20/22
Tel: 6732 5707
Mon–Fri 7am–8pm, Sat & Sun
10am–6pm
A French chef bakes
delicious pastries,
croissants and baguettes
here every day. Soups,
quiche and other light
French items are also on
offer. €
Emīls Gustavs Chocolate
Marijas 13 (Berga Bazārs)
Tel: 6728 7510
Mon–Sat 9am–9pm, Sun 11am–
8pm
This chain of chocolatiers
serves delicious home-
made sweets, cakes and
coffee. €
Harry Morgan
Dzirnavu 33
Tel: 6733 1042
www.harrymorgan.lv

Mon–Fri 9am–11pm, Sat & Sun
10am–11pm
This London chain of New
York-style delis offers great
breakfasts served all day, as
well as falafel, sandwiches,
matzah ball soup and
chopped liver. €-€€
Lidojošā varde
Elizabetes 31a
Tel: 6732 1184
Mon–Fri 10am–midnight, Sat &
Sun 11am–midnight
A staple of the Rīga dining
scene for several years, the
Flying Frog is often
frequented by expatriates
from surrounding
embassies. €€
Osīriss
Barona 31
Tel: 6724 3002
Mon–Fri 8am–midnight, Sat & Sun
10am–midnight
Owned by the Rīga Opera
director, this café has
managed to stay both
popular and trendy for over
10 years. Enjoy great
international cuisine and
all-day breakfasts. €-€€

BARS

Rīga

Četri Balti Krekli
Vecpilsētas 12
Tel: 6721 3885
www.krekli.lv
Wed–Sat 10pm–5am
The best place to see local
acts perform on weekend
nights. All of the music
played here is Latvian, and
the lively crowds often
include a number of poets
and politicians.
Cuba Café
Jauniela 15
www.cubacafe.lv
Sun–Thur 3pm–2am, Fri & Sat
3pm–5am
This cavernous bar and club
caters to students and
anyone else who likes
underground music. An
outdoor smoking courtyard
is also available as well as a
vintage accessories shop.
Krogs Aptieka
Mazā Miesnieku 1
Sun–Thur 5pm–1am, Fri & Sat
5pm–5am
The Pharmacy Bar is run by

an American-Latvian musician who owns a similar establishment in Washington, DC. The crowd is bohemian and the atmosphere friendly.

Nabaklab
Z.A. Meierovica bulv. 12
www.nabaklab.lv
Sun–Tue noon–2am, Wed–Sat noon–5am
This cavernous bar and club caters to students and anyone else who likes

underground music. An outdoor smoking courtyard is also available, as well as a vintage accessories shop.

Paddy Whelan's
Grēcinieku 4
Tel: 6721 0150
www.pub.lv
Mon–Thur 11am–1am, Fri–Sun 11am–4am
Rīga's first Irish pub has changed owners several times over the years, but

you're always guaranteed good service and a great selection of beers. You can also watch live sports and order Indian cuisine cooked in a real tandoor.

Paldies Dievam Piektdiena ir klāt
11 novembra krastmala 9
Tel: 6750 3964
Mon–Thur 9am–midnight, Fri 9am–4am, Sat 9am–4am, Sun 10am–midnight
Perhaps the best cocktails to

be had in town, served in a bright, lively Caribbean atmosphere where staff wear tropical gear and dancers in bikinis delight audiences on the bar at weekends.

PRICE CATEGORIES

For a three-course meal per person without drinks:
€ = under €7 (5Ls)
€€ = €7–14 (5–10Ls)
€€€ = over €14 (10Ls)

LITHUANIA

In Lithuania's cities you can find almost all major cuisines. Top hotels often have some of the city's best restaurants and can be a safe bet for those who wish to ease themselves slowly into the local cuisine.

Lithuanian cuisine, which is mainly based on potatoes and borrows heavily from Slavic and Jewish cuisine, is rich and rather fatty. The national dish, *cepelinai*, sticky potato rolls filled with meat or cottage cheese and usually dripping in a buttery bacon sauce (*spirgučiai*), probably made their way to the country with the Germans during World War I and are quite a mouthful in more ways than one. Although traditional Lithuanian food tends to be some combination of meat (usually pork), cabbage and potatoes, there are many pleasant exceptions to the rule. Lighter eaters will enjoy the array of salads and soups, which usually are more than just a fair sprinkling on the menu. Most menus are written in Lithuanian, Russian and English.

RESTAURANTS

Vilnius

Balti Drambliai
Vilniaus 41
Tel: 8-5 262 0875
Mon–Fri 11am–midnight, Fri 11am–4am, Sat noon–4am, Sun

noon–midnight
Vilnius's first vegetarian restaurant. The staff are friendly but the service is slow to say the least. The food is good though, and there's a very pleasant terrace for the warmer months. **€**

Čagino
Basanavičiaus 11
Tel: 8-5 261 5555
Daily noon–midnight
The only centrally located Russian restaurant in the city serves up some fabulous fare. Impromptu singing by inebriated Russian men adds an extra touch of authenticity. Čagino tends to close for a month or so during the summer and moves to its sister restaurant in Palanga. **€€**

Čili Kaimas
Vokiečių 8
Tel: 8-5 231 2536
Mon–Thur & Sun 11am–midnight, Fri & Sat 11am–2am
Wood and hearty portions are in abundance at this large, somewhat Disney-fied version of a traditional Lithuanian restaurant. Waiting for a table is not unusual at the weekend. **€€**

Forto Dvaras
Pilies 16
Tel: 8-5 261 1070
Daily 11am–midnight
Upstairs it is a faux cottage, downstairs a cellar and everywhere the music is loud. Music is courtesy of Lithuanian pop, with regional varieties of *cepelinai*. The meals are

great value and the service generally friendly and efficient. **€€**

La Provence
Vokiečių 22
Tel: 8-5 262 0257
www.laprovence.lt
Daily 11am–midnight
Simply one of the best restaurants in the country. Outrageously good French and Mediterranean restaurant and lovely service. **€€€€€**

Labuki
Didžioji 28
Tel: 8-5 261 1188
Mon–Fri 11am–midnight, Sat & Sun noon–midnight
The best Japanese food in town, close to the Town Hall and complete with a Korean chef in the kitchen. The sushi is better than most, and the noodle dishes are to die for. **€€€**

Lokys
Stiklių 8
Tel: 8-5 262 9046
www.lokys.lt
Daily noon–midnight
Open since 1972, squeeze down a narrow staircase to find this cellar where local game dishes abound. A Vilnius tourist favourite, booking is definitely recommended. **€€€**

Markus ir Ko
Antokolskio 11
Tel: 8-5 262 3185
Daily noon–midnight
Located on a small street off Stiklių is one of the oldest steakhouses in the city. Customers are guaranteed to get exactly what they want as they must choose their sauce, cut of beef

and accompanying side dishes. **€€€€**

Neringa
Gedimino 23
Tel: 8-5 261 4058
Mon–Wed 11am–11pm, Thur–Sat 11am–midnight, Sun 11am–10pm
A giant mural of hard-working peasants fits Neringa's former glorious past as the elite meeting spot during Soviet times. The butter sputtering around is from the signature dish, the chicken Kiev. **€€€**

Pegasus
Didžioji 11
Tel: 8-5 260 9430
www.restaurantpegasus.lt
Daily 11.30am–midnight
International food with an Asian twist in swish surroundings. Exclusive crowd on the late evening cocktail circuit. **€€€**

Riverside
Konstitucijos 20
Tel: 8-5 272 6272
Mon–Fri 6.30am–11pm, Sat & Sun 7am–11pm
Inside the Radisson Blu Hotel Lietuva, the chefs here respect food in a way not entirely common to the Baltics. Expect light flavours and a real dining experience. **€€€€**

Stikliai
Gaono 7
Tel: 8-5 264 9580

PRICE CATEGORIES

For a three-course meal per person without drinks:
€ under €20 (under 70 Lt)
€€ €20–35 (70–120 Lt)
€€€ €35–50 (120–175 Lt)
€€€€ over €50 (over 175 Lt)

Tue–Fri noon–3pm, 6pm–11pm, Sat noon–11.30pm, closed Sun, Mon
International food forms a happy marriage in this well-known spot for Vilnius's elite inside the glorious Stikliai hotel. €€€€€

Tores
Užupio 40
Tel: 8-5 6553 2626
Daily noon–midnight
Although named after a Spanish wine, the kitchen mostly sends out plates of Lithuanian cuisine. Summer days on their terrace overlooking the Old Town will make you feel like everything is right in the world. €€–€€€

Борщ!
Algirdo 5-2
Tel: 8-5 260 3344
Mon–Fri 10am–11pm, Sat & Sun 11am–11pm
Up the hill from the Old Town, Борщ! (Bortsch!) is the place to sample the Ukrainian take on the medley of potatoes, meat and cabbage. Their selection of vodkas makes the occasionally loud Ukrainian pop music less irritating. €€

Žemaičiai
Vokiečių 24
Tel: 8-5 261 6573
Daily 11am–midnight
This traditional cellar tavern/outdoor beer garden is great fun. The food is a delectable array of national dishes that are complemented best by their strong home-made brew. Highly recommended. €€€

Kaunas

Bernelių Užeiga
Valančiaus 9
Tel: 8-37 200 913
www.berneliuuziega.lt
Sun–Wed 11am–10pm, Thur

ABOVE: locally produced honeycomb.

11am–11pm, Fri & Sat 11am–1am
All the delightful trappings of a classic folk restaurant – the staff and the food are both dressed traditionally. Occasional live music. €€

Leonijos
Kurpių 11
Tel: 8-37 203 875
Mon–Sat 11am–10pm
A classic local affair selling hearty indigenous food made by matrons in aprons. Very cheap and equally cheerful. €

Lietuviški Patiekalai
Laisvės 21/13
Tel: 8-37 6553 5536
Mon–Wed 9am–9pm, Thur–Sat 9am–11pm, Sun 11am–9pm
A deliciously cheap affair offering classic national dishes either straight from hot metal containers for those in a hurry or from a small menu. €

Medžiotojų Užeiga
Rotušės 10
Tel: 8-37 320 956
Daily 11am–midnight
The Hunter's Tavern serves up all manner of local game dishes right on Town Hall Square. Look for the door with the antler handles. A bit on the stiff side. €€€–€€€€

Miesto Sodas
Laisvės 93
Tel: 8-37 424 424

Sun–Wed 10am–11pm, Thur–Sat 10am–midnight
One of the loveliest places to sit in Kaunas as the dining room is partially enclosed by glass, ensuring a good view onto the City Gardens or the people walking past. Food is exceptionally good. €€–€€€

Pas Paolo
S. Daukanto 17
Tel: 8-37 220 175
Mon–Thur 10am–midnight, Fri & Sat 10am–1am, Sun 11am–11pm
Found down a small alley, the atmosphere might be Lithuanian but the Italian food coming out of the kitchen certainly isn't. €€

Sushi Express
Laisvės 12a
Tel: 8-37 6999 6611
Sun–Thur 11am–9pm, Fri & Sat 11am–10pm
Surprisingly good sushi served in a small cabin at the very end of the city's most famous street. €

Žalias Ratas
Laisvės 36b
Tel: 8-37 200 071
Daily 11am–midnight
The huge fireplace in the centre of this thatched-roof restaurant aids the "step back in time" feel of this place. One of the better eateries in town, albeit fiendishly difficult to find down an alley. €€

Outside Kaunas

Bajorkiemis
Vilnius–Kaunas highway
Tel: 8-37 440 770
Mon 10am–10pm, Fri & Sat 11am–1am

This place somehow manages to attract all sorts of visitors. The huge roadside restaurant serves up hearty portions of Lithuanian standards. A lake, a petting zoo and crafts workshops round out the experience. €€–€€€

Klaipėda

Ararat
Liepų 48a
Tel: 8-46 410 001
Mon–Fri 11am–midnight, Sat noon–midnight, Sun 1pm–midnight
Inside the hotel of the same name, if you've never tried Armenian food before, then this is the place to begin the adventure. Grilled meats like you never tasted. €€€–€€€€

Delano
Taikos 61 (Akropolis)
Tel: 8-46 6595 5171
Daily 9am–10pm
Inside a vast shopping centre under the shade of a huge musical clock, Delano serves a vast range of ready-to-eat food for buttons. Excellent value and good food to boot. €

Ferdinandas
Naujoji Uosto 10
Tel: 8-46 313 681
Mon–Fri 10am–midnight, Sat & Sun noon–midnight
Authentic Russian cuisine in swish surroundings. Recommended. Occasional live music. €€€

Memelis
Žvejų 4
Tel: 8-46 403 040
www.memelis.lt
Sun–Thur noon–midnight, Fri & Sat noon–3am

FAST FOOD

McDonald's Baltic headquarters is in Lithuania, and there are outlets in every major town in the country. In Vilnius, the opening of their drive-in went hand-in-hand with a

thorough clean-up of the entire train station area. For inexpensive local food, see the café section on the next page.
For cheap pizza, look out for the ubiquitous **Čili Pizza** outlets.

TRANSPORT

ACCOMMODATION

EATING OUT

ACTIVITIES

A – Z

LANGUAGE

DRINKING SNACKS

Lithuania has some excellent beers. The main brands are Horn, Kalnapilis, Švyturys, Utenos and Tauras. Along with a beer-drinking culture, the Lithuanians have also perfected the beer snack. The most common is *kepta duona* (fried bread), which are pieces of dark bread deep-fried and accompanied by a massive amount of garlic. Some enjoy it *su sūriu* (with cheese) melted on top.

Meat products like smoked pig's ears (*rūkytos kiaulių ausys*), pig's leg (*kiaulės koja*), dried meats similar to jerky (*basturma*) and beef tongue (*jautienos liežuvis*) are also common.

This brewery/restaurant is a popular haunt usually filled with tourists. The Lithuanian menu has a German influence. €€€

Skandalas
Kanto 44
Tel: 8-46 411 585
Mon–Thur noon–midnight, Fri & Sat noon–1am, Sun noon–11pm
A bit out of the centre, but well worth the walk, this American-themed favourite churns out great food from burgers to pasta. Recommended. €€–€€€

Stora Antis
Tiltų 6
Tel: 8-46 493 910
Daily 11am–midnight
The Fat Duck is a small and slightly snobby affair serving classic Slavic dishes. Booking during the height of the holiday season is recommended. €€€

Nida

Ešerinė
Naglių 2
Tel: 8-469 527 57
Daily 10am–midnight
Sitting in a hut alongside the water while eating fish will make you wonder if you should just move here. €€

Seklyčia
Lotmiškio 1
Tel: 8-469 529 45
Daily 9am–midnight
The most upscale dining in this sleepy village. Its rooftop terrace has unbeatable views. €€€

Sena Sodyba
Naglių 6-2
Tel: 8-469 527 82
Daily 11am–11pm
This tiny garden makes the most charming "dining room". The menu, although diminutive, augments the delightful atmosphere. €€

Palanga

The pulse of Palanga is along Basanavičiaus, and the street is crammed with numerous restaurants, bars and cafés. With such competition, establishments tend not to slack on atmosphere, food or service.

Pušų Paunksnėje
Dariaus ir Girėno 25
Tel: 8-460 490 91
Daily 9am–11pm
A pleasant medley of international and Lithuanian food can be found inside this unpretentious but upscale hotel restaurant. €€€–€€€€

Svetainė
Vytauto 94
Tel: 8-460 532 59
Daily 8am–8pm
In the same building as the bus station, Svetainė may not be heading for any Michelin stars soon, but the instant buffet food on offer is at least filling. A classic east European institution, the key for the toilet is kept behind the bar. €

Vila Ramybė
Vytauto 54
Tel: 8-460 541 24
Daily 9am–11pm
The proprietor's love for food and music is undeniable. The attractiveness of this restaurant, where ordering anything from a full meal to just a drink is acceptable, is in its accommodating ambience. €€

Outside Palanga

Pas Juozą
Žibininkai village
Tel: 8-445 446 78
Tue–Sun 10am–midnight, Mon noon–midnight
A good old-fashioned brewery serving Lithuanian food and some Chinese flavours too. Although a bit odd, the brewery usually proves fun, especially for children, as its large grounds and play structures keep them entertained. €€

CAFÉS

Vilnius

Café de Paris
Didžioji 1
Tel: 8-5 261 1021
Sun–Tue 11am–midnight, Wed & Thur 11am–2am, Fri & Sat 11am–4am
Part of the French Cultural Centre, this is where the local young artists hang out. Surplus to decent coffee are pancakes and DJs several nights of the week. €

Coffee Inn
Vilniaus 17
Tel: 8-5 6557 7763
Mon–Wed 7am–10pm, Thur 7am–11pm, Fri 7am–midnight, Sat 9am–midnight, Sun 9am–10pm
A veritable Starbucks wanabee that's been hijacked by local students. Great coffee, excellent sandwiches and free WiFi. €

Ponių Laimė
Stiklių 14/1
Tel: 8-5 264 9581
Mon–Sat 9am–8pm, Sun 9am–6pm
More a patisserie than a café, there is drinkable coffee on the premises as well as a choice of ready-to-eat dishes at lunchtime during the week. €€

Kaunas

Vero Café
Vilniaus 18
Tel: 8-37 6071 4728
Mon–Fri 7.30am–9pm, Sat & Sun 10am–9pm
The best of the bunch in the Old Town, with devilishly strong coffee, wraps, cakes and students. Sit at the outside tables during summer. €

Klaipėda

Café Kubu
H. Manto 10
Mon–Thur 9am–10pm, Fri 9am–3am, Sun 11am–11pm
At last, a modern café comes to the city. Find the usual paper cups of brew plus DJs at the weekend. €

BARS

Vilnius

ŠMC
Vokiečiu 2
Mon–Thur 11am–midnight, Fri 11am–3am, Sat noon–2am, Sun noon–midnight
Around the back of the Contemporary Arts Centre, this is a bar where the arty crowd meets. Great outdoor seating in the summer.

Šnekutis
Šv Stepono 8
Mon–Sat noon–11pm
Beer from microbreweries all over the country served by a gentleman with a remarkable moustache. Some of the beers are 12 percent proof. Their other bar at Polocko 7a is more intimate and raucous.

Užupio Kavinė
Užupio 2
Mon–Thur 10am–11pm, Fri–Sun 10am–midnight
The breakaway republic's favourite spot, with a terrace overlooking the river. Good snacks, too.

Kaunas

Avilys
Vilniaus 34
Sun–Thur noon–midnight, Fri & Sat noon–2am
Three types of beer are brewed on the premises of this cellar bar, which also doubles as a restaurant.

PRICE CATEGORIES

For a three-course meal per person without drinks:
€ under €20 (under 70 Lt)
€€ €20–35 (70–120 Lt)
€€€ €35–50 (120–175 Lt)
€€€€ over €50 (over 175 Lt)

A CTIVITIES

FESTIVALS, THE ARTS, NIGHTLIFE, CHILDREN, SHOPPING AND SPORT

FESTIVALS

For Public Holidays, see A–Z, Page 369. For background information, see Folklore chapter, page 57.

January

New Year is celebrated throughout the Baltics, with fireworks and gatherings in town squares.
The Magi (6th). The Magi arrive in Vilnius Cathedral Square.
OpeNBaroque (late Jan or early Feb), long-standing series of concerts in Tallinn centred on Baroque and other early music.

February

Shrovetide. In Estonia, this day is called Vastlapäev, and is the day when children go sledging. In Lithuiania on the weekend before Lent, Užgavėnės takes place in Vilnius Old Town, when people wear costumes and masks; in the evening a large effigy of a woman is burnt.
International Ice-Sculpture Festival and art symposium (first week), Jelgava, Latvia.

March

St Casimir (4th, or closest weekend). The patron saint of Lithuania is celebrated with a large fair, Kaziukas, in Vilnius Old Town. Everyone carries *verbos*, a long stick of colourful dried flowers, grasses and/or herbs, used later at Palm Sunday services.
Rīga Fashion Week. This annual showcase features new talent from the whole of Europe.

April

Jazzkaar international jazz festival in

Tallinn, with world-class performers.
International Baltic Ballet Festival is held in Rīga and features the best performers from the Baltic Sea region.
Bimini International Animated Film Festival, Rīga.

May

Spring Student Days (early May), Tartu. Thousands of Tartu's students take part in creative and often silly competitions, including river races in bizarre, home-made boats.
Museum Day (24th). All museums free, with interactive night tours.
International Folklore Festival, Vilnius.
Go Blonde Festival. Two days of blonde events culminating in a parade in Old Rīga.
Rīga Marathon takes place.

June

Old Town Days Festival (first week). Entertaining mix of medieval tournaments, markets and concerts all over Tallinn's Old Town.
Annual Crafts Fair (first weekend) at Rīga's Ethnographic Museum.
Annual Cathedral Square Crafts Fair (22nd), Rīga. Large event with many stalls anticipating midsummer.
Midsummer's Eve (23rd–24th). The Baltic States' favourite national holiday is always celebrated on the actual date and never moved to the closest weekend for the sake of convenience. The pagan fertility celebrations consist of singing, dancing, lots of beer and bonfires in the countryside. Called Jaanipäev in Estonia, Jāņi in Latvia and Joninės in Lithuania, it is a festival of pagan origins, deeply rooted in peasant culture. The date marks the end of spring labours in the fields and used

to be seen as a night of omens and sorcery. One tradition that still exists is that of leaping over bonfires. A successful clearance of the flames used to indicate similar success for the year ahead. On the days leading up to this festival Tallinn is drained of people, as everyone heads for the countryside. At Jāņi in Latvia special beers and cheeses are made for the occasion and citizens sport floral wreaths. In Lithuania, the town of Kernavė, a small village about 24km (15 miles) north of Vilnius off the A2 motorway, is the best place to enjoy the festivities. The highlight of the evening is when young girls take off the wreaths from their heads, surround them with candles and set them afloat along the Neris, and the water, half-lit by moonlight and far-off bonfires, carries the hundreds of candles downstream.
Rīga Opera Festival (two weeks). Celebrities have included Warren Mok, Inese Galante and other international stars.
Rīgas Ritmi Rhythmic Music Festival R&B and Latin bands from around the world take part in this annual festival in Rīga.
Vilnius Festival celebrates classical music in many of Vilnius's venues and is overseen by the Vilnius Philharmonic.

July

Beer Summer (early July). Estonia's largest outdoor party. Four days of beer-tasting, concerts, carnival rides and games for children.
Mindaugas Coronation Day (6th). A Lithuanian national holiday; a large festival takes place in Kernavė.
Baltic Beach Party Annual International Rock Festival on the

beach in Liepāja, Latvia.

Pärnu Film Festival (early July), A major documentary and anthropology film event. See www.chaplin.ee.

Positivus Music Festival. Headliners of this two-day festival in Salacgrīva have included Muse, Moby and Stereophonics.

St Christopher Festival A large music festival throughout Vilnius. See www.kristupofestivaliai.lt.

International Organ Festival (late July or early August), Tallinn.

Viljandi Folk Music Festival (late July), Viljandi. In one of the largest events of the Estonian summer, folk music groups, both Estonian and international, gather to perform.

Rīgas Ritmi Rhythmic Music Festival. R&B and Latin bands from around the world take part in this annual festival in Rīga.

August

August Dance, Tallinn. Modern dance performances by cutting-edge groups from Estonia and abroad.

Song and Dance Festival

The next Song and Dance Festival will take place in the summer of 2013 in Latvia, and in 2014 in Estonia. The festival has been held roughly every five years since 1869 in Estonia and 1873 in Latvia, and its highlight is the final concert, during which hundreds of choirs from around the country sing together in front of tens of thousands of spectators who often join in on the most popular songs.

Banitis Festival (first weekend). Narrow-gauge railway festival at Ates Mills Gulbene, Latvia; www.banitis.lv.

Rīga Sacred Music Festival (Aug–Sept). Musicians from around Europe converge on Rīga to play religious music.

Annual Organ Music Festival at Dome Cathedral, Rīga (when restoration is completed).

Visagino Country International country music and bluegrass festival in Visaginas, Lithuania, the second weekend of the month. For details see the website www.visaginocountry.lt.

Feast of the Assumption (Žolinė, 15th). A Lithuanian public holiday with activities throughout the country. The Rumšiškės Open-Air Museum of Lithuania also hosts a celebration.

September

Homo Novus (Sept–Dec). International Festival of Contemporary

Theatre takes place every two years in Rīga.

Vilnius Capital Days is a week of folk concerts and fairs. For more information and latest dates see www. vilniusfestivals.lt.

Vilnius Jazz Festival, when music is heard throughout the city. See www. vilniusjazz.lt for more information and latest dates.

Orthodox Sacred Music Festival (Sept–Oct). Church and monastery choirs, secular and children's choirs perform in churches and halls throughout Tallinn; www.festivalcredo.com.

Arts and Lights (late Sept). Artists and designers take over Tallinn, presenting three days of avant-garde exhibitions and performances.

November

All Saints' Day (1st). People visit cemeteries, placing candles around graves.

Black Nights Film Festival (two weeks, beginning late Nov or early Dec). Tallinn. International feature films, with sub-festivals for student films, children's films and animation.

Rīga Shines (14th–18th). Rīga's most impressive buildings are illuminated and hundreds of thousands of people walk the streets at night to watch the spectacle.

December

Christmas Jazz (early Dec), Tallinn. An event similar to the April Jazzkaar but less ambitious in scale.

Christmas is celebrated throughout the Baltics with concerts, decorated trees and craft markets.

THE ARTS

The admission price to most state **museums** is nominal. Irrespective of the collection, it's often worth paying this fee just to look inside the

building. Several of the main museums are located in beautifully preserved medieval guild houses or merchants' buildings, while manor houses and churches provide other venues of architectural interest. Many museums close on Mondays, or sometimes Tuesdays, and they may have a free day of the week (usually Wednesday in Lithuania).

Information on current exhibitions can be found in the local *In Your Pocket* (www.inyourpocket.com) guides, and most galleries promote their exhibitions and events with posters around the town.

Estonia

Theatre

Theatre has enjoyed enormous popularity in this country since the 19th century, when the first Estonian plays arose out of the National Awakening. The centre of the nation's theatrical activity has traditionally been Tallinn, including several small experimental theatres, but there are well-established houses in Tartu, Pärnu and Viljandi too. Note that all performances, except those at the Russian Drama Theatre, are in Estonian. Full information on Estonia's theatre scene, as well as programmes, can be found at www.teater.ee.

Eesti Draamateater (Estonian Drama Theatre), Pärnu mnt. 5; tel: 6805 555; www.draamateater.ee. Tallinn's pre-eminent theatre since the 1950s, it has a repertoire stretching from Shakespeare to modern Estonian comedy. It is housed in a beautiful Art Nouveau building in central Tallinn.

Tallinna Linnateater (Tallinn City Theatre), Lai 23; tel: 6650 850; www. linnateater.ee. Three medieval buildings in the Old Town make up the City Theatre's house. In summer, plays are staged in the outdoor arena, in back.

Endla Teater, Keskväljak 1, Pärnu;

BELOW: ballet performance at the Estonian National Opera.

ABOVE: jazz festival, Vilnius.

tel: 4420 666; www.endla.ee. A time-honoured institution playing in a very modern house in central Pärnu.
Vanemuine Theatre, Vanemuine 6, Tartu; tel: 7440 165; www.vanemuine.ee. Tartu's all-in-one theatre is also the city's main venue for ballet, opera and classical music.

Music and Dance

Virtually every night from September to May, a classical performance is held at the Estonia Theatre and Concert Hall. More often than not the performances are given by the Estonian National Symphony or the Estonian National Opera. Guest orchestras, choirs and ensembles are also invited from around the world. These performances usually transfer to other concert halls, notably to Tartu's Vanemuine Theatre and the Pärnu Concert Hall. Churches, guild halls and other historic buildings also frequently serve as classical concert venues. Details of performances are posted on notice boards outside the concert halls and around city centres.
Estonia Concert Hall, Estonia pst. 4; tel: 6147 760; www.concert.ee, www.opera.ee. There are operas and ballets here as well as classical concerts. Look out for performances by the Tallinn Philharmonic Society (tel: 6699 940; www.filharmoonia.ee) and for Tallinn's early-music ensemble, Hortus Musicus, whose repertoire of Baroque and Renaissance music fits in well with the city's historic ambience.
    Other venues in Estonia include:
Mustpeade Maja (House of the Brotherhood of the Blackheads), Pikk 26; tel/fax: 6313 199; www.mustpeade maja.ee. The medieval Guild Hall is an intimate venue for smaller classical events.
Niguliste (St Nicholas's) Church, Niguliste 3; tel: 6449 911; www.ekm.ee.

Cinema

Cinema is an easy entertainment option in the Baltic countries as films are nearly always shown in their original language, with subtitles. The Forum Cinemas Plaza (www.forumcinemas.lv) in Rīga offers 14 cinema halls and a 260-sq-metre (2,800-sq-ft) film screen, the second-largest in northern Europe.

Organ concerts are held every Saturday and Sunday afternoon in a casual atmosphere. Concert times are posted outside.
Nokia Concert Hall, Estonia pst. 9; tel: 6261 111; www.tallinnconcerthall.ee. Everything from musicals to children's performances are staged in this spacious, modern venue.
Vanemuine Theatre. See *"Theatre" above*.
Pärnu Kontserdimaja (Pärnu Concert Hall), Aida 4; tel: 4455 800; www.concert.ee. Built in 2003, the high-tech, towering concert hall also serves as a catch-all cultural centre and houses a small art gallery.

Latvia

Theatre

Latvians have traditionally been seen as a nation of theatregoers, and hundreds of people from the countryside take buses to Rīga for the premieres of new plays.
Latvian National Theatre (Nacionālais teātris), Kronvalda bulv. 2; tel: 6700 6300; www.teatris.lv. This fantastic theatre was completely renovated in 2004 and continues to draw crowds for traditional Latvian plays.
Russian Drama Theatre (Krievu drāmas teātris), Kaļķu 16; tel: 6722 4660. New and classic plays in Russian.
New Rīga Theatre (Jaunais Rīgas teātris), Lāčplēša 25; tel: 6728 0765; www.jrt.lv. Avant-garde plays are often sold out at Rīga's most popular theatre.
Dailes Theatre (Dailes teātris), Brīvības 75; tel: 6729 4444; www.dailes teatris.lv. This large theatre shows classic plays from around the world in Latvian.
Valmiera Drama Theatre (Valmieras drāmas teātris), Lāčplēša 4; tel: 6420 7335, www.vdt.lv. This renowned theatre has been in operation under various names since 1919; and its extensive repertoire includes plays by Chekhov and Ibsen as well as Latvian classics and new drama.

Liepāja Theatre (Liepājas teātris), Teātra 4; tel: 6342 2121; www.liepajasteatris.lv. One of Latvia's oldest theatres still has regular performances of classic plays in autumn and winter.

Music and Dance

With such native sons as Mikhail Baryshnikov and Alexander Gudunov, it's no surprise that Rīga's ballet and opera draw crowds from around Europe. The city is never short of concerts and festivals, but organisers seldom know exact dates until only weeks and sometimes even days before an event.
House of Blackheads (Melngalvju nams), Rātslaukums 7; tel: 6704 4300. Venue of frequent chamber music concerts.
Latvian National Opera House (Latvijas Nacionālā opera), Aspazijas bulvāris 3; tel: 6707 3777; www.opera.lv. Opulently decorated with gilded ceilings, crystal chandeliers and priceless works of art.
Riga Cathedral (Doma baznīca), Doma laukums 1; tel: 6721 3213; www.doms.lv. Professionals from around the globe often waive their fees just to play on the magnificent organ, which has 6,718 pipes and is one of the world's largest.
Spīķeri Concert Hall (Spīķeru koncertzāle), Maskavas 4, korp. 2/3; tel: 6721 5018; www.sinfoniettariga.lv. The home of the Latvian National Chamber Orchestra is located in a renovated warehouse near the Central Market.
The Great Guild (Lielā Ģilde), Amatu 6; tel: 6722 4850; www.lnso.lv. Home to the Latvian National Symphony Orchestra, which has a host of national and international concert events.
The Small Guild (Mazā Ģilde), Amatu 3/5; tel: 6722 3772; www.gilde.lv/maza. Across the street from the Great Guild, it often hosts chamber music concerts and special events.

Lithuania

For tickets to many of Vilnius major events, see www.bilietai.lt or www.tiketa.lt.

Theatre

In spite of funding difficulties, the main theatres in Vilnius show a broad range of plays. The country has a strong acting tradition, and many players enjoy excellent reputations. Look out for performances at the university and by troupes such as the 15-strong Lithuanian National Theatre, which are particularly good. Performances usually start at 6 or

7pm, and résumés are sometimes available in English.

Lithuanian National Drama Theatre (Lietuvos nacionalinis dramos teatras), Gedimino 4; tel: 8-5 262 97 71; www.teatras.lt.

Vilnius Small State Theatre (Valstybinis Vilniaus mažasis teatras), Gedimino 4; tel: 8-5 249 98 69; www.vmt.lt.

Lithuanian Russian Drama Theatre (Lietuvos Rusų dramos teatros), Basanavičiaus 13; tel: 8-5 262 71 33. Puts on Russian-language plays and hosts occasional live music concerts.

State Youth Theatre (Valstybinis jaunimo teatras), Arklių 5; tel: 8-5 261 61 26; www.jaunimoteatras.lt. Ambitious productions of classical and modern works.

OKT, Ašmenos 8; tel: 8-5 212 20 99; www.okt.lt. The theatre director Oskaras Koršunovas's personal troupe.

Music and Dance

Siemens Arena, Ozo 14; tel: 8-5 247 7576; www.siemens-arena.com. A multi-purpose indoor arena where major concerts and basketball games are held.

Vingis Park (Vingio parkas). The park's marvellous outdoor amphitheatre stages all manner of shows throughout the summer.

Lithuanian National Philharmonic (Lietuvos Nacionalinė Filharmonija), Aušros Vartų 5; tel: 8-5 266 5213; www.filharmonija.lt.

Lithuanian National Opera and Ballet Theatre (Lietuvos Nacionalinis operos ir baleto teatras), Vienuolio 1; tel: 8-5 6155 1000; www.opera.lt. Opera and ballet productions are wide-ranging.

Vilnius Congressional Palace (Vilniaus kongresų rūmai); tel: 8-5 261 8828; www.lvso.lt. One of the best venues for classical music in the city.

NIGHTLIFE

Summer nights are long in the Baltic States, and there are few better ways to relax than to sit in an outdoor café, beer in hand, watching the world slowly meander past. The capitals in particular have a wide spectrum of nightlife to explore, from quiet, sophisticated lounges to pulsing dance clubs.

Estonia

Tallinn

Like everything else in Tallinn, most of the nightlife is squeezed into a few Old Town streets, giving rise to the custom of frequent bar-hopping. Since the bars are literally only a few paces apart, locals (and savvy visitors) will often change locations after every single drink, exploring all the options until they finally find the place they want to settle in.

Bars and pubs are easy to find in the Old Town – just follow the crowds and the noise. Beware, though, that annoying groups of British stag weekenders (bachelor partiers) infiltrate many of the central pubs, so the saner crowds tend to go elsewhere. **Molly Malone's** (Mündi 2; tel: 6313 016) on the square is still a safe bet and has good live music most weekends. **Hell Hunt** (Pikk 39; tel: 6818 333) has a good atmosphere and its own brand of beer. Local flavour can be found in the crowded **Karja-Kelder** (Väike-Karja 1; tel: 6441 008).

For more cosmopolitan, lounge-type surroundings, **Lounge 8** (Vana-Posti 8; tel: 6274 770) and **Deja Vu** (Sauna 1; tel: 6450 044) are both good choices. Cosy wine bars are also fashionable. Two highly recommended wine bars are **Musi** (Niguliste 6; tel: 6443 100) and **Gloria Veinikelder** (Müürivahe 2; tel: 6406 804).

Tallinn has an active local band scene, and many of the larger bars and pubs offer live music at the weekend. A couple of these, such as the downmarket and edgy **Von Krahli Baar** (Rataskaevu 10; tel: 6269 090) and the more sophisticated **Clazz** (Vana Turg 2; tel: 6279 022) build much of their business on live performance. Ask locals which of the bands are their favourites.

Nightclubs are also easy to find in Tallinn, but hard to recommend. Crowds are fickle, so what could be full of life on one night could be desolate the next. One that's always enormously popular, however, is the huge, central **Club Hollywood** (Vana-Posti 8; tel: 6274 770), which draws a young crowd. The scenes at nearby **Club Privé** (Harju 6; tel: 6310 545) and **Vabank** (Harju 13; tel: 6605 299) are more exclusive and mature.

Tartu

Tartu's student crowds give that city's nightlife a younger, more casual energy. The Mafia-themed **Ristiisa** (Küüni 7; tel: 7303 970) and the historic **Püssirohu Kelder** (Lossi 28; tel: 7303 560) are both popular live-music venues. **Nightclubs Atlantis** (Narva mnt. 2; tel: 7385 485) and **Pattaya Club** (Turu 12; tel: 7303 400) play mainstream dance hits. Those seeking more "club-style" sounds head to the trendy **Club Tallinn** (Narva mnt. 27a; tel: 7403 157).

Pärnu

Estonia's "summer capital" has a surprisingly trendy club scene for a town its size. Popular choices are the downtown **Sugar** (Vee 10; tel: 4421 100) and **Bravo** (Hommiku 3; tel: 53 443 887), as well as the beachside **Sunset Club** (Ranna pst. 3; tel: 4472 733). Generally though, Pärnu's nightlife is more rustic and down-to-earth than that of the larger cities. Pubs such as **Viies Villem** (Kuninga

BELOW: live music, Rīga.

11; tel: 4427 999) and **Postipoiss** (Vee 12; tel: 4464 864) offer live bands and an old-fashioned feel.

Latvia

Rīga
Trendy cocktail bars, chic clubs, 24-hour casinos and down-to-earth pubs occupy nearly every street corner in Rīga and, best of all, they seldom close their doors before everyone's had their fill.

For a glimpse of how life in the Baltics used to be; visit **Gauja** (Tērbatas 56; tel: 6727 5662), a retro Soviet bar made to look like a typical apartment in the USSR of the 1970s. Nearly its exact opposite is the bright, modern **Skyline Bar** on the 26th floor of the Radisson Blu Hotel Latvia, which has spectacular city views.

For live blues music at weekends visit **Bites Blues Club** (Dzirnavu 34a; tel: 6733 3125), but those out for a more local experience should take in a concert by a Latvian band at the popular **Četri Balti Krekli** (Vecpilsētas 12; tel: 6721 3885).

For dancing and seeing how the young and fashionable dress, try the huge techno club **PUSH** (Tērbatas 2; www.push.lv) or a hip alternative popular with bohemians, **Nabaklab** (Z.A. Meierovica bulv. 12; www.nabaklab.lv).

The **Olympic Voodoo Casino** at the Radisson Blu Hotel Latvia is stylish and open 24 hours.

Liepāja
In this coastal town, **First Rock Café** is a large, friendly club decorated with the posters and photographs of Latvian rock legends and different festivals. During the day it is a favourite place for families to have a

BELOW: winter transport.

meal. It's on three floors and there is an outdoor terrace in summer. Live concerts on Fridays in the basement. The **Fontaine Palace** (www.fontaine.lv) has a big stage and regular live bands, bar and dancing area, plus the biggest drum machine in the world – the owner's own invention.

Lithuania

Vilnius
Most bars in the centre of Vilnius are open until the early hours of the morning, and it is not uncommon to feel as though most people have been consuming high amounts of alcohol when roaming the streets of the Old Town after 10pm on a Friday or Saturday night.

Any time before midnight is a good time to visit one of the many beer tents that spring up along Pilies or Vokiečių. Later in the evening most patrons move inside for further drinking and discussion, or on to some of the city's clubs. New clubs practising face-control and charging exorbitant covers are rare.

For a quiet drink you can't beat **Būsi Trečias** (Totorių 18), with its home-made beer and wooden benches. Just down from the Gates of Dawn, two particularly good places to have drinks are the wine bar, **In Vino** (Aušros Vartų 7) and, just beyond the Town Hall, **Amatininkų Užeiga** (Didžioji 19/2), whose outdoor seating is among the city's liveliest. For a livelier atmosphere, a late night drink in **Cactus**, frequented by a younger crowd who visit to enjoy the range of tequila on offer, is hard to beat. The legendary **Brodvėjus** (Mėsinių 4; www.brodvejus.lt) is a large, high-energy place for dancing at the weekends and often hosts live music shows. An unpretentious but sophisticated lounge/club that stays open late at the weekends can be found at **Cozy** (Dominikonų 10; www.cozy.lt).

The recently renovated **Prie Parlamento** (Gedimino 46), a former expat favourite now making a name for itself among the locals, is a recommended wine bar and beer hall on two floors. Across the river on the 22nd floor of the Radison Blu Hotel Lietuva, **SkyBar** (Konstitucijos 20) serves up cocktails and has by far the best city view. Another club option in the Old Town, the Latin-themed **Pabo Latino** (Trakų 3/2; www.pabolatino.lt) operates face-control and is generally heaving at the weekend with the capital's more sophisticated millionaires.

Kaunas
One of the best places to visit is **Miesto Sodas** (Laisvės 93), where the restaurant/bar's glass windows look out onto the city garden. There is a nightclub, **Siena**, located downstairs.

Klaipėda
Kurpiai (Kurpių 1a) is considered one of the country's top venues for live jazz performances and is also a good bar in itself.

CHILDREN

Estonia

Tallinn
The most fun way to tour Tallinn's Old Town in summer is riding on **Toomas the Train**. The red-and-black electric locomotive departs from Kullassepa Street near Town Hall Square and makes a 20-minute circuit through the cobblestoned streets. Other entertainment in Tallinn includes: **AHHAA Science Centre**, Vabaduse väljak 9; tel: 6660 066. Young and old alike can try activities and see displays aimed at making science fun. **Estonian Puppet Theatre/Museum of Puppet Arts**, Lai 1; tel: 6679 555. The theatre offers short performances for tots. The language is Estonian, but the colourful action is universal. The theatre is also well worth visiting for the extensive, high-tech puppet museum opened here in 2010. **FK Centre**, Paldiski mnt. 229a; tel: 6870 101. Live out Formula 1 fantasies on a high-speed, motorised go-kart track.
Indoor play centres: HOPP! mängutuba, Mustamäe tee 5a; tel: 6559 671, and Riki-Tiki, Tartu mnt. 87d; tel: 5512 912. These offer ball pools, trampolines, climbing walls, crafts and organised entertainment. Here parents typically attend, but the play centres in the Viru Keskus and Ülemiste Keskus shopping malls are designed to watch your children while you shop. **Kalev Confectionery Museum**, Pikk 16. Discover the secrets of making traditional marzipan. **Miia-Milla-Manda Children's Museum**, L. Koidula 21c; tel: 6017 057. Set next to a playground in Kadriorg Park, this refurbished 1930s venue offers imaginative, hands-on activities for 3–11-year-olds. **Tallinn Zoo**, Paldiski mnt. 145; tel: 6943 300. Apart from the usual animals, an essential stop is the zoo's popular Tropical House, which

simulates rainforest conditions for alligators and chimpanzees, amongst others.

Pärnu

With its beach and parks, Pärnu is more naturally set up for children's enjoyment. The beachside promenades offer playgrounds, mini-golf, roller-skate hire and electric cars for tots.

Tervise Paradiis, Side 14; tel: 4451 666. This indoor water park is great for kids with its numerous water slides, climbing wall and a variety of swimming pools.

Tartu

Tartu has its own indoor water park, albeit small. It's the **Aura Keskus** (Turu 10; tel: 7300 280). For outdoor fun, there is a playground on Toomimägi, and the well-developed **Kaubamaja Mänguplats** along Küüni Street.

Tartu Mänguasjamuuseum (Tartu Toy Museum), Lutsu 8; tel: 7461 777. An amazing collection of toys, as well as a playroom.

Latvia

Rīga

Vairāk Saules (Dzirnavu 60; tel: 6728 2878) and **T.G.I. Friday's** (Kaļķu 6; tel: 6722 9071) offer games and colouring books.

No trip to Rīga would be complete without a short trip to the kitschy **Lido Recreation Centre** (Krasta 76; tel: 6750 4420; www.lido.lv). The complex's main attraction is a huge log cabin which offers three floors of Latvian restaurants and beer halls with live music and a supervised children's room with interactive games, colouring books and other activities. Outside is an amusement park that offers slides, games, go-karts, skating and ice-skating in the winter.

State Puppet Theatre K. Barona 16/18; tel: 6728 5418; www.puppet.lv. An excellent place for children to spend time, and although the plays are performed in either Latvian or Russian, the plot is generally easy enough to follow. The theatre is usually closed June and July.

The **Open-Air Ethnographic Museum**, Brīvības gatve 440; tel: 6799 4515 (see page 213).

The **Museum of Nature**, (Kr. Barona iela 4; tel: 6735 6024; www.dabasmuzejs.gov.lv) has interactive computer learning games in English on the top floor past the bizarre specimens in formaldehyde.

The **Rīga National Zoo** (see page 212). A quick tram ride from the centre will bring you in sight of lion,

leopard, musk ox and alligator.

Rīga Circus, Merķeļa 4; tel: 6721 3479; www.cirks.lv. Not quite what P.T. Barnum envisaged, but a good place to view animals. The circus is seasonal and is closed each year from Easter until the third Friday in October.

Līvu Akvaparks water park, Lielupe, Viestura 24; tel: 6775 5636; www.akvaparks.lv. Six water slides, a wave pool, children's pool, a tubing river and various other attractions guaranteed to keep the kids engaged for several hours.

Akvalande water park, Mūkusalas 45/47; tel: 6762 9700; www.akvalande.lv. Close to the centre of Rīga, it doesn't offer as many attractions as Līvu Akvaparks.

The coast

Latvia's coastal resorts are ideal for children. **Ventspils** is particularly well suited for families. The beach is well equipped and there are lots of festivals throughout the summer. The Open-Air Museum has a children's play area and a working steam train, and Children's World is dedicated to keeping them happy.

Jūrmala offers great beaches and loads of attractions for the kids in summer.

Lithuania

Vilnius

By far the most exciting place for children in the city is at any of the outdoor festivals. During summer the occasional carnival or circus comes to town. If all else fails, take them to the mall. In both of the city's most popular large shopping centres, Akropolis (Ozo 25) and Panorama (Saltoniškių 9), there are play areas for children. The former also has ice-skating and the latter an indoor go-kart track.

The **Vilnius Lėlė Puppet Theatre** (Vilniaus Teatras Lėlė; Arklių 5; tel: 8-5 262 8678), has adorable shows that will engage younger guests despite language barriers.

The **Open-Air Museum of Lithuania** (Lietuvos Liaudies Buities Muziejus) at Rumšiškės (see page 294) is littered with children's play structures made from wood. The kids might also learn something about farm life and crafts.

Kaunas

The **Lithuanian Zoological Gardens** (Lietuvos Zoologijos Sodas, Radvilėnų 21; tel: 8-5 332 540) features over 270 species of animals from around the world, all set in a pleasant woodland setting.

ABOVE: old-style toy shop, Tallinn.

SHOPPING

Estonia

Estonia is a great place to shop. Notable local products include art, knitwear, linen and a wide selection of handicrafts. Much of the delight of casual shopping here is not the goods but rather the shops themselves, many of which, particularly those in Tallinn's Old Town, possess great character. All shops listed here are in Tallinn unless otherwise stated.

Antiques

Antique shops seem to be everywhere, selling everything from 19th-century furniture, gramophones and jewellery to Soviet-era trinkets and military memorabilia. The trade in religious icons is still active here, although this has dropped off because it encourages their removal from isolated country churches.

Antikvaar, Rataskaevu 20; tel: 6418 269. A large shop with a varied assortment of furniture and distinctive metalworked items.

Reval Antiik, Harju 13; tel: 6440 747. Every item you can imagine, from Russian samovars to ceiling lamps.

Fine Art & Graphics

From its very beginnings, Estonian fine art has spanned a number of different media, and many of its brightest stars expressed themselves with applied art and graphics even more than with painting. These days it's just as common, if not more common, to see art shops selling innovative works in ceramics, jewellery, glass, metal and textiles, rather than framed pictures. That said, painters such as Jüri Arrak

(1936) and a younger generation of oil-on-canvas innovators have become well known internationally since independence was re-established.

Galerii 2, Lühike jalg 1; tel: 6418 308. Exquisitely crafted jewellery, ceramics, etched glasses and other items.

Haus Galerii, Uus 17; tel: 6419 471. Haus is a commercial gallery that features changing exhibitions of works by Estonia's finest painters.

Lühikese Jala Galerii, Lühike jalg 6; tel: 6314 720. An interesting place to shop, not only because it supplies a range of fun, fresh artistic gifts, but because it has a natural spring running through the wall in the back room.

Navitrolla Galerii, Sulevimägi 1; tel: 6313 716. Contemporary Estonian artist Navitrolla has become known for his strange animal creations. Prints are sold in his shop, as are T-shirts, coffee mugs, etc.

Skulptuuristuudio, Uus 20; tel: 6411 002. Works by Estonia's best-known sculptor, Tauno Kangro.

Books

A decent selection of English-language novels and non-fiction can be found in the larger shops, as can travel and gift books about Tallinn and Estonia. Books by Estonian author Jaan Kross can often be found in English.

Allecto, Juhkentali 8; tel: 6277 230. Specialising in foreign-language books, this shop has a small but respectable collection of novels and travel books.

Apollo Ramatumaja, Solaris Centre, Estonia pst. 9; tel: 6336 000. A large shop with several alcoves of material in English.

Raamatukoi, Harju 1; tel: 6837 710. Second-hand and antiquarian books, maps, postcards, magazines, etc.

Rahva Raamat, Viru väljak 4/6, on the 4th floor of the Viru Centre; tel: 6446 655. It probably has the largest collection of English-language books in Tallinn.

Handicrafts

You can find the best handmade sweaters, mittens and caps at the knitwear market on Tallinn's Müürivahe Street, Tallinn (see Markets, below). An equally fascinating place to pick up a gift or two is the **Katariina Guild**, in the Katariina Passage that runs from the knitwear market to Vene Street. In this string of small workshops, visitors can watch craftswomen at work creating quilts, ceramics, glass items, hand-

painted silk, jewellery and even hats. While the artists use time-honoured methods, their products are usually modern, even avant-garde.

Katariina Gild, Vene 12/Katariina käik; tel: 6418 476. Tallinn's most interesting place to shop . Glass, ceramics, textile items and more are produced in this string of open-studio handicraft workshops in the Old Town.

Kodukäsitöö, Pikk 22; tel: 6314 076; also at Pikk 15, Lühike jalg 6a and in the Viru Centre. These four shops run by the Estonian Handicraft Union sell authentic handicraft products, from toys to entire folk costumes.

Nukupood, Raekoja plats 18; tel: 6443 058. This tiny shop specialises in handmade dolls and toys.

VeTa, Pikk 6; tel: 6464 140. One of several shops on this stretch of Pikk Street selling woollens and linen.

Markets

Outdoor markets, while not common in Tallinn, present the most interesting shopping experience. First and foremost is the much-loved knitwear market along the old city wall on Müürivahe Street, near the Viru Gates. Since it doesn't have an official name, most foreigners simply refer to it as the **Wall of Sweaters**. Here local women sell just about every kind of knitted item you can imagine, with a better variation in styles than in most shops. A similar, but less spectacular craft market operates nearby on Mere Puiestee, just north of Vana-Viru Street. In summer, temporary markets also appear from week to week on or near Town Hall Square, where there is an enchanting Christmas Market.

Latvia

Latvians are renowned for their craftsmanship, and there is a wide

BELOW: knitwear.

range of paintings, ceramics, jewellery, glassware, porcelain, textiles, amber, leather, wooden crafts and locally made clothes. Shops listed are in Rīga unless otherwise stated.

Antiqua, Vaļņu 25. Mon–Fri noon–5pm, Sat 11am–3pm. Antique maps and lithographs, books, fine art and furniture.

Berga Bazārs, Marijas 13. Every second and fourth Saturday of the month you can buy antiques, including Soviet and Tsarist era memorabilia, here.

Galerija, Dzirnavu 53. Mon–Fri 10am–7pm, Sat 11am–5pm. Books, Soviet memorabilia, coins and knick-knacks.

Konvents, Kaļķu 9/11. Daily 10am–7pm. Mostly furniture, books, icons and porcelain.

Raritāte, Čaka 45. Mon–Fri 10am–6pm, Sat 10am–4pm. Religious icons, local porcelain, paintings, coins, stamps, silverware and furniture.

Retro A, Tallinas 54. Mon–Fri 10am–5pm, Sat 10am–2pm. Porcelain, World War II memorabilia and other antiques.

Volmar, Krāmu 4. Mon–Sat 10am–8pm, Sun 11am–6pm. Upmarket antiques shop specialising in religious icons.

Folk Art & Souvenirs

Best buys are the locally made woollen mittens and socks in bright patterns. Some lovely shawls are also available. Linen is a speciality – it comes in all shapes and sizes and is usually of especially high quality. Traditional leather shoes with long thong laces make good slippers.

Art Nouveau Rīga, Strēlnieku 9. Daily 10am–6pm. The only shop in Rīga completely dedicated to Art Nouveau merchandise.

Senā Klēts, Rātslaukums 1. Mon–Fri 10am–7pm, Sat & Sun 10am–5pm. The only shop in Rīga that specialises in Latvian folk costumes is worth a visit, even if you don't intend to buy anything.

Tine, Vaļņu 2. Mon–Sat 9am–7pm, Sun 10am–5pm. The city's best selection of traditional gifts and souvenirs.

Upe, Vāgnera 5; www.upett.lv. Mon–Fri 11am–7pm, Sat 10am–4pm. The best shop for traditional Latvian music, instruments and wooden folk souvenirs.

Jewellery

There are well-designed, locally made pieces available in Latvian shops

Buying Amber

Baltic amber is believed to have begun forming about 30–40 million years ago. It is fossilised tree resin, which dripped down the bark, perhaps caught a few insects or leaves, and hardened. It is rare to find bugs or leaves, called inclusions, inside an amber piece sold in one of the shops. Numerous types exist. Often the classification is by colour. In Vilnius you can find white, yellow, orange/red and green amber.

White amber, called King's Amber, is usually off-white with some yellow accents. Similarly, yellow amber is typically yellow with white swathes of colour throughout. The orange/red

varieties are the most common and green amber is the rarest, commanding a higher price.

The only real ways to tell if amber is not plastic is to see if it floats in sea water or turns to powder when scraped with a knife; neither of which any right-minded street vendor will allow you to do. The two best streets in Vilnius to search for amber are Pilies and Aušros Vartų.

Most amber is converted into jewellery, polished or left natural and strung as necklaces or inlaid with silver, or made into rings or bracelets. Houseware, such as glasses and cups, with amber decoration is becoming more popular.

are not open on Sundays; however, tourist-based shops in the Old Town tend to be open every day. All shops listed here are in Vilnius unless otherwise stated.

Antiques

Bear in mind customs regulations when buying items made pre-1945. An export licence is needed for antiques produced before this date. **Antikvaras**, Pilies 32–4. Walk through the courtyard to find this shop full to the brim with all sorts of antiques. Most notable are its selection of musical instruments. **Dominikonų Antiques**, Dominikonų 3-2. A few pieces of furniture crowd the interior of the shop, but mostly smaller items like books and postcards can be found here. **Senasis Kuparas**, Dominikonų 14. An impressive collection of paintings, furniture, icons and samovars makes this shop almost like a museum. The staff are knowledgeable and helpful.

Books

Foreign-language literature and guides are fairly easy to find. **Akademinų Knyga**, Universiteto 4. The first stop for those looking for reference books, although it has a small selection of paperbacks downstairs. **Humanitas**, Dominikonų 5. The English-language section tends towards books on art. There's also an excellent selection of guidebooks. **Oxford Centre**, Trakų 5a. The perfect place to find the next great paperback you'll need for the overnight bus or train trip. **Prie Halės**, Pylimo 53. A small selection of paperpacks in English. **Vaga**, Gedimino 50/2. Climb up to the top floor and then look for the English-language section in a back room. There you will find a satisfying amount of books.

Records

It is worth hunting out CDs of Čiurlionis's work, as well as local jazz and folk music for souvenirs. **Muzikos bomba** (Jakšto 24/3; tel: 8-5 262 4557) has a shop located right off of Gedimino. **Thelonious** (Stiklių 12; tel: 8-5 212 1076; www.thelonious.lt) is the best place to find independent and rare LPs.

Amber

The walk from Aušros Vartų through Didžioji and on to Pilies guarantees at least 7 billion chances to purchase amber. The street hawkers tend to have less ornate items, but they all

usually made of silver. The most interesting jewellery incorporates ancient pagan styles, including the distinctive designs of the interlocking Latvian ring, the Namejs. Amber is also relatively cheap. **A&E**, Jauniela 17. Daily 10am–6pm. Hillary Clinton shopped here for designer Baltic jewellery. **Amber Line**, Torņa 4. The largest selection of amber jewellery in nearly a dozen different shops in Old Rīga. **Līvs**, Kalēju 7. Mon–Fri 10am–6pm, Sat 10am–4pm. This shop specialises in jewellery based on ancient Baltic designs. **Tornis**, Grēcinieku 11-2; www.balturotas. lv. It sells handmade jewellery based on ancient designs, as well as contemporary pieces.

Books

You can find picture books, guides and maps in the following shops: **Globuss**, Vaļņu 26. Mon–Fri 10am–7pm, Sun 11am–5pm. **Jāņa Rozes**, Barona 5. Mon–Fri 10am–7pm, Sat 10am–5pm. **Jāņa Sēta**, Elizabetes 83/85; www.mapshop.lv. Mon–Fri 10am–7pm, Sat 11am–5pm. **Robert's Books**, Antonijas 12 (entrance from Dzirnavu). Daily 11am–7pm, Sun 11am–5pm. Second-hand books in English. **Valters un Rapa**, Aspazijas 24. Mon–Fri 9am–9pm, Sat 10am–9pm, Sun 10am–4pm.

Flowers

The best place to buy flowers in Rīga is the flower market on Tērbatas next to Vērmanes Garden. The market is open 24 hours. Note that a small bunch of flowers makes a very

welcome gift if you are visiting a Latvian home. Always buy an odd number of flowers unless attending a funeral or sad occasion.

Markets

Every town has its market, selling a wide selection of food and other trinkets and providing a fascinating view of local life. As in any market, watch out for pickpockets. In Rīga the main venues are: **Āgenskalna Market** Āgenskalna tirgus, Nometņu 64. Daily 8am–7pm. Rīga's oldest market. **Central Market** (Centrālais tirgus), Prāgas 1; www.centraltirgus.lv. Daily 8am–5pm. This vast market in five old Zeppelin hangars spills down across a flea market towards the river. Friday and Saturday are its busiest days. **Latgales Market**, Sadovņikova 9a. Daily 8am–4pm. You can buy anything here from tools to pirated CDs. **Vidzemes Market** Vidzemes tirgus, Matīsa 2. Mon–Sat 8am–7pm, Sun 8am–5pm. Like the central market, but smaller.

Lithuania

It is impossible to walk down Pilies or Aušros Vartų in Vilnius's Old Town without being made aware of local amber, linen goods or woodcarvings for sale. There is a small market where street vendors sell similar items usually for a bit less. In the Old Town, Žydų and Stiklių streets also have shops that are worth looking around. Gedimino is geared to those wanting to purchase Western clothing or shoes. As a rule, shops in Lithuania

ABOVE: basketball is big in Estonia.

sell the real deal. For decidedly more special pieces it is best to stop by the **Mažasis Gintaro Muziejus** (Didžioji 6), or the **Amber Museum-Gallery** (Šv Mykolo 8), where the staff will walk you through the 40-billion-year history of amber in about half an hour.

Souvenirs

There are countless souvenir shops along Pilies Street, the main tourist road in Vilnius. Look out for *verba*, dried-flower and twig willow, and yew bouquets, which are especially popular on Palm Sunday. **Linen & Amber Studio** (Stiklių 3; Didžioji 5, 6, 10, 11; Pilies 7, 10.) has somewhat taken over the Old Town. Their multiple stores ensure even the most confused tourist is likely to buy from them. Waiting in the wings is the **Sauluva** company (Literatų 3), selling a variety of amber, linen and wood sculptures. For something different check out **Dailininkų Sajungos Parodų Salė**, Vokiečių 2, in the Contemporary Arts Centre, and find some original paintings, drawings and jewellery.

Markets

With the exception of the Flower Market, all markets are closed on Mondays and open sunrise to mid-afternoon.

Gariūnai, the biggest market in Lithuania, is outside Vilnius along the A1, where large number of shacks are strung along the right side of the highway. Everything can be found here: cars, food items, household goods, tools, wedding dresses, wigs and much more. The magic of this place is in its intensity and high amount of traffic.

Kalvarijų Market (Kalvarijų turgus), across the river in the northern suburb of Šnipiškės, is a smaller version with a less arresting variety of

goods, though occasionally a rummage can produce some exceptionally good Soviet-made cameras and lenses.

The **Flower Market** (Gėlių turgus) in Vilnius is on Basanavičiaus 42. Lithuanians offer flowers on many occasions, for almost any reason. You can find flowers here around the clock.

The magnificent **Collectors' Club** (Kolekcininkų Klubas, Club Putino 5) opens for a few hours on Saturday mornings and is the best place in the country for bizarre antiques and Soviet-era bric-a-brac.

SPORT

See the Outdoor Activites chapter, pages 72–5, for what's on generally in the three countries.

Estonia

Spectator Sports

Basketball has long been the spectator sport of choice in Estonia. Tallinn's Kalev is the most recognised of the handful of teams based around the country. The national team plays tournaments in the Saku Suurhall stadium (Paldiski mnt. 104B; tel: 6261 111).

Football Though the Estonian team doesn't excel compared to its neighbours, football is fast catching up with basketball in popularity. Major games are held in A. Le Coq Arena (Asula 4c, Tallinn; tel: 6279 940).

Horse racing On some weekends, weather permitting, horse racing takes place in Tallinn's Hipodroom (Paldiski mnt. 50; tel: 6771 677).

Participation Sports

Golf Tallinn's only golf course is the 18-hole Niitvälja Golf (tel: 6780 454) located in Niitvälja, about 30 minutes from town. There are a number of new courses elsewhere in Estonia, most notably White Beach Golf (Valgeranna; tel: 53 624 476) near Pärnu.

Squash addicts can satisfy their needs at Metro Squash in Tallinn (Tondi 17; tel: 6556 392), which will also rent equipment. In Pärnu, try Mai Squash (Papiniidu 50; tel: 4420 103).

Tennis clubs in Estonia are visitor-friendly. Good choices in Tallinn are the Rocca-al-Mare Onistar Tennis Centre (Haabersti 5; tel: 6600 520), and the Kalevi Tenniseklubi (Herne 28; tel: 6459 229). In Tartu, there's the Tamme Indoor Tennis Hall (Tamme pst. 1; tel: 7428 194) and in Pärnu, the Pärnu Tennisehall (Tammsaare

pst. 39; tel: 4427 246). Reserve courts beforehand.

Windsurfing is practised by enthusiasts at just about every beach in the country. For information about lessons for beginners at Tallinn's Pirita Beach, contact Hawaii Express (Regati 1; tel: 6398 508).

Swimming The Kalev SPA's water park (Aia 18; tel: 6493 370) offers 25-metre and 50-metre pools right in the centre of Tallinn. The water centres in Pärnu and Tartu *(see Children, page 359)* also have pools for adults.

Ice-skating is popular in winter. In Tallinn the most picturesque venue by far is the outdoor Uisuplats along Harju street in the Old Town (tel: 6101 035), usually open Nov–Mar. In Tartu, try the Lõunakeskus Ice-Skating Rink in the Lõunakeskus shopping mall (Ringtee 75; tel: 7315 616).

Latvia

Spectator Sports

Ice hockey is a national obsession, and Latvians worship their hip-checking heroes, especially the ones that play in the National Hockey League. Each year at the end of April businesses close early and locals head out to their favourite pubs to watch their team strive for glory in the World Hockey Championship. A victory often leads to gatherings of hundreds of fans in Rīga, who parade about the city shouting slogans and singing songs, often ending their wanderings at the embassy of their vanquished foes.

Rīga also has its own hockey team, Dynamo Rīga (www.dinamoriga.eu), which competes in the Russian Federation's Kontinental Hockey League. With teams located across the entire breadth of Russia as well as in Latvia, Belarus and Kazakhstan, the league spans nearly a dozen time zones. Many of the teams have adopted their old names from the Soviet era, hence all of the metallurgists, dynamos and locomotives. Dynamo Rīga home games take place at Arena Rīga (Skanstes 21, www.arenriga.com).

Football doesn't command the same amount of respect that hockey does, but it became more popular in the aftermath of Latvia's surprising victory over Turkey to qualify for the Euro 2004 Football Championship in Portugal – a feat not since equalled. Latvia's most successful team is FC Skonto, which won the Latvian Championship every year since the club's founding in 1991 until 2005, a *Guinness Book* world record. FC Ventspils reached the group stage of the UEFA Europa League in 2009.

Matches in Rīga are held at the Skonto Stadium, E. Melngaiļa 1a, www.skontofc.lv, at the Ventspils Olympic Centre in Ventspils, Sporta 7/9; tel: 6362 2587; www.ocventspils.lv; and in Liepāja at the Daugava Stadium in the Seaside Park.

Participation Sports

Bobsleigh and luge The run at Sigulda, just a short ride from Rīga, hosts international events that draw huge numbers of spectators. When professionals aren't training on the difficult run at the weekend, an instructor will take you for a quick run down the mountain year-round at speeds in excess of 125km/h (80mph) for only 7–35Ls per person.

Golf Choose from an exclusive 18-hole lakeside course (OZO, Mīlgrāvja 16; tel: 6739 4399; www.ozogolf.lv) owned by millionaire hockey star Sandis Ozoliņš, the second Latvian to play in the NHL, another 18-hole course at Saliena (Egļuciems; www.salienagolf.com), near Jūrmala ,and a less challenging nine-hole course by the airport (Viesturi; tel: 2644 4390; www.golfsviesturi.lv).

Shooting Visitors can fire off rounds from weapons as diverse as World War II-era Lugers and AK-47s (Kalashnikovs) at the RegroS rifle range, Daugavgrīvas 23a, Rīga; tel: 6760 1705; www.regros.lv. Ex-military staff know enough English from their fairly frequent encounters with foreign tourists. It also has the added benefit of being located in an underground Cold War bomb shelter on the Pārdaugava side of the river.

Skiing and snowboarding Latvia's tiny hills won't challenge your downhill skills, but many resorts have created special parks for snowboarders with half pipes and other attractions. The best are: Baiļi (Valmiera, 107km/ 65 miles from Rīga); tel: 2928 4119; www.baili.lv; Gaiziņkalns (Madona county, 120km/75 miles from Rīga); tel: 6482 8176; www.gaizins.lv; Kaķīšu Trase (Sigulda, 50km/30 miles from Rīga); www.kakiskalns.lv; Žagarkalns (Cēsis, 90km/55 miles from Rīga); tel: 2626 6266; www.zagarkalns.lv; Zviedru Cepure (Sabile, 120km/75 miles from Rīga); tel: 2640 5405; www.zviedrucepure.lv.

Lithuania

Spectator Sports

Basketball is a national obsession, and arguments over teams are more likely to turn violent than ones over political issues. The Lithuanian Olympic basketball team regularly wins medals, their most recent honour being to become once again the European champions in 2010. The best-known national team is the Kaunas-based Žalgiris team, but Vilnius's Lietuvos Rytas have begun to make a name for themselves outside the country. Lietuvos Rytas (also the name of a popular Lithuanian newspaper) team's stadium should be contacted for ticket sales (Ozo 14; tel: 8-5 247 7551). Major local (for example Žalgiris versus Rytas) or international basketball events are held at Vilnius's Siemens Arena (Ozo 14; tel: 8-5 247 7576). To see league champions Žalgiris Kaunas requires a drive to Kaunas's Darius and Girėnas Sports Complex (Perkūno 3; tel: 8-37 200 514). A new stadium is currently under construction and is due to be completed in 2011.

Football is growing in popularity, with games often shown in a few of the city's establishments.

Participation Sports

Cycling, also growing in popularity, is best practised in parks or on the country's rural cycle paths. For information about routes and how to meet other serious cyclists, check out the Lithuanian-based BalticCycle site, www.balticcycle.lt, which also hires out bicycles in Vilnius and Klaipėda.

Bowling is also popular. Vilnius's bowling alleys include the small Boulingo Klubas (Jasinskio 16; tel: 8-5 249 6600) and the spacious and modern Cosmic Bowling Center (Vytenio 6/23; tel: 8-5 233 9909).

Go-karting (Savanorių 178; tel: 8-5 231 1507) is one of the more popular ways to pass the time during the warmer part of the year. A year-round indoor track can be found inside the Panorama shopping centre at Saltoniškių 9.

Golf is slowly gaining a following. There are now two courses in Vilnius (www.golfclub.lt, www.capitals.lt), one in Kaunas (www.elnias.lt) and one in Klaipėda (www.nationalgolf.lt).

Flying is another national obsession. Visitors can get in on the act by learning to fly a glider or light aircraft or by parachuting out of a plane at the Kaunas Flying Club (Kauno aeroklubas; Veiverių 132; www.aerokaunas.lt) inside the old city airport. Also, for a fee, you can fly in a fighter jet. Contact www.activeholidays.lt for more information.

Ice sports are perennially popular. Although not always the safest option, sledging attracts fair numbers to Vilnius's hills. The lack of mountains ensures that skiing is mostly of the cross-country variety. An ice rink can be found inside the large shopping complex Akropolis (Ozo 25; tel: 8-5 6599 1974), northwest of the centre.

Countryside Cycling and horse riding are great ways to see the countryside, and the numerous lakes are good for swimming or canoeing in the summer. For information about national parks contact the Vilnius Tourist Information centres (see page 371).

TOURS

Estonia

Around Tallinn

Until recently Tallinn was strictly orientated towards group travel, but now the city offers an increasing variety of tours for individuals, from pub tours to ghost walks. Tourist

BELOW: in the Lithuanian forest.

Information (see page 371) can provide a comprehensive list, as well as help you book your own guide (48 hours' notice required). In spring and summer a tent located across from the Old Town office provides separate, alternative-style tours for about €10.

One of the most popular general tours is the Tallinn Official Sightseeing Tour operated by Reisiekspert (tel: 6108 616), a combination bus and walking tour that covers all the city's major sights. It runs three times daily and costs €20 (free with Tallinn Card). Phone for schedules and meeting places.

Tallinn City Tour (Kadaka tee 62a; tel: 6279 080) uses London-style buses to run three different hop-on hop-off routes. A 24-hour ticket for all three lines costs €16 (free with Tallinn Card).

A more adventurous option is the Welcome to Tallinn bicycle tour organised by City Bike (tel: 5111 819). It departs from the City Bike Hostel (Uus 33) at 11am and 5pm daily in the warmer months. Phone ahead during the off-season. The tour covers the city's outlying green districts, the beach area and the Old Town. The €16 tour price includes bicycle rental and mineral water. Book at least one hour in advance.

Around Estonia

There are a number of travel companies that will organise pre-packaged or tailor-made trips to the various regions of the country, including the islands. Among these are Baltic Tours (Jõe 5; tel: 6300 460; www.baltictours.eu), which offers tours from the standard sightseeing to adventure trips with off-roading and ice climbing; Via Hansa (Rüütli 13; tel: 6277 870; www.viahansa.com), which also has thematic tours, as well as the all-inclusive country tours. In all cases, tours should be booked well in advance. Nature and rural tours have become particularly popular in the past few years. The non-profit Estonian Rural Tourism Organisation, Eesti Maaturism, lists over 100 specific tours and packages on its website, www.maaturism.ee. For bog-walking, canoeing or tracking wolves in Soomaa National Park, contact Soomaa.com (tel: 5061 896).

Latvia

Around Rīga

Rīga City Tours offers a tour of the city from the comfort of a red double-decker bus. Once you've paid for your ticket you can hop on or off at any stop for 48 hours. Tours begin at the Riflemen monument (www.citytour.lv). Amber Way, tel: 6727 1915, specialises in English-language tours of Rīga on foot, bus and boat. Tickets can be bought at the Rīga Information Centre, Rātslaukums 6. Visit www.sightseeing.lv. Rīga Out There (www.out-there.eu) is run by an Australian expat who has put together a wide variety of tours such as walking tours of Old Rīga and trips to Rundāle Palace, as well as more quirky activities that include nightlife tours, bungee-jumping, shooting with AK-47s, bobsleighing and even curling.

Boat tours depart nearly every hour from the Old Rīga bank of the River Daugava in the summer and usually cost no more than 3–5Ls. Longer boat rides may also include trips to Mežaparks and Jūrmala. You can also take boat tours on the Rīga Canal in retro wooden launches every 30 minutes in the summer from Bastion Hill (www.kmk.lv).

Bike tours. For cycling or even segway tours around Rīga contact

http:// Riga bike tours, www.rigabiketours.lv, or Segway tours at www.segway.lv.

Nature Tours

Latvia is famous for its rich nature and fauna and its great outdoors. The following travel agents arrange tailor-made nature/outdoor packages.

Country Holidays, Kalnciema 40, Rīga; tel: 6761 7600; www.celotajs.lv; and Makars Tourism Agency, Sigulda, Peldu 2; tel: 2924 4948; www.makars.lv.

Beer Tours

The following breweries offer tours of their facilities that include a tasting: Užavas Alus, Zaksi, Užava distr.; tel: 6363 0595; www.uzavas-alus.lv; Valmiermuižas Alus, Dzirnavu 2a, Valmiermuiža; http://valmiermuiza.lv.

Castle and Manor House Tours

Latvia's countryside is dotted with castles, palaces and elegant manor houses, many offering hotel rooms. For routes and descriptions, visit www.pilis.lv.

Lithuania

Around Vilnius

A great many Vilnius hotels have an arrangement with a tour company for specialised or even run-of-the-mill tours of the city or surroundings. Bus tours of the Old Town with explanations in English are also available. In good weather look for the open-top bus parked at the end of Didžioji outside the Town Hall.

Trips to Trakai and walking tours of the Old Town are the most popular and are offered by almost all agencies. Individual tours of specific interest, such as a tour of Jewish Vilnius, are also offered but usually by only a handful of people. For an authentic, unsanitised Jewish tour, contact Yulik Gurvitch (tel: 8-5 6999 0709), Ilya Lempertas (tel: 8-5 6871 3285), Regina Kopilevich (tel: 8-5 6990 5456), or Justina Petrauskaitė (tel: 8-5 6995 4064).

You can also take one-day cycling or canoe excursions.

Around Lithuania

Cultural, fishing and horse riding tours are offered by Lithuanian Tours, Šeimyniškių 18, Vilnius; tel: 8-5 272 4154; www.lithuaniantours.com

Nature Tours

A number of companies, such as Ave Vita (www.avevita.lt), offer nature tours. The Vilnius-based Lithuanian Ornithological Society (tel: 8-5 213 0498; www.birdlife.lt) are the people to contact for all bird-related activities.

The tourist information centre has details on all tour companies and operators.

Below: Daugava riverboat, Latvia.

A HANDY SUMMARY OF PRACTICAL INFORMATION, ARRANGED ALPHABETICALLY

A ccidents and Emergencies

An all-encompassing emergency number, **112**, works in all three countries. They try to staff with English-speaking personnel at all times, though a non-English-speaker may get your call.

You can also call:
Police in Estonia, **110**. In Latvia and Lithuania, **02**.
Paramedics in Latvia and Lithuania, **03**.

B udgeting for Your Trip

Food, transport and entertainment are all relatively inexpensive. Lithuania is, overall, the cheapest of the three countries, Estonia the most expensive, with Latvia in between. A meal, without drinks, will typically cost from €7 to €10. In the capitals' most expensive restaurants, it will be from €20 to €40 respectively. A large beer in a local pub costs €1.60–2.00, and in a touristy café €3–5. Soft drinks are €0.70–1.

The rate for a double room in a mid-range hotel is from €45 in Latvia to €90 in Estonia, with Lithuania in between, but quite decent rooms can

be found for under €35 in Lithuania and €50 in Estonia.

Museum tickets are nominal, and one- to three-day tourist cards, available at tourist offices, give discounts in the capitals.

C hildcare

Children take a central part in Baltic life and are welcomed in restaurants and other outings. Parks in the cities cater for children, but don't expect Disneyworld. *(For children's activities, see page 358.)*

Some hotels offer child-care facilities, and children under seven travel either half-price or free on public transport.

Climate and Clothing

July is by far the best time to visit. This is when the days are sunniest and it is least likely to rain. June, on the other hand, is usually rainy, especially around Midsummer's Eve in the third or fourth week of the month. In June the temperature is usually mild: the last of spring's icy spells having ended in May in Estonia and earlier in Lithuania. July is the hottest month,

when temperatures can reach up to 30°C (86°F). The average for the month is a pleasant 17°C (63°F).

In winter, temperatures as low as −30°C (−22°F) have been recorded in Estonia and −20°C (−4°F) in Lithuania. In recent years, with the exception of 2009, winter temperatures have tended to be milder, seldom falling below around the −5°C (23°F) mark, and temperatures inland are generally lower than near the coast. Despite this, winters can often seem extremely cold because of the piercing coastal winds. *(See climate charts overleaf.)*

Snow is most prolonged in Estonia, where it can fall from January through to March. The average fall had been decreasing for some time, but 2009 saw record snowfalls, and the Baltics were covered in the white stuff until mid-April.

The biggest drawback for visitors in winter is generally not the cold or the snow, but the lack of sunlight. From early November through until late March darkness never seems to lift completely, and the six or seven hours of daylight are often marred by overcast, misty conditions.

TRANSPORT

ACCOMMODATION

EATING OUT

ACTIVITIES

A – Z

LANGUAGE

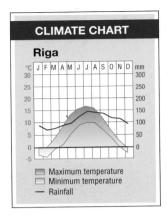

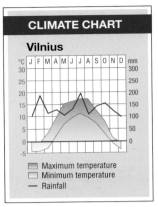

CLIMATE CHART

Riga

CLIMATE CHART

Tallinn

CLIMATE CHART

Vilnius

What to Wear

Although people tend to dress up for concerts, the theatre and official business, the dress code in all three countries is otherwise fairly informal. When packing, bear in mind how cold the winter climate can be. From November to April minimum requirements are a heavy woollen jumper, leggings and something thick-soled and waterproof on your feet. Thermal underwear can also be welcome. From January to March it is highly advisable to wear gloves and a hat and scarf.

In summer, lightweight garments and even shorts and T-shirts are adequate. Evenings can turn chilly, so bring a sweater and jacket to keep you warm. It is also advisable to pack waterproof clothing and an umbrella. Sensible, comfortable footwear is highly recommended as the cities' cobbled streets are uncomfortable in thin-soled shoes and treacherous in high heels.

Crime

Violent crime tends to be gangland-related, and assaults on foreigners are rare and usually involve excessive alcohol use at dodgy striptease clubs in Rīga. Take the usual precautions against theft that you would when travelling anywhere – anything that you are not physically attached to is liable to walk, so be watchful. Further good advice is to remain sober; nothing could present a more appealing target than an inebriated tourist staggering through dimly lit streets.

D isabled Travellers

The medieval Baltic capitals are a headache for anyone in a wheelchair.

Pavements can be rocky, kerbs steep, and many restaurants, cafés, shops and museums can only be accessed via cramped, narrow staircases. On the positive side, traffic in the Old Towns is usually restricted, leaving the streets wide open for pedestrian explorers.

Wheelchair-bound visitors will need to ask numerous, pointed and direct questions about a hotel's facilities in order to ensure they can be accommodated. The largest and newest hotels are fairly accessible, and almost always have rooms specially equipped for disabled guests.

Few buses, trams and trolleybuses have equipment to aid in boarding, but phone around the major taxi companies and you're likely to find a car that's designed for disabled passengers.

The situation gets progressively worse as you leave the capitals and go into more rural regions.

E lectricity

The electricity in all three countries is 220 volts AC, 50Hz. Plugs are the round, two-pinned variety used in Continental Europe. In Estonia, adaptors can be found in electronic shops and in department stores such as Tallinna Kaubamaja, and are readily available in Lithuania, but you are advised to take one with you if travelling in Latvia, or the countryside.

Embassies and Consulates

The embassies are all in the capital cities. When there is no local embassy, Australians, Irish, New Zealanders and South Africans should contact the UK Embassy, or their own embassy in a neighbouring country.

Tallinn
Canada (Representative office only), Toomkooli 13; tel: 6273 311.
Ireland Vene 2; tel: 6811 888.
UK Wismari 6; tel: 6674 700.
US Kentmanni 20; tel: 6688 100.
Riga
Canada Baznīcas 20/22; tel: 6781 3945; fax: 6781 3960
Ireland Alberta 13; tel: 6703 9370; fax: 670 393 71
UK Alunāna 5; tel: 6777 4700; fax: 6777 4707
US Raiņa bulvāris 7; tel: 6703 6200; fax: 6782 0047
Vilnius
Australia (Consulate) Vilniaus 23; tel: 212 3369; fax: 212 3369
Canada Jogailos 4; tel: 249 0950; fax: 249 7865
UK Antakalnio 2; tel: 246 2900; fax: 246 2901
US Akmenų 6; tel: 266 5500; fax: 266 5510

G ays and Lesbians

Though the situation is generally improving, especially in the cities, attitudes in the Baltic States towards homosexuality are not as liberal as those elsewhere in the West. Overt displays, such as holding hands, are not yet socially acceptable and may attract the wrong sort of attention.

Tallinn has a small but active gay night scene, which encompasses a handful of bars and clubs. X-Baar (Tatari 1) is the most established of these, but Angel (Sauna 1) is busier and more club-like.

In **Rīga** the hippest gay and lesbian club is Golden, www.mygoldenclub.com.

A small male gay scene does exist in **Vilnius**, but most gay organisations are underground and often geared simply towards providing a social and

Genealogy

Those wanting to track down information about their Baltic ancestry can get help from several agencies that specialise in such matters.

Estonia

Estonian Genealogical Society (Eesti Genealoogia Selts); www. genealoogia.ee. The society doesn't have an office, but its extensive website in English is an excellent starting point for research.
Estonian Biographical Centre (Eesti Isikuloo Keskus), Tiigi 10-51, Tartu; tel: 7420 882; www.isik.ee. The centre specialises in genealogical research and, for a fee, will track down relatives and create a family tree.
Estonian Historical Archives (Eesti Ajalooarhiiv), Liivi 4, Tartu; tel: 7387 555; fax: 7387 510; www.eha.ee. Archivists charge an hourly rate for researching and creating a family tree, but visitors can look through the archives at no expense.

Latvia

In Latvia contact the **State History Archive** (Valsts Vēstures Arhīvs) in Rīga, at Slokas 16; tel: 6761 3118; www.lvva.gov.lv.

Lithuania

In Lithuania there are several specialist agencies to assist you with your enquiries.
Lithuanian Central State Archive (Lietuvos centrinis valstybės archyvas), Milašiaus 21; tel: 247 7811. A directory of people living in Lithuania during the Nazi occupation (1941–2).
Lithuanian State Historical Archive (Lietuvos valstybės istorijos archyvas), Gerosios Vilties 10; tel: 213 7482. A Church registry until 1940.
Vilnius Civilian Archive (Vilnaus civilinės metrikacijos dokumentų archyvas), Kalinausko 21; tel: 233 7846. Birth, death and marriage certificates from 1940 to the present.

Tallinn

Pharmacies (apteek)
Tōnismäe Apteek, Tōnismägi 5, tel: 6442 282, in central Tallinn runs an all-night pharmacy window.
Hospitals (haigla)
Tallinn Central Hospital, Ravi 18; tel: 1900 or 6207 040. Open 24 hours.
The paramedic service in Tallinn runs a first-aid hotline (tel: 6971 145) that can give you advice or direct you to a hospital.
Dentists (hambaravi)
Baltic Medical Partners, Tartu mnt. 32; tel: 6010 550; fax: 6010 549.
Tallinna Hambapolikliinik, Toompuiestee 4; tel: 6119 230.
Sexually Transmitted Diseases
Aids Information and Support Centre, Kopli 32; tel: 6413 165.

Rīga

Pharmacies (aptiekas)
Ģimenes aptieka, Tallinas 57b; tel: 6731 4211. Open 24 hours.
Mēness aptieka, Aspazijas 20 (entrance from Audēju); tel: 6722 3826. Open 24 hours.
Hospitals (slimnīcas)
ARS, Skolas 5; tel: 6720 1007; www. ars-med.lv. For all emergencies.
Diplomatic Service Medical Centre, Elizabetes 57; tel: 6722 9942; www. dsmc.lv. Full English-speaking staff.
Paediatrics
Dr Tirāns, Bruņinieku 67; tel: 6731 5594. American-educated paediatrician.
Dentists (zobārsti)
Adenta, Skanstes 13; tel: 6733 9300; www.adenta.lv. Canadian and local dentists.
Diplomatic Service Medical Centre, Elizabetes 57; tel: 6722 9942; www.dsmc.lv.
Vaccinations
Veselības dienests, Brīvības gatve 195; www.vd.lv.

dating scene. The hugely controversial Gay Pride march in 2010 was heckled by swastika-waving neo-Nazis. Two members of parliament who actively tried to stop the march on the day were promptly arrested.

❐ ealth and Medical Care

No vaccinations are required. One concern, however, only applies to visitors who plan to spend time deep in the Estonian wilderness or in the wilds of the Latvian or Lithuanian countryside, in which case a vaccination against tick-borne encephalitis is recommended. People are advised to check themselves for ticks – tiny black mites in the skin – after tramping through tall brush.

There are no real problems with medical care, and most medicines are available in all three countries. If you feel unwell, your best first stop is a pharmacy, where you can often find most of what you might need to cure common, temporary ailments. Many pharmacies carry everything from Pepto Bismol, Advil and antibiotics to such goods as Visine, condoms and Slim Fast.

If over-the-counter medicines do not do the trick, it is advisable to seek help from a qualified doctor.

With the European reciprocation of treatment, UK visitors should theoretically need only to present a European Health Insurance Card (see www.ehic.org.uk, or apply for a card at a UK Post Office), for free treatment, but you are strongly advised to take out private insurance, too.

Although healthcare systems are undergoing crises due to budget cuts, foreigners with money are generally well-treated. Doctors and nurses are grossly underpaid but still try to provide an adequate service. If you want to, you can show your appreciation by giving a gift after you have been treated.

Hospitals are usually spartan but sanitary, and the healthcare is generally good. For an ambulance, dial 112 in all three countries.

BELOW: Lithuanian police.

ABOVE: rural bus stop, Lithuania.

Vilnius
Pharmacies (vaistinė)
Eurovaistinė Ukmergės 282; tel: 230 3759. A long way from the centre and best reached by taxi. Open 24 hours.
Vokiečių Vaistinė Didžioji 13; tel: 212 4232. Good Old Town pharmacy. Mon–Fri 9am–8pm, Sat & Sun 10am–6pm.
Hospitals
Baltic–American Clinic, Nemenčinės 54a; tel: 234 2020; www.bak.lt. Northeast of the city in a quiet forested suburb, the clinic is open 24 hours and is by far the most recommended and best known.
Vilnius University Emergency Hospital (Vilniaus Greitosios Pagalbos Universitetinė Ligoninė), Šiltnamių 29; tel: 216 9212.
Dentists (stomatologos or dantistas)
Dental care in Lithuania is of a very high quality and is considerably cheaper than in the West.
Dr Br. Sidaravičius, Klaipėdos 2/14-3; tel: 262 9760. Mon–Fri 8am–8pm.
Stomatologijos Gydykla, Dominikonų 3-45; tel: 262 8482. Daily 8am–7pm.
Gidenta, Vienuolio 14-3; tel: 261 7143. Mon–Fri 9am–7pm.
Sexually Transmitted Diseases
Lithuanian Aids Centre, Vytenio 37/59; tel/fax: 233 0111; www.aids.lt. Daily 8am–4pm.

Left Luggage
Estonia
In cities, left-luggage services can be found at all major transportation hubs.
In Tallinn Airport, it is in the main departure hall, next to the information desk. At the train station, the room is in the centre rear of the main hall, closest to the tracks. The passenger port's A and D terminals have both luggage rooms and lockers.

At the bus station, the left luggage office is in the basement, and there are also lockers immediately to the right of the ticket windows.

Latvia
Although many small stations in the Latvian countryside may lack left-luggage rooms or lockers, Rīga has proper facilities in each of its major transportation hubs.
At the airport, store luggage for 2Ls per item per day in the arrivals hall at the end of the corridor to the left of the exit (open 24 hours).
The luggage room at the bus station is located on the left side when entering from the platforms, and storage costs 0.40–1Ls per hour depending on the size and weight of your bag (5am–midnight). A luggage room for 0.50–1.50Ls per day is available in the basement of the train station (4.30am–midnight).

Lithuania
Most major transit points in Lithuania have left-luggage facilities (bagažinė). In Vilnius there are 24-hour left-luggage facilities at the airport and in the train station.
Left-luggage facilities in the Vilnius bus station (Mon–Sat 5.30am–9.45pm, Sun 7am–8.45pm) are also available.

Maps
In **Estonia**, free maps of Tallinn's Old Town are readily available in passenger ferries, hotel receptions and the tourist information office. More complete city maps, as well as maps of other cities and regions, produced by Regio, can be bought at bookshops and larger magazine kiosks.
In **Latvia**, city maps are readily available at the Rīga Tourist Information Centre. A wide selection

of inexpensive maps and guides of Latvia and its other cities can be purchased at the Jāņa Sēta Map Shop, Elizabetes 83/85; www.mapshop.lv.
In **Lithuania** Jāņa Sēta maps are available at tourist offices, bookshops and petrol stations. There are also maps by the Vilnius publishers Briedis. Several tourist information centres also publish free maps to their respective towns and cities.

Money
Estonians parted ways with their kroons and adopted the European single currency, the euro, at the beginning of 2011. Each euro is worth about £0.80–£0.90. Paper bills come in denominations of €500, €200, €100, €50, €20, €10 and €5. Coins come in €2, €1, and 50-, 20-, 10-, 5-, 2- and 1-cent varieties.
Latvia's lat is worth roughly £1.20 (1.40 euros). One lat consists of 100 santīmi, with 1, 2, 5, 10, 20 and 50 santīmi and 1 and 2 lat coins. Banknotes are available in denominations of 5, 10, 20, 50, 100 and 500 lats.
Lithuania's litas (Lt) is pegged to the euro at 3.45 to 1 euro. Currently there are about 4Lt to £1. Litas come in denominations of 10, 20, 50, 100, 200 and 500Lt notes. Coins are divided into the valuable – 1, 2 and 5Lt – and the nearly worthless centai, of which there are 50, 20, 10, 5, 2 and 1.
Currency exchange Tallinn's Old Town has recently become chock-full of brightly lit exchange offices, nearly all of which offer spectacularly bad rates. These can be avoided by exchanging currency in a bank, drawing cash from ATMs, or using credit cards, which are almost universally accepted.
In Vilnius, exchange bureaux are for the most part inside banks. This ensures that changing money between 9am and 5pm is relatively easy, but outside those times it can be a bit more difficult – although the Parex bank outside the train station in Vilnius is open 24 hours. At a pinch one can turn to exchanges at major hotels and a few tourist-targeting, after-hours exchanges. Rates will be less favourable than in the banks.
In Rīga, exchange booths are easier to find. Some may look questionably makeshift, but these are perfectly legitimate, and many are open all night.
Credit cards In the major cities almost all upmarket or mid-range

establishments such as hotels, restaurants, nightclubs, bars and shops will accept most major credit cards. However, it is always best to double-check before committing to or eating up all of your intended purchase. Outside the main towns and cites, cash remains the main currency.

ATMs are easy to find in the cities and accept all major credit and bank cards, but before leaving home check with your bank that your card will be acceptable.

Travellers' cheques The number of establishments accepting travellers' cheques are less frequent, but you can cash them at most banks. They cannot be used as currency.

N ewspapers and Magazines

The Baltic Times (Rupniecibas 1-5; tel: 722 9978; fax: 722 6041; editor@ baltictimes.com; www.baltictimes.com), printed in Rīga, is a weekly pan-Baltic English-language newspaper covering all three states. Formerly the standby of expats and visitors, it can still be found in some kiosks and hotels, but has been surpassed in quality by online sources such as *Baltic Reports* (http://balticreports.com).

Tallinn In Your Pocket, *Rīga In Your Pocket* and *Vilnius In Your Pocket* are handy English-language city guides, published six times a year with an updated calendar of events, full reviews about the cities' ever-changing restaurants, cafés and bars, and a selection of tourist sites. Once or twice per year the In Your Pocket team publishes *Pärnu In Your Pocket* and *Tartu In Your Pocket* (see also http://inyourpocket.com/estonia, http://inyourpocket.com/latvia, http://inyourpocket.com/lithuania).

The *International Herald Tribune*, the *Financial Times*, *The Times* and the *New York Times* are also on sale in the main hotels and at larger newsstands.

O pening Hours

With the exception of major shopping centres, which usually open seven days a week 10am–10pm (9pm in Estonia), most shops open 10am–7pm (6pm in Estonia), Sat 10am–5pm, and close on Sundays.

Banks and government offices are generally open weekdays 9am–5pm. Most museums are open 11am–5pm (6pm in Estonia) and many are closed on Mondays and Tuesdays.

Typical office hours are Mon–Fri 9am–5pm.

P ostal Services

There are good international postal links. Letters generally take about five days to reach the rest of Europe and around seven days to arrive in the US. Stamps can be bought at post offices or hotels, which are also the best places to post your letters.

Tallinn

Tallinn Central Post Office: Narva mnt. 1 (opposite the Viru Centre); tel: 661 6616/617 7037; info@post.ee; www.post.ee. Mon–Fri 8am–8pm, Sat 9am–5pm. Most services are handled in the main hall, upstairs. Packages, including those sent by EMS courier service, are sent and received in an office with an entrance around the left side of the building.
DHL Express Centre, Rävala pst. 5; tel: 6652 555.
Federal Express, Kesk-Sõjamäe 10a; tel: 8002 345; fax: 6068 690.
TNT Express Worldwide, Kesk-Sõjamäe 10a; tel: 627 1900; fax: 627 1901; info.ee@tnt.com
UPS, Valukoja 22; tel: 6664 700; fax: 6664 701; customer.service@upspartner.ee.

Rīga

Rīga Central Post Office, Brīvības bulv. 32; tel: 6750 2815; www.pasts.lv. Mon–Fri 8am–8pm, Sat 8am–6pm, Sun 10am–4pm.
Cargo Bus, Gogoļa 13 (entrance from Puškina); tel: 6722 5566; www.cargo bus.eu. Express parcel service in the Baltic and Scandinavian regions.
DHL, Mārupe, Plieņciema 35; tel: 6771 5500; www.dhl.lv.
FedEx, tel: 8000 5300.
TNT Express Worldwide, Mārupe, Plieņciema 11; tel: 6766 8000; www.tnt.lv.
UPS, Ulmaņa 2; tel: 6780 5650; www.ups.com.

BELOW: Lithuanian post box.

Vilnius

Central Post Office (Centrinis Paštas), Gedimino 7; tel: 262 5468. Mon–Fri 7am–7pm, Sat 9am–4pm. There's also a post office in the Akropolis shopping centre *(see page 359)* open daily 10am–10pm.
DHL, Dariaus ir Girėno 81; tel: 236 0700; www.dhl.lt. Mon–Fri 8am–6.30pm.
Express Mail Service, Geležinkelio 6; tel: 239 8333. Mon–Fri 8am–6pm.
FedEx, Gustaičio 1; tel: (8-800) 202 00; www.fedex.com. Mon–Fri 8am–5pm.
TNT, Dariaus ir Girėno 44; tel: (8-800) 252 22; www.tnt.lt. Mon–Fri 8am–5pm.
UPS, Eigulių 15; tel: 247 2222; www.ups.com. Mon–Fri 8am–6pm.

Public Holidays

Public holidays are cause for great celebration in the Baltics. Each state flies the flags of the other two nations on these special days, as well as their own flag – in Latvia the national flag must, by law, be displayed prominently on facades by the front door on public holidays.
(See also Festivals, pages 354–5.)

Estonia

January New Year's Day (1)
February Independence Day (24)
March/April Good Friday and Easter Sunday
May Spring Day (1)
June Victory Day (23), Midsummer (24)
August Day of Restoration of Independence (20)
December Christmas (24–25), Boxing Day (26)
Memorial Day
June First mass deportations to Siberia in 1941 (14)

Latvia

January New Year's Day (1)
March/April Good Friday and Easter Monday
May May Day (1)
May Proclamation of Independence (4)
June Līgo Day (23), Jāņi summer solstice (24)
November Independence Day (18)
December Christmas (24/25/26)
December New Year's Eve (31)
Memorial Days
March mass deportation of Balts to Siberia in 1949 (25)
May World War II Memorial Day (9)
June first mass deportation of Balts to Siberia, 1941 (14)
July Jewish Genocide Day (4)

November 1919 battle, during which invading German forces were repulsed from Rīga (11)

Lithuania

January New Year (1)
February Independence Day (1918) (16)
March Restoration of Lithuania's statehood (11)
March/April Easter
May Labour Day (1), Mothers' Day (first Sunday)
June St John's Day/Joninės (23–24)
July Crowning of Mindaugas, Day of Statehood (6)
August Feast of the Assumption (15)
November All Saints' Day (1)
December Christmas (25–26)

T elephones

You can direct dial to any country on the globe from almost any phone in the Baltic States. Public phones are card-operated and are also WiFi hotspots. Instructions are available inside the phone booths. Colourful chip-cards can be bought from post offices, kiosks, shops and hotels. Some card phones can also be used with your credit card, and all of them accept incoming calls. Near-universal mobile phone ownership has rendered public card phones increasingly rare. To call anywhere in Estonia and Latvia, just dial the full seven- or eight-digit number. In Lithuania, however, it's necessary to insert an 8 at the beginning of every number, except when calling within a city from one fixed line telephone to another, or if you're dialling from outside the country.

To call any of the countries from abroad, dial your country's international dialling code (00 in Europe) and the country code:
    Estonia 372
    Latvia 371
    Lithuania 370
followed by the number.

To call abroad dial 00, followed by the country code and then the number. You can call abroad from any phone.

Fax and Telegrams

Faxes and telegrams can be sent from central post offices. Faxes can also be sent from major hotels.

Mobile Phones

Mobile phones are popular in the Baltics, and the same GSM phone you use in Europe and the UK will also work here. You will automatically be switched over to a local service once you arrive. Check with your provider at home to see if there are

partnership agreements that will make roaming cheaper. To avoid roaming charges altogether, you can get a local number by buying an inexpensive starter kit, sold in kiosks and shops, which comes with prepaid credit.

Estonian mobile numbers start with 50–57. To call a mobile phone, simply dial the subscriber's number. From abroad, dial Estonia's country code (372), followed by the subscriber's number.

Latvian mobile phone numbers have eight digits, starting with 2 or 6. Digital rules apply (see above). From abroad, dial Latvia's country code (371), followed by the subscriber's mobile phone number.

Lithuanian mobile phone numbers always begin with an 8. To dial a mobile phone, dial 8, wait for the changed tone, then dial the number. When calling a Lithuanian mobile from abroad, dial the country code (370), but drop the 8 so that the number begins with 6. All cities in Lithuania have a code. When calling from abroad or from one city to another the code must be dialled. For example, when calling from Kaunas to Vilnius one must press 8, wait for the changed tone and then dial 5 (Vilnius city code) followed by the number. A prepaid SIM card can be purchased in order to use your own mobile phone in the country. Bitė (Žemaitės 15, www.bite.lt), Omnitel (Jasinskio 16b, www.omnitel.lt) and TELE2 (Vytenio 9/25, www.tele2.lt) provide such services.

Internet

Most hotels have websites and accept reservations through them. Public internet access points and internet cafés charge about £1–1.50 per hour

of surfing time. Many hotels and cafés in the Baltic capitals offer free WiFi as standard. In city centres, free access is also widely available in pubs, shopping malls and many public parks.

Television and Radio

Most major hotels have rooms with radios and satellite televisions; the majority of them will come with BBC World, CNN, SkyNews, plus a clutch of other channels such as Eurosport, Discovery and Cartoon Network. Much of the entertainment programming on local channels is in English with subtitles in Estonia, but not so often the case in Latvia or Lithuania. You may also be able to pick up channels from the neighbouring countries.

Television stations

Estonia There are five channels broadcasting domestically, as well as a handful of cable-based entertainment channels. Eesti Televisioon (ETV and ETV2), the public channels, broadcast mainly cultural and documentary programming. Kanal 2 is a commercial station whose programming leans heavily towards soap operas and reality TV. Higher-quality entertainment programmes appear on TV3 and TV6. Nearly all households and businesses use digital, cable or satellite TV systems.

Latvia The two state-owned channels LTV1 and 7 show a variety of dated sitcoms from the US as well as local programming which is rarely of interest, even to Latvians and Russians. Privately owned LNT, TV3 and TV5 often broadcast good films, reality shows and even sporting

BELOW: modern communications.

events, but most are dubbed in Latvian with Russian subtitles.

Lithuania The three local channels are LTV (the national broadcasting station) and the privately owned and more popular LNK and TV3. Foreign movies or television shows are almost always dubbed into Lithuanian.

Radio

Estonia There are 18–21 radio stations on Tallinn's FM band. The state-owned Eesti Raadio airs the BBC World Service on 103.5FM every day midnight–6am, 7am–8am and 7pm–8pm.

Latvia There are over 15 FM radio stations in the capital, notably Radio Latvia (Latvijas Radio), which has three channels including Radio Klasika, a classical radio station on 103.7FM. The BBC World Service can be picked up 24 hours a day on 100.5FM. Of the private music and news radios, SWH on 105.2FM, SWH Rock on 89.2FM and 101 Radio at 101FM are well worth a listen.

Lithuania You can pick up more than a dozen FM radio stations in Vilnius. For news in English tune to the BBC World Service on 95.5 FM, VOA Europe on 105.6 FM or the French Radio France Internationale on 98.3 FM.

Time Zone

The Baltic States are in the eastern European time zone which is GMT +2 hours. An hour is added between the end of March and October for daylight savings, so during the summer local time is GMT +3 hours, known as Eastern European Summer Time or EEST for short.

Tourist Information Centres

Note that tourist office opening hours often vary from year to year.

Estonia

Tallinn

Tallinn City Tourist Office & Convention Bureau, Vabaduse Väljak 7, 15199 Tallinn; tel: 6404 411; fax 6404 764; www.tourism.tallinn.ee; for conference organisers only.
Tallinn Tourist Information Centre, Niguliste 2/Kullaseppa 4, 10146 Tallinn; tel: 645 7777; fax: 645 7778; turismiinfo@tallinn.ee; www.tourism.tallinn.ee.
May–14 June Mon–Fri 9am–7pm, Sat–Sun 10am–5pm; 15 June–14 Aug Mon–Fri 9am–8pm, Sat & Sun 10am–6pm; 15 Aug–Sept Mon–Fri 9am–6pm, Sat & Sun 10am–5pm;

Oct–Apr Mon–Fri 9am–5pm, Sat 10am–3pm.
Tourist Information in the Viru Centre, Viru väljak 4; tel: 6101 557; fax: 6101 559. Daily 9am–9pm.

Elsewhere in Estonia

Hiiumaa Island, Hiiu tn 1, Kärdla; tel/fax: 4622 232; hiiumaa@visitestonia.com; www.hiiumaa.ee.
Kuressaare (Saaremaa Island), Tallinna 2; tel/fax: 4533 120; tourism@kuressaare.ee; www.saaremaa.ee.
Narva, Puškini 13; tel/fax: 3560 184; narva@visitestonia.com; tourism.narva.ee.
Pärnu, Rüütli 16; tel: 447 3000; fax: 447 3001; parnu@visitestonia.com; www.parnu.ee.
Tartu, Raekoja plats (in Town Hall); tel/fax: 7442 111; info@visittartu.com; www.tartu.ee.
Võru, Tartu tn. 31; tel/fax: 7821 881; voru@visitestonia.com; www.visitvoru.ee.

Latvia

Rīga Information Centre, Rātslaukums 6; Rīga, tel: 6703 7900; fax: 6703 7910; www.riga tourism.com.

Elsewhere in Latvia

For a full list of Latvian information centres visit http://latviatourism.lv/info.php?id=51.
Balvi, Bērzpils1a; tel: 6452 2356; www.balvi.gov.lv.
Bauska, Rātslaukums 1; tel: 6392 3797; www.tourism.bauska.lv.
Cēsis, Pils laukums 1; tel: 6412 1815; www.tourism.cesis.lv.
Daugavpils, Rīgas 22a; tel: 6542 2818; www.visitdaugavpils.lv.
Dundaga, Dundaga Castle, Pils 14; tel: 6323 7858; www.dundaga.lv.
Jelgava, Pasta 37; tel/fax: 6302 2751; www.jelgava.lv.
Jūrmala, Lienes 5; tel: 6714 7900; www.jurmala.lv.
Kandava, Kūrorta 1b; tel: 6318 1150; fax: 6318 1194; www.kandava.lv.
Kolka Information Centre; tel: 2914 9105; www.kolkasrags.lv.
Kuldīga, Baznīcas 5; tel/fax: 6332 2259; www.kuldiga.lv.
Liepāja Regional Tourism Information Bureau, Roža laukums 5/6; tel: 6348 0808; www.liepaja.lv.
Rēzekne, Atbrīvošanas aleja 98; tel: 6460 5005; www.rezekne.lv.
Roja, Selgas 33; tel: 6326 9594; www.roja.lv.
Sabile, Pilskalna 6; tel: 6325 2344; www.sabile.lv.
Sigulda, Valdemāra 1a; tel: 6797 1335; fax: 6797 1372; www.sigulda.lv.
Talsi, Lielā 19/21; tel: 6322 4165; www.talsi.lv.
Tukums, Pils 3; tel: 6312 4451; www.tukums.lv.

ABOVE: advertising kiosk.

Valmiera, Rīgas 10; tel/fax: 6420 7177; www.valmiera.lv.
Ventspils, Tirgus 7; tel: 6362 2263; fax: 6360 7665; www.tourism.ventspils.lv.

Lithuania

Lithuanian State Department of Tourism, Švitrigailos 11m, Vilnius; tel: 210 8796; www.tourism.lt.
Vilnius Tourist Information Centres,
Vilniaus 22; tel: 262 9660; www.vilnius-tourism.lt.
Didžioji 31 (Town Hall); tel: 262 6470; www.vilnius-tourism.lt.
Geležinkelio 16 (Train Station); tel: 269 2091; www.vilnius-tourism.lt.
Kaunas
Kaunas Region Tourist Information Centre, Laisvės 36; tel: 323 436; www.kaunastic.lt.
Klaipėda
Klaipėda Tourist Information Centre, Turgaus 7; tel: 412 186; www.klaipedainfo.lt.
Palanga
Tourist Information Centre, Kretingos 1 (bus station); tel: 488 11; www.palangatic.lt.
Nida
Nida Culture and Tourism Information Centre, Taikos 4; tel: 523 45; www.visitneringa.com.
Trakai
Tourist Information Centre, Vytauto 69; tel: 519 34; www.trakai.lt.

Websites

The best Baltic-related internet resources are:
www.ee (search the Estonian-wide web);
www.lv (search the Latvian web);
www.all.lv (all Latvian links);
www.on.lt (Lithuanian links);
http://inyourpocket.com (contents of the print guides are available online free of charge; events updated monthly).

TRANSPORT

ACCOMMODATION

EATING OUT

ACTIVITIES

A – Z

LANGUAGE

L ANGUAGE

UNDERSTANDING THE LANGUAGE

ESTONIAN

Estonian, the official language of the Republic of Estonia, is closely related to Finnish and Hungarian. Although it uses a Latin alphabet, and each letter represents only one sound, it is a difficult language to master. There are 14 different cases of any noun, verb conjugation is complex, and the verb's meaning may also change according to how its root is pronounced. There are, however, no articles or genders in Estonian. If you can manage to pick up a few of the words listed below, this will be appreciated by the locals.

Numbers

1	üks
2	kaks
3	kolm
4	neli
5	viis
6	kuus
7	seitse
8	kaheksa
9	üheksa
10	kümme
11	üksteist
12	kaksteist
13	kolmteist
20	kakskümmend
21	kakskümmend-üks
30	kolmkümmend
100	sada
200	kaksada
1,000	tuhat

Days of the Week

Sunday pühapäev
Monday esmaspäev
Tuesday teisipäev
Wednesday kolmapäev
Thursday neljapäev
Friday reede
Saturday laupäev

Estonian Sounds

Vowels
a – as in car
e – as in bed
i – as in beet
o – as in phone
u – as in moon
ä – as in cat
ö – as in hurt
õ – as in girl
ü – as in shoot.
When a vowel is doubled its sound is lengthened.

Consonants
These have the same sound values as in English, except:
g – always hard, as in gate
j – as the y in yet
š – tch as in match
ž – as in pleasure

Common Expressions

hello tere
good morning tere hommikust
good evening tere õhtust
goodbye head aega
see you nägemist
thanks aitäh or tänan
please palun
sorry vabandust
excuse me vabandage palun
yes/no jah/ei
fine hästi
a toast terviseks
bon appétit head isu
The general purpose negative – ei ole – is used to encompass every inconvenience from "we're sold out" to "she's not here".

Useful Words

airport lennujaam
train station raudteejaam
(in Tallinn the station is known as Balti jaam)
harbour sadam
shop kauplus/pood
town centre kesklinn
market turg
hairdresser juuksur
pharmacy apteek
street/road tänav tn./maantee mnt./puiestee pst.
every day iga päev
holiday puhkepäev

LATVIAN

Latvian is the native language of about 60 percent of the 2.2 million people living in Latvia and one of the world's endangered languages. It is one of two surviving Baltic languages of the Indo-European language group, the other being Lithuanian. Remotely related to the Slavic languages Russian, Polish and Ukrainian, Latvian has 48 phonemes – speech sounds distinguishing one word from another – 12 vowels, 10 diphthongs and 26 consonants. Stress is placed on the first syllable.

Numbers

1	viens
2	divi
3	trīs
4	četri
5	pieci

Latvian Sounds

Vowels
These have the same sound values as in English, with several additions:
a – as in cat
e – as in bed
i – as in hit
o – as in floor
u – as in good
a line over a vowel lengthens it:
ā – as in car
ē – as in there
ī – as in bee (Riga = Rīga)
ū – oo as in cool

Diphthongs
au – ow as in pout
ie – e as in here
ai – I as in sight
ei – ay as in sway

Consonants
Consonants have the same sound values as in English with the following exceptions:
c – ts as in tsar
č – ch as in chin
g – always hard, as in gate
ģ – as in logical. The accent can also be a "tail" under the letter.
j – as the y in yet
ķ – tch as in hatch
ļ – as in failure
ņ – as in onion
r – always rolled as in Spanish
š – sh as in shoe
ž – as in pleasure

6   seši
7   septiņi
8   astoņi
9   deviņi
10 desmit
11 vienpadsmit
12 divpadsmit
20 divdesmit
30 trīsdesmit
100 simts
200 divi simti
1,000 tūkstotis

Days of the Week
Sunday svētdiena
Monday pirmdiena
Tuesday otrdiena
Wednesday trešdiena
Thursday ceturtdiena
Friday piektdiena
Saturday sestdiena

Common Expressions
hello, hi sveiki
good morning labrīt

good afternoon labdien
good evening labvakar
goodbye uz redzēšanos/visu labu
yes jā
no nē
Please; You're welcome lūdzu
Thank you paldies
I am sorry! Excuse me Atvainojiet!
That's all right Nekas
May I ask a question? Vai drīkstu jautāt?
May I come in? Vai drīkstu ienākt?
Where can... be found? Kur atrodas...?
How much is it? Cik tas maksā?
Would you please tell me/show me? Vai Jūs lūdzu man nepateiktu/neparādītu?
Pleased to meet you Patīkami ar Jums iepazīties
Let me introduce myself Atļaujiet stādīties priekšā
My name is... Mani sauc...
Do you speak English? Vai Jūs runājiet angliski?
I don't understand/speak Latvian Es nesaprotu/nerunāju latviski
We need an interpreter Mums ir vajadzīgs tulks

Useful Words
doctor ārsts
hospital slimnīca
first aid ātrā palīdzība
hotel viesnīca
restaurant restorāns
shop veikals
airport lidosta
bus station autoosta
railway station dzelzceļa stacija
petrol station degvielas uzpildes stacija
post office pasts
street iela
boulevard bulvāris
square laukums
closed slēgts
open atvērts

LITHUANIAN

Lithuanian and Latvian both belong to the Baltic family of the Indo-European languages. With some resemblance to Sanskrit, Lithuanian is one of the oldest surviving languages, and it has kept its sound system and many archaic forms and sentence structures. When the written language was first formalised in the first half of the 20th century, there were a variety of distinctive dialects across the country, and the Suvalkiečiai, the southern sub-dialect of Western High Lithuania, was adopted as the official

dialect. Today, local dialects have been largely assimilated. There are 32 letters in the alphabet. One of Lithuanian's idiosyncrasies is the tail that appears beneath its vowels.

Numbers
1   vienas
2   du
3   trys
4   keturi
5   penki
6   šeši
7   septyni
8   aštuoni
9   devyni
10 dešimt
11 vienuolika
12 dvylika
20 dvidešimt
30 trisdešimt
100 šimtas
200 du šimtai
1,000 tūkstantis

Common Expressions
hello laba diena
hello Mr... laba diena, pone...
hi labas, sveikas
please prašom
excuse me atsiprašau
sorry atsiprašau, atleisk
good morning labas rytas
good evening labas vakaras

Lithuanian Sounds

Vowels
a – as in back
e – as in peck
i – as in sit
o – as in shot
u – as in should
ė – as in make
ū – oo as in stool
y – ee as in see
ą, ę, į and ų appear in special cases and are slightly longer than the equivalent letters without a "tail".

Diphthongs
ai – as in i (sometimes as in bait)
au – as in now
ei – as in make
ie – as in yellow
uo – as in wonder

Consonants
c – ts as in rats
č – ch as in chin
j – as in yes
š – sh as in she
z – as in zoo
ž – as in vision

good night *labanakt*
goodbye *Sudie, viso gero*
welcome *sveiki atvykę*
How are you? *Kaip sekasi?*
Pleased to meet you *Malonu susipažinti*
See you later *Iki pasimatymo*
yes/no *taip/ne*
okay *gerai*
when? *kada?*
where? *kur?*
who? *kas?*
why? *kodėl?*
Do you understand me?
Ar mane supranti?

I don't speak Lithuanian
Aš nekalbu lietuviškai
I understand Lithuanian
Aš suprantu lietuviškai
Do you speak English, German, French, Russian, Polish? *Ar kalbate angliškai, vokiškai, prancuziskai, rusiškai, lenkiškai?*
I speak English, German...
Aš kalbu angliškai, vokiškai...
I would like... *Prašyčiau...*
What time is it? *Kiek valandų?*
How much is it? *Kiek kainuoja?*
Where is the nearest shop, hotel, restaurant, café, bar, toilet? *Kur*

arčiausia (s) parduotuvė, viešbutis, restoranas, kavinė, baras, tualetas?
thank you (very much) *Ačiū (labai)*

Useful Words

left *kairė*
right *dešinė*
bread *duona*
butter *sviestas*
cheese *sūris*
beer *alus*
wine *vynas*
tea *arbata*
coffee *kava*

FURTHER READING

General

Baltic Countdown, by Peggie Benton. Centaur Press, 1985. An extraordinary account of the wife of a British diplomat caught up in Rīga at the outbreak of World War II.
The Baltic Nations and Europe, by John Hiden & Patrick Salman. Longman, 1995. A history of the 20th century in the three countries.
The Baltic Revolution, by Anatol Lieven. Yale, 1993. A fine background to the cultural, economic and political life in the region by a member of one of the foremost Baltic families, and a contributor to this book.
The Baltic States: Years of Dependence (1940–1990), by Romanuld J. Misiunas, Rein Taagepera. C. Hurst & Co., London; and University of California Press, 1983. This is a follow up to the classic **Years of Independence (1917–1940)**, by Georg von Rauch.
The Czar's Madman, by Jaan Kross. Harvill, 2001. Estonia's premier writer brilliantly evokes life in the times of the Russian occupation in the 19th century. Also by Kross: **Professor Marten's Departure**, 1994; **Treading Air**, 2003.
The Good Republic, by William Palmer. Minerva, 1990. An excellent and imaginative novel about an émigré returning to the Baltic city he fled during World War II and encountering some ghosts on his return 40 years later.
Racundra's First Cruise and **Racundra's Third Cruise**, by Arthur Ransome, Brian Hammett (Editor). Fernhurst Books, 2003. Reprint of 1920s boating tales from the Baltic – the first around Estonia's islands, the third upriver in Latvia – from the

creator of *Swallows and Amazons*.
The Singing Revolution, by Clare Thompson. Michael Joseph, 1992. Personal account of the rebirth of the Baltics by a British journalist who was there in 1989–90.
To the Baltic with Bob: An Epic Misadventure, by Griff Rhys Jones. Penguin, 2003. The humorist's adventures from the Thames to St Petersburg.
Walking since Daybreak, by Modris Eksteins. Papermac, 2000. An

Send Us Your Thoughts

We do our best to ensure the information in our books is as accurate and up to date as possible. The books are updated on a regular basis using local contacts, who painstakingly add, amend and correct as required. However, some details (such as telephone numbers and opening times) are liable to change, and we are ultimately reliant on our readers to put us in the picture.

We welcome your feedback, especially your experience of using the book "on the road". Maybe we recommended a hotel that you liked (or another that you didn't), or you came across a great bar or new attraction we missed.

We will acknowledge all contributions, and we'll offer an Insight Guide to the best letters received.

Please write to us at:
    Insight Guides
    PO Box 7910
    London SE1 1WE
Or email us at:
    insight@apaguide.co.uk

account of a Latvian family through the 20th century.
War in the Woods: Estonia's Struggle for Survival, 1944 –1956, by Mart Laar. 1992. The courageous story of the "Forest Brothers", freedom fighters who took to the woods after the second Soviet occupation.

Other Insight Guides

More than 120 **Insight Guides** and **Insight City Guides** cover every continent, providing information on culture and all the top sights, as well as superb photography and detailed maps. In addition, **Insight Smart Guides** present comprehensive listings in a snappy, easy-to-find way, held together by an A–Z theme and with a street atlas showing major attractions, hotels and public transport; while **Insight Step By Step Guides** deliver self-guided walks and tours. **Insight Fleximaps** highlight all the main tourist sights and provide essential facts about the destination, while being printed on durable paper with a laminated finish – write on the map with a non-permanent marker pen and wipe it off later.

ART AND PHOTO CREDITS

Alamy 6BL, 49, 60, 230, 239, 297, 299/T, 300T, 304
Jose Antonia Alonso 7ML
AKG London 29, 264
AWL Images 225T, 227, 231
Axiom 38, 174
Bridgeman Art Library 42
Central Independent Television 214T
Corbis 9TR, 33, 34/35, 107, 192, 193, 226, 232, 258, 265
Crabapple Archive 52, 210T
courtesy Devil Museum 293
Druskininkai Spa Centre 7TR
Estonia State Tourism Dept 155T, 156
ESTD Jarek Joepera 75, 95B, 157, 159, 169, 175
ESTD/Toomas Olvey 88/89
ESTD/Andreas Meichsner 141
ESTD/Lembit Michelson 71, 151, 154, 157T, 160, 163
ESTD/Tiit Motus 171
ESTD/Jaak Nilson 136, 137, 363
ESTD/Aivar Ruukel 65, 147T
ESTD/Marin Sild
ESTD/Andrus Teemant 69
ESTD/Toomas Tuul 8T, 9M, 115, 136T, 155, 168, 358
ESTD/Kati Vaas 147
ESTD/Sven Zachek
Eesti Ralva Museum 98
Mary Evans 26B, 38, 102, 105, 263
Focus Baltic 54, 55, 152, 167
Fotolia 289T
Getty Images 39, 223, 298
Lina Guiter 169T
John Hansen 243T
Istockphoto 7M, 217T, 220, 318T
Jarek Joepera 140
Donald Judge 247/T
Jun Kwang Han 202
Latvia Tourist Organisation 216, 219, 222T, 226T, 236, 237, 244/T, 246
Leonardo 337
Lyle Lawson 28, 40, 43, 44, 46, 47, 50, 51, 56, 57, 61, 100, 106, 135T, 146, 147, 153, 158, 162, 172,

173/T, 218, 220T, 221, 222, 228, 229, 234T, 234, 247, 248, 249, 254, 277, 283, 294/T, 302, 303, 306R, 327
Loosusemees 139
Matisons 233
APA Mockford/Bonetti 72, 73, 76, 79, 116/T, 117L, 118/T, 119, 212/T, 123/T, 126/T, 130, 131, 133/T, 135, 142, 143, 144, 145, 149, 150/T, 166, 170/T, 180, 196/197, 201/T, 202T, 23L/R, 204, 207L/R, 209T, 210, 212, 214, 215, 241T, 252/253, 268, 271, 272L/R, 273T, 274/T, 275, 276L/T, 278, 279T, 280T, 281L/R/T, 282T, 284, 285, 286, 287, 288, 289, 290, 291/T, 292, 295, 301, 308/T, 309, 335, 350,
Lithuania State Dept of Tourism 6BR, 7B, 8B, 84/85, 86/87, 314T, 319, 320, 354, 356
Courtesy The London Hotel 338B
Dainis Jürgens Osts + Europa Photo 101
Reeksts 190
Courtesy Relais & Chateaux Stikliai 342
Rex Features 21, 316
Riga Museum of History and Navigation 184, 185, 187, 188, 189
Robert Harding 321T
Specialist Stock 7TL
APA Micah Sarut 1, 2/3, 4T, 5B, 6M, 7MR, 8BR, 9B, 12/13, 14/15, 16, 17B/M/T, 18B/M/T, 19/T, 20, 22, 23, 24, 27, 36, 45, 58, 59, 67, 74, 77, 78, 80, 81, 82, 83, 91/T, 92/93, 95M/T, 110/111, 112, 113, 117R, 124T, 125, 129L/R/T, 132, 134, 151T, 161T, 164, 165, 176/177, 178/179, 181B/T, 198, 199, 205, 206, 207T, 208, 209, 211, 213, 217, 223T, 224, 225, 235, 237/T, 238, 240, 241, 242, 243, 248T, 250/251, 255B/M/T, 266/267, 269, 273, 276R, 280, 282, 296, 300, 303T, 305, 307, 312,

133, 314, 315/T, 317L/R/T, 321L/R/T, 322, 324L/R, 325/T, 326/T, 327, 328, 330, 332, 338T, 339, 341, 345, 346, 349, 352, 357, 359, 362, 367, 368, 369, 370, 371, 372
Tallinn City Tourist Office & Convention Bureau 68
TCCB/Tavi Greep 25
TCCB/ Toomas Volmer 6T, 37, 94, 120, 124, 128
TCCB/Allan Alajaan 10/11
TCCB Meelia Lokk 41
TCCB/Kaido hagen 122
TCCB/Maret Poldveer 127
TCCB/Harri Rospu 355
Courtesy The Three Sisters 336
Topfoto 48, 53, 262

PHOTO FEATURES

62–63: APA Micah Sarut 62/63, 62BL/BR, 63BR/ML, Estonia State Tourism Dept 63BL, Parnu Spa 63T

108–109: Estonia State Tourism Dept 108/109, APA Micah Sarut 108BL, 109B/TR, Lithuania State Dept of Tourism 109BR/M

194–195: all Pictures APA Micah Sarut

310–311: APA Micah Sarut 310-311, 310BL/BR, 311BL/M, Estonian State Tourism Board 311BT, Tallinn City Tourist Office & Convention Bureau 310M, Getty Images 311TR

Map Production: original cartography Stephen Ramsey, updated by Apa Cartography Department

© 2011 Apa Publications (UK) Limited

Production: Tynan Dean, Linton Donaldson and Rebeka Ellam

INDEX

Main references are in bold type

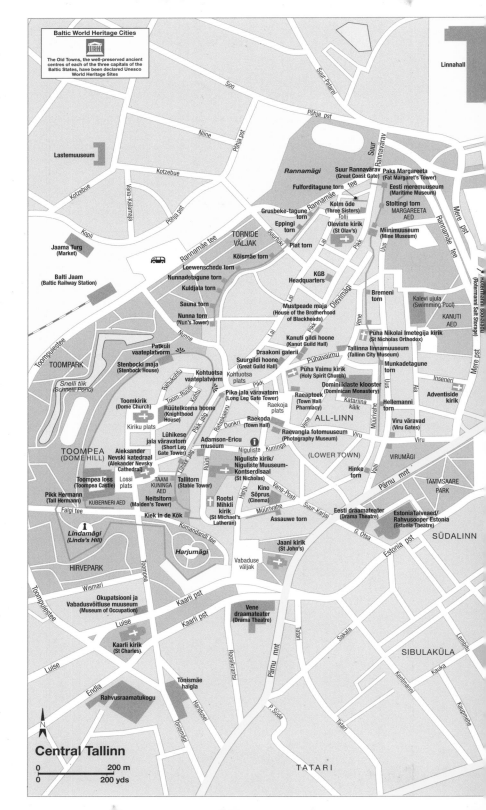

Baltic World Heritage Cities

The Old Towns, the well-preserved ancient centres of each of the three capitals of the Baltic States, have been declared Unesco World Heritage Sites

Linnahall

Lastemuuseum

Rannamägi

Suur Rannavärav (Great Coast Gate)

Paks Margareeta (Fat Margaret's Tower)

Fulforditagune torn

Eesti meremuuseum (Maritime Museum)

Kolm õde (Three Sisters)

Stoltingi torn

Grusbeke-tagune torn

MARGAREETA AED

Oleviste kirik (St Olav's)

Eppingi torn

Jaama Turg (Market)

TORNIDE VÄLJAK

Plat torn

Miinimuuseum (Mine Museum)

Balti Jaam (Baltic Railway Station)

Köismäe torn

KGB Headquarters

Bremeni torn

Kalevi ujula (Swimming Pool)

Loewenschede torn

Nunnadetagune torn

KANUTI AED

Kuldjala torn

Mustpeade maja (House of the Brotherhood of Blackheads)

Püha Nikolai Imetegija kirik (St Nicholas Orthodox)

Sauna torn

Nunna torn (Nun's Tower)

Kanuti gildi hoone (Kanut Guild Hall)

Tallinna linnamuuseum (Tallinn City Museum)

Munkadetagune torn

Patkuli vaateplatvorm

Draakoni galerii

Suurgildi hoone (Great Guild Hall)

Püha Vaimu kirik (Holy Spirit Church)

Adventiside kirik

Inseneri

TOOMPARK

Stenbocki maja (Stenbock House)

Kohtuotsa vaateplatvorm

Kohtuotsa plats

Dominiiklaste klooster (Dominican Monastery)

Snelli tiik (Schnelli Pond)

Toomkirik (Dome Church)

Rüütelkonna hoone (Knighthood House)

Pika jala väravatorn (Long Leg Gate Tower)

Raeapteek (Town Hall Pharmacy)

Hellemanni torn

Katariina käik

Raekoja plats

Viru väravad (Viru Gates)

Kiriku plats

Lühikese jala väravatorn (Short Leg Gate Tower)

Raekoda (Town Hall)

ALL-LINN

Viru

TOOMPEA (DOME HILL)

Aleksander Nevski katedraal (Alekander Nevsky Cathedral)

Adamson-Ericu museum

Raevangla fotomuuseum (Photography Museum)

(LOWER TOWN)

VIRUMÄGI

Lossi plats

Tallitorn (Stable Tower)

Niguliste kirik/ Niguliste Muuseum-Kontserdisaal (St Nicholas)

Hinke torn

TAANI KUNINGA AED

Pikk Hermann (Tall Hermann)

Toompea loss (Toompea Castle)

Neitsitorn (Maiden's Tower)

TAMMSAARE PARK

Kino Sõprus (Cinema)

Eesti draamateater (Drama Theatre)

EstoniaTalveaed/ Rahvusooper Estonia (Estonia Theatre)

KUBERNERI AED

Kiek in de Kök

Rootsi Mihkli kirik (St Michael's Latheran)

Assauwe torn

SÜDALINN

Lindamägi (Linda's Hill)

HIRVEPARK

Harjumägi

Jaani kirik (St John's)

Vabaduse väljak

Okupatsiooni ja Vabadusvõitluse muuseum (Museum of Occupation)

Vene draamateater (Drama Theatre)

SIBULAKÜLA

Kaarli kirik (St Charles)

Tõnismäe haigla

Rahvusraamatukogu

N

Central Tallinn

| 0 | 200 m |
| 0 | 200 yds |

TATARI